COOK
Quick

Oxmoor
House®

Copyright 1986 by Oxmoor House, Inc.
Book Division of Southern Progress Corporation
P.O. Box 2463, Birmingham, Alabama 35201

Library of Congress Catalog Number: 86-60215
ISBN: 0-8487 0685-4

Manufactured in the United States of America

COOK QUICK

Senior Foods Editor: Katherine M. Eakin
Senior Editor: Joan E. Denman
Assistant Foods Editors: Janice L. Krahn,
    Helen R. Turk
Editor: Olivia Wells
Director, Test Kitchen: Laura N. Massey
Test Kitchen Home Economists: Kay E. Clarke,
    Bonnie Echols, Rebecca J. Riddle,
    Elise Wright Walker
Copy Editor: Melinda West
Editorial Assistants: Donna A. Rumbarger,
    Karen Parris, Joan Winstead
Photographer: Jim Bathie
Photo Stylists: Sara Jane Ball, Kay E. Clarke
Designer and Illustrator: Carol Middleton
Editorial Consultant: Nao Hauser
Production Manager: Jerry R. Higdon
Art Director: Bob Nance

Cover: *A tasty Chicken and Vegetable Stir-Fry
is complemented by quick-to-fix French
Breadsticks and Summer Fruit Compote in
the Stir-Fry Surprise menu (page 82).*

Page i: *Not one succulent bite of this Rum Berry
Trifle (page 257) will betray its ease of
preparation.*

Page ii: *A flavorful sauce enhances Snapper
Veracruz which is served with a tossed
salad and Quick Parmesan Loaf in
the Snappy Red Snapper menu (page 62).*

Contents

Guide to COOK Quick

Think about what you'd like to eat, and anticipate the pleasure. Think about the sharing, and what it means to your family. Think about the abundant choices in any American market—the heaps of bright, fresh vegetables, the long rows of ready-to-cook meats, the aisles of already prepared foods, and the natural goodness of milk, cheese, and eggs.

Think about all this, and you'll be ready to celebrate—quickly! And that's what *Cook Quick* is all about. It's a gathering of recipes and menus that promise results fast enough to allow you and your family to enjoy favorite foods every day. The ingredients are readily available. The cooking techniques are basic and streamlined. And the tastes are sufficiently varied to make even the weariest work-day survivor or harried dinner host eager to savor some morsel—fast!

Cook Quick is for all those times when the eating, and the togetherness, are more important than the cooking. It's for the days

when dinner preparations must be sandwiched between a rush and a flurry, between arrival home and hunger pangs. It's for the evenings you'd love to invite friends over—if only you had time to cook. And it's for those odd minutes when what you really want is a panful of fudgy brownies . . . or a loaf of hot-from-the-oven bread . . . or a batch of creamy potato salad . . . or a great chicken salad sandwich . . . or a pizza . . . or some pasta—and you want it in a hurry!

There are two kinds of recipes in *Cook Quick*: fast and faster. Some take additional time to marinate, bake, or freeze, but every cook knows that's "stolen time"—the time when something's getting done but you don't have to do it. The menus have been coordinated so that none takes more than an hour, and many take less. Just pick any food that sounds tempting with the assurance that you'll be eating soon, for *Cook Quick* is the shortest path to those happiest words, "Everything's ready now!"

1

STRATEGIES
FOR
EVERYDAY COOKING

When you're hungry, the last thing you want to do is sit down and think about meal preparations. So don't. Proceed right to the recipes—they are all simple and self-explanatory. But when you do have time to browse, you might want to tuck some of the following thoughts into your strategy for everyday cooking.

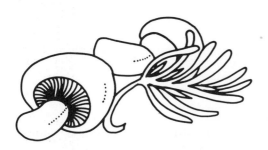

What to Cook

First and foremost, cook what you and your family like. This seems like the most obvious thought in the world. Yet when five o'clock rolls around it's easy to forget the obvious answers to "What should I make tonight?" Here are some ways to keep yourself reminded:

● **Make a List of Favorites.** Take time when you have it to write down the foods each family member—including yourself—especially likes. Keep your list close at hand, like wallet snapshots, to remind you of what's special in your household. Once you've searched all crannies of memory you may be surprised to realize how long it's been since you've prepared some of the dishes—and the realization may send you to the *Cook Quick* index for versions fast enough to serve often.

● **Keep a "Shop Quick" Notebook.** Use a notebook small enough to keep in a pocket, purse, or car glove compartment. Divide it into categories, such as meat, poultry, fish, vegetables, and desserts. Then jot down your favorite recipes in each category along with a brief notation of the nonstaple ingredients needed to prepare the dish. Refer to your notes while you're shopping, so that if you want to cook chicken or if you see a fine bunch of broccoli on sale, you can make sure you have whatever is needed to prepare it the way you like it before you get home.

● **List Menu "Inspirations" from the Family.** Meal planning shouldn't be the cook's responsibility alone. Family members will look forward to meals more if they anticipate the foods they like. They'll also be more apt to help with shopping and preparations. Some suggestions may be a bit offbeat—but so what! Nobody is going to perish from malnutrition if you dine on a youngster's requested hot dogs and chocolate cake one night. And you might all have a lot of fun delving into Chinese or Mexican cooking, if that's somebody's choice. Once everyone begins participating in menu-making, it's a lot easier to begin discussing the next topic of mutual concern, which is . . .

Satisfying Nutritional Needs

The more you know about the nutrient content of foods, the more flexibility you'll have in meal planning. If you know, for example, that average portions of beef, cottage cheese, fish, boiled ham, and cheese pizza all supply at least 15 grams of protein, you'll feel more confident about using them interchangeably in menus. You might explain to the child who requests hot dogs and cake that it would be wise, for the sake of everyone's eyesight and skin, to add some vitamin A to the menu; then you can present some choices, such as carrot sticks, canteloupe wedges, a glass of tomato juice, or a small spinach salad. Since children do worry about growing up, and teenagers tend to worry about their attractiveness, it's not hard to interest them in the benefits of balanced nutrition, especially if they are aware of how many different foods fall into any given nutrient category. The U.S. government publishes many free or inexpensive booklets on the subject; you can ask for a publication list from the Consumer Information Center, U. S. General Services Administration, Washington, D.C. 20405.

Time's on Your Side

Appetite is urgent, but most cooking isn't. Very few recipes—and these are usually the simplest—need to be prepared just before serving. Many people like to cook when they have time to take things slowly. Others like to cook sporadically—maybe just once a week rather than every day. Both preferences can be met with a little advanced thought given to scheduling preparations in the following ways:
- **Make Double Batches.** By doubling recipes, you can make enough food for more than one meal—with only one shopping trip and one cleanup. Refrigerate or freeze the surplus for another meal.
- **Cook Ahead.** Since almost any kind of food can be held in the refrigerator at least overnight, you can use time the night before, or even the weekend before, to get a head start on weekday cooking. Salad dressings, soups, stews, breads, and cakes keep especially well. Often you can protect quality by preparing parts of a recipe ahead, storing them separately, and heating them just before serving. Cooked chicken and meat will hold at least four days in the refrigerator; for the sake of fresh flavors, it's better to precook these ingredients than to refrigerate them uncooked for the same length of time. Wrap them well so that they won't dry out.

- **Put Some Things By.** Containers of homemade chicken broth, homemade jam and applesauce, seasoned butters (see page 28), fresh-picked berries, and vegetable purees in the freezer can make all the difference in the world between delicious and ho-hum meals. You can make any of these items only once or twice a year and reap the rewards year-round. The preparations don't have to be large-scale or elaborate. You can put a few pounds of chicken wings in a large pot with carrots, celery, onions, and parsley and as much water as the pot will hold and leave it to simmer over low heat overnight; then strain and freeze the broth. The pot doesn't need to be tended, but the broth will give you a great headstart on a homemade soup or sauce. Berries can be washed and frozen on baking sheets and then transferred to plastic bags. Apples can be cut up, simmered over low heat without anything else, pressed through a food mill, seasoned, and frozen. There are many simple recipes in standard reference cookbooks for freezer jams and soups based on vegetable purees that will provide similar bounty. If you lack both time and freezer space, don't feel that you have to prepare large quantities.

STOCK UP ON CONVENIENCE

The simplest ways to save time are to use packaged and prepared foods when they present adequate substitutes for home-made products and to keep these foods on hand—so that you don't squander the time on supermarket trips! No doubt you have your own list of such essentials, ranging from peanut butter to frozen waffles. Here are shopping lists of some other non-perishable convenience items that you might want to try, with suggestions for making the most of them.

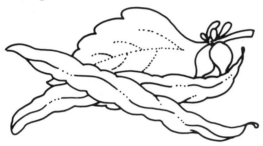

The Quick Change-of-Pace List

● **Vinegars.** Substitute raspberry or blueberry vinegar in fruit and chicken salad dressings and tarragon or sage vinegar in tossed salad vinaigrettes. Balsamic vinegar is deliciously rich and sweet in salads and as marinating liquid for grilled beef and onions. Rice wine vinegar is very mild—perfect for cooked vegetables and spinach salads.

● **Nut Oils.** Walnut, hazelnut, and sesame oils are more expensive than vegetable oils, but a little goes a long way. These oils are too strong and sweet to be used by themselves. Mix a vinaigrette of 1 part nut oil, 2 parts vegetable oil, 1 part raspberry vinegar, and dried tarragon leaves for a quick "gourmet" salad dressing that's great with watercress and other dark greens, green beans, and cold poultry. Use a blend of 1 part sesame oil, 2 parts vegetable oil, 1 part rice wine vinegar, and toasted sesame seeds to sauce cooked broccoli or asparagus with Oriental flavor. Keep nut oils refrigerated; they may become cloudy and thick, but they'll clear up again at room temperature.

● **Grains.** Serve buckwheat groats, pearl barley, bulgar wheat, or couscous instead of rice. The buckwheat groats and pearl barley cook in about the same amount of time as rice. Bulgar wheat and couscous are sold precooked and need only be softened in boiling water.

● **Frozen Burritos, Tacos, and Enchiladas.** Add a big topping of shredded lettuce, chopped tomatoes and onions, and a sprinkling of lime juice to these products to give them fresh flavor and textural contrast. If you add a garnish of chopped fresh cilantro, you'll have something that tastes, well . . . almost Mexican!

● **Ethnic Sauces.** Use Chinese hoisin sauce, Japanese steak sauce (sometimes labeled "bulldog sauce" or tenkatsu), or Mexican picante sauce to baste grilled or roast meat and poultry. Stir a few spoonfuls of Chinese oyster sauce into stir-fried broccoli. Mix soy sauce with a little bit of Japanese horseradish powder to make a great dipping sauce for cold shrimp.

● **Chopped Nuts and Granola.** All of these can be frozen to maintain freshness. Spread them on a baking sheet and toast them for 10 minutes in a moderate oven to bring out the best flavor. Chopped pecans add richness to buttered steamed carrots, hazelnuts are terrific with green beans or asparagus, and walnuts do wonders for broccoli. Try almonds with cauliflower or fish, pine nuts with spaghetti, zucchini, or spinach. Pistachio nuts, cashews, peanuts, and granola can be counted on to turn fresh fruit or ice cream into a treat. Cashews are especially good with fresh pineapple chunks, pistachio nuts with orange sections or melons.

● **Grated and Crumbled Cheeses.** These, too, can be frozen for prolonged storage. Stir a couple of tablespoons of grated Parmesan or Asiago cheese into any cooked vegetable, grain, or pasta for rich, intense flavor. Romano cheese is stronger; mix it with an equal quantity of toasted bread crumbs to season vegetables. Melt crumbled blue cheese on broiled steaks for an excellent robust combination. Or mash blue cheese with milk or cream to make a paste; stir this into cooked vegetables.

SUBSTITUTIONS THAT WORK

No matter how carefully you shop, there are bound to be times when you don't have an ingredient specified in a recipe. So here are some substitutions that will work in a pinch.

For Baking:

If recipe calls for:	You may use:
1 square unsweetened chocolate	3 tablespoons cocoa plus 1 tablespoon butter or margarine
2 large eggs	3 small or medium eggs
1 large egg	1 medium egg
1 cup sifted cake flour	1 cup sifted all-purpose flour minus 2 tablespoons
1 cup honey	¾ cup sugar plus ¼ cup liquid
1 cup whole milk	½ cup evaporated milk plus ½ cup water; or 1 cup reconstituted non-fat dry milk plus 2½ teaspoons butter or margarine; or 1 cup fruit juice
1 cup buttermilk	1 cup plain yogurt
1 cup sour cream	1 cup plain yogurt
1 cup brown sugar, firmly packed	1 cup granulated sugar
Whole wheat flour	All-purpose flour
1 teaspoon grated lemon or orange rind	½ teaspoon lemon or orange extract

For other Cooking:

If you don't have:	Substitute:
Heavy cream to thicken a sauce or soup	Light cream or plain yogurt (do not boil)
Wine	Broth or fruit juice
Tomato juice	Equal parts of tomato sauce and water
Tomato sauce	Equal parts of tomato paste and broth
1 cup rich chicken broth	1½ teaspoons chicken-flavored bouillon granules dissolved in 1 cup water; for extra richness, simmer with sliced carrot and dillweed
1 cup rich beef broth	1½ teaspoons beef-flavored bouillon granules dissolved in 1 cup water; for extra richness, simmer with chopped onion
Fresh herbs	½ the quantity of dried herbs
1 clove fresh garlic	⅛ teaspoon garlic powder
1 teaspoon lemon juice	½ teaspoon vinegar
1 tablespoon cornstarch for thickening	2 tablespoons flour
Shredded Cheddar cheese	Shredded provolone, Muenster, brick, or mozzarella cheese

● **Vermouth and Other Fortified Wines.** If you don't drink wine often, it's hard to keep a good wine around for cooking, since it will spoil in a few days once opened. But dry white vermouth keeps indefinitely and can be substituted for white wine in sauces and marinades. Port and dry Marsala wine will also keep and can be substituted for red wine; use half the quantity and add water, if necessary, to make up the difference. A few drops of port, sherry, or Marsala wine will enhance many cooked vegetables; heat the wine with butter before pouring over the food to evaporate some of the alcohol.

The Ready-for-Company List

● **Marinated Artichokes, Mushrooms, and Roasted Red Pepper or Pimiento Strips.** Arrange these three ready-to-serve antipastos on a platter; they'll banner the colors of the Italian flag and take the edge off appetites when accompanied by some crusty bread and a glass of red wine. Or serve any of them with an assortment of cold cuts and cheese for a heartier antipasto platter.

● **Canned Shrimp and Smoked Oysters.** Rinse the shrimp, and drain well; mix with mayonnaise, curry powder, and dillweed for a quick canapé topping or dip. Set out wooden picks, and the oysters become instant hors d'oeuvres.

● **Specialty Mustards and Tiny Gherkins.** Keep an assortment of coarse-grain mustard, Dijon-style mustard, and honey or lemon mustard ready to set out with salami, ham, smoked turkey breast, or other cold cuts and cheeses. The gherkins will add a pleasant tanginess, crispness, and color to your hors d'oeuvres platter.

● **Fresh Pasta.** Many supermarkets now sell fresh pasta. It will keep in the freezer for up to 6 months and can be cooked without thawing. The sauce can be as simple as melted butter with any chopped fresh herb, chopped seeded tomatoes and Parmesan cheese, or cream and Parmesan cheese. The delicate flavor of fresh pasta will make the simply prepared dish both elegant and irresistible.

● **Canned White Asparagus and Hearts of Palm.** These are little luxuries that take no work at all, but will turn a salad into something special. Just drain them and arrange on greens; top with vinaigrette dressing and, if you wish, some pimiento strips for color contrast.

● **Frozen Puff Pastry.** Use the recipe for Baked Camembert in Puff Pastry (see page 154) to create a party appetizer. Or turn the pastry into a quick impressive dessert by baking it in strips and sandwiching them around whipped cream and berries.

● **Frozen Raspberries.** Thaw them and puree in the blender with any fruit-flavored liqueur—et voilà! A marvelous topping for fresh fruit, ice cream, or sherbet.

● **Liqueurs.** Keep the cabinet stocked with all flavors—coffee, orange, raspberry, mint, chocolate, almond, and more—to provide a choice of ice cream toppings or coffee enhancements.

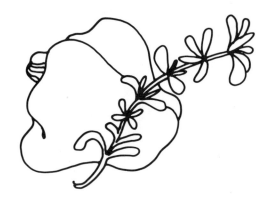

The Spice-of-Life List

● **Garlic.** Buy jars of pre-chopped garlic to save time. Or chop a lot of fresh garlic in the food processor and refrigerate in a covered jar filled with oil.

● **Ginger.** Keep gingerroot in a jar filled with sherry for indefinite storage. Grate it into salad dressings or mix with butter to baste grilled meats or toss with cooked broccoli or asparagus.

● **Prepared Horseradish.** Add a spoonful to the same-old-pot roast to spark the flavor of the gravy.

- **Dried Basil, Oregano, Tarragon, and Dillweed.** These are the most versatile dried herbs—good with all vegetables, tossed salads, and butter or cream sauces.
- **Ground Cumin, Coriander, and Cardamom.** It takes only ¼ teaspoon or so of these pungent spices to make almost any vinaigrette or butter sauce taste better.
- **Whole Cinnamon Sticks, Cloves, and Allspice.** Simmer these with red wine, apple cider, or tea for a delicious spiced beverage. Strain and serve hot in winter or over ice in summer, or as a tasty marinade for pork, beef, or lamb.
- **Soy Sauce and Worcestershire Sauce.** Substitute a few drops of either sauce for plain salt in vegetable, meat, and grain dishes. The taste will be livelier.

MAKING YOUR KITCHEN WORK FOR YOU

Every busy cook deserves a few "servants"—like a food processor to chop or slice foods, a blender to whip them to a froth, and a microwave oven to cook them fast. Here are some tips for maximizing the convenience of these appliances and other kitchen helpers.

- **Food Processor.** The best thing about the food processor is that it saves hours of chopping. The worst thing is that it has to be cleaned after use. The way to reconcile the two is to chop enough of commonly used ingredients at one time to last for several cooking sessions. Chopped onions, peppers and parsley, and grated cheese can all be refrigerated in covered containers for up to one week or frozen for longer storage. A large food processor is terrific for kneading bread dough, slicing or pureeing vegetables for soups, and throwing everything into one bowl to make a dip. But you may find that a very small processor or electric mini-chopper is more convenient for small everyday chopping chores.
- **Microwave Oven.** The key to mastering microwave cooking is to do it often. It's an easy, nutritious way to cook vegetables and produces superior results with grains. It protects the moistness of fish and

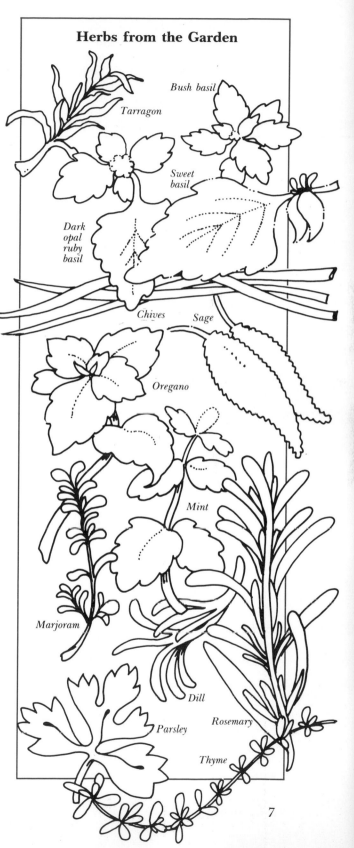

Herbs from the Garden

Tarragon
Bush basil
Sweet basil
Dark opal ruby basil
Chives
Sage
Oregano
Mint
Marjoram
Dill
Parsley
Rosemary
Thyme

chicken and cuts simmering time by one-third to one-half for soups and stews. Consult your microwave owner's manual for basic directions for any of these foods. Use wooden spoons to stir; you can leave them in the dish for short cooking periods. Invest in some bowls, platters, and casseroles that you would enjoy seeing on the table every day, so that you can take advantage of the oven's big bonus—no pot to wash, no separate serving dish needed.

● **Blender.** Though it's better known for milk shakes and cocktails, the blender excels at salad dressings. Whip a vinaigrette in the blender, and it will come out creamier; add some chunks of ripe avocado, canned artichoke hearts, blue cheese, or seeded tomato, and you'll have a special "house dressing."

● **Electric Skillet.** Keep this appliance out on the counter, especially if you don't have a microwave oven. It is terrific for steaming vegetables. Place 1 inch of water in the pan and heat to simmering; then place a collapsible steamer basket in the pan, add the vegetables, and cover. The vegetables will cook quickly and retain tempting color and crisp-tender texture.

● **Wok.** The ancient Chinese cook pot was designed to hasten cooking by concentrating heat at the bottom of the pot. So it's better than a skillet for stir-fried dishes because the speed seals in the flavorful juices of meat and vegetables. Its well-like shape makes it excellent for deep-frying and steaming.

● **Mixers.** If you have counter space, a tabletop mixer is the best choice, since it's strong enough for bread dough and doesn't require a free hand for beating egg whites or cream. But if you have to take the big mixer out of the cabinet every time you need it, you'll find a hand mixer to be much more convenient.

● **Cutting Tools.** Everyone knows that sharp knives make for easier food preparation. But don't forget that other tools with cutting edges, especially vegetable peelers, graters, and food processor blades, become dull, too. Since these cutting edges can't be sharpened, replace them when necessary—and save yourself a lot of frustration.

● **Cutting Boards.** Why do you need several cutting boards? So that there's no excuse for other people not sharing chopping and slicing chores! Your kitchen space may be limited, but a cutting board, knife, and a cook's helper can always be moved into another room.

● **Pots and Pans.** A very big pot—at least 10-quart capacity—will enable you to double most recipes for soups and stews. A large flat-bottom roasting pan will allow you to do the same for casseroles and roasts. Thus you can cook enough for two or more meals at once. For everyday use, it's handy to have 1-quart, 2-quart, and 4-quart saucepans with covers. A large oven-proof skillet gives you the flexibility to cook some ingredients on top of the stove and then finish a dish in the oven without transferring the food.

● **Helpful Accessories.** A salad spinner makes cleaning greens a pleasure; children can easily accomplish this task. An extra-large colander will save the day when there's a big batch of spaghetti or potatoes to drain. Sturdy tongs are the ideal implement for removing corn from the boiling water, turning a steak under the broiler, retrieving fried foods from hot fat, and moving pieces of meat around in a sauté pan. Kitchen shears make quick work of snipping parsley and other fresh herbs. A small plastic juicer with an attached container will inspire you to use fresh lemon and lime juice instead of bottled juice; you can put the juicer in the refrigerator to store extra juice. A kitchen timer or two will allow you to complete preparations, start cooking . . . and walk away from the kitchen!

Menus to COOK Quick

All cooks know that fast is a relative term. If you get home from work at five o'clock and your children clamor for supper at five-thirty, fast isn't fast enough. A meal that takes only half an hour to prepare but doesn't supply needed vitamins and minerals may be fast, but it isn't smart. And, of course, a supper that lands lickety-split on the table but doesn't look tempting could be said to have regrettably exceeded the speed limits!

So the minutes allotted to each *Cook Quick* menu have been counted accordingly. None of the menus requires more than an hour of preparation prior to serving. But if an hour is too long to wait in your home, you can divide any of the preparations into do-ahead and finish-up segments of half an hour or less. All of the menus have been designed to supply protein, carbohydrates, and the vitamins, minerals, and fiber of vegetables and fruits. As for the flavors and colors. . . these menus sparkle!

Each menu chapter has been developed to meet a different set of serving requirements. About half of the menus supply solutions to the everyday dinner dilemma in the *What's for Supper?* section. These are the simplest meals to prepare—unless you'd rather simmer a potful of something delicious whenever time allows and just reheat it when needed. In that case, you'll want to turn straight to the section called *All in One Dish*. If stove-top simmering sounds too hot or too slow, consider the alternatives in *Making the Most of the Microwave*—a section that highlights the ways in which microwave recipes can be coordinated to produce the most pleasure in the least amount of time. But what about those days when any cooking at all seems like too much? Think light, as in salads and sandwiches, and turn the recipes in *Time Out for Lunch* into anytime refreshment. Or ask any cook's helper who is capable of scrambling eggs to show off his or her talents with one of the easy dishes in the section called *Brunch or Breakfast*. After all, every cook deserves a break now and then.

No matter how experienced they are, most cooks think twice about any mealtime improvisations when guests are due to arrive. The nervousness may be natural and unavoidable—but it doesn't have to be time-consuming! Look at the menus in the section called *Fast But Fancier*, and you'll recognize the little tricks that can make a meal seem special without demanding more of the cook. The recipes feature ingredients that have a natural elegance, such as seafood, boneless meats and chicken breasts, and the brightest fruits and vegetables. The seasonings are a bit more complex because intrigue goes hand in hand with festivity. The presentations display a little more consideration for distinct colors and shapes. All of these refinements are derived from the one big difference you should allow for when you entertain, and that is that diners will sit around the table longer than the "regular crew" usually does. This fact doesn't imply that you should prepare more food; in fact, lighter fare can be more pleasant when you're sitting for a longer time. It does mean that anything that invites lingering—such as a vase of flowers that catches the eye or a cup of coffee good enough to savor slowly—will contribute to the "company" mood.

How to Use Cook Quick Menus

Make *Cook Quick* menus work best for you by following these steps to maximize time efficiency:

● **Read Through the Entire Menu Before You Start to Cook.** No ingredient or preparation step will take you by surprise halfway through the cooking.

● **Look to Other Menus**. If you would like to make part of the menu but not all of it, check other menus as well as the *Cook Quick* recipe section for appropriately fast substitutions. The easiest way to choose complementary recipes is to turn to other menus that feature a similar main dish. You'll find chicken recipes, for example, in every menu chapter except *Brunch or Breakfast*; by browsing through all the chicken menus, you'll come across dozens of side dishes that taste good with any kind of chicken.

● **Read the Preparation Schedule for Each Menu Ahead of Time.** Most of the schedules are divided into two parts: Make Ahead and Prepare & Serve. Under Make Ahead, you'll find some steps that must be done in advance, such as marinating, and others that could be done several days ahead, such as making a dessert. There's enough leeway in the Make Ahead part for you to decide just how far ahead you'd like to work, whether two hours or two days.

Take Time to Enjoy

The best-laid plans of busy cooks sometimes go awry, and that need not be disastrous! Menus are meant to inspire—not to mire you in details that can detract from the enjoyment of food. There's always more than one way to supply nutrients and sate appetites. Here are just a few possibilities:

● **Start the Meal Before You Start the Cooking.** A glass of juice or milk, a cup of canned soup, melon or tomato wedges, lettuce with a bottled salad dressing, cheese and crackers, carrot and celery sticks, or even an apple or pear—all of these snacks can provided a predinner bonus of vitamins and minerals as well as an opportunity to relax before you go into the kitchen.

● **Celebrate the Best of Each Season.** When the corn is high and tomatoes are ripe and juicy, artichokes are abundant, or new potatoes have just come to market, rejoice and eat your fill! Add an assortment of cold cuts or cheese to the menu, if you wish. Or just set out an herb butter that will highlight the bounty, pass the bread, and dig in.

● **Indulge in a Great Dessert.** Make time to bake a cake, pie, or cookies now and then—even if it means there's not much time to prepare anything else for dinner. You can pack a lot of nutrients into thick sandwiches, especially if you layer them with lettuce and tomatoes. And you'll certainly be able to enlist other family members to fix the sandwiches when they see that you're up to your elbows in a delicious dessert!

What's for Supper?

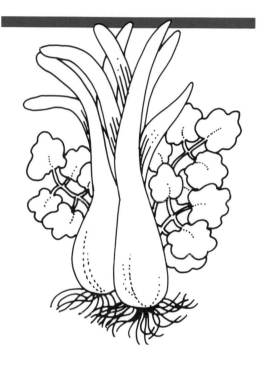

The question gets asked so often that not a few cooks begin to think their name is "What's for supper"! Well, the question may be routine in your home, but the answer doesn't have to be. You can say you're flying south of the border for Taco Casseroles or visiting Italy for Savory Scallopini. Tell them something tantalizing, like Oriental Steak. Or bring a round of cheers by mentioning a Backyard Barbecue or a Fast Shrimp Feast.

Whatever response you choose, it can be prepared and served in an hour or less. These are uncomplicated menus that flatter familiar ingredients with readily available seasonings. Use them to renew appreciation for chicken with, say, tangy Lemon-Caper Butter Chicken or couldn't-be-simpler Italian Grilled Chicken. Turn to them for fresh approaches to ground beef, such as Spaghetti Squash with Meat Sauce. Let them show off the marvelous flavors of fish in recipes such as Snapper Veracruz or Salmon Poached in Wine.

When you're looking for the fastest replies, try Lamb Kabobs or Chicken Chop Suey. If you'd like to come home to a dinner that's just about ready, plan ahead for Peppered Steak or Ham and Sweets. Cold days can make you hungry for a Hearty Pork Supper or Gourmet Meatballs and Spaghetti. Hot days welcome the outdoors approach to Grilled Pork Chops or Skewered Shrimp. And what about didn't-have-time-to-shop days? Keep the ingredients for Country-Style Steak or Broiled Cornish Hens menus in the freezer and pantry, and you'll be all set.

Many menus include breads and desserts that you may or may not have time to prepare at suppertime. Packaged breads and ice cream or fruit can always be substituted. But don't overlook these recipes, for they are all very fast, and most can be made ahead. Some of them, such as Frozen Brandy Alexander Pie or Glazed Fruit Tart will turn an everyday meal into company fare. Others, such as Refrigerator Yeast Biscuits, Coconut Snowdrops or Fudge-Topped Chocolate Cake, will remind you with their aromas of how comforting easy dishes can be.

Menu of Menus

TACO CASSEROLES

Individual Taco Casseroles
Overnight Slaw

Serves 8

Make Ahead: Prepare and refrigerate Overnight Slaw.
Prepare & Serve: Prepare and bake Individual Taco Casseroles. If you haven't made Overnight Slaw, serve a salad of shredded lettuce, chopped tomatoes, and green onions with the casseroles. For a refreshing dessert, try topping fresh fruit with lemon yogurt.

INDIVIDUAL TACO CASSEROLES

1 **pound lean ground beef**
1 **cup chopped onion**
1 **clove garlic, minced**
1 **(29-ounce) can pinto beans, drained**
1 **(28-ounce) can tomatoes, undrained and chopped**
1 **(6-ounce) can tomato paste**
1 **(2¼-ounce) can sliced ripe olives, drained**
½ **cup water**
2 **tablespoons chili powder**
1 **teaspoon salt**
½ **teaspoon dried whole oregano**
¼ **teaspoon ground cumin**
8 **(6-inch) corn tortillas**
1 **cup (4 ounces) shredded Cheddar cheese**

1. Combine ground beef, onion, and garlic in a large Dutch oven; cook until meat is browned, stirring to crumble. Drain and discard pan drippings. Add beans, tomatoes, tomato paste, olives, water, chili powder, salt, oregano, and cumin to Dutch oven. Bring to a boil. Reduce heat, and simmer, uncovered, 30 minutes, stirring mixture occasionally.

2. Cut four 2-inch slashes, 3 inches apart, around edge of each uncut tortilla. Fit one tortilla into each of 8 (10-ounce) individual casseroles, overlapping cut edges of tortilla.

3. Spoon beef mixture evenly into prepared casseroles. Bake at 350° for 20 minutes or until thoroughly heated.

4. Sprinkle with cheese; bake 5 minutes or until cheese melts.

5. Serve warm. Yield: 8 servings.

Note: If you don't have individual casseroles, spoon beef mixture into center of each tortilla. Roll tortilla around filling and place seam-side down in a lightly greased 12- x 8- x 2-inch baking dish. Bake as directed.

◆ OVERNIGHT SLAW

1 **large cabbage (about 2¾ pounds), cored and shredded**
1 **large onion, sliced and separated into rings**
1 **cup vinegar**
¾ **cup vegetable oil**
3 **tablespoons sugar**
1 **tablespoon dry mustard**
1½ **teaspoons salt**
1½ **teaspoons celery seeds**

1. Layer cabbage and onion in a large serving bowl.

2. Combine remaining ingredients in a small saucepan; bring to a boil.

3. Pour over vegetables. Cover and refrigerate overnight.

4. Toss lightly, and drain before serving. Yield: 8 servings.

An easy make-ahead in this Steak and Potatoes menu (page 19) is Marinated Squash Salad. And while the potatoes bake, the Mustard-Topped Steak can be sauced and broiled.

SPAGHETTI SQUASH WITH MEAT SAUCE

Spaghetti Squash with Meat Sauce
Cauliflower Salad
Cheese-Herb Loaf

Serves 4

Make Ahead: Marinate Cauliflower Salad.
Prepare & Serve: Prepare Cheese-Herb Loaf while spaghetti squash cooks. Cook meat sauce. Microwave or bake Cheese-Herb Loaf. For a refreshing follow-up, serve chunks of honeydew melon sprinkled with melon-flavored liqueur.

SPAGHETTI SQUASH WITH MEAT SAUCE
(pictured at left)

1 (2½-pound) spaghetti squash
½ pound ground chuck
1 (15½-ounce) jar prepared
   spaghetti sauce
3 tablespoons butter or margarine
   Chopped fresh parsley (optional)

1. Pierce squash in several places. Place in a Dutch oven; add water to cover. Bring to a boil; cover and simmer 30 minutes or until slightly tender. Remove from Dutch oven, and drain well. Set aside.
2. Cook ground chuck in a small skillet over medium heat until brown, stirring to crumble. Remove from skillet; drain.
3. Combine ground chuck and spaghetti sauce in a medium saucepan. Cover

This Spaghetti Squash with Meat Sauce menu (above) features Cheese Herb-Loaf and Cauliflower Salad with the entrée.

and cook over medium heat, stirring occasionally, until thoroughly heated.
4. Cut reserved squash in half lengthwise; remove and discard seeds. Melt butter in a large skillet over low heat. Pull "spaghetti-like" strands from squash. Add strands to hot butter; toss gently.
5. Transfer spaghetti squash to a serving platter; pour meat sauce over top. Sprinkle with chopped parsley, if desired. Serve hot. Yield: 4 servings.

MicroNote: To microwave step 1, pierce squash; place on a paper towel. Microwave at HIGH for 6 to 8 minutes or until squash feels soft.

CAULIFLOWER SALAD
(pictured at left)

1 (1½-pound) head cauliflower
1 medium-size red onion, thinly
   sliced
6 pitted ripe olives, coarsely
   chopped
6 pimiento-stuffed olives,
   sliced
4 small sweet pickles, coarsely
   chopped
1 tablespoon capers, drained
⅓ cup white wine vinegar
⅓ cup olive oil
2 tablespoons chopped fresh
   basil
¼ teaspoon salt
   Dash of pepper
   Lettuce leaves

1. Wash cauliflower, and break into flowerets. Cover and cook in boiling water 5 minutes. Drain and immediately plunge into cold water. Drain thoroughly.
2. Combine cauliflowerets, onion, olives, pickles, and capers. Combine remaining ingredients, except lettuce, and pour over salad, tossing lightly.
3. Cover with plastic wrap, and chill 8 hours or overnight.
4. Toss just before serving. Serve on lettuce-lined plates. Yield: 4 servings.

☐ CHEESE-HERB LOAF
(pictured on page 14)

1 (3-ounce) package cream cheese
¾ cup (3 ounces) shredded sharp
    Cheddar cheese
½ teaspoon dry mustard
2 slices bacon
1 tablespoon plus 1½ teaspoons
    milk
1½ teaspoons chopped fresh chives
1 (16-ounce) loaf French bread

1. Soften and combine cream cheese with Cheddar cheese and mustard in a medium mixing bowl; beat well.
2. Cook bacon in a small skillet until crisp. Drain bacon. Crumble bacon, and set aside.
3. Heat milk in a small saucepan. Pour warm milk into cheese mixture; beat until fluffy. Add chives and bacon to cheese mixture, mixing well.
4. Cut bread into 1-inch slices, cutting to, but not through, bottom crust. Spread slices with cheese mixture.
5. Wrap Cheese-Herb Loaf in heavy-duty aluminum foil. Bake at 400° for 10 to 12 minutes or until thoroughly heated.
6. Serve warm. Yield: one loaf.

MicroMethod

1. Place cream cheese in a small bowl; microwave at MEDIUM-LOW (30% power) for 2 to 3 minutes. Combine cream cheese, Cheddar cheese, and mustard in a medium mixing bowl; beat well.
2. Place bacon slices on a rack in a 12- x 8- x 2-inch baking dish; cover with paper towels. Microwave at HIGH for 2 to 3 minutes. Crumble bacon.
3. Heat milk in a 1-cup glass measure at HIGH for 15 seconds. Pour into cheese mixture; beat until fluffy. Add chives and bacon, mixing well.
4. Same as step 4.
5. Place loaf on waxed paper. Cover with paper towels, and microwave at HIGH for 2 to 3 minutes or until thoroughly heated.
6. Same as step 6.

BEEF RAGOUT

Ground Beef-Zucchini Ragout
Lettuce Wedges with
Italian Country Salad Dressing
French Bread
Pear Upside-Down Ginger Cake

Serves 6

Make Ahead: Make Italian Country Salad Dressing, and refrigerate overnight. Bake Pear Upside-Down Ginger Cake.
Prepare & Serve: If cake has not been made ahead, it can be prepared now, and baked during other meal preparation. While Ground Beef-Zucchini Ragout cooks, wash lettuce and cut into wedges. Chill lettuce until serving time. Warm commercial French bread.

The Italian Country Salad Dressing needs to stand for the flavors to blend; so if you don't have it ready, substitute Vinaigrette Dressing (page 75).

☺ GROUND BEEF-ZUCCHINI RAGOUT

½ pound ground chuck
1 cup chopped onion
1 cup chopped green pepper
½ pound fresh mushrooms, sliced
    Vegetable cooking spray
1 (24-ounce) can tomato juice
1 bay leaf
½ teaspoon salt
½ teaspoon dried whole thyme
6 ounces corkscrew pasta, uncooked
2 medium zucchini, thinly sliced

1. Combine ground chuck, onion, green pepper, and mushrooms in a large Dutch oven coated with cooking spray. Cook over medium heat 5 minutes or until meat is browned, stirring to crumble.

2. Add tomato juice, bay leaf, salt, thyme, and pasta. Cover and cook 5 minutes, stirring occasionally. Add zucchini and cook 5 minutes or until zucchini is tender.

3. Remove and discard bay leaf before serving. Yield: 6 servings.

ITALIAN COUNTRY SALAD DRESSING

½ **cup garlic-flavored red wine vinegar**
⅓ **cup olive oil**
2 **tablespoons firmly packed brown sugar**
1 **tablespoon grated Parmesan cheese**
2 **tablespoons catsup**
1 **tablespoon prepared mustard**
½ **teaspoon salt**
½ **teaspoon dried whole Italian herbs**
¼ **teaspoon paprika**
⅛ **teaspoon pepper**
 Lettuce wedges

1. Combine all ingredients, except lettuce wedges, in a glass jar. Cover tightly, and shake well.

2. Chill at least 2 hours. Shake well before serving over lettuce wedges. Yield: 1¼ cups.

PEAR UPSIDE-DOWN GINGER CAKE

2 **tablespoons butter or margarine**
½ **cup firmly packed light brown sugar**
1 **(16-ounce) can pear halves in light syrup, drained**
1 **(14.5-ounce) package gingerbread mix**
 Frozen whipped topping, thawed (optional)

1. Place butter in an 8-inch square baking pan; heat in a 375° oven 2 minutes or until butter melts.

2. Remove pan from oven. Stir in brown sugar. Spread mixture evenly over bottom of pan. Arrange pears, cut side down, over sugar mixture.

3. Prepare gingerbread mix according to package directions. Pour gingerbread batter over pears.

4. Bake at 375° for 35 minutes or until a wooden pick inserted in center comes out clean. Remove from oven, and cool in pan 2 minutes.

5. Invert cake onto a serving platter. Cut cake into squares, and top each serving with a dollop of whipped topping, if desired. Yield: 6 servings.

QUICK HOT BREADS

The fastest way to serve an enticing hot bread is to start with purchased bread and add some extra savor. Here are just some of the possibilities that you can pop into the toaster oven or under the broiler. They're all easy to serve appetite-appeasers.

● Cut French bread in half lengthwise. Spread with butter. Sprinkle lavishly with grated Parmesan cheese. Place bread under the broiler until cheese is lightly browned.

● Slice bagels in half. Place cut-side down under the broiler to lightly toast. Turn halves over, spread with butter, and sprinkle with sesame seeds. Place under broiler until seeds are toasted.

● Cut pita bread rounds in half to make two flat discs from each loaf. Brush lightly with olive or vegetable oil. Sprinkle with chopped or sliced pitted ripe olives, a pinch of dried oregano, and shredded mozzarella cheese. Place under broiler until cheese melts.

COUNTRY-STYLE STEAK

Braised Steak with Onions
Brussels Sprouts Creole
Luscious Light Pineapple-Cheese Pie

Serves 6

Make Ahead: Prepare pie, and chill.
Prepare & Serve: Cook Braised Steak with Onions. Prepare Brussels Sprouts Creole. If you had no time to make the pie the night before, prepare Chocolate Cupcakes (page 267) while the meat is cooking. Or put a loaf of Easy Cheese Bread (page 131) in the oven before you prepare the meat, and serve purchased spice cookies for dessert.

BRAISED STEAK WITH ONIONS

¼ cup all-purpose flour
¾ teaspoon salt
½ teaspoon paprika
¼ teaspoon pepper
 1 (1½-pound) boneless round steak,
       cut ½-inch thick
 1 tablespoon plus 1½ teaspoons
       vegetable oil
 1 cup water
 1 tablespoon red wine vinegar
 1 clove garlic, minced
 1 bay leaf
¼ teaspoon dried whole thyme,
       crushed
 2 medium onions, sliced

1. Combine first 4 ingredients. Trim excess fat from steak, and sprinkle with half of flour mixture. Pound steak, using a meat mallet or rolling pin, to ⅜-inch thickness. Turn steak over, and repeat procedure, pounding steak to ¼-inch thickness. Cut into 6 serving-size pieces.

2. Heat oil in a large skillet; add steak, and brown on all sides. Remove steak from skillet, and drain on paper towels; add remaining ingredients to skillet. Stir well, scraping brown particles from bottom of skillet; bring mixture to a boil.

3. Return meat to skillet; reduce heat. Cover and simmer 45 minutes or until tender. Remove and discard bay leaf.

4. Serve steak and onions directly from skillet. Spoon cooking liquid over top of each serving. Yield: 6 servings.

BRUSSELS SPROUTS CREOLE

1½ pounds fresh brussels sprouts or
       2 (10-ounce) packages frozen
       brussels sprouts
 1 quart cold water
1½ teaspoons salt, divided
¼ cup finely chopped onion
¼ cup chopped green pepper
 2 tablespoons butter or margarine
 2 cups (about 2 medium) peeled,
       diced tomatoes
¼ teaspoon poultry seasoning
¼ teaspoon pepper

1. Trim base of brussels sprouts, and discard yellowed outer leaves. Soak brussels sprouts in water and 1 teaspoon salt for 20 minutes. Drain well, and cut a small cross in base of each brussels sprout to hasten cooking. Set aside.

2. Sauté onion and green pepper in butter in a large skillet until tender. Stir in tomatoes, remaining ½ teaspoon salt, poultry seasoning, and pepper. Add reserved brussels sprouts, and cook over medium heat 5 minutes, uncovered.

3. Cover and continue to cook 15 to 20 minutes or until sprouts are tender.

4. Transfer to a serving bowl, and serve immediately. Yield: 6 servings.

MicroNote: To microwave steps 2 and 3, place onion, green pepper, and butter in a 3-quart casserole; microwave at HIGH for 1 minute. Add remaining ingredients. Cover and microwave at HIGH for 6 to 8 minutes or until brussels sprouts are tender.

♦ LUSCIOUS LIGHT PINEAPPLE-CHEESE PIE

1 (15¼-ounce) can unsweetened pineapple tidbits, undrained
1 envelope unflavored gelatin
2 tablespoons sugar
1 (8-ounce) package Neufchâtel cheese, softened
Graham cracker crust, chilled

1. Drain pineapple, reserving juice. Reserve 3 tablespoons pineapple tidbits for garnish.

2. Add water to reserved juice to equal 1 cup. Place in a small non-metal saucepan; bring to a boil.

3. Combine gelatin and sugar, stirring well; add to boiling liquid, stirring until dissolved. Remove from heat, and cool mixture slightly.

4. Beat Neufchâtel cheese in a medium mixing bowl until smooth; add gelatin mixture; beat well. Cover and chill for 1 hour or until gelatin mixture reaches the consistency of unbeaten egg white.

5. Press any excess juice out of pineapple. Fold well-drained pineapple into chilled mixture, and pour into chilled crust. Cover with plastic wrap, and chill.

6. Garnish pie with reserved 3 tablespoons pineapple, and cut into wedges to serve. Yield: one 9-inch pie.

STEAK AND POTATOES

Mustard-Topped Steak
Baked Potatoes
Marinated Squash Salad
Kiwi-Lime Tarts

Serves 6 to 8

Make Ahead: Make Kiwi-Lime Tarts. Prepare Marinated Squash Salad.
Prepare & Serve: Bake potatoes. Broil Mustard-Topped Steak. If you didn't prepare the tarts, serve fresh kiwifruit slices with raspberry yogurt.

MUSTARD-TOPPED STEAK
(pictured on page 13)

1 (2-pound) boneless top round steak, cut 1¼-inch thick
¾ cup mayonnaise
¼ cup seasoned dry breadcrumbs
2 tablespoons prepared mustard
½ teaspoon onion salt
⅛ teaspoon paprika
Cherry Tomatoes
Fresh parsley sprigs (optional)

1. Place steak on rack in a broiler pan. Place pan 5 to 6 inches from heating element. Broil steak 10 minutes on each side or until desired degree of doneness.

2. Combine mayonnaise, breadcrumbs, mustard, onion salt, and paprika in a small mixing bowl, stirring well; spread mustard mixture over top of steak. Broil an additional 3 minutes or until mustard topping is bubbly.

3. To serve, place steak on a serving platter, and cut across the grain into thin slices. Garnish with cherry tomatoes and parsley sprigs, if desired. Yield: 6 to 8 servings.

MARINATED SQUASH SALAD
(pictured on page 13)

4 cups yellow squash, sliced
4 cups zucchini, sliced
1 medium-size red onion, sliced and
    separated into rings
1 (8-ounce) bottle commercial
    Italian salad dressing
½ teaspoon salt
¼ teaspoon pepper

1. Combine all ingredients in a large bowl. Cover and refrigerate overnight.
2. Drain vegetables, discarding marinade. Arrange vegetables on a serving platter. Yield: 6 to 8 servings.

Note: For a quicker side dish, sauté onion in 2 tablespoons Italian salad dressing over medium heat until soft. Stir in yellow squash and zucchini; cover and cook until squash is tender. Season with additional salad dressing, salt, and pepper.

KIWI-LIME TARTS

1 (8-ounce) package cream cheese,
    softened
½ cup sifted powdered sugar
½ teaspoon grated lime rind
3 tablespoons lime juice
8 (2¾-inch) tart shells, baked
2 kiwifruit, peeled and sliced
1 tablespoon plus 1 teaspoon apple
    jelly, melted (optional)

1. Beat cream cheese until light and fluffy in a medium mixing bowl; add powdered sugar, lime rind, and juice, beating well. Spoon mixture into tart shells.
2. Arrange kiwifruit slices on tarts; spoon ½ teaspoon melted jelly on each tart, if desired. Chill tarts thoroughly. Yield: 8 tarts.

MicroNote: To soften cream cheese, remove from wrapper, and microwave at LOW (10% power) for 1 to 2 minutes.

PEPPERED STEAK

Peppered Steak
Marinated Tomatoes
New Potato Salad

Serves 8

Make Ahead: Marinate steaks overnight. Boil or microwave potatoes for New Potato Salad.
Prepare & Serve: Marinate tomatoes. Complete potato salad; broil steaks. For a quick dessert, serve ice cream with chocolate sauce and coffee liqueur.

PEPPERED STEAK

½ cup brandy
¼ cup water
¼ cup lemon juice
¼ cup vegetable oil
2 tablespoons sugar
1 teaspoon onion salt
2 (1½-pound) blade chuck steaks,
    ¾-inch-thick
2 tablespoons cracked black pepper

1. Combine first 6 ingredients in a 13- x 9- x 2-inch pan. Add steaks to marinade; turn to coat well. Cover and marinate in refrigerator overnight.
2. Remove steaks from marinade; discard marinade. Press pepper into surface on both sides of steaks.
3. Place steaks on rack of broiler pan. Broil 6 inches from heating element 7 minutes on each side or until desired degree of doneness.
4. Serve warm. Yield: 8 servings.

Note: Steaks may be cooked 6 inches from medium coals 10 minutes on each side or until desired degree of doneness.

◆ MARINATED TOMATOES

½ pound fresh spinach, chopped
6 medium tomatoes, peeled and
  thinly sliced (about 3 pounds)
½ cup vegetable oil
⅓ cup chopped fresh parsley
⅓ cup chopped green onions
3 tablespoons red wine vinegar
1 teaspoon salt
¼ teaspoon pepper
  Dash of sugar

1. Line a 10- x 6- x 2-inch dish with chopped spinach; arrange tomato slices attractively over top.
2. Combine remaining ingredients, mixing well. Pour marinade over tomatoes. Cover with plastic wrap; chill 1 hour.
3. Serve tomatoes, using a slotted spoon. Yield: 8 servings.

▣ NEW POTATO SALAD

2 pounds new potatoes, unpeeled
⅓ cup mayonnaise
⅓ cup commercial sour cream
¼ cup finely chopped fresh parsley
1 teaspoon prepared horseradish
¾ teaspoon Dijon mustard
  Juice of half a lemon
⅛ teaspoon salt
  Dash of pepper

1. Place potatoes in a small Dutch oven with water to cover. Cover and bring to a boil; reduce heat, and cook for 15 minutes or just until fork-tender. Drain and cool.
2. Combine remaining ingredients in a large mixing bowl; stir until well blended.
3. Cut potatoes into quarters; add to mayonnaise mixture. Toss gently. Cover with plastic wrap; chill 25 minutes.
4. Serve chilled. Yield: 8 servings.

MicroNote: To microwave step 1, prick potatoes. Place in a 2-quart casserole with 2 tablespoons water. Cover and microwave at HIGH for 8 to 10 minutes. Let stand 3 minutes.

COME TO THE "BAR" FOR DESSERT

A choice of fixings makes things festive, especially at dessert-time. Set up any of these "bars":

● The Fresh Fruit Bar. Cut up four or more kinds of fresh fruit—oranges, pineapple, melon, mango, grapes, bananas, and strawberries are good choices, because they won't darken as quickly as apples and pears. Set fruit out in separate bowls with a choice of toppings: toasted chopped almonds, walnuts, pecans, toasted coconut, granola, fruit yogurts, or brown sugar.

● The Cheese Bar. The key to serving cheese for dessert is a variety of tastes and textures. Offer at least one firm cheese, such as aged Cheddar or Gruyère; one semi-firm, such as Port Salut or Muenster; and one softer cheese, such as Brie, herbed cream cheese, or fresh goat cheese. Or compose a cheese platter based on a theme, such as "Tastes of Italy" using imported Parmesan, Fontina, provolone, Mascarpone, and fresh mozzarella cheeses. Add two or three kinds of bread—French, raisin toast points, and wheatmeal biscuits provide a good variety of flavors.

● The Chocolate-Lovers' Bar. Rely on purchased desserts to give chocolate-lovers a choice of everything they ever wanted to dive into! Include chocolate, chocolate-mint, and mocha ice creams; chopped chocolate bars and mint wafers for topping; fudge sauce, melted chocolate, and chocolate-flavored liqueur to drizzle on top; toasted chocolate pound cake slices or chocolate sandwich cookies; and chocolate sprinkles, of course. Serve whipped cream flavored with melted chocolate or chocolate-flavored liqueur, only if you dare!

ORIENTAL STEAK

Oriental Grilled Steak
Grilled Zucchini
Salad Greens with Roquefort Dressing

Serves 6

Make Ahead: Marinate steak. If time allows, you might want to bake a quick batch of Easy Surprise Brownies (page 270) for dessert the night before or earlier in the day. Make Roquefort Dressing and refrigerate.
Prepare & Serve: Prepare salad greens of your choice; prepare zucchini for grilling. Grill steak and zucchini.

ORIENTAL GRILLED STEAK

¼ cup vegetable oil
2 tablespoons soy sauce
1 teaspoon grated lemon rind
2 tablespoons lemon juice
1 tablespoon sugar
½ teaspoon ground oregano
½ teaspoon salt
⅛ teaspoon pepper
1 medium onion, sliced
1 (1½-pound) flank steak

1. Combine oil, soy sauce, lemon rind, lemon juice, sugar, oregano, salt, pepper, and onion in a 12- x 8- x 2-inch baking dish, mixing well.
2. Score steak in a diamond pattern, making ¼-inch-deep cuts. Place steak in dish. Cover and refrigerate at least 2 hours, turning steak frequently.
3. Remove steak from marinade. Remove onion from marinade, using a slotted spoon; set aside. Reserve marinade.

4. Place steak on grill 5 inches from medium coals; grill 5 minutes on each side or until desired degree of doneness. Baste frequently with reserved marinade.
5. Cut steak in thin slices diagonally across the grain.
6. Cook reserved onion in a small skillet over low heat until tender. Serve with Oriental Grilled Steak. Yield: 6 servings.

GRILLED ZUCCHINI

3 medium zucchini
  Reserved marinade from Oriental
  Grilled Steak

1. Split zucchini in half lengthwise; brush with reserved marinade.
2. Place zucchini on grill 5 inches from medium coals; grill 5 minutes on each side or until tender, basting frequently with marinade.
3. Transfer zucchini to a serving platter; serve warm. Yield: 6 servings.

Note: Italian salad dressing may be substituted for the reserved marinade.

ROQUEFORT DRESSING

4 ounces Roquefort cheese,
  crumbled
1 (8-ounce) carton commercial sour
  cream
½ cup mayonnaise
2 tablespoons white wine vinegar
¼ teaspoon salt
⅛ teaspoon garlic salt
  Dash of pepper

1. Combine all ingredients in a medium mixing bowl; stir well. Cover and refrigerate until ready to use.
2. Serve dressing over salad greens. Yield: 1¾ cups.

GRILLED PORK CHOPS

Apricot-Stuffed Pork Chops
Green Bean Bundles
Baked Onions
Frozen Brandy Alexander Pie

Serves 6

Make Ahead: Cook and marinate green beans overnight. Prepare pie several hours or several days ahead.

Prepare & Serve: If you haven't made the pie, you may want to make instant "tartlets." (See recipe note.) Stuff pork chops, and grill while onions are baking. No time to marinate the beans? Cook beans as directed in the recipe, and serve hot with this simple sauce: ¼ cup melted butter mixed with 1 to 2 tablespoons Dijon mustard and 1 teaspoon dried dillweed.

APRICOT-STUFFED PORK CHOPS
(pictured on page 31)

  1 **(6-ounce) package dried apricots, coarsely chopped**
  1 **cup water**
  ¼ **cup chopped walnuts**
  2 **tablespoons sugar**
  2 **tablespoons butter or margarine**
  ¼ **teaspoon ground ginger**
  ¼ **teaspoon ground cinnamon**
  6 **(1¼-inch-thick) pork chops, cut with pockets**

1. Combine apricots and water in a saucepan; bring to a boil. Reduce heat, and simmer, uncovered, 5 minutes. Drain.

2. Combine apricots, walnuts, sugar, butter, ginger, and cinnamon in a medium mixing bowl; stir well. Stuff pockets of pork chops with apricot mixture.

3. Place pork chops 5 to 6 inches from low to medium coals; grill 30 to 35 minutes, turning frequently.

4. Remove pork chops to individual serving plates. Yield: 6 servings.

Note: To make a pocket in a pork chop, cut into the chop with a small sharp knife on the rib side, parallel to the surface of the chop. Be careful not to cut through the opposite side.

◆ ⬚ GREEN BEAN BUNDLES
(pictured on page 31)

  1 **pound fresh green beans**
  ¼ **cup water**
  1 **tablespoon lemon juice**
  1 **tablespoon red wine vinegar**
  1 **tablespoon Dijon mustard**
  ¼ **teaspoon salt**
  ⅛ **teaspoon coarsely ground black pepper**
  ½ **cup vegetable oil**
  1 **medium-size red pepper, seeded and cut into 6 rings**

1. Remove tips and strings from beans. Wash in cold water. Combine whole beans and ¼ cup water in a saucepan; bring to a boil. Reduce heat, and simmer, uncovered, 4 to 5 minutes or until crisp-tender. Drain. Place in 2-quart casserole.

2. Combine lemon juice, vinegar, mustard, salt, and pepper in a small mixing bowl, stirring well. Gradually add oil; stir constantly, using a wire whisk.

3. Pour dressing over beans. Cover and chill.

4. To serve, drain beans. Divide into 6 portions; circle each portion with a pepper ring. Yield: 6 servings.

MicroNote: To microwave step 1, combine beans and ¼ cup water in a 2-quart casserole. Cover with heavy-duty plastic wrap, and vent to allow steam to escape. Microwave at HIGH for 7 to 9 minutes or until crisp-tender.

BAKED ONIONS

(pictured on page 31)

12 small onions (about 1½ pounds)
2 tablespoons sherry
2 tablespoons honey
1 tablespoon butter or margarine, melted
1 teaspoon soy sauce
¼ teaspoon ground ginger

1. Place onions in a 9-inch square baking dish.
2. Combine sherry, honey, butter, soy sauce, and ginger in a small mixing bowl, stirring well. Pour mixture over onions.
3. Cover and bake at 350° for 40 minutes or until tender.
4. Serve warm. Yield: 6 servings.

◆ FROZEN BRANDY ALEXANDER PIE

1 quart vanilla ice cream, softened
3 tablespoons brandy
2 tablespoons crème de cacao
1 (9-inch) prepared graham cracker or chocolate crumb crust
Chocolate curls

1. Combine ice cream, brandy, and crème de cacao in a medium mixing bowl, stirring well.
2. Spoon mixture into crust. Cover and freeze overnight or until firm.
3. Garnish pie with chocolate curls, and serve immediately. Yield: one 9-inch pie.

Note: Frozen Brandy Alexander Pie melts quickly; serve directly from the freezer. To make instant Brandy Alexander "tartlets," line 6 or 8 muffin cups with paper liners. Divide 8 ounces chocolate cookie crumbs evenly among liners. Scoop ice cream into cups, turning to coat with crumbs. Freeze. At serving time, drizzle brandy and crème de cacao over ice cream, and garnish with grated chocolate.

HEARTY PORK SUPPER

Pork Chops with Applesauce Cream
Steamed Red Cabbage
Fudge-Topped Chocolate Cake

Serves 4

Make Ahead: Bake Fudge-Topped Chocolate Cake several hours ahead or day before serving.

Prepare & Serve: Cook Pork Chops with Applesauce Cream. Cook noodles and cabbage. The Fudge-Topped Chocolate Cake is extremely easy to make, but if you need something even faster, make parfaits by layering crushed chocolate-mint sandwich cookies with coffee or mint chip ice cream, and drizzle with chocolate sauce.

PORK CHOPS WITH APPLESAUCE CREAM

4 (¾-inch-thick) pork loin chops
2 tablespoons butter or margarine
1 tablespoon apple brandy
1 clove garlic, finely chopped, or 1 teaspoon garlic paste
2 tablespoons finely chopped onion
½ cup applesauce
1½ teaspoons all-purpose flour
1½ teaspoons Dijon mustard
½ cup commercial sour cream
Hot buttered noodles
4 thinly sliced apple wedges (optional)

1. Brown pork chops on both sides in butter in a large skillet over medium heat. Remove chops; set aside.

2. Add brandy, garlic, onion, applesauce, flour, and mustard to skillet; cook 3 minutes. Stir in sour cream with a wire whisk. Return chops to skillet; cover and simmer 20 minutes or until chops are tender.

3. Serve pork chops with applesauce cream over hot buttered noodles. Garnish each pork chop with an apple wedge, if desired. Yield: 4 servings.

⊘ STEAMED RED CABBAGE

**1 small head red cabbage, cored and
    very thinly sliced
½ cup toasted chopped walnuts**

1. Cook cabbage in steamer basket over simmering water 10 to 15 minutes or until wilted.

2. Remove cabbage to a serving bowl; stir in walnuts.

3. Serve cabbage with Pork Chops with Applesauce Cream, spooning some of the sauce over cabbage. Yield: 4 servings.

Note: An electric fry pan makes an excellent steamer; place a collapsible steamer basket or a small colander inside to hold the vegetables.

FUDGE-TOPPED CHOCOLATE CAKE

**1 cup butter or margarine, softened
    and divided
2 cups sugar, divided
4 eggs
1 cup all-purpose flour
1 teaspoon baking powder
⅛ teaspoon salt
1 (16-ounce) can chocolate syrup
1 teaspoon vanilla extract
⅓ cup evaporated milk
½ cup semisweet chocolate morsels**

1. Combine ½ cup butter, 1 cup sugar, eggs, flour, baking powder, salt, chocolate syrup, and vanilla in a large bowl. Beat with an electric mixer until just blended.

2. Pour batter into a well-greased 13- x 9- x 2-inch baking pan. Bake at 350° for 40 minutes or until a wooden pick inserted in center comes out clean. Remove from oven; set aside.

3. Combine remaining 1 cup sugar, milk, and remaining ½ cup butter in a medium saucepan. Bring to a boil; let boil 2 minutes, stirring constantly.

4. Remove from heat; add chocolate morsels, and stir morsels, using a wire whisk, until melted. Spoon icing immediately over warm cake.

5. Let cake cool before serving. Yield: one 13- x 9-x 2-inch cake.

FASTER THAN FROSTING

If you don't have time to fuss with making a frosting, try these faster alternative toppings for single-layer cakes:

● Sift powdered sugar through a paper doily to decorate a chocolate cake. Use cocoa on a yellow cake.

● Cut cooled cake crosswise in half. Return bottom half of cake to cake pan. Spread with softened ice cream. Replace top half of cake. Place in freezer until serving time. To serve, cut into squares, and spoon chocolate sauce over cake.

● Turn any cake mix into an upside-down cake. Melt ¼ cup butter in the bottom of a baking pan; stir in ½ cup brown sugar until dissolved. Arrange pecan halves and any drained canned fruit in bottom of pan, placing pieces upside down. Pour cake batter over fruit and bake. When cake tests done, remove from oven and invert onto a plate; let stand 5 minutes before removing pan.

BACKYARD BARBECUE

Barbecued Country-Style Ribs
Herbed New Potatoes
or
Potato Patties
Nutty Slaw
Sliced Tomatoes
Almond-Blueberry Cake

Serves 4

Make Ahead: Prepare and chill Nutty Slaw. Bake Almond-Blueberry Cake.
Prepare & Serve: Precook country-style ribs. Cook Potato Patties; slice tomatoes. Barbecue ribs on grill or cook in microwave. If there's no time to bake, serve watermelon for dessert.

Double the ribs and potatoes recipes, and you'll have the makings of a backyard barbecue party. Pick a quick dip from the appetizers chapter, and prepare it while the ribs are precooking.

BARBECUED COUNTRY-STYLE RIBS

3 to 4 pounds country-style ribs
3 cups water
1 (12-ounce) bottle chili sauce
1 (10-ounce) jar orange marmalade
3 cups red wine vinegar
1 tablespoon Worcestershire sauce
1 teaspoon celery seeds
   Orange slices

1. Combine ribs and water in a large Dutch oven. Bring to a boil. Reduce heat; cover and simmer 30 minutes. Drain.
2. Combine chili sauce, marmalade, vinegar, Worcestershire sauce, and celery seeds in a small saucepan. Bring to a boil.

Reduce heat, and simmer, uncovered, 10 minutes.
3. Place ribs on grill over medium coals. Grill 15 minutes, turning and basting with sauce as needed.
4. Serve remaining sauce with ribs. Garnish with orange slices. Yield: 4 servings.

MicroMethod

1. Combine ribs and water in a 3-quart casserole. Cover with heavy-duty plastic wrap, and vent to allow steam to escape; microwave at HIGH for 5 minutes. Reduce to MEDIUM (50% power); microwave 25 minutes, turning ribs once halfway through cooking time. Drain. Place ribs in a 13- x 9- x 2-inch baking dish.
2. Combine chili sauce, marmalade, vinegar, Worcestershire sauce, and celery seeds in a 2-quart glass measure. Cover and microwave at HIGH for 5 minutes. (At this point you may proceed with step 3 below or grill ribs as directed above. The microwave doesn't save a lot of time in this recipe, but it does ensure moist meat and easy cleanup.)
3. Pour sauce over ribs. Cover with heavy-duty plastic wrap, and vent to allow steam to escape; microwave at MEDIUM for 15 minutes, turning ribs after 7 minutes. Let stand, covered, 10 minutes.
4. Same as step 4.

HERBED NEW POTATOES

1 pound new potatoes
2 tablespoons plus 2 teaspoons
   butter or margarine, melted
2 tablespoons chopped fresh parsley
2 teaspoons chopped fresh or
   freeze-dried chives
2 teaspoons lemon juice
1 teaspoon chopped fresh dillweed
   or ¾ teaspoon dried dillweed
   Salt and pepper to taste

1. Pare a 1-inch strip around center of each potato. Cover potatoes, and cook in boiling salted water 25 minutes or until tender. Drain potatoes, and set aside.

2. Combine remaining ingredients, stirring well. Pour dressing over potatoes, coating thoroughly.

3. Serve warm. Yield: 4 servings.

POTATO PATTIES

2 **medium potatoes**
4 **slices bacon**
2 **green onions, minced**
1 **egg**
½ **teaspoon salt**
¼ **teaspoon pepper**
2 **tablespoons vegetable oil**

1. Drop potatoes into boiling water. Cook 6 to 8 minutes. Drain; peel and shred potatoes.

2. Cook bacon in a large skillet until crisp; drain. Crumble and set aside; reserve pan drippings in skillet.

3. Combine shredded potatoes, crumbled bacon, onion, egg, salt, and pepper, mixing well. Shape into 8 patties.

4. Add oil to reserved pan drippings. Place over medium heat. Add patties, a few at a time; cook patties on both sides until browned and crisp. Repeat procedure with remaining patties. Drain.

5. Serve patties immediately. Yield: 4 servings.

☺ ✦ NUTTY SLAW

4 **cups shredded cabbage**
1 **red apple, cored and shredded**
¼ **cup milk**
2 **tablespoons lemon juice**
2 **tablespoons mayonnaise**
½ **teaspoon salt**
½ **teaspoon pepper**
¼ **cup chopped dry roasted peanuts**
2 **tablespoons chopped fresh parsley**

1. Combine cabbage and apple in a medium bowl. Add milk, lemon juice, mayonnaise, salt, and pepper; toss lightly.

2. Sprinkle with peanuts and parsley; toss lightly. Serve immediately or refrigerate up to 24 hours. Yield: 1 quart.

ALMOND-BLUEBERRY CAKE

½ **cup plus 2 tablespoons butter or margarine, softened and divided**
½ **cup plus 2 tablespoons sugar, divided**
2 **eggs**
1 **teaspoon lemon juice**
1½ **cups all-purpose flour, divided**
1 **teaspoon baking powder**
¼ **cup slivered almonds, toasted**
1 **cup fresh blueberries**

1. Cream ½ cup softened butter in a large mixing bowl; gradually add ½ cup sugar, beating well. Add eggs, one at a time, beating well after each addition; stir in lemon juice.

2. Combine 1 cup flour and baking powder; stir into creamed mixture, mixing well. Spread batter evenly in a greased and floured 9-inch square baking pan.

3. Combine remaining ½ cup flour, 2 tablespoons sugar, and almonds in a small mixing bowl; cut in remaining 2 tablespoons butter with a pastry cutter until mixture resembles coarse meal. Gently stir in blueberries.

4. Sprinkle top of batter with almond-blueberry mixture. Bake at 325° for 40 minutes or until a wooden pick inserted in center comes out clean.

5. Cut Almond-Blueberry Cake into 2-inch squares. Place on individual serving plates. Yield: 16 servings.

BETTER THAN PLAIN BUTTER

Add seasonings to butter to make delicious sauces for all kinds of vegetables and broiled, grilled, or baked poultry, fish, and meats. Melt the butter with the seasonings just before serving, or make it anytime and store it as you would plain butter—in the refrigerator or the freezer. Usually you won't have to re-melt a frozen butter; just cut off a piece and let it melt atop the hot cooked food. Use unsalted butter or margarine, if possible, so salt won't dominate the other seasonings. And don't be afraid to use a lot of herbs and spices.

The following mixtures are all based on ½ cup of butter; double or triple the quantities to store for later use:

● Melt butter with 1 to 2 tablespoons minced fresh gingerroot and 1 teaspoon soy sauce; use to baste broiled chicken or serve with broccoli.

● Add grated rind of one lemon to butter; serve with asparagus, broccoli, or brussels sprouts.

● Mince 3 peeled cloves garlic, 2 green onions, and 5 sprigs parsley in food processor; blend in butter. Serve this all-purpose herb butter with broiled steaks, fish, or chicken.

● Melt butter with 2 tablespoons dried tarragon or rosemary leaves, or a combination; use to baste broiled or baked chicken, or roasts.

● Stir ¼ cup toasted chopped walnuts, pecans, almonds, or hazelnuts with melted butter. It's well worth keeping this mixture on hand to serve over cooked carrots, cauliflower, asparagus, winter squash, or cabbage. Almond butter tastes especially good with green beans; pecan butter is extremely complementary to beets.

SHERRIED PORK CUTLETS

Sherried Pork Cutlets
Orange Broccoli
Beet-Walnut Salad
Cheddar Pear Pie

Serves 6

Make Ahead: Prepare Beet-Walnut Salad.
Prepare & Serve: Bake Cheddar Pear Pie. Prepare cutlets for cooking. Cook Sherried Pork Cutlets, and prepare Orange Broccoli. Arrange salad on serving plate. If you didn't make salad ahead of time, you may wish to heat canned pickled beets to serve with the meat.

Brown rice would go well with pork, and there's time to simmer a potful while the pie cooks. For best flavor, substitute beef broth for all or part of the water called for in the package directions, and omit salt. For a speedier accompaniment, serve long grain and wild rice mix.

SHERRIED PORK CUTLETS

6 (¼-inch-thick) pork cutlets
2 eggs
½ cup all-purpose flour
¼ teaspoon salt
⅛ teaspoon pepper
¼ cup butter or margarine
¾ cup water
2 tablespoons sherry
1 tablespoon chopped fresh
    parsley

1. Flatten pork to ⅛-inch thickness, using a meat mallet or rolling pin. Beat eggs in a small mixing bowl. Combine flour, salt, and pepper in a shallow dish, mixing well. Dip pork in beaten eggs; dredge in flour mixture.

2. Melt butter in a large skillet over low heat. Add pork cutlets, a few at a time; cook over medium-high heat 2 minutes on each side or until lightly browned. Remove from skillet, and drain. Repeat procedure with remaining cutlets, reserving drippings in skillet.

3. Add water and sherry to skillet, scraping bottom of skillet with wooden spoon to loosen pan drippings. Bring to a boil; cook 2 minutes, stirring occasionally.

4. Transfer cutlets to a serving platter, and pour sauce over top. Sprinkle with parsley. Serve warm. Yield: 6 servings.

ORANGE BROCCOLI

1 (1½-pound) bunch broccoli
¼ cup butter or margarine, softened
1 tablespoon grated orange rind
2 tablespoons orange juice

1. Trim broccoli; pare stalks, using a vegetable peeler. Cut into long, thin stems. Transfer broccoli to a steamer basket; cover and steam 8 to 10 minutes or until tender. Place broccoli in a serving bowl.

2. Mix butter, orange rind, and orange juice in a small mixing bowl. Top broccoli with butter mixture. Yield: 6 servings.

Note: Orange butter may be refrigerated or frozen like plain butter.

BEET-WALNUT SALAD

1 (16½-ounce) jar sliced pickled beets, undrained
1 medium-size red onion, sliced
Watercress
¾ cup coarsely chopped walnuts
Orange slices

1. Combine beets and sliced onion in a large mixing bowl, tossing lightly. Cover tightly with plastic wrap, and refrigerate overnight.

2. Arrange watercress on a serving platter. Arrange pickled beets and onion slices over watercress, using a slotted spoon. Sprinkle salad with walnuts, and garnish platter with orange slices. Serve chilled. Yield: 6 servings.

CHEDDAR PEAR PIE

¼ cup butter or margarine, softened
½ cup (2 ounces) shredded sharp Cheddar cheese
½ cup all-purpose flour
¼ cup sugar
¼ teaspoon salt
⅓ cup sugar
1 tablespoon cornstarch
⅛ teaspoon salt
4 large Bartlett pears, peeled, cored, and thinly sliced
1 unbaked (9-inch) pastry shell

1. Combine butter and cheese in a small mixing bowl. Combine flour, ¼ cup sugar, and ¼ teaspoon salt in a medium mixing bowl; cut in cheese mixture with a pastry blender until mixture resembles coarse meal. Set aside.

2. Combine ⅓ cup sugar, cornstarch, and ⅛ teaspoon salt in a large mixing bowl; stir well. Add pears, tossing lightly to coat well.

3. Spoon pear mixture into unbaked pastry shell, and crumble reserved cheese mixture over top. Bake at 425° for 20 minutes. Reduce heat to 375°, and continue baking for 20 minutes.

4. Cool pie slightly before cutting into 8 wedges. Serve warm. Yield: one 9-inch pie.

Note: A food processor may be used to shred the Cheddar cheese and to thinly slice the pears.

HAM AND SWEETS

Honey-Glazed Ham Slice
Caraway Cabbage
Sweet Potatoes with Pecans

Serves 4

Make Ahead: Bake sweet potatoes.
Prepare & Serve: Make glaze for ham. Complete Sweet Potatoes with Pecans and Honey-Glazed Ham Slice. Make Caraway Cabbage.

HONEY-GLAZED HAM SLICE

1 (1½-pound) fully cooked ham
    slice (about 1-inch thick)
½ cup firmly packed brown sugar
½ cup honey
½ teaspoon dried mustard
6 whole cloves
2 slices canned pineapple
4 maraschino cherries, halved

1. Bake ham at 325° for 10 minutes.
2. Combine brown sugar, honey, mustard, and cloves in a small saucepan; mix well. Bring to a boil; boil 2 to 3 minutes, stirring constantly. Remove from heat.
3. Arrange pineapple and cherries on top of ham; spoon on glaze. Bake 15 minutes, basting twice with drippings.
4. Serve warm. Yield: 4 servings.

☺ CARAWAY CABBAGE

2 tablespoons vegetable oil
1 medium head cabbage, cored and
    shredded
1 tablespoon caraway seeds
¾ teaspoon salt
¼ teaspoon pepper

1. Heat oil in a large skillet; add remaining ingredients, stirring well.
2. Cook cabbage over medium heat, stirring constantly, 10 to 12 minutes or until tender.
3. Serve Caraway Cabbage immediately. Yield: 6 servings.

▣ SWEET POTATOES WITH PECANS

4 medium-size sweet potatoes
¼ cup butter or margarine, melted
¼ cup firmly packed brown sugar
¼ teaspoon ground nutmeg
¼ teaspoon salt
¼ teaspoon pepper
¼ cup chopped pecans

1. Wash sweet potatoes; pierce with a fork 3 times. Bake at 400° for 40 minutes or until tender, but firm.
2. Peel potatoes; cut into ½-inch slices. Place in a 10- x 6- x 2-inch baking dish.
3. Combine remaining ingredients; pour over potatoes. Bake at 325° for 20 minutes.
4. Serve warm. Yield: 6 servings.

MicroMethod

1. Wash sweet potatoes; pierce with a fork 3 times. Arrange potatoes on a paper towel in a circular pattern in the microwave. Microwave at HIGH for 8 to 10 minutes or until tender, but firm.
2. Same as step 2.
3. Combine remaining ingredients; pour over potatoes. Microwave at HIGH for 3 to 5 minutes or until hot.
4. Same as step 4.

The blend of fruit, nuts, and spices in the pockets of Apricot Stuffed Pork Chops is complemented by onions baked with sherry, honey, and soy sauce. Marinated Green Bean Bundles complete this delectable Grilled Pork Chop menu (page 23).

LAMB CHOPS À L'ORANGE

Orange Lamb Chops
Hot Cooked Brown Rice
Spinach and Mushrooms
Coconut Pudding

Serves 4

Make Ahead: Prepare Coconut Pudding several hours ahead or the night before. **Prepare & Serve:** Marinate lamb chops while rice is cooking; wash spinach. Broil lamb chops, and cook Spinach and Mushrooms. Garnish pudding with toasted coconut. If you anticipate being rushed at supper time, marinate lamb the night before, and serve it with couscous, cooked according to package directions.

ORANGE LAMB CHOPS

½ cup orange juice
1 tablespoon vegetable oil
1 tablespoon lemon juice
1 teaspoon onion salt
½ teaspoon dry mustard
¼ teaspoon ground cinnamon
⅛ teaspoon garlic powder
8 (4-ounce) lamb loin chops
Orange slices

1. Combine first 7 ingredients in a 13- x 9- x 2-inch baking dish; add chops. Cover; refrigerate 30 minutes.

Delicious accompaniments in this Gourmet Meatballs and Spaghetti menu (page 37) are Mozzarella and Mushroom Salad, and Garlic Bread. Peach-Lemon Frost is the easy make-ahead dessert.

2. Drain marinade into a small saucepan; transfer chops to a lightly greased rack of a broiler pan. Bring marinade to a boil, and boil 4 minutes or until slightly thickened. Remove from heat, and brush over chops; set remaining marinade aside.
3. Broil chops 6 inches from heating element, 4 to 5 minutes on each side, basting several times with marinade.
4. Transfer chops to a serving platter, and garnish with orange slices. Serve Orange Lamb Chops immediately. Yield: 4 servings.

Note: Lamb chops may be cooked over medium coals on the grill.

SPINACH AND MUSHROOMS

1½ pounds fresh spinach
¼ cup butter or margarine
½ pound fresh mushrooms, thinly sliced (about 3 cups)
½ cup finely chopped onion
Salt and pepper to taste
⅛ teaspoon ground nutmeg

1. Discard any wilted or yellowed leaves and pulpy stems of spinach. Wash spinach well, and set aside to drain.
2. Melt butter in a large Dutch oven over low heat; add mushrooms and onion, and sauté until tender. Gradually add reserved spinach, stirring constantly until spinach wilts.
3. Stir in salt, pepper, and nutmeg. Cook, uncovered, over high heat 5 minutes, stirring frequently until most of the liquid evaporates.
4. Serve warm. Yield: 4 servings.

Note: Packaged spinach tends to be less gritty than bulk spinach, but you're also more apt to find some wilted leaves in the bag. Whichever you use, immerse it in a sinkful or large bowl of cool water, and let stand a few minutes. Lift the spinach into a colander. Repeat once or twice, or until there's no sand left in the water.

◆▢ COCONUT PUDDING

1 (3½-ounce) can flaked coconut,
  divided
¼ cup all-purpose flour
½ cup sugar
1 cup milk, divided
2 eggs, well beaten
2 tablespoons butter or margarine,
  melted
½ teaspoon vanilla extract

1. Spread ½ cup coconut on a baking sheet. Bake at 350° for 5 minutes or until lightly toasted; set aside.

2. Combine flour, sugar, and ⅓ cup milk in a large mixing bowl, stirring well. Scald remaining milk in a heavy saucepan. Stir hot milk into flour mixture, using a wire whisk. Return mixture to saucepan; cook over medium heat, stirring constantly, until thick and bubbly.

3. Gradually stir one-fourth of hot mixture into eggs; add to remaining hot mixture, stirring constantly. Cook 5 minutes. Whisk in remaining coconut, butter, and vanilla. Spoon into individual serving bowls. Cover and chill several hours.

4. To serve, sprinkle top of pudding with toasted coconut. Yield: 4 servings.

MicroMethod

1. Sprinkle ½ cup coconut in a thin layer in a 9-inch pieplate. Microwave at MEDIUM-HIGH (70% power) for 4 to 5 minutes, tossing with a fork every minute.

2. Combine flour, sugar, and ⅓ cup milk, stirring well. Microwave remaining milk at HIGH for 2 to 3 minutes, until boiling. Stir hot milk into flour mixture, using a wire whisk. Microwave at HIGH for 1½ to 2 minutes, stirring every two minutes or until thick and bubbly.

3. Gradually stir one-fourth of hot mixture into eggs; add to remaining hot mixture, stirring constantly. Microwave at HIGH for 1 to 2 minutes. Whisk in remaining coconut, butter, and vanilla. Spoon into individual serving bowls. Cover with plastic wrap, and chill several hours.

4. Same as step 4.

LAMB CHOPS AND MASHED POTATOES

Braised Lamb Rib Chops
Buttered Carrots
Mashed Potatoes Au Gratin
Strawberry Fool

Serves 4

Prepare & Serve: Simmer or microwave potatoes. Cook lamb chops. Cook carrots. Complete Mashed Potatoes Au Gratin. Make Strawberry Fool just before serving. Serve packaged wafers with dessert to add a crisp accent.

BRAISED LAMB RIB CHOPS

8 (¾-inch-thick) lamb rib chops
  Vegetable cooking spray
¼ cup plain low-fat yogurt
¼ cup firmly packed brown sugar
1 tablespoon instant minced onion
1 teaspoon dried whole thyme
½ teaspoon salt
  Dash of pepper
1 cup sliced fresh mushrooms

1. Sauté chops in a large skillet, lightly coated with cooking spray, over medium heat until browned.

2. Combine yogurt, brown sugar, onion, thyme, salt, and pepper in a medium mixing bowl, stirring well. Spread yogurt mixture over chops, and top with sliced fresh mushrooms. Cover and simmer 15 minutes.

3. Serve warm. Yield: 4 servings.

Note: Yogurt mixture may be prepared ahead and refrigerated until ready to use.

MASHED POTATOES
AU GRATIN

4 medium potatoes (about 1½
   pounds), peeled and cut into
   eighths
½ teaspoon salt
2 tablespoons butter or margarine
½ cup milk
   Salt and pepper to taste
¼ cup (1 ounce) shredded Cheddar
   cheese

1. Place potatoes, ½ teaspoon salt, and water to cover in a large saucepan. Bring to a boil; reduce heat, and cook 15 to 20 minutes or until potatoes are tender. Drain, reserving potatoes in saucepan. Add butter to potatoes, stirring until butter is melted.
2. Place milk in a small saucepan. Cook over low heat until thoroughly heated. Add warmed milk and salt and pepper to taste to potatoes, stirring until smooth.
3. Spoon potatoes into a 1½-quart baking dish, and sprinkle with shredded cheese. Broil for 2 minutes or until lightly browned. Yield: 4 servings.

☺ STRAWBERRY FOOL

2 cups fresh strawberries, washed
   and hulled
¼ cup sugar
1 cup whipping cream, whipped
4 fresh strawberries, washed

1. Place 2 cups fresh strawberries and sugar in container of a food processor or an electric blender; process until smooth. Pour strawberry mixture into a large mixing bowl.
2. Fold whipped cream into strawberry mixture. Spoon into individual serving bowls. Garnish each with a strawberry. May be served immediately or refrigerated 1 hour. Yield: 4 servings.

Note: Frozen strawberries, thawed and drained, may be substituted for fresh.

AMERICA'S FAVORITE VEGETABLE!

Potatoes win, hands down, as a preferred side dish. Fortunately, white potatoes are also low in fat and calories, and high in minerals and vitamin C. Sweet potatoes are an excellent source of vitamin A. Here are some ways to make the most of these assets:

● Store potatoes in a dark, dry place-never in the refrigerator or under the sink. You can keep them up to three months if your storage area is about 45° to 50°. If your storage area is warmer than that, buy only as many potatoes as you can use in one week.

● New potatoes are the best choice for potato salads because they retain their shape when cooked. For best texture, cut potatoes into salad-size pieces and steam. Or simmer potato pieces covered in about ½-inch of chicken broth just until tender. If you like very firm potatoes in salads, arrange potato pieces in a ring in a round baking dish, leaving the center empty. Cover with heavy-duty plastic wrap, and vent to allow steam to escape. Microwave at HIGH for 5 to 6 minutes per pound or until tender, rotating dish a half-turn every 2 minutes.

● Many people believe that sour cream is a baked potato's true soul mate! To vary this great combination, mix the sour cream with crumbled bacon or blue cheese, grated Parmesan cheese, fresh or dried dillweed, minced anchovies or anchovy paste, shredded Cheddar or Swiss cheese, minced ham, caraway seeds, chopped ripe olives, chopped green onions, chopped fresh parsley, or chili powder. To top baked sweet potatoes, sprinkle the sour cream with nutmeg and black pepper, curry powder, or pumpkin pie spice. If you're counting calories, try plain low fat yogurt or cottage cheese instead of sour cream.

LAMB KABOBS

Lamb and Vegetable Kabobs
Artichoke Salad
Almond Rice

Serves 6

Make Ahead: Marinate lamb several hours or overnight.
Prepare & Serve: Prepare salad. Broil Lamb and Vegetable Kabobs while Almond Rice is cooking.

For a quick dessert, sprinkle sliced, peeled oranges with cinnamon. Brush with honey, and broil oranges just until glazed.

LAMB AND VEGETABLE KABOBS

½ cup olive oil
¼ cup lemon juice
1 teaspoon salt
½ teaspoon onion powder
½ teaspoon dried whole thyme
½ teaspoon paprika
1½ pounds boneless lamb, cut into 1¼-inch cubes
12 large fresh mushrooms (about ½ pound)
1 large green pepper, cut into 12 ½-inch squares
3 medium onions, peeled and quartered

1. Combine olive oil, lemon juice, salt, onion powder, thyme, and paprika in a 12- x 8- x 2-inch baking dish. Add lamb; cover and refrigerate overnight.
2. Drain marinade from lamb; set marinade aside. Thread lamb, mushrooms, green pepper, and onion alternately on 6 skewers.

3. Arrange skewers on a lightly greased rack of a broiler pan. Broil 6 inches from heating element 4 to 5 minutes on each side or until desired degree of doneness; baste frequently with remaining marinade.
4. Serve warm. Yield: 6 servings.

Note: Kabobs may be grilled over medium coals until desired degree of doneness. Baste kabobs frequently with remaining marinade.

ARTICHOKE SALAD

2 (6-ounce) jars marinated artichoke hearts, undrained
1 (½-pound) head Bibb lettuce, separated into leaves
3 tomatoes, cut into eighths
3 tablespoons capers
Pimiento strips

1. Drain artichoke hearts, and reserve ½ cup marinade.
2. Arrange lettuce leaves on six salad plates; divide artichoke hearts and tomato wedges evenly among plates.
3. Spoon reserved marinade over artichokes and tomatoes; sprinkle with capers. Garnish with pimiento. Yield: 6 servings.

ALMOND RICE

1 (10¾-ounce) can chicken broth, undiluted
1¼ cups water
1 cup regular rice, uncooked
2 tablespoons butter or margarine
½ cup slivered almonds

1. Combine broth and water in a heavy saucepan; bring to a boil, and add rice. Reduce heat; cover and simmer 20 minutes or until liquid is absorbed.
2. Melt butter in a small skillet. Sauté almonds in butter until lightly browned; stir into rice.
3. Serve warm. Yield: 4 to 6 servings.

GOURMET MEATBALLS AND SPAGHETTI

Veal with Pasta
Mozzarella and Mushroom Salad
Garlic Bread
Peach-Lemon Frost

Serves 6

Make Ahead: The Peach-Lemon Frost can be made up to 2 weeks ahead. Lemon Vinaigrette Dressing for the salad can be made up to 2 weeks ahead, and refrigerated until ready for use.
Prepare & Serve: Make veal meatballs. Cook spaghetti, and arrange salads while meat is cooking. Prepare bread.

VEAL WITH PASTA
(pictured on page 32)

1 pound ground veal
1 (10-ounce) package frozen spinach, thawed and drained
1 egg white
1 cup finely chopped onion
2 cloves garlic, crushed
1½ teaspoons dried whole basil, crushed and divided
1 teaspoon salt, divided
½ teaspoon red pepper, divided
2 ounces low-fat mozzarella cheese, cut into ½-inch cubes
1 (16-ounce) can whole tomatoes, undrained and chopped
1 (15-ounce) can tomato sauce
1 medium green pepper, seeded and sliced
½ cup water
3 tablespoons burgundy or other dry red wine
1 (12-ounce) package whole wheat spaghetti, cooked

1. Combine veal, spinach, egg white, onion, garlic, 1 teaspoon basil, ½ teaspoon salt, and ¼ teaspoon red pepper; mix well. Shape into 1½-inch balls. Insert 1 cheese cube into center of each meatball. Brown in electric skillet over medium heat. Remove meatballs from skillet; drain and discard pan drippings.
2. Combine tomatoes, tomato sauce, green pepper, water, wine, remaining ½ teaspoon basil, remaining ½ teaspoon salt, and remaining ¼ teaspoon red pepper in skillet. Simmer, uncovered, 10 minutes, stirring frequently. Add meatballs; cover and cook 10 minutes.
3. Serve meatballs and sauce over hot spaghetti. Yield: 6 servings.

◆ MOZZARELLA AND MUSHROOM SALAD
(pictured on page 32)

4 ounces mozzarella cheese
Red leaf lettuce
2 medium tomatoes (about 1 pound) sliced
3 large fresh mushrooms, cut in half
6 leaves basil, fresh
Lemon-Vinaigrette Dressing

1. Slice cheese ¼-inch thick, and cut into triangles.
2. Arrange lettuce and cheese evenly on 6 salad plates. Top each with 2 tomato slices, a mushroom half, and a basil leaf.
3. Serve topped with Lemon Vinaigrette Dressing. Yield: 6 servings.

Lemon Vinaigrette Dressing:

½ cup lemon juice
¼ cup plus 2 teaspoons vegetable oil
1 large clove garlic, minced
2 tablespoons minced fresh parsley

1. Combine ingredients in a jar. Cover tightly with lid; shake well and chill.
2. Shake before serving. Yield: ⅔ cup.

GARLIC BREAD
(pictured on page 32)

6 cloves garlic, unpeeled
¼ cup melted butter or olive oil
1 (16-ounce) loaf Italian bread

1. Simmer garlic cloves in water to cover 20 minutes or until soft. Rinse under cold water; drain.
2. Peel garlic; place in a small bowl, and mash, using a fork. Stir in butter.
3. Slice bread into 1-inch slices. Spread each slice with garlic mixture. Wrap loaf in heavy-duty aluminum foil; bake at 350° for 15 minutes or until thoroughly heated.
4. Serve warm. Yield: 1 loaf.

Note: Garlic cloves become very mild when simmered and will peel easily. Garlic mixture may be refrigerated or frozen. Try stirring 1 tablespoon dried whole oregano into the garlic mixture for extra flavor.

◆ PEACH-LEMON FROST
(pictured on page 32)

5 medium peaches, peeled and
    sliced
1 tablespoon plus 1½ teaspoons
    lemon juice
2 tablespoons plus 1½ teaspoons
    peach brandy or rum
¼ cup sifted powdered sugar
    (optional)
½ cup half-and-half
    Additional peach slices

1. Place sliced peaches in a single layer on a baking sheet; cover and freeze.
2. Place frozen peaches in container of a food processor or blender; process until smooth. Add lemon juice, brandy, and sugar, if desired; pulse twice. Slowly add half-and-half, processing until smooth.
3. Spoon into small cups; serve or freeze until ready to use. Top with an additional peach slice. Yield: 6 servings.

VEAL BIRDS IN ORZO NESTS

Veal Birds
Orzo with Pine Nuts
Romaine Salad
Easy Lemon Ice Cream

Serves 6

Make Ahead: Make Easy Lemon Ice Cream at least 4 hours ahead. The salad dressing can be made up to 1 week ahead, and stored in the refrigerator. Double the quantities of ingredients for the vinaigrette if you want to have an extra batch of this all-purpose vinaigrette handy.
Prepare & Serve: Make Veal Birds. Cook orzo. Complete salad. Finish Orzo with Pine Nuts. Toss Romaine Salad with vinaigrette dressing.

VEAL BIRDS

6 (¼-inch-thick) veal scallops (about
    2 pounds)
½ teaspoon salt
¼ teaspoon white pepper
    Grated rind of 1 lemon
1 (8-ounce) package frozen broccoli
    cuts, thawed
1 teaspoon chicken-flavored bouillon
    granules
1 cup water
1 tablespoon plus 1½ teaspoons
    tomato paste
1 tablespoon minced fresh parsley

1. Pound veal between two sheets of waxed paper to ⅛-inch thickness, using a meat mallet or rolling pin.
2. Sprinkle veal scallops evenly with salt,

pepper, and grated lemon rind. Place several broccoli cuts in center of each scallop. Roll up jellyroll fashion, and secure with wooden picks.

3. Combine bouillon granules, water, and tomato paste in a large skillet. Bring to a boil, stirring constantly to dissolve granules. Reduce heat, and simmer 3 minutes. Add veal rolls; cover and simmer 15 minutes or until veal is tender.

4. Transfer veal rolls to a serving platter, and remove wooden picks; reserve tomato sauce in skillet. Garnish Veal Birds with parsley, and serve over Orzo with Pine Nuts with tomato sauce reserved from skillet. Yield: 6 servings.

☺ ORZO WITH PINE NUTS

2 **tablespoons butter**
3 **tablespoons pine nuts**
1 **tablespoon dried whole basil**
3 **cups cooked orzo**
 Salt and pepper

1. Melt butter in a medium skillet over medium heat. Stir in nuts; cook, 3 to 5 minutes or until nuts are golden, stirring occasionally.

2. Stir basil into butter mixture. Add orzo to butter mixture, stirring to coat well. Season with salt and pepper to taste. Yield: 6 servings.

Note: Other types of pasta, such as spaghetti or small shells, can be substituted for orzo. One-half pound dried pasta will yield about 3½ cups cooked.

☺ ROMAINE SALAD

½ **cup olive or vegetable oil**
2 **tablespoons red wine vinegar**
1 **tablespoon fresh lemon juice**
2 **teaspoons dried whole oregano**
½ **teaspoon garlic powder**
1 **head romaine lettuce, torn into bite-size pieces**
2 **medium tomatoes, cut into thin wedges**
1 **medium cucumber, peeled, seeded, and sliced**
½ **purple onion, sliced very thin**
½ **cup ripe pitted olives, sliced**
2 **tablespoons grated Parmesan cheese (optional)**
 Salt and pepper

1. Combine olive oil, vinegar, lemon juice, oregano, and garlic powder in a small jar; cover tightly and shake vigorously. Set salad dressing aside.

2. Combine lettuce, tomatoes, cucumber, onion, and olives in a salad bowl. Sprinkle with cheese, if desired; sprinkle with salt and pepper to taste.

3. Serve dressing over salad. Yield: 6 servings.

◆ EASY LEMON ICE CREAM

3 **cups half-and-half**
1½ **cups sugar**
2 **teaspoons grated lemon rind**
½ **cup freshly squeezed lemon juice**
 Fresh mint leaves (optional)
 Fresh strawberries (optional)

1. Combine half-and-half and sugar in a large bowl; stir until sugar dissolves. Add lemon rind and juice; stir well.

2. Pour into a 9-inch square pan. Cover with heavy-duty plastic wrap. Freeze 4 hours or until firm, stirring every hour.

3. Scoop ice cream into dessert glasses or cups, and garnish each serving with mint leaves and a strawberry, if desired. Serve immediately. Yield: 6 servings.

THE SECOND TIME AROUND...

Anyone who has ever picked at the Thanksgiving turkey or holiday ham after all the guests have gone, knows how good leftovers can be. Here are some ways to stretch holiday dinner leftovers into next-day lunches:

• *Roast Pork.* It's worth cooking an extra-large pork loin or fresh ham just to have the leftover meat for sandwiches. Heat sliced pork under the broiler or in a skillet to render the fat a bit, and it will be irresistible. Then wrap in warm corn tortillas and top with taco sauce. Or mix mayonnaise with orange juice and grated orange rind; spread the blend lavishly on crusty rolls or French bread, and sandwich the pork with thin slices of tomato. The fresh orange flavor is wonderful with pork.

• *Pot Roast or Roast Beef.* For a great salad, toss strips of leftover beef with freshly minced onion, parsley, and capers. Sprinkle with vinegar to make the mixture very tangy; then add mayonnaise to taste. Or pull roast apart into large shreds, heat under the broiler, wrap in warm wheat tortillas, and top with picante sauce, shredded lettuce, and chopped tomatoes.

• *Roast Lamb.* Slice lamb thinly and place on an aluminum foil-lined pan. Spread with a combination of yogurt, mustard, curry powder, and a pinch of allspice; broil just until topping bubbles. Spoon the flavorful mixture into pita pockets and enjoy!

• *Fish.* To make a Mexican-style salad, combine flaked fish with diced green pepper, chopped seeded tomato, chopped avocado, and sliced ripe olives. Make a complementary spicy dressing of 1 part fresh lime juice to 2 parts olive oil, and ground cumin and chili powder to taste.

SAVORY SCALLOPINI

Veal Scallopini with
Cheese and Walnuts
Sautéed Peppers
Baked Rice
Strawberry Sorbet (page 89)
Coconut Snowdrops

Serves 4

Make Ahead: Bake Coconut Snowdrops when it's convenient.
Prepare & Serve: Prepare Baked Rice, and keep covered until serving time. Prepare Veal Scallopini with Cheese and Walnuts. Sauté peppers. At serving time, scoop out sorbet and serve with Coconut Snowdrops.

VEAL SCALLOPINI WITH CHEESE AND WALNUTS

4 ounces Gorgonzola cheese or blue cheese, softened
½ cup chopped walnuts
2 tablespoons whipping cream
¼ cup plus 1 tablespoon Madeira, divided
8 (⅛-inch-thick) veal cutlets
Salt and pepper to taste
1 egg, beaten
¾ cup fine dry breadcrumbs
¾ cup water
1 (.75-ounce) package mushroom gravy mix

1. Combine cheese, walnuts, whipping cream, and 1 tablespoon Madeira in a small mixing bowl; set aside.
2. Flatten veal slightly, using a meat mallet or rolling pin. Sprinkle 4 cutlets with salt and pepper. Spoon ¼ cup of

cheese mixture in center of each cutlet. Brush edge of cutlet with egg. Top each cutlet with a second cutlet; press to seal edges. Dip in egg; dredge in breadcrumbs. Place in a large covered skillet.

3. Combine water, gravy mix, and remaining Madeira. Pour over meat in skillet. Cover and place over medium heat. Cook 20 minutes or until veal is tender.

4. Remove cutlets and gravy to a serving platter; serve warm. Yield: 4 servings.

MicroMethod

1. Same as step 1.

2. Same as step 2, except place veal cutlets in a 12- x 8- x 2-inch baking dish.

3. Combine water, gravy mix, and remaining Madeira in a 2-cup glass measure. Microwave at HIGH for 2 minutes, stirring well after 1 minute. Pour into baking dish. Cover with heavy-duty plastic wrap, and vent to allow steam to escape. Microwave at MEDIUM (50% power) for 15 to 18 minutes, rotating dish every 5 minutes.

4. Same as step 4.

SAUTÉED PEPPERS

2 tablespoons olive oil
1 green pepper, seeded and cut into thin strips
1 yellow pepper, seeded and cut into thin strips
1 red pepper, seeded and cut into thin strips
½ cup sliced pitted ripe olives
2 teaspoons Balsamic or red wine vinegar
Garlic salt

1. Heat oil in large skillet over high heat. Add peppers, stirring to coat. Cook, stirring often, 6 minutes or until edges of peppers are lightly browned.

2. Reduce heat to medium; stir in olives, vinegar, and garlic salt to taste. Cook 3 minutes, stirring often.

3. Serve immediately. Yield: 4 servings.

BAKED RICE

¼ cup chopped onion
2 tablespoons chopped green pepper
2 stalks celery, sliced diagonally
2 tablespoons butter or margarine, melted
1 cup regular rice, uncooked
1½ cups water
½ cup white wine
2 teaspoons chicken-flavored bouillon granules
1 teaspoon salt
¼ teaspoon pepper

1. Sauté onion, green pepper, and celery in butter in a large skillet until vegetables are tender. Add rice; cook over medium heat, stirring constantly, until rice is lightly browned. Add remaining ingredients, stirring well.

2. Pour into a lightly greased 1½-quart casserole. Cover and bake at 350° for 25 minutes or until liquid is absorbed.

3. Serve warm. Yield: 4 servings.

COCONUT SNOWDROPS

2 cups all-purpose flour
1 cup butter, softened
1 cup flaked coconut
½ cup sugar
¼ cup milk
1 egg
1 teaspoon vanilla extract
Sifted powdered sugar

1. Combine all ingredients, except powdered sugar, in a large mixing bowl. Beat at medium speed of an electric mixer 2 minutes.

2. Drop dough by heaping teaspoonfuls 2 inches apart onto ungreased cookie sheets. Bake at 350° for 10 minutes. (Cookies should still be white when done.) Remove cookies from cookie sheets, and cool on wire racks.

3. Dust with powdered sugar. Store in airtight containers. Yield: about 4 dozen.

ITALIAN GRILLED CHICKEN

Italian Grilled Chicken
Vegetable Kabobs
Herbed Bread
Almond Crunch Dessert

Serves 4

Make Ahead: Prepare and freeze Almond Crunch Dessert.

Prepare & Serve: Marinate chicken. Prepare Herbed Bread and Vegetable Kabobs. Grill chicken and kabobs. Heat Herbed Bread in the oven or on the grill.

If you need a super-fast alternative to the Almond Crunch Dessert, toast the almonds as directed in the recipe, and stir in the coconut during the last minute of cooking time. Let the mixture cool while you prepare the chicken. Spoon the coconut mixture over vanilla or strawberry ice cream at serving time.

ITALIAN GRILLED CHICKEN

½ cup butter or margarine, melted
⅓ cup fresh lime juice
1 (0.6-ounce) package Italian salad dressing mix
4 chicken breast halves

1. Combine first three ingredients in a 12- x 8- x 2-inch baking dish. Add chicken; cover and marinate one hour.

2. Remove chicken from marinade; discard marinade. Place chicken 5 to 6 inches from medium-hot coals. Grill 30 minutes or until done, turning frequently.

3. Serve warm. Yield: 4 servings.

VEGETABLE KABOBS

¼ cup butter or margarine, melted
¼ teaspoon ground cumin
2 medium onions, quartered
1 medium zucchini, cut into 1-inch slices
2 medium-size yellow squash, cut into 1-inch slices
8 medium-size fresh mushrooms
8 cherry tomatoes

1. Combine melted butter and cumin.

2. Arrange vegetables on 4 skewers. Brush with butter mixture.

3. Grill kabobs over medium-hot coals 20 minutes or until zucchini and yellow squash are crisp-tender, turning occasionally and brushing with butter mixture.

4. Serve warm. Yield: 4 servings.

HERBED BREAD

½ cup butter or margarine, softened
1 teaspoon fennel seeds
½ teaspoon dried whole basil
½ teaspoon dried whole oregano
1 (16-ounce) loaf Italian bread

1. Slice bread into 1-inch slices. Set aside.

2. Combine butter, fennel seeds, basil, and oregano in a small mixing bowl. Spread butter mixture on one side of each slice of bread.

3. Wrap the slices in heavy-duty aluminum foil; bake at 350° for 15 minutes or until thoroughly heated.

4. Serve warm. Yield: 1 loaf.

◆ □　ALMOND CRUNCH
DESSERT

¼ **cup butter or margarine**
2 **(2¼-ounce) packages slivered almonds**
1 **cup oven-toasted rice cereal**
½ **cup firmly-packed brown sugar**
½ **cup flaked coconut**
⅛ **teaspoon salt**
½ **gallon vanilla ice cream, softened**
Chocolate syrup (optional)

1. Melt butter in a medium skillet. Add almonds; toss in butter until toasted. Remove half the almonds; drain.

2. Add cereal, sugar, coconut, and salt to remaining almond mixture. Stir to combine. Pat mixture in bottom of a 12- x 8- x 2-inch baking dish. Spread softened ice cream over top. Sprinkle with reserved almonds. Freeze overnight.

3. To serve, cut into 4- x 2-inch bars. Top with chocolate syrup, if desired. Yield: 12 servings.

MicroMethod

1. Place butter in a 12- x 8- x 2-inch baking dish. Microwave at HIGH for 55 seconds. Add slivered almonds; microwave at HIGH for 4 to 5 minutes or until almonds are toasted, stirring after 2 minutes. Remove half the toasted almonds; drain and set aside.

2. Stir cereal, sugar, coconut, and salt into remaining almond mixture. Spread almond mixture evenly in bottom of baking dish. Spread softened ice cream on top of almond mixture. Sprinkle with reserved almonds. Freeze overnight.

3. Same as step 3.

FAMILY GET-TOGETHER

*Lemon-Caper Butter Chicken
Herbed Green Beans
Refrigerator Yeast Biscuits*

Serves 8

Make Ahead: Prepare the biscuit dough, and refrigerate overnight. For a delicious do-ahead dessert, try Apple Clafouti (page 252).

Prepare & Serve: Prepare Lemon-Caper Butter Chicken and Herbed Green Beans. Bake biscuits.

LEMON-CAPER BUTTER CHICKEN

¼ **cup butter or margarine**
2 **tablespoons lemon juice**
2 **tablespoons capers**
1 **tablespoon caper juice**
2 **cloves garlic, crushed**
½ **teaspoon paprika**
½ **teaspoon salt**
⅛ **teaspoon pepper**
8 **boneless and skinless chicken breast halves**
½ **pound fresh mushrooms, sliced**
4 **cups hot cooked rice**
1½ **teaspoons all-purpose flour**
Fresh parsley sprigs

1. Combine first 8 ingredients in a large skillet; bring to a boil. Add chicken and sliced mushrooms; reduce heat, cover, and simmer 20 minutes. Uncover and simmer 10 minutes.

2. Place rice on a serving platter. Remove chicken and mushrooms from skillet, using a slotted spoon; serve over rice.

3. Add flour to pan drippings; cook, stirring constantly, until mixture thickens.

4. Spoon sauce over chicken to serve. Garnish with parsley. Yield: 8 servings.

HERBED GREEN BEANS

2 (10-ounce) packages frozen green
    beans
½ cup white wine
2 teaspoons dried rosemary leaves
¼ cup butter, melted

1. Cook beans according to package directions; drain.
2. Combine wine and rosemary in a small saucepan; simmer until reduced by half. Whisk in butter.
3. Spoon sauce over beans in serving bowl; toss to coat. Yield: 8 servings.

REFRIGERATOR YEAST BISCUITS

1 package dry yeast
3 tablespoons sugar, divided
2 tablespoons warm water (105° to
    115°)
2 cups buttermilk
5 cups all-purpose flour
1 tablespoon baking powder
1 teaspoon baking soda
1 teaspoon salt
¾ cup shortening

1. Combine yeast, 1 teaspoon sugar, and warm water in a small mixing bowl, stirring to dissolve; let stand 5 minutes or until bubbly. Add remaining sugar and buttermilk to yeast mixture; stir well.
2. Combine flour, baking powder, baking soda, and salt in a large mixing bowl, stirring well; cut in shortening with a pastry blender until mixture resembles coarse meal. Add buttermilk mixture, stirring with a fork until dry ingredients are moistened. Cover tightly and refrigerate overnight.
3. Turn dough out onto a lightly floured surface, and knead 4 to 5 times. Roll dough to ½-inch thickness; cut with a 2-inch biscuit cutter. Place biscuits on a lightly greased baking sheet. Bake at 425° for 12 minutes or until golden brown.
4. Serve hot. Yield: about 2½ dozen.

CHICKEN CHOP SUEY

Chicken Chop Suey
Individual Orange Alaskas

Serves 6

Make Ahead: Assemble Individual Orange Alaskas.
Prepare & Serve: Cook Chicken Chop Suey. Just before serving, bake Individual Orange Alaskas. Instead of making Individual Orange Alaskas, try mandarin oranges mixed with fresh or dried mint leaves over orange sherbet. Either way, oranges signify good luck in China!

CHICKEN CHOP SUEY

2 tablespoons butter or margarine
1½ pounds boneless and skinless
    chicken breasts, cut into 1-inch
    cubes
1 cup diagonally sliced carrots
1 (10-ounce) package frozen
    Chinese-style vegetables, thawed
1 (8-ounce) can sliced water
    chestnuts, drained
4 ounces fresh bean sprouts
1½ cups chicken broth
¼ cup soy sauce
1 tablespoon plus 1½ teaspoons
    cornstarch
3 cups hot cooked rice
1 can chow mein noodles

1. Melt butter in a wok or large skillet. Add chicken to skillet; stir-fry over medium-high heat 3 minutes. Add carrots; stir-fry 3 minutes. Add Chinese-style vegetables, water chestnuts, and bean sprouts; stir-fry vegetable mixture 2 minutes.
2. Combine chicken broth, soy sauce, and cornstarch, stirring until smooth. Add

to vegetable mixture; cook, stirring constantly, 5 minutes or until thickened.

3. Serve over hot cooked rice; sprinkle with chow mein noodles. Yield: 6 servings.

Variations: Pork and Pepper Chop Suey: Substitute boneless pork, cut into cubes, for the chicken, and sliced red or green pepper for the carrots.
Beef and Asparagus Chop Suey: Substitute beef flank steak, sliced thinly, for the chicken, sliced celery for the carrots, and frozen asparagus cuts for the Chinese-style vegetables.
Almond Chop Suey: Substitute 1 cup whole almonds or walnut pieces for the water chestnuts, omitting bean sprouts.
Chicken Lo Mein: Serve the chop suey over thin egg noodles or buckwheat noodles instead of rice, omitting the chow mein noodles.

INDIVIDUAL ORANGE ALASKAS

3 medium oranges
1 quart orange sherbet
3 egg whites
¼ cup plus 2 tablespoons sugar

1. Cut a thin slice from both the top and bottom of each orange. Cut oranges in half crosswise; scoop out pulp, and reserve for other uses. Place a scoop of orange sherbet in each shell; cover and freeze.
2. Beat egg whites (at room temperature) until frothy. Gradually add sugar, 1 tablespoon at a time, beating until stiff peaks form and sugar dissolves. Spread meringue evenly over sherbet in each orange shell, sealing to edge of shell; freeze.
3. Before serving, place Individual Orange Alaskas on a baking sheet; broil 6 inches from heat 1 minute or until meringue is lightly browned.
4. Serve immediately. Yield: 6 servings.

Note: Place sherbet-filled orange shells in muffin pans for easy handling.

NO-BAKE DESSERTS

A little "fancifying" can turn convenience foods into very attractive desserts. Here are some combinations that look and taste especially good:

● Toast round frozen waffles, and cut into quarters. Arrange on plates pinwheel fashion, raising one edge of each quarter with a small mound of whipped cream and berries. Garnish center with more cream and berries. Sift powdered sugar over waffles.

● Top slices of packaged banana cake with either diced ripe papaya, sliced bananas, or strawberries. Add a sprinkling of fresh lime juice. Serve sliced packaged orange cake with unsweetened fresh or frozen raspberries or blueberries; top with whipped cream, if desired.

● Serve packaged applesauce or spice cake with apple or pear slices that have been sautéed in butter, and lightly sprinkled with a liqueur such as Amaretto or Grand Marnier.

● Sprinkle sliced pound cake with grated coconut or sliced almonds. Place under broiler to toast. Top with scoops of orange or raspberry sherbet.

● Top ice cream or sherbet with a complement of crushed packaged cookies: orange sherbet with chocolate-mint sandwich cookies; coffee ice cream with chocolate-fudge sandwich cookies; chocolate ice cream with orange-chocolate sandwich cookies; cookies 'n cream ice cream with chocolate-cream sandwich cookies; lemon sherbet with iced lemonade cookies; strawberry ice cream with almond crescents. Crush cookies in the food processor, or place cookies in a plastic bag and crush with a rolling pin. Cookies should be just crushed—not crumbed!

CHICKEN PAPRIKASH

Chicken-Mushroom Paprikash
Buttered Brussels Sprouts
Pineapple Crunch
or
Cranberry-Pear Crisp

Serves 4

Make Ahead: Prepare topping for Pineapple Crunch.

Prepare & Serve: Combine fruit mixture for Pineapple Crunch and chill. Boil water for noodles. Cook Chicken-Mushroom Paprikash, Buttered Brussels Sprouts, and noodles.

To enhance the flavor of brussels sprouts, cook them in chicken or beef broth instead of water. Remove the cooked sprouts, using a slotted spoon. Boil the broth until reduced to ¼ cup; stir in 1 to 2 tablespoons butter, and pour broth over sprouts.

CHICKEN-MUSHROOM PAPRIKASH
(pictured on page 49)

  4 **boneless and skinless chicken**
     breast halves
  ½ **cup water**
  ½ **pound fresh mushrooms, sliced**
  2 **tablespoons dried onion flakes**
  1 **tablespoon paprika**
  1 **teaspoon dried marjoram, crushed**
  ½ **teaspoon salt**
  ⅛ **teaspoon pepper**
  1 **clove garlic, crushed**
  2 **tablespoons water**
  1 **teaspoon cornstarch**
  ⅓ **cup plain low-fat yogurt**
     Fresh parsley sprigs
     Hot cooked egg noodles

1. Place chicken breast halves, ½ cup water, sliced mushrooms, onion flakes, paprika, marjoram, salt, pepper, and garlic in a large skillet. Bring to a boil. Reduce heat; cover and simmer 15 minutes or until juices of chicken run clear when chicken is pierced with a fork.

2. Combine 2 tablespoons water and cornstarch in a small bowl, stirring until smooth. Stir into skillet. Cook over medium heat 2 minutes or until thickened and bubbly.

3. Stir yogurt into chicken mixture. Remove from heat.

4. Garnish with fresh parsley sprigs, and serve immediately over hot cooked egg noodles. Yield: 4 servings.

BUTTERED BRUSSELS SPROUTS
(pictured on page 49)

  1 **pound fresh brussels**
     sprouts
  2 **tablespoons melted butter**
     or margarine
     Salt to taste

1. Wash brussels sprouts, and remove discolored leaves. Trim ends of brussels sprouts, slashing bottom of each sprout with a shallow X.

2. Arrange brussels sprouts in a steaming rack. Place steaming rack over boiling water; cover and steam 10 to 12 minutes or until sprouts reach desired degree of doneness.

3. Place brussels sprouts in a serving dish. Add melted butter and salt to brussels sprouts; toss mixture gently. Serve warm. Yield: 4 servings.

MicroNote: To microwave step 2, place prepared brussels sprouts in a 2-quart casserole, and add ¼ cup water. Cover with heavy-duty plastic wrap, and vent to allow steam to escape. Microwave at HIGH for 6 to 8 minutes or until brussels sprouts are tender. Let sprouts stand, covered, for 3 minutes.

PINEAPPLE CRUNCH
(pictured on page 49)

2 teaspoons butter or margarine
1 tablespoon sugar
¼ cup plus 2 tablespoons chopped
    pecans
1 (20-ounce) can pineapple tidbits,
    drained
2 to 3 tablespoons rum

1. Melt butter in a skillet; add sugar and pecans. Cook over medium-low heat 4 minutes, stirring constantly, until pecans are lightly browned. Pour onto lightly greased aluminum foil. Cool completely.
2. Combine pineapple and rum in a small bowl; toss lightly. Cover and chill.
3. To serve, spoon pineapple mixture into 4 dessert dishes; sprinkle with nut mixture. Yield: 4 servings.

CRANBERRY-PEAR CRISP

½ cup plus 2 tablespoons
    all-purpose flour, divided
1 cup sugar
1 teaspoon ground cinnamon
1 (12-ounce) package fresh or frozen
    cranberries, thawed
2 pears, cored and sliced
½ cup firmly packed brown sugar
⅓ cup butter or margarine, softened
¾ cup regular oats, uncooked
¾ cup chopped pecans

1. Combine 2 tablespoons flour, sugar, and cinnamon. Place cranberries and pears in a 12- x 8- x 2-inch baking dish. Sprinkle with flour mixture; toss gently.
2. Combine remaining ½ cup flour and brown sugar in a medium mixing bowl; cut in butter with a pastry blender until mixture resembles coarse meal. Add oats and pecans; mix well. Sprinkle evenly over fruit mixture.
3. Bake at 350° for 35 minutes or until juice is bubbly.
4. Spoon into individual serving bowls; serve warm or cold. Yield: 4 to 6 servings.

CHICKEN AND PEPPERS

Quick Chicken and Peppers
Layered Potato Salad
Corn-On-The-Cob
Double-Crust Strawberry Pie

Serves 4

Make Ahead: Prepare Layered Potato Salad and Double-Crust Strawberry Pie.
Prepare & Serve: Prepare chicken. While chicken is cooking, cook corn.

QUICK CHICKEN AND PEPPERS

1 (3- to 3½-pound) broiler-fryer, cut
    up
1 teaspoon celery salt
1 teaspoon chili powder
¼ cup vegetable oil
1 large green pepper, seeded and
    cut into strips
1 large red pepper, seeded and cut
    into strips
2 medium onions, sliced and
    separated into rings

1. Sprinkle chicken pieces with celery salt and chili powder. Heat oil in a skillet over medium-high heat. Add chicken. Cook 5 minutes on each side or until chicken is browned.
2. Reduce heat to medium-low. Cover and continue cooking about 15 minutes or until juices of chicken run clear when pierced with a fork.
3. Remove chicken from skillet, and keep warm. Drain off fat from skillet.
4. Add peppers and onion; sauté until tender.
5. Arrange vegetables on a serving platter. Top with chicken. Yield: 4 servings.

◆ LAYERED POTATO SALAD

⅓ cup mayonnaise
⅓ cup commercial sour cream
¾ teaspoon prepared horseradish
½ teaspoon celery seeds
¼ teaspoon salt
½ cup chopped onion
⅓ cup chopped fresh parsley
¼ teaspoon minced fresh dillweed
3 medium-size baking potatoes
   (about 1½ pounds), cooked,
   peeled, and sliced

1. Combine first 5 ingredients in a small bowl, stirring well; set aside.
2. Combine onion, parsley, and dillweed in a small bowl; stir well. Set aside.
3. Layer one-third each of potato slices, reserved mayonnaise mixture, and reserved onion mixture in a 1-quart serving bowl; repeat layers twice. Cover; chill.
4. Yield: 4 to 6 servings.

▢ CORN-ON-THE-COB

1 teaspoon sugar
4 ears fresh corn, cleaned

1. Combine sugar and enough water to half fill a large saucepan. Bring water to a boil; add corn.
2. Return to a boil; cover, and cook 10 minutes or until tender. Drain well.
3. Serve hot. Yield: 4 servings.

MicroNote: To microwave steps 1 and 2, arrange 4 ears of corn in the oven. Microwave at HIGH for 10 to 17 minutes, turning over and rearranging every 4 minutes. Let stand for 5 minutes.

Note: To make a quick sauce for corn, place ¼ cup butter in a 1-quart glass measure; microwave at HIGH for 55 seconds or until melted. Stir in 1 tablespoon white wine, 1 teaspoon crushed dried basil leaves, ¼ teaspoon garlic powder, and ¼ teaspoon salt; microwave at HIGH for 30 seconds or until thoroughly heated.

◆ DOUBLE-CRUST STRAWBERRY PIE

1 cup sugar plus 1½ teaspoons,
   divided
3 tablespoons cornstarch
1 tablespoon lemon juice
3 pints fresh strawberries, washed,
   hulled, and halved
½ teaspoon almond extract
   Double-Crust Pastry
2 tablespoons milk
¼ teaspoon ground cinnamon

1. Combine 1 cup sugar and cornstarch in a small Dutch oven; stir until well blended. Add lemon juice and strawberries, stirring well. Bring to a boil; reduce heat and cook, stirring constantly, until thickened. Remove from heat, and stir in almond flavoring. Let cool.
2. Roll half of pastry to ⅛-inch thickness on a lightly floured surface; fit into a 9-inch pieplate. Spoon filling into pastry; roll remaining pastry to ⅛-inch thickness, and place over filling. Trim edges; seal and flute. Cut slits in top crust.
3. Brush pastry with milk. Combine remaining sugar and cinnamon; sprinkle over pastry. Bake at 425° for 20 minutes or until lightly browned.
4. Let cool. Yield: one 9-inch pie.

Double-Crust Pastry:

2 cups all-purpose flour
½ teaspoon salt
⅔ cup shortening
5 to 6 tablespoons cold water

1. Combine flour and salt; cut in shortening with a pastry blender until mixture resembles coarse meal.
2. Sprinkle water over surface; stir with a fork until dry ingredients are moistened. Shape into a ball; chill.

Pineapple Crunch is the perfect ending to the Chicken Paprikash menu (page 46), which includes chicken in a rich mushroom sauce and Buttered Brussels Sprouts.

CHICKEN SKILLET SUPPER

Skillet Chicken and Broccoli
Beets Lancaster
Whole Wheat Rolls
Chocolate Pecan Pie

Serves 4

Make Ahead: Bake Chocolate Pecan Pie.
Prepare & Serve: The Chocolate Pecan Pie is easy enough to pop into the oven before you start preparing the chicken if you haven't had the time to make it ahead. Prepare and cook Skillet Chicken and Broccoli. Cook Beets Lancaster. Warm whole wheat rolls.

SKILLET CHICKEN AND BROCCOLI
(pictured at left)

  1 chicken-flavored bouillon cube
  1 cup hot water
  1 (3- to 3½-pound) broiler-fryer, cut up
  1 small onion, sliced
  1 pound fresh broccoli, cut into spears
1½ teaspoons lemon and pepper seasoning salt

1. Dissolve bouillon cube in hot water; set aside.
2. Heat an electric skillet to 400°. Brown chicken on each side 1 to 2 minutes. Reduce heat to 300°; add sliced onion and

---

In the Chicken Skillet Supper menu (above), the broccoli is quick-cooked with the chicken to be served with Beets Lancaster, hot or cold. A tempting dessert, Chocolate Pecan Pie, provides a sweet ending.

dissolved bouillon. Cover and simmer 10 minutes.
3. Add broccoli to skillet; sprinkle chicken and broccoli with seasoning salt. Reduce heat to 200°; cover and cook 15 minutes. Uncover and continue cooking 5 minutes or until tender.
4. Serve warm. Yield: 4 servings.

☺ BEETS LANCASTER
(pictured at left)

  2 tablespoons cider vinegar
  1 tablespoon honey
  ½ teaspoon onion powder
  ¼ teaspoon salt
  1 (16-ounce) can sliced beets, drained

1. Combine first 4 ingredients in a saucepan; stir well. Add beets. Cook over medium heat until thoroughly heated.
2. Serve hot or cold in a small serving bowl. Yield: 4 servings.

◆ CHOCOLATE PECAN PIE
(pictured at left)

  3 eggs, well beaten
  1 cup sugar
  ¾ cup light corn syrup
  ¼ cup butter or margarine, melted
  1 teaspoon vanilla extract
  ½ cup semisweet chocolate morsels
  ½ cup chopped pecans
  1 unbaked (9-inch) pastry shell
     Pecan halves
     Frozen whipped topping (optional)

1. Combine first 5 ingredients in a large mixing bowl; mix well. Stir in chocolate morsels and chopped pecans.
2. Pour pecan mixture into pastry shell. Garnish with pecan halves. Bake at 350° for 55 minutes or until set.
3. Cool before slicing; dollop with frozen whipped topping, if desired. Yield: one 9-inch pie.

CHICKEN AT ITS BEST

Nutritious, low in fat, economical, and very flavorful, chicken is the champion of quick-cooking entrées. Follow these simple procedures to enjoy all the attributes of chicken:

• Take advantage of supermarket sales to save money on chicken. You can always substitute any kind of chicken parts for cut-up chicken, and vice versa. To serve 4 people, you'll need 1 whole or cut-up chicken, 4 breast halves, 4 whole legs, or 8 thighs or drumsticks.

• Raw chicken can be frozen safely for several months if well wrapped. But the freezer temperature must be kept at around 0°. However, a chicken that has been frozen will never taste quite as good as a fresh one, and there is likely to be some harmless discoloration around the bones. Your best bet for freezing is boneless chicken breasts, as these keep quite well and offer great convenience. Wrap them individually, so that you can remove only as many as you need. If you want to slice or dice the meat, it's easiest to do so while the meat is still partially frozen.

• Soaking chicken in a seasoned liquid is an easy way to enhance flavor. The time can be as little as half an hour or as long as overnight. Many cooks like to soak chicken in buttermilk before frying. For broiling or grilling you can use any vinaigrette dressing.

• To season a roast chicken, fill the cavity with several lemon or onion slices, several bay leaves, and a small bunch of fresh parsley or dillweed; skewer closed. During the roasting procedure, baste the chicken with chicken broth, melted butter, or a combination of the two every 15 to 20 minutes.

MEXICAN CHICKEN

Mexican Chicken
Fiesta Salad with
Chili-Avocado Dressing
Sliced Fresh Fruit

Serves 4

Prepare & Serve: Prepare Chili-Avocado Dressing. Cook Mexican Chicken. If desired, prepare rice or corn to serve with the chicken. Arrange Fiesta Salad. Slice fruit of your choice.

For an even speedier supper, season chicken with cumin, chili powder, and fresh lime juice. Broil or grill outdoors. Top with Chili-Avocado Dressing. Serve with corn-on-the-cob and sliced tomatoes.

MEXICAN CHICKEN

1 large onion, chopped
1 cup chopped celery
2 cloves garlic, chopped, or 2 teaspoons garlic paste
1 tablespoon vegetable oil
1 (3- to 3½- pound) broiler-fryer, cut up and skinned
1 (28-ounce) can whole tomatoes, undrained and chopped
1 (4-ounce) can chopped green chiles, undrained
½ teaspoon chili powder
½ teaspoon ground cumin

1. Sauté onion, celery, and garlic in oil in an electric skillet until tender. Add chicken; brown on all sides.
2. Stir in tomatoes, chiles, chili powder, and cumin. Cover and simmer 20 minutes, stirring occasionally, until chicken is tender.

3. Remove chicken; place on a warmed platter. Cook sauce, stirring constantly, until thickened. Pour sauce over chicken to serve. Yield: 4 servings.

FIESTA SALAD WITH CHILI-AVOCADO DRESSING

½ medium head iceberg lettuce, shredded
1 (8-ounce) can red kidney beans, rinsed, drained, and chilled
1 (8-ounce) package tortilla chips, crumbled
½ cup (2 ounces) shredded Cheddar cheese
1 (2¼-ounce) can sliced ripe olives
1 large tomato, peeled and chopped Chili-Avocado Dressing

1. Arrange lettuce on a large serving platter. Layer beans, chips, cheese, olives, and tomato on top of lettuce in order given.
2. Serve salad with Chili-Avocado Dressing. Yield: 4 servings.

Chili-Avocado Dressing:

2 medium-size ripe avocados, peeled and coarsely chopped
¼ cup commercial sour cream
1 tablespoon lemon or lime juice
1 tablespoon onion juice
1½ teaspoons salt
1 teaspoon chili powder
⅛ teaspoon ground coriander
⅛ teaspoon hot sauce
1 medium tomato, peeled, cored, seeded, and chopped

1. Combine first 4 ingredients in container of an electric blender. Blend until smooth. Stir in remaining ingredients.
2. Cover with plastic wrap, and chill. Serve over Fiesta Salad. Yield: 2½ cups.

Note: Avocado seed may be placed in dressing to prevent it from darkening.

BROILED CORNISH HENS

Peppered Cornish Hens
Creamed Peas And Celery
Long Grain and Wild Rice Mix
Pear Harvest Pleaser

Serves 6

Make Ahead: Bake Pear Harvest Pleaser, and set aside to serve at room temperature. Or prepare pears before you start supper and microwave or bake them during dinner.
Prepare & Serve: Cook long grain and wild rice mix according to package directions. Prepare Cornish hens. While hens are cooking, prepare Creamed Peas and Celery.

PEPPERED CORNISH HENS

3 (1- to 1¼-pound) Cornish hens
Salt
3 tablespoons Dijon mustard
Cracked black pepper
Fresh parsley sprigs
Cherry tomatoes

1. Remove giblets from hens; reserve for other uses. Rinse hens with cold water, and pat dry. Split each hen lengthwise.
2. Sprinkle cavity and skin side of each hen with salt; brush each side with mustard. Sprinkle with pepper.
3. Place hens, cavity side up, on a rack in a shallow roasting pan 5 inches from heating element. Broil 10 minutes; turn hens. Broil an additional 8 minutes or until browned. Turn broiler off, leaving hens in oven 5 minutes.
4. Transfer to a warm serving platter; garnish with parsley sprigs and cherry tomatoes. Yield: 6 servings.

CREAMED PEAS AND CELERY

2 cups buttermilk
1 tablespoon cornstarch
½ cup chopped celery
2 tablespoons chopped celery leaves
1 tablespoon grated onion
1 teaspoon salt
⅛ teaspoon pepper
2 tablespoons orange juice
2 (10-ounce) packages frozen green
  peas
  Additional celery leaves

1. Combine buttermilk and cornstarch in a large skillet, stirring well; add celery, chopped celery leaves, onion, salt, and pepper. Cook over low heat, stirring frequently, until mixture comes to a boil.
2. Add orange juice and peas, stirring well. Cover and simmer 10 minutes or until peas are tender.
3. Transfer Creamed Peas and Celery to a serving bowl; garnish with additional celery leaves. Yield: 6 servings.

PEAR HARVEST PLEASER

6 ripe Bartlett pears (about 2
  pounds), peeled
½ cup dry sherry
2 tablespoons honey
½ teaspoon vanilla extract
½ teaspoon grated lime rind
  Whipping cream

1. Cut pears in half lengthwise, and remove the core. Place pear halves, cut side down, on counter or cutting board; make lengthwise cuts through pears, leaving stem ends intact. Place pear halves, cut side down, in a lightly greased 13- x 9- x 2-inch baking dish.
2. Combine sherry, honey, vanilla, and lime rind in a small saucepan, stirring well; cook over low heat until sauce is thoroughly heated.
3. Pour sauce over pears. Cover and bake at 350° for 40 minutes or until tender, basting frequently. Gently press

cut portion of pears during cooking to separate slices.
4. Transfer pear halves to individual dessert plates; serve with cream. Yield: 6 servings.

MicroMethod

1. Same as step 1. Use a 13- x 9- x 2-inch baking dish, and place thicker ends of pears towards edge of dish.
2. Combine sherry, honey, vanilla, and lime rind in 2-cup glass measure. Microwave at HIGH for 1½ minutes or until boiling. Pour over pears; cover with heavy-duty plastic wrap, and vent to allow steam to escape.
3. Microwave pears at HIGH for 6 to 9 minutes or until pears are tender, 6 to 12 minutes, rearranging pears and rotating dish halfway through cooking time.
4. Same as step 4.

Note: Cooking times for pears will vary depending on degree of ripeness.

FRUITS OF THE HARVEST

Here are some helpful hints for making the most of autumn's bounty of apples and pears:

● A mixture of several types of apples yields the most flavorful pies and sauces. Combine sweet apples, such as Delicious and Rome varieties, with tart ones, such as Jonathan, Winesap, and McIntosh. Rome apples, as well as Bartlett and Bosc pears, are excellent for baking.

● Choose Delicious apples or Bartlett, Anjou, Bosc, or Comice pears for poaching. Watch cooking time carefully, as it will vary according to the ripeness of the fruit. Poach fruit in a rosé or sweet white wine instead of water to enhance the flavor.

CHICKEN LIVER SPECIAL

Sherried Livers and Mushrooms
Winter Vegetable Medley
Poached Apples with
Ginger Whipped Cream

Serves 4

Make Ahead: Poach apples; refrigerate.
Prepare & Serve: Slice vegetables for
Winter Vegetable Medley. Cook rice if
serving with chicken livers. Cook Sherried
Chicken Livers and Mushrooms. Stir-fry
vegetables. At dessert time, whip cream
and pipe around individual servings of
Poached Apples.

well. Combine remaining ½ cup water and
bouillon granules, stirring well; add
bouillon mixture, mushrooms, sherry, tomato paste, and salt to liver mixture. Cook,
stirring frequently, 5 minutes or until
sauce thickens.

3. To serve, spoon Sherried Livers and
Mushrooms over toast points or hot
cooked rice. Yield: 4 servings.

Note: To give Sherried Livers and Mushrooms an Italian accent, substitute dry
Marsala wine for the sherry. Serve sauce
over spaghetti, and sprinkle with Parmesan cheese.

SHERRIED LIVERS AND MUSHROOMS

1 medium onion, chopped
2 tablespoons butter or margarine
1 pound chicken livers
1 tablespoon plus 1½ teaspoons
   all-purpose flour
¾ cup water, divided
½ teaspoon beef-flavored bouillon
   granules
1 (4½-ounce) jar whole mushrooms,
   undrained
3 tablespoons sherry
1 tablespoon tomato paste
⅛ teaspoon salt
4 slices toasted bread or hot cooked
   rice

1. Sauté onion in butter in a large skillet
10 minutes or until tender. Add chicken
livers; cook over medium heat, stirring
frequently, 5 minutes or until tender.

2. Combine flour and ¼ cup water, stirring well; add to liver mixture, stirring

☺ WINTER VEGETABLE MEDLEY

¼ cup butter or margarine
1 cup julienned turnips
1 cup julienned sweet potato
1 cup julienned green pepper
2 tablespoons lemon juice
¼ teaspoon salt
⅛ teaspoon pepper

1. Melt butter in a large skillet or wok;
add turnips, and stir-fry 3 minutes. Add
sweet potato and green pepper; stir-fry an
additional 5 minutes.

2. Remove from heat; stir in remaining
ingredients. Yield: 4 servings.

Note: Substitute carrots, red pepper, yellow squash, and zucchini for a Summer
Vegetable Medley. To julienne vegetables,
slice them ¼-inch thick. Cut turnips and
potatoes crosswise; cut zucchini and carrots lengthwise. Then stack 3 or 4 slices
and julienne.

♠ POACHED APPLES WITH GINGER WHIPPED CREAM

1 cup sugar
1 cup water
½ teaspoon vanilla extract
¼ teaspoon salt
4 medium Golden Delicious apples, peeled and cored
  Ginger Whipped Cream

1. Combine sugar and water in a small Dutch oven; bring to a boil. Reduce heat, and simmer, uncovered, 5 minutes. Add vanilla and salt, stirring well.

2. Place apples in syrup. Cover and simmer 20 minutes or until tender, turning apples frequently. Remove apples from syrup; cover and chill overnight.

3. Spoon Ginger Whipped Cream into a pastry bag fitted with a star tip; pipe into centers and on tops of apples. Yield: 4 servings.

Ginger Whipped Cream:

½ cup whipping cream
2 tablespoons sugar
½ teaspoon ground ginger

1. Beat whipping cream until foamy in a medium mixing bowl; gradually add sugar and ginger, beating until soft peaks form.
2. Yield: about 1 cup.

Note: For a quick change of flavor, stir any of these seasonings into the whipped cream, and pipe or spoon into the poached apples: 2 tablespoons almond-flavored liqueur; 2 ounces peppermint or cinnamon candies, crushed; 2 tablespoons Grenadine or créme de cassis syrup (either one will tint the cream pink!); 1 ounce crushed walnuts, 1 tablespoon sugar, and ½ teaspoon cinnamon.

If you're counting calories, use wine instead of water for poaching, reduce the sugar to ¼ to ½ cup, and add ½ teaspoon ground cinnamon with the vanilla. After removing apples, boil poaching liquid until it is thick and syrupy; spoon over apples instead of whipped cream.

CREOLE FLAVORS

Creole Snapper
Hot Cooked Rice
Carrots Caribbean
Lemon Sherbet
with Blueberry Sauce
(page 118)

Serves 4

Make Ahead: Make Blueberry Sauce, and chill.
Prepare & Serve: Cook rice and Carrots Caribbean; microwave or simmer fish.

Fresh herbs will make any Creole or Caribbean dish sparkle. Add 2 tablespoons chopped fresh basil or thyme to the fish during the last minute of cooking, or stir the same amount of mint into the carrots or rice. If you don't have fresh herbs, chop flat-leaf parsley, and mix with dried herbs to use in the same way.

▯ CREOLE SNAPPER

1 large green pepper, seeded and cut into thin strips (about ¼ pound)
1½ cups chopped green onions
2 tablespoons butter or margarine
1 (14½-ounce) can whole tomatoes, drained and chopped
1 (8-ounce) can tomato sauce
½ teaspoon ground thyme
¼ teaspoon salt
⅛ teaspoon pepper
1 bay leaf
1 pound red snapper fillets
  Hot cooked rice

1. Sauté green pepper and green onions in butter in a large skillet; add tomatoes, tomato sauce, thyme, salt, pepper, and bay leaf to skillet.

2. Arrange fillets in sauce. Simmer, uncovered, 10 minutes or until fish flakes easily when tested with a fork.

3. Remove and discard bay leaf. Serve fish and sauce over hot cooked rice. Yield: 4 servings.

MicroMethod

1. Combine green pepper, green onion, and butter in a 2-quart dish. Cover and microwave at HIGH for 3 to 4 minutes.

2. Stir tomatoes, tomato sauce, thyme, salt, pepper, and bay leaf into cooked vegetables. Arrange fillets in sauce.

3. Cover with heavy-duty plastic wrap, and vent to allow steam to escape; microwave at HIGH for 6 to 8 minutes. Let stand, covered, for 5 minutes.

4. Same as step 3.

Note: Grouper fillets may be substituted for the red snapper fillets.

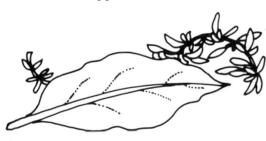

CARROTS CARIBBEAN

> 1 **pound carrots, cleaned and cut into thin strips**
> 1½ **cups unsweetened pineapple juice**
> 1½ **teaspoons ground cinnamon**
> ¼ **teaspoon ground nutmeg**
> **Dash of pepper**

1. Combine all ingredients in a medium saucepan. Bring to a boil. Reduce heat; cover and simmer 15 minutes or until carrots are tender.

2. Spoon into a serving bowl. Serve warm. Yield: 4 to 6 servings.

SIMPLY DELICIOUS FISH

Dill and Lemon Flounder Rolls
Buttered Spinach Noodles
Squash Medley
Gingersnap Peaches

Serves 6

Prepare & Serve: Prepare Gingersnap Peaches; bake just before serving. Make Dill and Lemon Flounder Rolls and cook spinach noodles. Prepare squash while fish is baking.

Try seasoning the noodles with dillweed. If you have fresh dill, substitute 1 to 2 tablespoons of the chopped fronds for the dried dill in the fish recipe, and add the same amount of fresh dill to the noodles.

DILL AND LEMON FLOUNDER ROLLS

> 1 **teaspoon grated lemon rind**
> ½ **teaspoon dried whole dillweed**
> ⅛ **teaspoon pepper**
> 6 **flounder fillets (about 4 ounces each)**
> ½ **cup dry vermouth**
> 3 **tablespoons lemon juice**
> 6 **slices lemon**

1. Combine lemon rind, dillweed, and pepper in a small mixing bowl. Rub both sides of fillets with lemon mixture. Roll up each fillet jellyroll fashion. (Secure with wooden picks, if needed.) Place in a 10- x 6- x 2-inch baking dish.

2. Combine vermouth and lemon juice. Pour over fish; cover with aluminum foil. Bake at 350° for 18 minutes or until fish flakes easily when tested with a fork.

3. Garnish flounder rolls with lemon slices. Yield: 6 servings.

SQUASH MEDLEY

2 tablespoons butter or margarine
1 medium onion, thinly sliced
1 large zucchini, thinly sliced
4 medium-size yellow squash, thinly sliced
1 medium-size green pepper, cut into strips
3 medium tomatoes, peeled and quartered
1 teaspoon dried whole basil
1 teaspoon salt
  Dash of pepper
1 cup grated Parmesan cheese

1. Melt butter in preheated wok or a large skillet, coating sides and bottom; heat at medium-high for 2 minutes. Add onion; stir-fry for 1 minute or until tender.
2. Stir in zucchini, yellow squash, and green pepper; cook 2 to 3 minutes or until vegetables are crisp-tender.
3. Add tomatoes, basil, salt, and pepper to wok; stir well to combine.
4. Sprinkle Parmesan cheese over stir-fried vegetables, and toss gently until the cheese melts.
5. Transfer Squash Medley to a serving bowl; serve warm. Yield: 6 servings.

GINGERSNAP PEACHES

6 gingersnaps, crushed
1½ teaspoons sugar
¼ teaspoon ground cinnamon
6 canned peach halves
3 tablespoons butter or margarine, melted
6 scoops vanilla ice cream

1. Combine gingersnap crumbs, sugar and cinnamon.
2. Place peach halves in a 2-quart casserole. Fill each peach cavity with crumb mixture; drizzle with butter.
3. Bake at 400° for 8 minutes or until peaches are thoroughly heated.
4. Serve in dessert bowls; top servings with ice cream. Yield: 6 servings.

A NEW FASHION FOR FISH

Surprise Steamed Fish
Twice-Baked Potatoes
Sautéed Spinach
Fresh Lime Pie

Serves 4

Make Ahead: Prepare Twice-Baked Potatoes through recipe's step 3. Prepare Fresh Lime Pie.
Prepare & Serve: Bake fish and potatoes. Sauté spinach. For a refreshing alternative to the Fresh Lime Pie, serve lime sherbet with raspberry puree and crisp packaged cookies, such as Brown-Edge Wafers. To make raspberry puree, process 1 (10-ounce) package frozen raspberries in syrup, thawed, in container of a food processor or blender until pureed; add ¼ cup apple or grape juice if blender requires more liquid to puree.

SURPRISE STEAMED FISH

1 (16-ounce) package frozen cod, flounder, or haddock, thawed
  Vegetable cooking spray
1 tablespoon plus 1½ teaspoons fresh lemon juice
1 medium tomato, chopped
½ medium zucchini, shredded (about 1 cup)
⅛ teaspoon dried whole basil
⅛ teaspoon dried whole tarragon leaves
⅛ teaspoon dried whole thyme
⅛ teaspoon salt
1 tablespoon butter or margarine
4 slices lemon

1. Cut fish into 4 servings. Place each serving on lower half of a 15-inch square sheet of heavy-duty aluminum foil that has been lightly coated with cooking spray. Sprinkle with lemon juice.

2. Combine tomato, zucchini, basil, tarragon, thyme, and salt; gently toss. Divide tomato mixture evenly over fish. Dot each piece of fish with butter.

3. Fold upper half of foil over fish to bottom edge of foil. Seal edges to make a tight ½-inch fold. Fold again. Allow space for circulation and expansion.

4. Place foil packets on a baking sheet; bake at 450° for 12 minutes.

5. To serve, transfer foil packets to dinner plates. Cut an X in top of packet; fold foil back. Garnish with lemon slices. Yield: 4 servings.

TWICE-BAKED POTATOES

4 medium baking potatoes, washed
¼ cup milk
¼ cup chopped green onions
½ teaspoon parsley flakes
¼ teaspoon salt
⅛ teaspoon pepper
¼ cup (1 ounce) shredded Cheddar
   cheese

1. Bake potatoes on center oven rack at 450° for 45 minutes or until tender.

2. Cut a ¼-inch slice from the top of each potato; carefully scoop pulp from shell. Reserve potato shells.

3. Mash potato pulp; add milk, green onions, parsley flakes, salt, and pepper, stirring well. Stuff mixture into reserved potato shells; sprinkle with cheese.

4. Bake at 450° for 10 minutes or until golden brown.

5. Serve warm. Yield: 4 servings.

Note: Vary the cheese in Twice-Baked Potatoes to create a different flavor. Try Swiss cheese, mozzarella cheese or a combination of cheeses.

SAUTÉED SPINACH

1 pound fresh spinach
2 tablespoons olive or vegetable oil
2 cloves garlic, minced
2 teaspoons red wine vinegar

1. Remove stems from spinach; wash leaves thoroughly.

2. Heat oil in large skillet over high heat. Add garlic; sauté 1 minute. Add half of spinach; cook until wilted. Push cooked spinach to side of pan; add remaining spinach, and cook until wilted.

3. Stir in vinegar; cook 1 minute. Yield: 4 servings.

FRESH LIME PIE

1 cup vanilla wafer crumbs
3 tablespoons butter or margarine,
   melted
   About 15 vanilla wafers
1 (14-ounce) can sweetened
   condensed milk
½ cup fresh lime juice
4 eggs, separated
2 drops green food coloring
½ teaspoon cream of tartar
¼ cup plus 2 tablespoons sugar

1. Combine wafer crumbs and butter, stirring well with a fork. Press into bottom of a 9-inch pieplate. Arrange whole wafers around edge of pieplate. Bake at 350° for 10 minutes. Cool.

2. Combine sweetened condensed milk, lime juice, egg yolks, and food coloring, beating well. Pour into pie shell.

3. Beat egg whites (at room temperature) and cream of tartar until frothy. Gradually add sugar, 1 tablespoon at a time, beating until stiff peaks form. Spread over filling, sealing to edge of pie shell.

4. Bake at 350° for 12 minutes or until meringue is golden brown. Cool to room temperature. Chill.

5. Serve chilled. Yield: one 9-inch pie.

LIGHT, ELEGANT SALMON

Salmon Poached In Wine
Leeks Mimosa
Broiled Tomatoes
Glazed Fruit Tart

Serves 4

Make Ahead: Prepare Glazed Fruit Tart several hours ahead or night before.
Prepare & Serve: Make Leeks Mimosa, and prepare tomatoes. Place tomatoes under broiler just before adding salmon to poaching liquid.

Want a quick sauce for the salmon? Melt ¼ cup butter with 1 to 2 tablespoons chopped fresh dill, basil, chives, or parsley while the fish is cooking. Feel free to combine herbs. Fresh chives and dried tarragon go well together; so do fresh parsley and dried dillweed or basil.

SALMON POACHED IN WINE
(pictured on page 68)

1 cup Chablis or other dry white wine
1 cup water
1 tablespoon vinegar
½ teaspoon salt
4 (5- to 6-ounce) salmon steaks
Fresh dill sprigs

1. Combine Chablis, water, vinegar, and salt in a large skillet, stirring well; bring to a boil. Reduce heat to low; add salmon. Cover and simmer 4 minutes or until fish flakes easily with a fork.
2. Remove salmon from liquid; transfer to a serving platter. Garnish with fresh dill sprigs. Yield: 4 servings.

LEEKS MIMOSA
(pictured on page 68)

6 leeks (about 2¼ pounds), cleaned
1½ teaspoons butter or margarine
¼ cup plus 2 tablespoons water
½ teaspoon chicken-flavored bouillon granules
1 teaspoon lemon juice
⅛ teaspoon garlic powder
1 hard-cooked egg, finely chopped

1. Slice leeks in half lengthwise. Sauté leeks in butter in a large skillet 2 minutes, turning once.
2. Combine water, bouillon granules, lemon juice, and garlic powder in a small bowl; stir well. Pour over leeks. Cover; simmer 25 minutes or until tender.
3. Transfer leeks to a warm serving platter. Spoon pan drippings over leeks; sprinkle with egg. Yield: 4 servings.

Note: You may substitute 1 head cauliflower, cored and broken into flowerets; 1 head broccoli, cut into slim stems; Belgian endive, cored, trimmed, and left whole; celery, cut into 4-inch lengths; or brussels sprouts, trimmed. Cooking time may need to be reduced.

BROILED TOMATOES
(pictured on page 68)

4 medium tomatoes
¼ cup fine dry Italian-style breadcrumbs
2 tablespoons butter or margarine, melted
2 teaspoons chopped fresh parsley

1. Remove stems from tomatoes, and cut a ¼-inch slice from top of each.
2. Combine breadcrumbs, butter, and parsley; spoon evenly over tomatoes.
3. Broil 6 inches from the heating element 7 minutes or until lightly browned.
4. Remove to a serving dish, and serve warm. Yield: 4 servings.

♦ ⊡ GLAZED FRUIT TART

(pictured on page 68)

1 cup all-purpose flour
¼ cup cornstarch
¼ cup sugar
⅓ cup butter or margarine
1 egg, beaten
1 cup fresh strawberry halves
1 cup sliced peaches
½ cup green grapes, halved
½ cup fresh blueberries
   Citrus Glaze

1. Combine first 3 ingredients in a medium bowl; cut in butter with a pastry blender until mixture resembles coarse meal. Add egg; stir with a fork until dry ingredients are moistened. Shape dough into a ball; chill one hour.
2. Press dough into a 9-inch tart pan with lightly floured hands. Bake at 400° for 8 minutes or until lightly browned. Cool 5 minutes. Remove crust from tart pan to a serving platter. Cool completely.
3. Arrange fruit on pastry. Spoon Citrus Glaze over fruit. Refrigerate 1 to 2 hours. Yield: one 9-inch tart.

Citrus Glaze:

1½ teaspoons cornstarch
 2 tablespoons water
¼ cup plus 2 tablespoons orange juice
⅛ teaspoon grated lemon rind
1½ teaspoons lemon juice

1. Combine cornstarch and water in a small saucepan, stirring until blended. Stir in orange juice. Bring to a boil over medium heat, stirring constantly. Boil 1 minute or until thickened.
2. Remove mixture from heat. Stir in lemon rind and lemon juice. Cover and chill. Yield: ½ cup.

MicroNote: To microwave steps 1 and 2, combine all ingredients in a 1-quart glass measure. Microwave at HIGH for 2 to 5 minutes or until thickened and clear, stirring after 1 minute.

EASY FISH PARMESAN

Fish Fillets Parmesan
Spinach-Tomato Stacks
Steamed New Potatoes
Caramel Pecan Bars

Serves 4

Make Ahead: Bake Caramel Pecan Bars; cool and cut into squares.
Prepare & Serve: Prepare Spinach-Tomato Stacks. Cook potatoes. Make Fish Fillets Parmesan. Place tomatoes in oven with fish for last 10 minutes of baking.

The sweetness of grapes would substitute well for the Caramel Pecan Bars.

FISH FILLETS PARMESAN

1 pound sea bass or flounder fillets, cut into 4 equal portions
½ cup commercial sour cream
2 tablespoons grated Parmesan cheese
2 tablespoons minced onion
1 tablespoon lemon juice
½ teaspoon garlic powder
½ teaspoon salt
¼ teaspoon pepper
   Paprika
   Fresh parsley sprigs

1. Place fillets in a lightly greased 13- x 9- x 2-inch baking dish.
2. Combine remaining ingredients, except paprika and parsley, in a small mixing bowl, stirring well. Spread mixture evenly over fillets.
3. Bake at 375° for 20 minutes or until fish flakes easily with a fork. Transfer fish to a serving platter; sprinkle with paprika, and garnish with parsley.
4. Serve warm. Yield: 4 servings.

SPINACH-TOMATO STACKS

3 green onions, chopped
1 teaspoon vegetable oil
1 (10-ounce) package frozen
    chopped spinach, cooked and
    drained
½ cup soft breadcrumbs
1 egg, beaten
¼ teaspoon dried whole thyme
¼ teaspoon pepper
2 medium tomatoes, cut in half
    crosswise

1. Sauté onion in oil in a medium skillet. Remove from heat. Add spinach, breadcrumbs, egg, thyme, and pepper; stir well.

2. Place tomato halves in a buttered 10- x 6- x 2-inch baking dish. Top each half with one-fourth of spinach mixture.

3. Bake at 375° for 10 minutes or until thoroughly heated. Yield: 4 servings.

CARAMEL PECAN BARS

1 (18.5-ounce) package yellow cake
    mix with pudding
⅓ cup butter or margarine, softened
1 egg
1 (14-ounce) can sweetened
    condensed milk
1 egg
1 teaspoon vanilla extract
1 cup chopped pecans
½ cup almond brickle chips

1. Combine cake mix, butter, and 1 egg in a large mixing bowl; beat at high speed of an electric mixer until crumbly. Press cake mixture evenly into a greased 13- x 9- x 2-inch baking pan.

2. Combine milk, remaining egg, and vanilla in a small mixing bowl, beating well. Stir in pecans and brickle chips. Spread milk mixture evenly over cake mixture. Bake at 350° for 35 minutes.

3. Cool completely. Cut into 2- x 1½-inch bars. Store in airtight containers. Yield: about 3 dozen.

SNAPPY RED SNAPPER

Broccoli Soup (page 226)
Snapper Veracruz
Tossed Green Salad
Quick Parmesan Loaf
Melon Ice

Serves 6

Make Ahead: Prepare soup through recipe's step 3 and refrigerate for up to 1 week ahead. Make Melon Ice.

Prepare & Serve: Make salad. Heat soup. Marinate fish; prepare sauce. Make Quick Parmesan Loaf. Serve soup while fish is in the oven.

If Melon Ice was not prepared ahead of time, a fast and refreshing dessert alternative would be fresh mango, papaya, or melon with lime wedges.

SNAPPER VERACRUZ
(Pictured on page ii)

2 pounds red snapper fillets
2 tablespoons lime juice
1 medium onion, chopped
2 cloves garlic, minced
1 tablespoon olive oil
1 (28-ounce) can tomatoes, drained
    and chopped
2 canned mild green chile peppers,
    chopped
¼ cup sliced green olives
¾ teaspoon dried oregano
1 bay leaf
½ teaspoon salt
¼ teaspoon pepper

1. Place fish in a 13- x 9- x 2-inch baking dish. Sprinkle lime juice over fish. Cover and refrigerate 30 minutes.

2. Sauté onion and garlic in olive oil in a large skillet until vegetables are tender. Add tomatoes, peppers, olives, oregano, bay leaf, salt, and pepper. Bring to a boil. Remove from heat. Discard bay leaf.

3. Spoon mixture evenly over fish. Bake at 350° for 10 minutes or until fish flakes easily when tested with a fork.

4. Serve warm. Yield: 6 servings.

QUICK PARMESAN LOAF
(pictured on page ii)

2 **(7.5-ounce) cans refrigerated flaky biscuits**
¼ **cup plus 2 tablespoons butter or margarine, melted**
Grated Parmesan cheese
Sesame seeds

1. Separate each biscuit into 2 round pieces. Dip each piece in melted butter; sprinkle with Parmesan cheese.

2. Stand each piece on side in a greased 8½- x 4½- x 3-inch loafpan, making 2 rows. Sprinkle with Parmesan cheese and sesame seeds.

3. Bake at 350° for 20 to 25 minutes or until golden brown. Serve warm. Yield: one 8½-inch loaf.

◆ MELON ICE

1½ **cups cubed honeydew melon**
1 **(10-ounce) package frozen strawberries, unthawed**

1. Place honeydew in a single layer on a baking sheet. Place in freezer 1 hour or until frozen.

2. Position knife blade in food processor bowl; add honeydew and strawberries. Process until mixture is pureed and smooth.

3. Place mixture in tightly covered container. Freeze until firm.

4. Scoop into serving dish to serve. Serve immediately. Yield: 6 servings.

SUMMER REFRESHMENT

Three Citrus Seviche
Vegetable-Rice Salad
Assorted Crackers
Quick and Cool Peach Pie

Serves 4

Make Ahead: Make salad, and refrigerate overnight. Make pie, and marinate scallops at least 4 hours ahead.

Many other recipes in this book also invite you to "cook cool." Free yourself at supper time by making a whole meal ahead of time, serving Fusilli Salad (page 222) and Cold Lime Soufflé (page 113) or Chicken Salad in Pineapple Boats (page 221) and Chocolate Coffee Pie (page 261).
Prepare & Serve: Nothing left to do but set the table!

◆ THREE CITRUS SEVICHE

½ **teaspoon grated lemon rind**
½ **teaspoon grated lime rind**
½ **teaspoon grated orange rind**
¼ **cup lemon juice**
¼ **cup lime juice**
¼ **cup orange juice**
2 **tablespoons minced green pepper**
1 **tablespoon chopped green onion**
1 **pound bay scallops**
Leaf lettuce
Green onion fan

1. Combine first 8 ingredients in a medium mixing bowl. Add scallops, and stir to coat well.

2. Cover with plastic wrap, and refrigerate at least 4 hours, stirring occasionally.

3. Transfer scallops, using a slotted spoon, to a lettuce-lined serving bowl. Garnish scallops with green onion fan. Yield: 4 servings.

♠ VEGETABLE-RICE SALAD

2 cups cooked rice, chilled
¾ cup diced celery
⅓ cup diced green pepper
1 medium tomato, diced
2 tablespoons chopped onion
⅓ cup mayonnaise
2 teaspoons Dijon mustard
1 tablespoon commercial creamy
   garlic salad dressing
Lettuce leaves

1. Combine rice, celery, green pepper, tomato, and onion; toss lightly. Combine mayonnaise, mustard, and dressing. Pour over rice mixture; toss lightly.

2. Pack into a lightly oiled 3½-cup mold. Chill overnight.

3. To serve, unmold onto a lettuce-lined platter. Yield: 4 servings.

♠ QUICK AND COOL PEACH PIE

1 (14-ounce) can sweetened
   condensed milk
½ cup lemon juice
1 (4-ounce) container frozen
   whipped topping, thawed
1 (9-inch) graham cracker crust
3 medium peaches, peeled and
   sliced

1. Combine condensed milk and lemon juice in a medium mixing bowl; beat until well blended. Fold in whipped topping.

2. Spoon half of mixture into pie crust; arrange three-fourths of peach slices over top. Spread remaining whipped topping mixture over peaches.

3. Garnish top of pie with remaining peach slices. Cover and refrigerate 4 hours or until thoroughly chilled.

4. Slice into wedges, and serve. Yield: one 9-inch pie.

Note: Sliced strawberries or kiwi fruit may be substituted for remaining sliced peaches to garnish top of pie.

SUPER-QUICK SCALLOPS

Sautéed Scallops
Asparagus with Garlic Butter
Fruit Pizza

Serves 6

Prepare & Serve: Bake cookie dough for Fruit Pizza. Steam asparagus. Make Sautéed Scallops. Just before serving, toss asparagus with butter. Complete Fruit Pizza at dessert time.

☺ SAUTÉED SCALLOPS

2 pounds fresh sea scallops, cut into
   quarters
   Vegetable cooking spray
2 tablespoons butter or margarine
¼ cup Chablis or other dry white
   wine
2 tablespoons lemon juice
2 tablespoons chopped fresh chives
¼ teaspoon garlic salt
⅛ teaspoon white pepper
1 pound angel hair pasta, cooked
   Fresh parsley sprigs

1. Rinse scallops in cold water; drain.

2. Coat a large skillet with cooking spray. Add butter; melt over low heat. Add scallops; cook over high heat 5 to 8 minutes, stirring constantly. Remove scallops using a slotted spoon; set aside.

3. Add wine, lemon juice, and chives to skillet. Cook over medium heat 2 minutes, stirring occasionally. Add garlic salt and pepper. Remove from heat.

4. To serve, spoon sauce over pasta; spoon scallops over sauce. Garnish with parsley sprigs. Yield: 6 servings.

ASPARAGUS WITH GARLIC BUTTER

2 pounds fresh asparagus or 2 (10-ounce) packages frozen asparagus
3 tablespoons butter
2 cloves garlic, minced
1 teaspoon soy sauce

1. Cut asparagus on the diagonal into 1-inch pieces.
2. Cook asparagus, covered, in boiling water 4 to 6 minutes or until crisp-tender.
3. Melt butter in a large saucepan, and add garlic and soy sauce. Cook over low heat, stirring constantly, for 1 minute. Add asparagus; toss to coat.
4. Reheat before serving, if necessary. Yield: 6 to 8 servings.

FRUIT PIZZA
(pictured on page 67)

1 (20-ounce) roll refrigerated sugar cookie dough
1 (8-ounce) container frozen non-dairy whipped topping, thawed
1 cup fresh strawberries, hulled and halved
½ cup fresh blueberries
1 banana, sliced
1 kiwi, peeled and sliced
½ cup mandarin orange slices
½ cup canned sliced peaches
½ cup canned pineapple chunks

1. Press cookie dough evenly into a 12- or 14- inch pizza pan. Bake at 375° for 12 minutes or until browned. Remove from oven, and cool completely.
2. Spread whipped topping over cookie crust. Arrange fruit over topping. Serve immediately or chill thoroughly. Yield: 10 to 12 servings.

Note: Substitute 1 (8-ounce) package cream cheese, softened, for frozen non-dairy whipped topping, if desired.

FRESH CAUGHT FLAVOR

Fresh seafood offers speedy, low-fat cooking and delicate flavor, but you can't reap the benefits unless the seafood is in peak condition. Follow these guidelines for buying, storing, and cooking fresh seafood:

• Fresh fish should be cooked the day it is purchased. If you have to keep fish overnight, rinse under cold water, pat dry, and wrap in waxed paper. Place the wrapped fish in a plastic bag and close tightly. Place the bag in a bowl of ice cubes in the refrigerator, or freeze water in a metal baking pan and place in pan in the refrigerator.

• The key to using frozen seafood is not to defrost it completely. Frozen shrimp, scallops, and individually glazed small fillets don't need to be thawed; just rinse under cold water to separate pieces and remove ice crystals. Thaw blocks of frozen fish in the refrigerator overnight or in a bowl of cold water. To defrost in the microwave, use LOW (10% power) or MEDIUM LOW (30% power), allowing 3 minutes per pound, turning the block over every minute. Defrost only until you can separate fillets.

• A whole fish grilled outdoors takes the heat off any dinner party host. It's very elegant, and it couldn't be easier. Brush the fish with a combination of vegetable oil and soy sauce; grill 10 minutes for each inch of thickness (measured at the thickest point, just behind the head), turning once. Serve with melted butter seasoned with any combination of fresh or dried herbs. It's important that the heat from the coals be even and the fish cold when it goes onto the grill. To prevent sticking, oil the grate first and place a few lemon slices between the fish and the grate.

SCALLOPS AU GRATIN

Scallops au Gratin
Saucy Broccoli Spears
Blueberries and Cointreau

Serves 6

Prepare & Serve: Make sauce for broccoli. Cook broccoli. Make Scallops au Gratin. Prepare Blueberries and Cointreau.

Keep a bag of frozen peeled shrimp in the freezer for those times when you need to serve something hot in a hurry. Substitute the shrimp for scallops, if desired.

⊙ SCALLOPS AU GRATIN

- ¼ cup butter or margarine
- ¼ cup all-purpose flour
- 1 (.6-ounce) package Italian salad dressing mix
- 1½ cups milk
- 2 (4-ounce) cans sliced mushrooms, drained
- 2 teaspoons grated lemon rind
- 1½ pounds bay scallops, rinsed and drained
- 1½ cups (6 ounces) shredded Cheddar cheese
- 3 English muffins, halved and toasted
- 6 slices tomato
  Fresh parsley sprigs (optional)

1. Melt butter in a large skillet over medium heat; add flour and salad dressing mix, stirring well. Cook 1 minute, stirring constantly. Gradually stir in milk. Add mushrooms and lemon rind; cook, stirring constantly, until thickened and bubbly. Add scallops; cook, stirring occasionally, 5 to 7 minutes. Remove from heat; add cheese, stirring until cheese melts.

2. Top each English muffin half with a tomato slice; spoon ½ cup scallop mixture on top. Garnish with a parsley sprig, if desired. Yield: 6 servings.

⊙ SAUCY BROCCOLI SPEARS

- 2 (10-ounce) packages frozen broccoli spears
- 3 tablespoons butter or margarine, melted
- 3 tablespoons lemon juice
- 2 teaspoons prepared white horseradish
- ¼ to ½ teaspoon salt
- 1 teaspoon paprika

1. Cook broccoli according to package directions; drain. Place in a serving dish.

2. Combine remaining ingredients.

3. Spoon sauce over broccoli. Serve immediately. Yield: 6 servings.

⊙ BLUEBERRIES AND COINTREAU

- 3 cups fresh blueberries, rinsed and drained
- ¼ cup plus 2 tablespoons Cointreau or other orange-flavored liqueur
- 1 cup whipping cream
- ¼ cup sifted powdered sugar

1. Place ½ cup blueberries in each of 6 stemmed glasses; pour about 1 tablespoon Cointreau over each serving.

2. Beat whipping cream until foamy; gradually add powdered sugar, beating until soft peaks form.

3. Top each serving with a dollop of whipped cream. Yield: 6 servings.

A delightful variation on the pizza theme, Fruit Pizza, provides a grand finale to a menu that is also elegant but easy to prepare, Super-Quick Scallops (page 64).

GRILLED SEAFOOD

Skewered Shrimp
Zucchini with Corn Stuffing
French Bread

Serves 6

Make Ahead: Scoop out zucchini shells; fill with corn stuffing, and refrigerate. Peel and devein shrimp.

Prepare & Serve: Bake Zucchini with Corn Stuffing; keep covered with foil while you broil shrimp. You might want to serve Rocky Road Sundaes for dessert—ice cream topped with miniature marshmallows, nuts, and warm chocolate sauce.

SKEWERED SHRIMP

36 **jumbo shrimp (about 1½ pounds), peeled and deveined, or sea scallops**
30 **cherry tomatoes**
6 **lemon wedges**
1 **(8-ounce) bottle commercial French salad dressing**

1. Alternate shrimp and tomatoes on 6 skewers; place a lemon wedge at the end of each skewer.
2. Place kabobs on a greased rack in a shallow roasting pan. Broil 4 to 5 inches from heating element, 2 to 3 minutes on each side, basting frequently with French dressing.
3. Transfer kabobs to a serving platter; serve warm. Yield: 6 servings.

The star of this Light, Elegant Salmon menu (page 60) is Salmon Poached in Wine. Sharing the spotlight are Leeks Mimosa, Broiled Tomatoes, and Glazed Fruit Tart.

ZUCCHINI WITH CORN STUFFING

3 **medium zucchini**
3 **tablespoons butter or margarine**
⅓ **cup chopped onion**
⅓ **cup chopped red or green pepper**
1 **12-ounce can vacuum-packed whole kernel corn, drained**
½ **teaspoon dried whole basil**
¼ **teaspoon pepper**

1. Cook zucchini in boiling water 3 minutes. Remove zucchini from water, and cool slightly.
2. Cut zucchini in half lengthwise, and gently scoop out pulp; finely chop pulp, and transfer zucchini shells to a lightly greased 13- x 9- x 2-inch baking dish. Set baking dish aside.
3. Melt butter in a large skillet over low heat. Add onion, red pepper, and zucchini pulp; sauté until tender. Stir in corn, basil, and pepper; cook until thoroughly heated, stirring frequently. Remove vegetable mixture from heat.
4. Spoon vegetable mixture into zucchini shells. Bake at 350° for 20 minutes or until thoroughly heated.
5. Transfer to a serving plate, and serve warm. Yield: 6 servings.

MicroMethod

1. Cut zucchini in half lengthwise, and gently scoop out pulp; finely chop pulp, and transfer zucchini shells to a 13- x 9- x 2-inch baking dish. Set aside.
2. Place butter in a 1-quart bowl. Microwave vegetable mixture at HIGH for 50 seconds or until butter melts. Stir in zucchini pulp, onion, and red pepper; microwave at HIGH for 3 minutes. Add corn, basil, and pepper; stir well. Microwave at HIGH for 2 minutes.
3. Spoon vegetable mixture into reserved zucchini shells. Cover with waxed paper, and microwave at HIGH for 6 to 8 minutes or until zucchini shells are tender. Let stand, covered, 3 to 5 minutes.
4. Same as step 5.

Fish and Shellfish 69

FAST SHRIMP FEAST

Shrimp Scampi
Green Peas with Mushrooms
Apricot Baked Bananas

Serves 4

Prepare & Serve: Make apricot sauce for Apricot-Baked Bananas. Prepare Shrimp Scampi. Make Green Peas with Mushrooms. Reheat apricot sauce, if necessary, and bake bananas just before serving.

SHRIMP SCAMPI

¼ cup butter or margarine, melted
2 tablespoons Sauterne or other dry, white wine
2 tablespoons freeze-dried chives
1 clove garlic, crushed, or 1 teaspoon garlic paste
2 drops hot sauce
2 pounds medium shrimp, uncooked, peeled, and deveined
Toast points

1. Combine first 5 ingredients in a 2-quart baking dish. Add shrimp to mixture, stirring well.
2. Bake at 450° for 10 to 12 minutes, stirring occasionally.
3. Spoon over toast points to serve. Yield: 4 servings.

MicroNote: To microwave step 2, cover with waxed paper, and microwave at HIGH for 6 to 7 minutes, stirring every 2 minutes. Let stand, covered, 1½ minutes before serving.

GREEN PEAS WITH MUSHROOMS

1 (10-ounce) package frozen green peas
1 (6-ounce) can sliced mushrooms, drained
1 tablespoon butter or margarine
Salt and pepper

1. Cook peas according to package directions. Drain.
2. Toss peas with mushrooms and butter; add salt and pepper to taste.
3. Transfer to a serving bowl, and serve warm. Yield: 4 servings.

APRICOT-BAKED BANANAS

1 tablespoon margarine
2 tablespoons apricot preserves
2 tablespoons orange juice
⅛ teaspoon ground cinnamon
2 medium bananas
Lemon juice
2 tablespoons slivered almonds, toasted
Vanilla ice cream

1. Melt margarine in a small saucepan over low heat. Add apricot preserves, orange juice, and cinnamon, stirring until mixture is melted and well blended. Remove from heat.
2. Slice bananas, and sprinkle with lemon juice. Divide banana slices evenly among four custard cups; spoon apricot sauce over top, and sprinkle with toasted almond slivers.
3. Bake at 400° for 10 minutes.
4. Top banana mixture in each custard cup with a scoop of vanilla ice cream. Serve warm. Yield: 4 servings.

Note: To reduce calories, substitute low sugar apricot spread for apricot preserves and ice milk for ice cream. For a change of pace, substitute sliced apples or pears for the bananas.

LOUISIANA GARLIC SHRIMP

Louisiana Garlic Shrimp
Green Salad with Dill Dressing
Buttered Peas and Pearl Onions
Fudge Pie

Serves 4

Make Ahead: Dill Dressing can be made up to 5 days in advance.

Prepare & Serve: Make Fudge Pie. While pie is baking, prepare green salad, and toast French bread. Bake Louisiana Garlic Shrimp, and cook Buttered Peas and Pearl Onions. You may want to serve the salad while the shrimp bakes.

LOUISIANA GARLIC SHRIMP

    2 pounds medium shrimp,
        uncooked, peeled, and
        deveined
  ¼ cup unsalted butter or margarine,
        melted
    2 cloves garlic, crushed
  ¼ teaspoon hot sauce
    8 slices (about ½-inch thick) French
        bread, toasted
  ¼ cup chopped fresh parsley

1. Place shrimp in a 10- x 6- x 2-inch baking dish.

2. Combine butter, garlic, and hot sauce in a small mixing bowl, stirring well. Pour mixture over shrimp. Bake at 450° for 10 minutes or until shrimp are opaque.

3. To serve, spoon shrimp mixture over toasted French bread. Sprinkle with chopped fresh parsley. Serve immediately. Yield: 4 servings.

MicroNote: To microwave steps 1 and 2, combine shrimp and butter sauce in a 10- x 6- x 2-inch baking dish. Cover with waxed paper. Microwave at HIGH for 6 to 7 minutes or until shrimp are opaque, stirring halfway through cooking time.

DILL DRESSING

  ½ cup commercial sour cream
  ½ cup mayonnaise
    2 tablespoons plus 1½ teaspoons
        white wine vinegar
    1 teaspoon sugar
    1 teaspoon dried whole dillweed
  ½ teaspoon salt
  ¼ teaspoon pepper

1. Combine all ingredients in a small mixing bowl; stirring until well blended.

2. Cover and chill dressing at least 2 hours before serving. Yield: 1 cup.

FUDGE PIE

  ½ cup butter or margarine, melted
    1 cup sugar
    2 eggs, lightly beaten
  ¼ cup all-purpose flour
  ¼ cup cocoa
  ½ cup chopped pecans
    1 teaspoon vanilla extract
    1 (9-inch) frozen pastry shell,
        thawed

1. Combine butter, sugar, and eggs; beat well with a wire whisk. Add flour cocoa, pecans, and vanilla, beating well with wire whisk.

2. Pour batter into pastry shell, and bake at 350° for 40 minutes or until a knife inserted in center comes out clean.

3. Let pie cool before slicing into wedges. Yield: one 9-inch pie.

Note: Fudge Pie may be served warm with vanilla ice cream.

EASY CLAM LINGUINE

Linguine with Clam Sauce
Italian Dinner Salad
Angel Food Trifle

Serves 4

Make Ahead: Make and refrigerate Angel Food Trifle.

Prepare & Serve: Make Italian Dinner Salad. Cook Linguine with Clam Sauce.

If you had no time to make Angel Food Trifle, you might want to cook the pudding mixture (steps 1 and 2) before you begin other dinner preparations. Refrigerate the pudding until dessert time; then spoon over cut-up fruit, and top with toasted almonds.

LINGUINE WITH CLAM SAUCE

 8 ounces linguine, uncooked
 1 large clove garlic, minced
 2 tablespoons butter or margarine
 1 (10¾-ounce) can cream of shrimp soup, undiluted
 2 (6½-ounce) cans minced clams, rinsed and drained
 ½ cup water
 ¼ cup Chablis or other dry white wine
 ¼ cup commercial sour cream
 1 tablespoon chopped fresh parsley

1. Cook linguine according to package directions; drain.

2. Sauté garlic in butter in a large skillet until lightly browned. Stir in soup, clams, water, wine, sour cream, and parsley. Cook over low heat until bubbly.

3. Toss clam sauce and linguine together. Serve hot. Yield: 4 servings.

ITALIAN DINNER SALAD

 ½ cup white wine vinegar
 ½ cup olive oil
 2 tablespoons sugar
 1 teaspoon salt
 ½ teaspoon dried whole oregano
 ¼ teaspoon pepper
 5 small onions, quartered
 2 medium carrots, scraped and sliced at an angle
 2 stalks celery, cut into 3-inch strips
 1 small head cauliflower, broken into flowerets
 1 (3-ounce) jar pimiento-stuffed olives, drained

1. Combine first 6 ingredients in a small Dutch oven, stirring well. Add remaining ingredients; toss gently.

2. Bring to a boil. Reduce heat to medium; cover and cook 15 minutes, stirring occasionally.

3. Serve hot. Yield: 4 servings.

ANGEL FOOD TRIFLE

 1 (3.5-ounce) package vanilla pudding mix
 ½ teaspoon almond extract
 1 (10-ounce) jar strawberry or raspberry preserves
 1 (10¾-ounce) angel food loafcake, sliced
 ½ cup sherry
 ½ cup whipping cream, whipped
 2 tablespoons toasted slivered almonds

1. Prepare pudding mix according to package directions. Stir in almond extract.

2. Spread preserves on one side of cake slices. Place a layer of cake slices in bottom of a large glass serving bowl, preserve side up. Sprinkle with sherry; spoon pudding mixture over cake. Repeat layers with remaining ingredients ending with pudding. Cover and refrigerate until chilled.

3. To serve, top with whipped cream; sprinkle with almonds. Yield: 8 servings.

All in One Dish

All busy cooks share the same fantasy from time to time: tossing everything into one pot and letting the cooking take care of itself! These menus fit that frame of mind, but the recipes have been calculated to provoke all kinds of taste fantasies, too. You'll find here the inimitable freshness of Pasta Primavera, the spicy goodness of New Orleans Seafood Supper, and the cold-weather solace of Braised Chicken with Julienne Vegetables.

Because one-dish meals are everyday fare all over the world, the recipes feature international flavors. German Pork and Potato Bake, Italian Eggplant and Cheese, and Poached Eggs Provençal are quite "Continental." But it's hard to beat the all-American joys of Hearty Fish Stew with Blueberry-Walnut Cobblers for dessert, or Southwestern Beef Combo with Jalapeño Pepper Bread and Apple Slaw.

The side dishes suggested with the main attractions were selected because their timing coordinates easily with the toss-into-the-pan rhythm of one-dish cooking. But none of them is essential. A one-dish meal can remain just that, with nothing more than the nutrients of vegetable relishes or fresh fruit needed to round out the menu.

Look to these recipes to stock your freezer when time allows, for the hearty casseroles and simmer dishes keep well and may taste even better after reheating because the flavors will have had more of a chance to blend. Defrost stews and casseroles in the refrigerator or in the microwave oven. If you don't have time to defrost in the refrigerator, place the food in a saucepan with tall sides; then place the saucepan in a roasting pan. Half fill the roasting pan with water, heat to simmering over medium-low heat, and simmer until the food is thawed. You can then put the saucepan over low direct heat to finish warming the food.

Every cook who loves hearty one-pot fare should give some thought to owning just the right pot. An enameled cast-iron Dutch oven is excellent for such cooking, because it will hold a steady simmer with least risk of scorching. Heavy stainless steel and aluminum are also good choices.

Menu of Menus

CHEESE CRUST PIZZAS

Cheese Crust Pizzas
Green Salad
with Vinaigrette Dressing
Ice Cream with Chocolate-Mint Sauce

Serves 6

Prepare & Serve: Prepare and bake Cheese Crust Pizzas. Make salad and dressing. Cook Chocolate-Mint Sauce.

To save time, start with two 9- or 10-inch purchased unbaked pizza crusts, and proceed with the recipe from step 4. You may also start with one purchased cheese pizza, omit the pizza sauce, and top the pizza with half of the meat mixture and half of the cheeses. Bake as directed.

To freeze one pizza for later, cool completely, and wrap the pizza tightly in heavy-duty aluminum foil.

CHEESE CRUST PIZZAS
(pictured on page 85)

2½ cups all purpose flour, divided
1 package rapid-rise yeast
⅔ cup plus 2 tablespoons grated
    Parmesan cheese, divided
½ teaspoon salt
¼ teaspoon pepper
1 cup very warm water (120° to
    130°)
    Vegetable cooking spray
1 pound ground chuck
¼ cup chopped onion
½ teaspoon cumin
    Pizza Sauce
1 (8-ounce) package shredded
    mozzarella cheese
1 (8-ounce) package shredded sharp
    Cheddar cheese

1. Combine 1 cup flour, yeast, ½ cup Parmesan cheese, salt, and pepper in a large mixing bowl; stir well. Add warm water, stirring well. Gradually add remaining flour to make a soft dough.

2. Turn dough out onto a lightly floured surface; knead 2 to 3 minutes. Cover dough; let rest 7 minutes. Divide dough in half.

3. Coat two 12-inch pizza pans with cooking spray; set aside. Lightly coat hands with cooking spray, and pat dough evenly into pizza pan. Set aside.

4. Combine ground chuck, onion, and cumin in a large skillet. Cook over medium heat until meat is browned and onion is tender, stirring to crumble. Drain.

5. Spread half of Pizza Sauce evenly over one pizza, leaving a ½-inch border around edges. Sprinkle half the meat mixture on top of Pizza Sauce. Sprinkle half the remaining Parmesan, mozzarella, and Cheddar cheeses on top of meat mixture. Repeat procedure for remaining pizza. Place pizzas on lowest racks in oven.

6. Bake at 425° for 10 minutes. Move pizzas to opposite racks, and bake an additional 15 minutes or until edges of pizzas are crisp.

7. Remove from oven; cool slightly before serving. Yield: two 12-inch pizzas.

Pizza Sauce:

1 (15-ounce) can tomato sauce
1½ teaspoons Italian seasoning

1. Combine ingredients.
2. Set aside. Yield: about 2 cups.

Note: You can "personalize" Cheese Crust Pizzas by adding or substituting other ingredients. Here are some choices:
1. Use 1 pound Italian sausage, removed from casing, instead of the ground chuck.
2. Sauté 1 chopped green pepper and/or 4 ounces sliced fresh mushrooms with meat.
3. Stir 2 teaspoons dried whole oregano, basil, or 2 cloves minced garlic into the meat mixture.
4. Substitute 8 ounces shredded smoked

Cheddar or smoked mozzarella for the sharp Cheddar cheese.

5. Sprinkle 4 ounces sliced pitted ripe or green olives over the cheese before you bake the pizzas.

◆ **GREEN SALAD WITH VINAIGRETTE DRESSING**

1 small head romaine lettuce, torn into pieces
6 ounces fresh mushrooms, sliced
1 small cucumber, pared and sliced
1 large tomato, sliced
Salt and pepper to taste
Vinaigrette Dressing

1. Combine lettuce, mushrooms, cucumber, and tomato in a large salad bowl. Add salt and pepper.
2. Toss salad with Vinaigrette Dressing just before serving. Yield: 6 servings.

Vinaigrette Dressing:

1⅓ cups vegetable oil
1 cup tarragon vinegar
1 clove garlic, peeled and halved
1 teaspoon salt
½ teaspoon pepper

1. Combine oil, vinegar, garlic, salt, and pepper in a jar with a tight fitting lid. Cover and shake vigorously. Chill at least 2 hours.
2. Remove and discard garlic. Serve Vinaigrette Dressing over a tossed green salad. Yield: 2⅓ cups.

◒ **CHOCOLATE-MINT SAUCE**

1 (6-ounce) package semisweet chocolate morsels
⅔ cup light corn syrup
1 (5⅓-ounce) can evaporated milk
¼ cup crème de menthe
Vanilla ice cream

1. Combine chocolate morsels and corn syrup in a small saucepan. Cook over low heat until chocolate melts. Remove from heat and gradually add milk, stirring constantly with a wire whisk. Stir in crème de menthe.
2. Serve Chocolate-Mint Sauce warm over ice cream. Store remaining sauce in refrigerator. Yield: 2 cups.

PIZZA PIZZAZZ!

How many ways can you bake a pizza? As many ways as there are breads and toppings. Here are a few ideas:

● Start with the plainest, least expensive type of frozen cheese pizza. Add one of the following combinations, and bake in a preheated 375° oven. To ensure a crisp crust, preheat a large baking sheet in the oven and slide the pizza directly onto it. To a 1-pound pizza add:

8 ounces shredded mozzarella cheese; 2 ounces grated Parmesan cheese; 1 tablespoon dried whole oregano; 8-ounces bulk pork sausage, cooked and crumbled; and freshly ground pepper.

8 ounces shredded smoked provolone cheese; 1 large tomato, thinly sliced; 1 tablespoon dried whole basil; and freshly ground pepper to taste.

● Start with a purchased refrigerated pizza crust, spread with olive oil or vegetable oil. Add toppings, and bake as directed above. Choose one of the following combinations:

8 ounces shredded mozzarella cheese; 1 (2-ounce) can anchovies, rinsed and patted dry; ¼ cup sliced ripe olives; and 2 ounces grated Parmesan cheese.

One or 2 thinly sliced medium-size tomatoes; 4 ounces crumbled feta cheese; 1 teaspoon dried whole basil; ¼ cup sliced ripe olives; and 1 teaspoon dried whole rosemary, crushed.

ONE-DISH GOULASH

Beef-Vegetable Goulash
Tomato Wedges
Double Quick Whole Wheat Rolls

Serves 6

Prepare & Serve: Start making rolls, and while the batter is rising, prepare goulash. Slice tomatoes while rolls are baking. Cherries Jubilee (page 258) is a no-bake alternative for a crowning dessert.

BEEF-VEGETABLE GOULASH

- 1 **pound ground chuck**
- 1 **medium-size green pepper, seeded and coarsely chopped**
- 1 **medium-size red sweet pepper, seeded and coarsely chopped**
- 1 **medium onion, coarsely chopped**
- 1 **medium-size yellow squash, cut into ½-inch cubes**
- 2 **cloves garlic, minced**
- 1 **tablespoon paprika**
- ¾ **teaspoon salt**
- ½ **cup commercial sour cream**
- 2 **teaspoons prepared mustard**
- 1 **(8-ounce) package egg noodles, cooked according to package directions**

1. Brown ground chuck in a large Dutch oven over medium heat, stirring to crumble. Drain meat in a colander, reserving pan drippings in Dutch oven. Set crumbled meat aside.

2. Add chopped peppers, onion, squash, garlic, paprika, and salt to Dutch oven, stirring well. Sauté vegetable mixture until tender.

3. Stir meat, sour cream, and mustard into vegetable mixture. Cook over low heat, stirring frequently, until mixture is thoroughly heated.

4. Place egg noodles on a serving platter; spoon beef mixture over top. Yield: 6 servings.

MicroMethod

1. Combine ground chuck, peppers, onion, squash, and garlic in a 2-quart casserole. Cover with heavy-duty plastic wrap, and vent to allow steam to escape; microwave at HIGH for 4 minutes, stirring after 2 minutes. Drain.

2. Add paprika and salt, stirring well. Cover and microwave at HIGH for 5 minutes, stirring after 2½ minutes.

3. Stir in sour cream and mustard. Cover and microwave at HIGH for 3 minutes or until mixture is thoroughly heated. Stir beef mixture well.

4. Same as step 4.

DOUBLE QUICK WHOLE WHEAT ROLLS

- 1¼ **cups whole wheat flour**
- 2 **tablespoons sugar**
- 1 **teaspoon salt**
- 1 **package dry yeast**
- 1 **cup warm water (120° to 130°)**
- 2 **tablespoons shortening**
- 1 **egg**
- 1 **cup all-purpose flour**

1. Combine whole wheat flour, sugar, salt, and yeast in a large mixing bowl. Add water, shortening, and egg; beat until smooth. Stir in remaining flour until smooth. Cover and let rise in a warm place (85°), free from drafts, 30 minutes or until doubled in bulk.

2. Stir batter down, beating 25 strokes. Spoon batter evenly into 12 greased muffin cups. Let rise 15 minutes or until batter reaches tops of cups.

3. Bake at 400° for 15 minutes or until golden brown.

4. Serve warm. Yield: 1 dozen.

TEX-MEX COMBO

Southwestern Beef Combo
Jalapeño Pepper Bread
Apple Slaw
Blender Chocolate Mousse

Serves 6

Make Ahead: Prepare Blender Chocolate Mousse, and refrigerate.
Prepare & Serve: Prepare Jalapeño Pepper Bread. Cook Southwestern Beef Combo. Make Apple Slaw.

SOUTHWESTERN BEEF COMBO

1 **pound lean ground beef**
1 **(1¾-ounce) package chili seasoning mix, divided**
¼ **cup soft breadcrumbs**
1 **egg, beaten**
1 **tablespoon vegetable oil**
1 **(15-ounce) can red kidney beans, undrained**
1 **(8-ounce) can whole kernel corn, undrained**
¼ **cup tomato paste**
¼ **cup chopped green pepper**
¼ **teaspoon dried whole oregano**

1. Combine beef, 1 tablespoon chili seasoning mix, breadcrumbs, and egg. Shape beef mixture into 18 meatballs. Brown meatballs in oil in a large skillet, turning frequently; drain on paper towels. Discard pan drippings in skillet. Set meatballs aside.
2. Add beans, corn, tomato paste, green pepper, oregano, and remaining chili seasoning mix to skillet; stir well. Place reserved meatballs over mixture in skillet.

3. Bring mixture to a boil. Reduce heat; cover and simmer 15 minutes, stirring occasionally. Uncover and simmer an additional 5 minutes.
4. Ladle beef combo into serving bowls. Yield: 6 servings.

MicroMethod

1. Combine beef, 1 tablespoon chili seasoning mix, breadcrumbs, and egg. Shape mixture into 18 meatballs. Place meatballs in a 12- x 8- x 2-inch baking dish, omitting oil. Cover with heavy-duty plastic wrap, and vent to allow steam to escape; microwave at MEDIUM (50% power) for 6 to 8 minutes, rotating dish after 3 minutes. Set aside.
2. Combine beans, corn, tomato paste, green pepper, oregano, and remaining seasoning mix in a 2-quart casserole. Cover with a glass lid or heavy-duty plastic wrap, and microwave at HIGH for 4 to 5 minutes, stirring after 2 minutes.
3. Remove meatballs from drippings; stir into vegetable mixture. Cover; microwave at MEDIUM (50% power) for 5 to 6 minutes, stirring every 2 minutes.
4. Same as step 4.

JALAPEÑO PEPPER BREAD

1½ **cups self-rising cornmeal**
1 **(8-ounce) carton commercial sour cream**
½ **cup shortening, melted**
3 **eggs, beaten**
1 **(7-ounce) can whole kernel corn, undrained**
2 **jalapeño peppers, seeded and chopped**

1. Combine cornmeal, sour cream, shortening, eggs, corn, and peppers in a medium mixing bowl, mixing well.
2. Pour batter into a well-greased 10½-inch cast-iron skillet. Bake at 425° for 20 minutes or until golden brown.
3. Serve warm. Yield: 6 to 8 servings.

APPLE SLAW

¼ cup plus 2 tablespoons
    commercial sour cream
¼ cup plus 2 tablespoons plain
    low-fat yogurt
1½ teaspoons prepared horseradish
2 medium-size red Delicious apples,
    coarsely chopped
½ small cabbage, shredded (about 2
    cups)
2 medium carrots, shredded (about
    ½ cup)
  Bibb lettuce leaves

1. Combine sour cream, yogurt, and horseradish in a medium mixing bowl; stir until well blended. Stir in apples, cabbage, and carrots; toss until well coated.
2. Cover with plastic wrap, and chill. Serve slaw on lettuce-lined serving plates. Yield: 6 servings.

BLENDER
CHOCOLATE MOUSSE

2 (12-ounce) packages semisweet
    chocolate morsels
4 eggs
2 tablespoons Grand Marnier or
    other orange-flavored liqueur
1½ cups milk
¼ cup plus 2 tablespoons strong
    coffee
  Frozen whipped topping, thawed
  Orange zest

1. Combine chocolate morsels, eggs, and liqueur in container of an electric blender. Set aside.
2. Combine milk and coffee in a saucepan; cook over high heat until thermometer registers 180°. Remove from heat.
3. Pour hot liquid into blender container. Process at high speed for 2 minutes.
4. Pour mixture into 6 stemmed dessert dishes. Chill overnight.
5. Garnish Blender Chocolate Mousse with whipped topping and orange zest. Yield: 6 servings.

STIR-FRY SPECIAL

Stir-Fried Beef and Vegetables
Overnight Oriental Salad
Cherry-Chocolate Cake

Serves 8

Make Ahead: Prepare Oriental Salad and refrigerate overnight.
Prepare & Serve: Bake Cherry-Chocolate Cake. Cook rice. Prepare ingredients for Stir-Fried Beef and Vegetables. Stir-fry the beef and vegetables. Frost cake. If you don't feel like baking, serve fruit kabobs for dessert. Skewer any combination of your favorite fruits you wish on toothpicks. Serve with one or two kinds of fruit yogurt for dipping.

STIR-FRIED BEEF
AND VEGETABLES

2 tablespoons vegetable oil
2 pounds top round beef steak, cut
    across grain into 3- x ⅛-inch
    strips
8 green onions, cut into 1½-inch
    pieces
3 carrots, scraped and sliced
    diagonally
2 green peppers, seeded and cut
    into 1-inch pieces
½ pound fresh mushrooms, halved
1 (8-ounce) can sliced water
    chestnuts, drained
1 clove garlic, minced
1 cup water
⅓ cup soy sauce
1 tablespoon plus 1½ teaspoons
    cornstarch
2 teaspoons sugar
¼ teaspoon pepper
  Hot cooked rice

1. Heat oil in a large skillet. Brown beef strips. Remove beef; set aside.

2. Add green onion, carrots, green pepper, mushrooms, water chestnuts, and garlic to skillet. Cook over medium-high heat 2 to 3 minutes, stirring constantly, or until vegetables are crisp-tender.

3. Combine water, soy sauce, cornstarch, sugar, and pepper; stir well. Return beef to skillet; add cornstarch mixture.

4. Cook, stirring constantly, 3 to 4 minutes or until thickened and bubbly.

5. Serve over hot cooked rice. Yield: 8 servings.

OVERNIGHT ORIENTAL SALAD

1 (17-ounce) can tiny green peas, drained
1 (14-ounce) can bean sprouts, drained
1 (12-ounce) can white shoe peg corn, drained
1 (6-ounce) jar sliced mushrooms, drained
1 (8-ounce) can sliced bamboo shoots, drained
1 (4-ounce) jar sliced pimiento, drained
1 large green pepper, seeded and cut into strips
1 large onion, sliced and separated into rings
1 cup sliced celery
1 cup vegetable oil
1 cup water
1 cup sugar
½ cup vinegar
  Lettuce leaves

1. Place peas, sprouts, corn, mushrooms, bamboo shoots, pimientos, green pepper, onion, and celery in a large bowl; toss lightly.

2. Combine vegetable oil, water, sugar, and vinegar in a 2-quart measuring cup; stir well. Pour dressing over vegetable mixture. Cover and refrigerate mixture overnight.

3. Line serving bowl with lettuce leaves. Drain vegetable mixture and spoon Overnight Oriental Salad into bowl. Yield: 8 servings.

CHERRY-CHOCOLATE CAKE

1 (18.25-ounce) package devil's food cake mix with pudding
1 (21-ounce) can cherry pie filling
2 eggs, beaten
1 teaspoon almond extract
1 cup sugar
¼ cup plus 1 tablespoon butter or margarine
⅓ cup milk
1 (6-ounce) package semisweet chocolate morsels

1. Grease and flour a 13- x 9- x 2-inch baking pan. Set aside.

2. Combine cake mix, cherry pie filling, eggs, and almond flavoring in a large mixing bowl. Stir, using a wooden spoon, until all ingredients are well mixed.

3. Pour batter into prepared pan, and bake at 350° for 30 minutes or until a wooden pick inserted in center comes out clean. Set aside to cool.

4. Combine sugar, butter, and milk in a small saucepan. Bring mixture to a boil; reduce heat, and simmer 1 minute, stirring constantly.

5. Remove saucepan from heat, and stir in chocolate morsels. Continue to stir until mixture is smooth and well blended. Pour mixture over cooled cake. Let frosting set before serving. Cut Cherry-Chocolate Cake into 3-inch squares. Yield: one 13- x 9-inch cake.

GERMAN CASSEROLE

German Pork and Potato Bake
Twist-of-Lemon Pie

Serves 4

Make Ahead: Bake Twist-of-Lemon Pie.
Prepare & Serve: Prepare German Pork and Potato Bake. For a crisp accompaniment make Apple Slaw (page 78) while the casserole is in the oven. Or slice a cucumber, green pepper, and green onions, and toss with olive oil, lemon juice, and dillweed for a salad.

GERMAN PORK AND POTATO BAKE

4 new potatoes, cooked, peeled, and
    sliced
½ pound hot bulk pork sausage,
    cooked, crumbled, and drained
1 tablespoon butter or margarine
2 tablespoons all-purpose flour
1 cup milk
2 cups (8 ounces) shredded sharp
    Cheddar cheese
¼ teaspoon salt
¼ teaspoon red pepper (optional)
½ cup fine dry breadcrumbs
2 tablespoon butter or margarine,
    melted

1. Place potato slices in a lightly greased 8-inch square baking dish; sprinkle sausage over potatoes. Set aside.
2. Melt 1 tablespoon butter in a heavy saucepan over low heat; add flour, stirring until smooth. Cook 1 minute, stirring constantly. Gradually add milk; cook over medium heat, stirring constantly, until thickened and bubbly. Remove from heat;

add cheese, salt, and red pepper, if desired, stirring until cheese melts. Spoon sauce evenly over sausage mixture.
3. Combine breadcrumbs and melted butter in a small mixing bowl, stirring well. Sprinkle mixture evenly over sauce. Bake at 350° for 25 minutes or until bubbly.
4. Serve immediately. Yield: 4 servings.

MicroMethod

1. Same as step 1.
2. Microwave 1 tablespoon butter in a 1-quart glass measure at HIGH for 45 seconds. Stir in flour until smooth. Blend in milk. Microwave at HIGH for 6 to 8 minutes or until thickened. Add cheese, salt, and pepper, stirring until cheese melts. Spoon over sausage mixture.
3. Combine breadcrumbs and melted butter in a small bowl; sprinkle evenly over sauce. Microwave at MEDIUM (50% power) for 10 to 12 minutes or until bubbly and thoroughly heated.
4. Same as step 4.

TWIST-OF-LEMON PIE

½ cup sugar
3 tablespoons all-purpose flour
3 eggs, beaten
½ cup light corn syrup
2 tablespoons butter or margarine,
    melted
2 teaspoons grated lemon rind
3 tablespoons lemon juice
1 unbaked (9-inch) frozen pastry
    shell, thawed
Lemon slices

1. Combine sugar and flour in a large bowl; stir well. Add eggs, syrup, and butter, stirring until well blended; add lemon rind and juice, stirring well.
2. Pour mixture into pastry shell. Bake on lowest rack of oven at 375° for 40 minutes or until center is set. Cool to room temperature; chill thoroughly.
3. Garnish each piece of pie with a lemon slice. Yield: one 9-inch pie.

HEARTY HAM CASSEROLE

Hot Cheese and Ham Potatoes
Mushroom Salad
Sliced Apples
Carrot Cookies

Serves 4 to 6

Make Ahead: Bake Carrot Cookies.
Prepare & Serve: Prepare Hot Cheese and Ham Potatoes. While the casserole is baking, slice apples, and prepare salad.

HOT CHEESE AND HAM POTATOES

4 large potatoes (about 2 pounds), peeled and cut into 1½-inch cubes
1 cup chopped onion
¾ cup chopped celery
½ cup beer
¼ cup butter or margarine
1 tablespoon Worcestershire sauce
½ teaspoon salt
2 cups cubed cooked ham
1 cup (4 ounces) shredded Cheddar cheese
¼ cup chopped fresh parsley

1. Combine first 7 ingredients in a large saucepan; bring to a boil. Reduce heat; cover and simmer 25 minutes, stirring mixture occasionally.
2. Add ham, cheese, and parsley, stirring until cheese melts.
3. Transfer mixture to a large serving bowl; serve hot. Yield: 4 to 6 servings.

MicroNote: To microwave step 1, reduce beer to ¼ cup. Combine first 7 ingredients in a 3-quart casserole. Cover and microwave at HIGH for 10 minutes.

MUSHROOM SALAD

¼ cup fresh lemon juice
¼ cup vegetable oil
¼ cup olive or vegetable oil
1 tablespoon dried mint leaves, crushed
1 teaspoon dried whole dillweed
¼ teaspoon salt
½ medium-size red onion, thinly sliced
6 ounces fresh mushrooms, sliced
8 ounces romaine lettuce, torn into pieces
6 ounces curly endive, spinach, or watercress, torn into pieces

1. Combine first 6 ingredients in a small bowl. Stir with a wire whisk.
2. Combine onion, mushrooms, and greens in a salad bowl; toss with dressing. Yield: 4 to 6 servings.

CARROT COOKIES

1 cup butter or margarine, softened
1 cup firmly packed brown sugar
1 cup shredded carrots
½ cup chopped pecans
½ cup raisins
½ cup molasses
1 egg
1 teaspoon vanilla extract
2 tablespoons grated orange rind
2½ cups all-purpose flour
1½ teaspoons baking powder

1. Cream butter in a large mixing bowl; gradually add sugar, beating well. Add carrots, pecans, raisins, molasses, egg, vanilla, and orange rind, mixing well.
2. Combine flour and baking powder in a small bowl, stirring well. Add to creamed mixture; stir until well blended.
3. Drop batter by teaspoonfuls 2 inches apart onto lightly greased cookie sheets.
4. Bake at 375° for 7 to 10 minutes or until lightly browned. Remove from cookie sheets, and cool completely on wire racks. Yield: 6 dozen.

STIR-FRY SURPRISE

Chicken and Vegetable Stir-Fry
French Breadsticks
Summer Fruit Compote

Serves 4

Make-Ahead: Make compote and chill.
Prepare & Serve: Prepare Chicken and Vegetable Stir-Fry. Bake breadsticks.

CHICKEN AND VEGETABLE STIR-FRY
(pictured on front cover)

- 2 tablespoons soy sauce
- 1 tablespoon dry sherry
- 2 teaspoons cornstarch
- 1 pound boneless and skinless chicken breast halves, cut into ½-inch-thick strips
- ¼ cup peanut oil, divided
- 2½ cups fresh broccoli flowerets
- 1 (8-ounce) can sliced water chestnuts, drained
- 4 medium carrots, thinly sliced
- ½ medium-size green pepper, seeded and sliced
- 2 medium-size sweet red peppers, seeded and sliced
- ½ medium-size sweet yellow pepper, seeded and sliced
- ½ pound fresh mushrooms, sliced
- ¼ cup water
  Hot cooked rice or 1 (5-ounce) can chow mein noodles

1. Combine first 3 ingredients in a medium mixing bowl; add chicken, tossing lightly to coat. Cover and marinate in refrigerator 20 minutes.
2. Place 2 tablespoons oil in a preheated wok or electric skillet, coating sides; heat at high (375°) for 2 minutes. Add vegetables; stir-fry 2 to 3 minutes. Remove vegetables from wok; set aside, and keep warm.
3. Drain chicken, reserving marinade. Place remaining 2 tablespoons oil in wok; add chicken, stir-frying for 2 minutes. Stir in reserved marinade, vegetables, and water. Cover and cook over low heat (225°) 2 minutes or until thickened.
4. Serve over rice. Yield: 4 servings.

FRENCH BREADSTICKS
(pictured on front cover)

- 1 (16-ounce) loaf French bread
- 1 cup butter or margarine, melted

1. Slice loaf crosswise into 3 equal sections. Cut each section lengthwise into 12 sticks about 1½ inches thick.
2. Dip breadsticks in butter to coat.
3. Arrange on baking sheets; broil 6 inches from heating element 8 minutes or until golden brown, turning often.
4. Serve warm. Yield: 3 dozen.

SUMMER FRUIT COMPOTE
(pictured on back cover)

- ¼ cup sugar
- 2 tablespoons rum
- 1 teaspoon grated lime rind
- 2 tablespoons fresh lime juice
- 1 medium nectarine
- 1 medium plum
- 1 small pear
- 1 small peach
- 4 small strawberries

1. Combine sugar, rum, lime rind and juice. Seed and slice fruit, except strawberries. Pour dressing over fruit in a medium mixing bowl; toss lightly. Cover and chill.
2. Spoon into individual serving bowls; garnish each serving with a strawberry. Yield: 4 servings.

PASTA POULET

Pasta with Chicken and Vegetables
Herb-Seasoned French Bread
Peaches with Raspberry Sauce

Serves 4

Make Ahead: Raspberry Sauce may be prepared, covered, and refrigerated up to 10 days. Warm over low heat or in the microwave before serving.
Prepare & Serve: Prepare ingredients for Pasta with Vegetables and Chicken. Make Herb-Seasoned French Bread. Cook vegetables and chicken.

PASTA WITH CHICKEN AND VEGETABLES

4 boneless and skinless chicken
    breast halves, cut into strips
½ cup chopped green onions
2 cloves garlic, minced
1 teaspoon dried whole basil
2 tablespoons vegetable oil
2 medium zucchini, thinly sliced
    (about 2 cups)
2 medium carrots, scraped and
    thinly sliced (about 2 cups)
½ cup dry white wine
¼ cup chopped fresh parsley
1 teaspoon salt
⅛ teaspoon hot sauce
8 ounces Rigatoni pasta, cooked

1. Sauté chicken, onion, garlic, and basil in oil in a large skillet 3 minutes or until chicken turns opaque.
2. Add zucchini, carrots, wine, parsley, salt, and hot sauce. Cover; simmer 5 minutes or until crisp-tender.
3. Toss chicken mixture and Rigatoni together. Serve hot. Yield: 4 servings.

HERB-SEASONED FRENCH BREAD

1 (16-ounce) loaf unsliced French
    bread
⅓ cup butter or margarine, softened
1 teaspoon Worcestershire sauce
2 teaspoons dried parsley flakes
½ teaspoon dried whole basil
¼ teaspoon garlic powder

1. Slice French bread into 1-inch slices. Combine butter, Worcestershire sauce, parsley, basil, and garlic powder, mixing well; spread between bread slices.
2. Wrap loaf in aluminum foil; bake at 350° for 15 minutes or until heated.
3. Serve warm. Yield: one loaf.

PEACHES WITH RASPBERRY SAUCE

1 (10-ounce) package frozen
    raspberries
2 teaspoons cornstarch
½ teaspoon grated lemon rind
3 (16-ounce) cans peach halves,
    drained

1. Thaw frozen raspberries. Drain; reserve raspberries and juice.
2. Combine raspberry juice, cornstarch, and lemon rind in a medium saucepan; mix well. Bring to a boil. Reduce heat; cook, stirring constantly, until thickened. Gently stir in reserved raspberries.
3. Place 2 peach halves on each of 4 serving dishes. Reserve remaining peach halves for other uses.
4. Spoon raspberry mixture evenly over peach halves. Yield: 4 servings.

MicroNote: To microwave step 1, thaw frozen raspberries in an all-paper package by placing box in a bowl in the oven. Microwave at HIGH until paper carton feels warm to touch. Let stand 10 to 12 minutes. Pour raspberries into bowl; stir to break up remaining icy pieces. Drain; reserve raspberries and juice.

ONE-POT CHICKEN

Braised Chicken With Julienne Vegetables
Hot Cooked Chicken-Flavored Rice
Chess Cake

Serves 4

Make Ahead: Bake Chess Cake.
Prepare & Serve: Cook Braised Chicken with Julienne Vegetables. While chicken is cooking, prepare rice mix according to package directions. Strawberry or blueberry shortcake, made with purchased sponge cake, would be a good spur-of-the-moment substitute for Chess Cake. Toss berries with a teaspoon of orange-flavored liqueur to enhance the flavor.

BRAISED CHICKEN WITH JULIENNE VEGETABLES

1 (3- to 3½ pound) broiler-fryer, cut up
1 teaspoon paprika
¾ teaspoon salt
¼ teaspoon dried whole marjoram
1 tablespoon vegetable oil
1 medium onion, chopped
1 clove garlic, minced
1 cup dry white wine
4 medium carrots, cut into julienne strips
4 stalks celery, cut into julienne strips

1. Sprinkle chicken pieces with paprika, salt, and marjoram. Heat oil in a large skillet over medium-heat. Brown chicken on all sides. Remove chicken; set aside, and keep warm.
2. Sauté onion and garlic in pan drippings in a large skillet until tender. Add chicken and wine. Cover and cook over medium-low heat 15 minutes or until juices of chicken run clear when pierced with a fork.
3. Add carrots and celery. Cover and cook 5 to 7 minutes or until vegetables are crisp-tender.
4. Transfer to a serving platter, and serve warm. Yield: 4 servings.

CHESS CAKE

1 (18.25-ounce) package yellow cake mix, without pudding
½ cup butter or margarine, melted
4 eggs, divided
1 (16-ounce) package powdered sugar, sifted
1 (8-ounce) package cream cheese, softened

1. Combine cake mix, butter, and 2 eggs in a large mixing bowl; mix until well blended. Spread batter in a greased 13- x 9- x 2-inch baking pan.
2. Position knife blade in food processor bowl; add 2 eggs, powdered sugar, and cream cheese. Process until smooth. Pour mixture over cake batter.
3. Bake at 350° for 45 minutes or until browned and set.
4. Let cool to serve. Yield: one 13- x 9-inch cake.

Right: *Made with Parmesan Cheese, the crust of this pizza from the Cheese Crust Pizza menu (page 74) is sure to become a family favorite.*

Page 86: *Use your microwave to whip out this Beefed-Up Eggplant menu (page 94) featuring a savory beef mixture in eggplant, Sautéed Peppers and Mushrooms, and Special Swirl Cheesecake.*

NEW ORLEANS SEAFOOD SUPPER

New Orleans Seafood Supper
Avocado-Grapefruit Salad
with Honey Vinaigrette Dressing

Serves 6

Prepare & Serve: Make New Orleans Seafood Supper. Cook rice. Make Avocado-Grapefruit Salad with Honey Vinaigrette Dressing. If there's time the night before, you might make Crème de Menthe Chocolate Parfaits (page 255) or Mud Pie with Chocolate Sauce (page 107) for dessert.

NEW ORLEANS SEAFOOD SUPPER

- 4 slices bacon
- 2 tablespoons all-purpose flour
- 1 teaspoon browning and seasoning sauce
- 1½ cups chopped celery
- 1 medium-size green pepper, seeded and chopped
- 6 green onions, chopped
- 2 cloves garlic, crushed
- 4 medium tomatoes, seeded and chopped
- 1 (4-ounce) can chopped chili peppers, undrained
- 2 bay leaves
- 1½ teaspoons salt
- ½ teaspoon pepper
- ½ teaspoon dried whole basil
- ¾ pound medium shrimp, uncooked, peeled, and deveined
- ¾ pound scallops, uncooked, rinsed, and drained
- ½ cup chopped fresh parsley
  Hot sauce to taste
  Hot cooked rice

1. Cook bacon in a small Dutch oven until crisp; drain on paper towels, reserving 2 tablespoons drippings in pan. Crumble bacon; set aside.

2. Add flour and browning and seasoning sauce to reserved pan drippings in Dutch oven; cook over medium heat 1 minute, stirring constantly. Add celery, green pepper, green onions, and garlic; cook 10 minutes, stirring frequently. Add tomatoes, chili peppers, bay leaves, salt, pepper, and basil; cook, uncovered, 45 minutes, stirring occasionally. Add shrimp, scallops, reserved bacon, chopped parsley, and hot sauce; cook 3 minutes. Remove and discard bay leaves.

3. Serve over hot cooked rice. Yield: 6 servings.

AVOCADO-GRAPEFRUIT SALAD WITH HONEY VINAIGRETTE DRESSING

- 1 large avocado, peeled and sliced
- 1 large grapefruit, peeled and sectioned
  Lettuce leaves
  Honey Vinaigrette Dressing

1. Arrange avocado slices and grapefruit sections on individual lettuce-lined salad plates.

2. Serve with Honey Vinaigrette Dressing. Yield: 6 servings.

Honey Vinaigrette Dressing:

- ½ cup lemon juice
- ½ cup vegetable oil
- ½ cup honey
- ¾ teaspoon salt
- ¼ teaspoon paprika

1. Combine all ingredients in a glass jar; cover and shake vigorously. Chill dressing thoroughly.

2. Shake well before serving with salad. Yield: 1½ cups.

HOT AND HEARTY FISH STEW

Hearty Fish Stew
Blueberry-Walnut Cobblers

Serves 8

Prepare & Serve: Prepare Blueberry-Walnut Cobblers. Make Hearty Fish Stew. Bake cobblers while stew is being served.

A simple salad of lettuce wedges or other greens with an herb vinaigrette would be a great start for this menu.

HEARTY FISH STEW

½ pound fresh mushrooms, sliced
2 medium onions, chopped
2 medium carrots, grated
¼ cup butter or margarine, melted
½ cup diced cooked country ham
3 tablespoons all-purpose flour
1 cup fish bouillon or clam juice
1 cup milk
1 cup half-and-half
2 teaspoons Worcestershire sauce
¼ teaspoon pepper
1½ pounds flounder fillets, cut into
     1-inch pieces
   Thick slices of toasted French
     bread

1. Sauté mushrooms, onion, and carrot in butter in a small Dutch oven 3 to 4 minutes or until tender. Stir in ham and flour; cook 2 minutes, stirring constantly. Add bouillon; cook and stir until slightly thickened and smooth.
2. Bring mixture to a boil. Reduce heat; add milk, half-and-half, Worcestershire sauce, pepper, and flounder. Cover and simmer for 6 minutes or until fish flakes easily with a fork.

3. Ladle stew into individual bowls, and top each serving with a slice of toasted French bread. Serve immediately. Yield: about 2 quarts.

Note: To substitute frozen haddock or cod fillets, thaw in the refrigerator, and drain well before cutting into pieces.

BLUEBERRY-WALNUT COBBLERS

⅔ cup sugar
2 tablespoons cornstarch
1 cup water
3 cups fresh blueberries
1 teaspoon lemon juice
⅛ teaspoon ground nutmeg
2 cups buttermilk baking mix
½ cup chopped walnuts
¼ teaspoon ground cinnamon
¼ cup butter or margarine
⅓ cup milk
⅓ cup orange juice

1. Combine sugar and cornstarch in a small saucepan, stirring until well blended. Stir in water until mixture is smooth.
2. Bring mixture to a boil; cook 1 minute or just until thickened, stirring constantly. Add blueberries, lemon juice, and nutmeg; stir well. Spoon mixture evenly into eight lightly greased 6-ounce custard cups or individual baking dishes.
3. Combine baking mix, walnuts, and cinnamon in a medium mixing bowl. Cut in butter, using a pastry blender, until mixture resembles coarse meal. Add milk and orange juice, stirring until mixture is stiff and slightly sticky.
4. Drop 3 tablespoonfuls mixture over top of each individual serving of blueberry mixture. Bake at 400° for 20 minutes or until golden brown.
5. Remove from oven, and serve Blueberry-Walnut Cobblers warm or cool completely. Yield: 8 servings.

Note: A (1.25-ounce) can blueberry pie filling may be used, omitting steps 1 and 2.

PASTA PRIMAVERA

Pasta Primavera
Breadsticks
Strawberry Sorbet

Serves 6

Make Ahead: Prepare Strawberry Sorbet.
Prepare & Serve: Blanch vegetables, and
cook linguine. While breadsticks are heating, complete Pasta Primavera.

A quickly arranged antipasto platter will
appease appetities while the pasta is cooking. Use any combination of cold cuts and
cheeses; garnish with black and green
olives, tomato wedges, and celery hearts.
Drizzle with olive oil and red wine vinegar
or Italian dressing.

PASTA PRIMAVERA

1 **pound fresh broccoli, broken into**
   flowerets
1 **pound fresh green beans, trimmed**
   and cut into 1-inch pieces
2 **medium-size sweet red peppers,**
   seeded and cut into strips
½ **(16-ounce) package linguine**
1 **cup chopped onion**
3 **cloves garlic, minced**
¼ **cup butter or margarine, melted**
12 **ounces fresh mushrooms, sliced**
⅓ **cup grated Parmesan cheese**

1. Cook broccoli, green beans, and red
peppers in boiling water to cover in a large
saucepan 5 minutes or until crisp-tender.
Drain and set aside.

2. Break linguine into 3-inch pieces.
Cook, according to package directions,
omitting salt. Drain; place cooked linguine
in a large serving bowl. Set aside.

3. Sauté onion and garlic in butter in a
large skillet until tender. Add mushrooms,
and sauté an additional 5 minutes or until
mushrooms are tender.

4. Add reserved vegetable mixture, sautéed vegetable mixture, and Parmesan
cheese to linguine; toss to mix well.

5. Serve immediately or chill and serve.
Yield: 6 servings.

Note: Other vegetables, such as asparagus, summer squash, peas, and cauliflower
may be substituted for the broccoli and
green beans. Slice or cut into small pieces;
cook as above just until crisp-tender.

♦ STRAWBERRY SORBET

6 **cups fresh strawberries, hulled**
½ **cup sugar**
1 **cup lemon juice**
1 **cup orange juice**
½ **cup Grand Marnier**
   Fresh mint leaves (optional)
   Additional fresh strawberries
   (optional)

1. Combine 6 cups strawberries and
sugar in container of an electric blender or
food processor; process until smooth.
Transfer mixture to a large mixing bowl;
add lemon juice, orange juice, and Grand
Marnier, stirring well.

2. Pour mixture into a 13- x 9- x 2-inch
baking pan. Freeze until mixture reaches
consistency of a sherbet, stirring every
hour during freezing.

3. Scoop Strawberry Sorbet into individual serving dishes; garnish with mint
leaves and additional fresh strawberries, if
desired. Yield: about 2½ quarts.

EATING LESS MEAT— AND ENJOYING IT MORE!

Cut down on fat and calories by serving 2- to 3-ounce portions of meat instead of thick steaks and chops. Here are some quick ways to make smaller meat servings appealing and satisfying:

● Instead of grilling a whole steak, cut the meat into cubes and make kabobs. Skewer meat cubes, alternating with a colorful combination of peppers, corn, zucchini, yellow squash, purple onion, and mushrooms. Baste kabobs with a vinaigrette dressing. You'll enjoy a double bonus—less saturated fat and no need to prepare a vegetable dish.

● Serve potatoes with meat instead of "meat and potatoes." Bake one large potato for each serving. Sauté 2 ounces of diced meat per serving; season with chili powder, curry powder, or any herbs you desire. Remove meat from skillet, and add wine to the pan drippings; cook, stirring constantly, until thickened. Return meat to skillet, and cook until thoroughly heated. Spoon meat mixture over potato.

● Serve main-dish salads often, especially in warm weather. Add 2 ounces of julienne-cut beef or ham per serving to tossed green salad. Mix the same amount of pork into your favorite potato salad. Add any kind of meat to a pasta salad. To enhance the flavor of cold meat, heat meat briefly in a skillet, with no added fat, before adding it to the salad, even if the salad is chilled.

● Turn small servings of meat into tacos. A taco is any combination of meat, beans, cheese, salsa, and chopped vegetables, wrapped in a warm corn tortilla. A burrito is the same combination rolled up in a flour tortilla.

SUNDAY NIGHT SUPPER

Poached Eggs Provençal
Whole Wheat English Muffins
Crusty Peach Dessert

Serves 8

Prepare & Serve: While Crusty Peach Dessert is baking, prepare Poached Eggs Provençal, and toast English muffins.

This menu would also make a lovely casual brunch. For a sparkling starter, serve tall glasses of grapefruit or orange juice fizzed with club soda; stir a spoonful of frozen raspberries in syrup into each glass, and garnish with mint, if desired. Spoon heavy cream or sour cream over the Crusty Peach Dessert instead of ice cream. You might also want to accompany the eggs with smoked sausage links, fried ham, or Canadian bacon.

POACHED EGGS PROVENÇAL

1 (14½-ounce) can tomato wedges, undrained
1 medium onion, thinly sliced and separated into rings
1 medium zucchini, thinly sliced
1 medium-size green pepper, seeded and coarsely chopped
2 teaspoons chili powder
½ teaspoon celery salt
4 drops hot sauce
8 eggs
 Salt and pepper to taste
4 whole wheat English muffins, split and toasted

1. Combine tomato, onion, zucchini, green pepper, chili powder, celery salt, and hot sauce in a 10-inch skillet. Bring to

a boil over medium heat; reduce heat, and simmer 5 minutes. Stir occasionally.

2. Make 8 indentions in tomato mixture, using the back of a spoon. Add 1 egg to each indention; sprinkle each with salt and pepper. Cover and cook an additional 10 minutes or until eggs reach desired degree of doneness.

3. To serve, spoon an egg with vegetables onto a toasted muffin half. Serve immediately. Yield: 8 servings.

CRUSTY PEACH DESSERT

  1 (16-ounce) package frozen sliced peaches, thawed
½ cup sugar
½ cup butter or margarine, softened
½ cup firmly packed brown sugar
  1 egg
  1 cup self-rising flour
  1 teaspoon vanilla extract
½ cup chopped pecans
   Vanilla ice cream (optional)

1. Place peaches in a lightly greased 8-inch square baking dish. Sprinkle with ½ cup sugar.

2. Cream butter in a large mixing bowl; gradually add brown sugar. Add egg; beat well. Add flour; mix just until blended. Stir in vanilla and pecans. Spoon mixture onto peaches. Bake at 350° for 35 minutes.

3. Spoon peach mixture into individual serving bowls. Top with a scoop of ice cream, if desired. Yield: 8 servings.

Note: One cup self-rising flour equals 1 cup all-purpose flour plus 1½ teaspoons baking powder and ½ teaspoon salt.

MEATLESS ITALIAN SUPPER

Italian Eggplant and Cheese
Fresh Broccoli Salad
Parmesan Breadsticks
Chocolate Cake Roll

Serves 4

Make Ahead: Prepare Chocolate Cake Roll; chill. Make salad dressing; chill.
Prepare & Serve: Assemble salad. While salad chills, prepare and bake Italian Eggplant and Cheese. Increase the oven temperature, and bake Parmesan Breadsticks.

ITALIAN EGGPLANT AND CHEESE

  1 large eggplant (about 1¼ pounds)
  2 tablespoons olive oil
  1 (15-ounce) can chunky tomato sauce
¼ teaspoon dried whole basil
¼ teaspoon dried whole oregano
¼ teaspoon dried whole thyme
  1 (8-ounce) package thinly sliced mozzarella cheese

1. Cut eggplant into 12 slices. Brush both sides of slices with olive oil. Arrange eggplant in a single layer on rack of a broiler pan. Broil 3 to 4 inches from heating element 2 to 3 minutes on each side.

2. Combine tomato sauce, basil, oregano, and thyme in a small saucepan. Bring to a boil. Remove from heat.

3. Arrange a single layer of broiled eggplant in bottom of a lightly greased 9-inch baking dish. Spread with one-third of sauce and cheese. Repeat layers with remaining eggplant, sauce, and cheese.

4. Bake at 375° for 20 minutes or until hot and bubbly.

5. Serve hot. Yield: 4 servings.

◆ FRESH BROCCOLI SALAD

1¼ pounds fresh broccoli
1 quart water
3 tablespoons Dijon mustard
2 teaspoons red wine vinegar
2 teaspoons chopped fresh dillweed
⅛ teaspoon salt
⅛ teaspoon pepper
¼ cup olive oil
¼ cup vegetable oil
Lettuce leaves

1. Remove and discard the bottom 2 inches from broccoli stalks. Separate broccoli into flowerets with stems attached.

2. Bring water to a boil in a 3-quart saucepan. Add broccoli; cover and cook 2 minutes. Drain and plunge into ice water. Drain well on paper towels, and blot dry. Cover and chill thoroughly.

3. Combine mustard, vinegar, dillweed, salt, and pepper in container of an electric blender. Process until smooth. With blender running, add oil in a slow steady stream; process until smooth. Cover and chill thoroughly.

4. Arrange broccoli on 4 lettuce-lined salad plates; pour dressing over broccoli, and serve immediately. Yield: 4 servings.

◔ PARMESAN BREADSTICKS

4 slices whole wheat bread
¼ cup cornflake crumbs
2 tablespoons grated Parmesan cheese
¼ cup butter or margarine, melted

1. Trim crust from bread; cut each slice into 4 sticks.

2. Combine cornflake crumbs and cheese. Brush bread with butter; dip in crumb mixture. Place breadsticks on a baking sheet.

3. Bake at 425° for 6 to 7 minutes.

4. Serve warm. Yield: 16 breadsticks.

Note: Other types of bread, such as rye or white, may be substituted for wheat.

◆ CHOCOLATE CAKE ROLL

5 eggs, separated
¾ cup plus 3 tablespoons sifted powdered sugar, divided
½ cup cocoa, divided
1 teaspoon vanilla extract
1 (2½-ounce) package whipped topping mix
½ cup cold milk
Grated chocolate (optional)

1. Grease a 15- x 10- x 1-inch jellyroll pan. Line pan with waxed paper; grease paper, and set pan aside.

2. Beat egg yolks 5 minutes or until thick and lemon colored in a small mixing bowl. Gradually add ¾ cup sugar, ¼ cup cocoa, and vanilla, beating until well blended.

3. Beat egg whites (at room temperature) until stiff peaks form. Gently fold chocolate mixture into beaten egg whites. Spread batter evenly into prepared jellyroll pan. Bake at 350° for 15 minutes or until a wooden pick inserted in center comes out clean.

4. Sift remaining 3 tablespoons powdered sugar in a 15- x 10-inch rectangle on a linen towel. When cake has finished baking, remove from oven, and immediately loosen cake from sides of pan. Turn cake out onto powdered sugar on linen towel. Peel waxed paper off bottom of cake. Starting at narrow end, roll up cake and towel together. Cool cake on a wire rack, seam side down.

5. Combine remaining ¼ cup cocoa, whipped topping mix, and cold milk in a medium mixing bowl; beat cocoa mixture at high speed of an electric mixer until stiff peaks form.

6. Unroll cake, and remove linen towel. Spread cake with 1¼ cups whipped topping mixture and reroll. Place Chocolate Cake Roll on a serving plate, and spread with remaining topping mixture. Garnish cake with grated chocolate, if desired. Chill cake until serving time.

7. Serve chilled. Slice Chocolate Cake Roll into 1-inch-thick pieces to serve. Yield: 10 servings.

Make the Most of the Microwave

Menu of Menus

Speed is only one part of the pleasure of microwave cooking. Quick cleanup counts, too—no pots to scrub, no stove to clean. Reheating without loss of moisture and flavor is another big plus. Defrosting meat becomes less time-consuming. Moreover, vegetables retain bright color and more nutrients, sauces come out smoother, chicken tastes juicier, seafood stays moister, grains cook fluffier . . . the list of benefits goes on and on.

Coordinate these attributes, and the microwave oven can provide great menu-planning flexibility. The speed makes it possible to cook Mexican Pot Roast, Sweet-Sour Pork, or Savory Beefed-Up Eggplant at the end of a work day, and continue on with a grand finale, such as Bananas Foster. The minimal cleanup can tempt you to make delicious desserts, such as Special Swirl Cheesecake or Raspberry Tart Squares the night before. The reheating invites you to double any conventional recipe, freeze the surplus, and feel confident that the dish will taste just as good the second time around. Slightly stale bread and rolls get a new lease on life when they are reheated in the microwave oven. You can also reheat leftover rice, noodles, and vegetables without fear that they'll become mushy. And as for the quality of the food . . . well, you'll taste the extra freshness and moistness in Hot German Potato Salad, Sautéed Peppers and Mushrooms, and Perch with Lemon.

Sometimes the greatest time savings and flexibility comes from using the microwave oven and conventional oven or grill simultaneously. This principle is applied here in several menus, such as Curried Chicken, where Lemon Squares are baked conventionally in order to free the microwave oven for use in preparing other menu items. But you may wish to take it further by mixing the microwave recipes with others in this book, especially breads and desserts that can be baked conventionally while the main course is in the microwave oven. All microwave recipes were tested in 650- and 700-watt ovens, so if your oven has a lower wattage, you may have to add some extra cooking time.

BEEFED-UP EGGPLANT

Savory Beefed-Up Eggplant
Sautéed Peppers and Mushrooms
Special Swirl Cheesecake

Serves 4

Make Ahead: Microwave cheesecake, and refrigerate several hours or overnight.
Prepare & Serve: Prepare and microwave Savory Beefed-Up Eggplant. Prepare peppers and mushrooms. Cover eggplant with aluminum foil while you microwave Sautéed Peppers and Mushrooms.

A quick dessert alternative: Prepare packaged vanilla pudding, according to directions, but add ½ teaspoon ground cinnamon and ⅛ teaspoon ground nutmeg. Garnish with fresh orange slices.

SAVORY BEEFED-UP EGGPLANT
(pictured on page 86)

2 small eggplant (about 1¼ pounds)
1 pound ground beef
½ cup chopped onion
1 clove garlic, minced
½ teaspoon salt
½ cup (2 ounces) shredded Swiss cheese
¼ cup grated Parmesan cheese
¼ cup chopped fresh parsley
¼ cup soft breadcrumbs
¾ teaspoon dried whole rosemary, crushed
Fresh parsley sprigs
Additional grated Parmesan cheese

1. Cut eggplant in half lengthwise; scoop out and reserve pulp, leaving ¼-inch shell. Place eggplant shells, cut side down, in a shallow dish. Cover with heavy-duty plastic wrap, and vent to allow steam to escape; microwave at HIGH for 2 minutes.

2. Remove eggplant shells, and invert onto paper towels. Chop enough reserved eggplant pulp to yield 2 cups. Combine chopped eggplant, beef, onion, and garlic in a plastic colander. Place colander over a bowl. Microwave at HIGH for 2 minutes. Stir to crumble beef. Continue microwaving at HIGH for 1 to 2 minutes.

3. Sprinkle salt over beef mixture. Combine beef mixture, Swiss cheese, ¼ cup Parmesan cheese, chopped parsley, breadcrumbs, and rosemary. Spoon evenly into eggplant shells.

4. Place filled shells in a shallow dish. Cover with heavy-duty plastic wrap, and vent to allow steam to escape. Microwave at HIGH for 6 to 8 minutes or until eggplant is tender.

5. Garnish with parsley sprigs and additional Parmesan cheese before serving. Yield: 4 servings.

SAUTÉED PEPPERS AND MUSHROOMS
(pictured on page 86)

1 medium-size green pepper, seeded and cut into strips
1 medium-size sweet red pepper, seeded and cut into strips
½ pound fresh mushrooms, sliced
1 tablespoon olive oil
1 clove garlic, minced
¼ teaspoon salt

1. Combine peppers and mushrooms in a 10- x 6- x 2-inch baking dish. Add remaining ingredients; toss lightly.

2. Cover with heavy-duty plastic wrap, and vent to allow steam to escape; microwave at HIGH for 3 to 4 minutes or until peppers are crisp-tender, stirring after 1½ minutes.

3. Serve warm. Yield: 4 servings.

◆⬒

SPECIAL SWIRL CHEESECAKE

(pictured on page 86)

20 chocolate wafers
 2 (8-ounce) packages cream cheese
 3 eggs
½ cup sugar
 1 teaspoon vanilla extract
⅓ cup semisweet chocolate morsels
   Fresh raspberries (optional)
   Fresh mint sprig (optional)

1. Line bottom of a 9-inch pieplate with chocolate wafers; fit remaining wafers around sides of pieplate. Set aside.

2. Unwrap cream cheese and place in a medium bowl; microwave at MEDIUM-LOW (30% power) for 2 to 3 minutes or until softened.

3. Position knife blade in food processor bowl; add softened cream cheese. Process until smooth. Scrape sides of bowl with rubber spatula. Add eggs, sugar, and vanilla; process until smooth.

4. Transfer mixture to 2-quart glass measure. Microwave at HIGH for 4 minutes, whisking after every minute. Pour mixture into prepared crust.

5. Place chocolate morsels in a 1-cup glass measure. Microwave at HIGH for 1 to 1½ minutes; stir until chocolate completely melts. Drop chocolate by spoonfuls over cheesecake filling; swirl through mixture with a knife.

6. Microwave cheesecake at MEDIUM (50% power) for 4 to 6 minutes, rotating a quarter-turn after every 1½ minutes. Remove cheesecake from oven. Cool to room temperature. Chill 3 to 4 hours.

7. Garnish with raspberries and a mint sprig before serving, if desired. Yield: one 9-inch cheesecake.

MICRO-QUICK DESSERTS

The speed and indirect heat of microwave cooking takes the fuss out of these mouthwatering desserts:

● Chocolate Fondue. Microwave 1 (6-ounce) package semisweet chocolate morsels with ¼ cup whipping cream until chocolate morsels are not quite melted; stir in 1 tablespoon brandy, rum, or cherry-flavored liqueur. Stir in additional whipping cream to thin, if necessary. Chunks of fruit and plain cake, strawberries, and miniature marshmallows are all good for dipping.

● Chocolate-Dipped Cream Sandwich Cookies (These are truly sinful!). Using tongs, dip chocolate-cream sandwich cookies in microwave-melted semisweet or milk chocolate. Refrigerate or freeze coated cookies on waxed paper until chocolate sets. Repeat procedure for a thicker coating.

● Nutty-Baked Apples. Core apples, and pare a thin strip of skin from the top of each apple. Place apples in a baking dish or custard cups. Microwave butter to soften; mix in any desired amount of chopped walnuts or pecans, brown sugar, nutmeg, and cinnamon. Spoon mixture into apple cavities; cover with waxed paper. Microwave at HIGH for 2 to 3 minutes per apple; let stand 5 minutes before serving.

● Your-Own-Flavor Ice Cream. Place any size ice cream container in a baking dish; microwave at LOW (10% power) just until softened. Stir in any delicious flavoring you desire. Some possibilities: instant expresso coffee powder and chopped semisweet chocolate in coffee ice cream; chopped candied ginger in peach ice cream; chopped candy bars in fudge ripple ice cream; crushed peppermint sticks in vanilla ice cream. Return to freezer to firm before serving.

MEXICAN POT ROAST

Mexican Pot Roast
Hot Cooked Saffron Rice
Green Salad with Dilly Dressing
Heavenly Coconut Cake

Serves 6 to 8

Make Ahead: Bake Heavenly Coconut Cake, and prepare Dilly Dressing.
Prepare & Serve: Prepare Mexican Pot Roast. Make saffron rice according to package directions. Toss vegetables of your choice for green salad, and serve with Dilly Dressing.

No time to bake? Split a purchased angel food cake into 3 or 4 layers. Fill and frost as directed for Heavenly Coconut Cake. To enhance the coconut flavor, spread coconut in a baking dish, and microwave at HIGH for 2 minutes or until toasted, stirring after 1 minute. If you wish, sprinkle coconut very lightly with an orange-flavored liqueur before toasting to add an extra rich flavor.

MEXICAN POT ROAST

1 (3-pound) boneless chuck roast
2 (12-ounce) jars picante sauce
1 (12-ounce) can beer
1 medium onion, thinly sliced
1 green pepper, seeded and
    chopped

1. Prick roast thoroughly with tines of a fork; place roast in a 3-quart casserole. Pour picante sauce and beer over roast.
2. Cover and microwave at MEDIUM (50% power) for 1 hour to 1 hour and 15 minutes, rotating every 20 minutes.
3. Add onion and green pepper to casserole. Cover and microwave at MEDIUM

for 15 minutes. Let stand, covered, 15 minutes.
4. Transfer roast to a serving platter; slice. Spoon vegetables over roast. Yield: 6 to 8 servings.

DILLY DRESSING

½ cup plain low-fat yogurt
½ cup mayonnaise
2 tablespoons plus 1½ teaspoons
    red wine vinegar
2 teaspoons minced fresh dillweed
1½ teaspoons sugar
½ teaspoon salt
¼ teaspoon pepper

1. Combine all ingredients in a small mixing bowl, whisking until well blended. Cover with plastic wrap, and chill.
2. Serve dressing over tossed green salads. Yield: about 1⅓ cups.

HEAVENLY COCONUT CAKE

1 (18.5-ounce) package white cake
    mix, without pudding
1 (16-ounce) carton commercial sour
    cream
1 (6-ounce) package frozen grated
    coconut
2 tablespoons sugar
1 cup frozen whipped topping

1. Bake cake in two 8-inch round layers according to package directions. Split cooled layers horizontally.
2. Combine sour cream, coconut, and sugar in a mixing bowl, stirring well. Spread 1¼ cups of mixture between cake layers.
3. Combine remaining sour cream mixture with whipped topping, stirring well. Spread on top and sides; chill cake.
4. Slice to serve. Yield: one 4-layer cake.

Note: Store leftover cake, tightly covered, in the refrigerator.

CHINESE-STYLE PORK

Sweet-Sour Pork
Bananas Foster

Serves 4

Prepare & Serve: If you wish to serve rice with the Sweet-Sour Pork, cook rice conventionally. Microwave Sweet-Sour Pork. Microwave Bananas Foster just before serving. Add stir-fried pea pods to the menu for a complementary vegetable accompaniment.

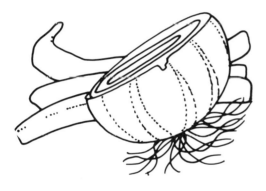

SWEET-SOUR PORK

 1 (20-ounce) can unsweetened
    pineapple chunks, undrained
 1 tablespoon vegetable oil
1½ pounds boneless pork loin, cut
    into 1-inch cubes
 ½ teaspoon salt
 ½ medium onion, sliced
 ½ medium-size green pepper, seeded
    and thinly sliced
 3 tablespoons cornstarch
 ½ cup water
 ¼ cup firmly packed brown sugar
 2 tablespoons soy sauce
 1 tablespoon red wine vinegar
    Hot cooked rice

1. Drain pineapple, reserving juice; set pineapple aside.

2. Place oil and pork in a 13- x 9- x 2-inch baking dish; cover with heavy-duty plastic wrap, and vent to allow steam to escape. Microwave at MEDIUM-HIGH (70% power) for 7 minutes, giving dish a half-turn after 3½ minutes. Add reserved pineapple juice and salt, stirring well. Microwave at MEDIUM-HIGH for 7 minutes, giving dish a half-turn after 3½ minutes.

3. Add onion, green pepper, and reserved pineapple; cover and microwave 1 minute at MEDIUM-HIGH, stirring well. Dissolve cornstarch in water; stir in sugar, soy sauce, and vinegar, and add to pork mixture, stirring well. Microwave 7 minutes at MEDIUM-HIGH, stirring well every 3½ minutes.

4. Serve over rice. Yield: 4 to 6 servings.

BANANAS FOSTER

 ¾ cup butter or margarine
 ¾ cup firmly packed brown sugar
 ⅛ teaspoon ground cinnamon
 ¼ cup plus 2 tablespoons dark rum
 2 tablespoons banana-flavored
    liqueur
 6 small bananas, peeled and halved
    lengthwise, then crosswise
    Vanilla ice cream

1. Combine butter and sugar in a 10- x 6- x 2-inch baking dish. Cover with waxed paper, and microwave at HIGH for 1½ to 2 minutes, stirring after 1 minute.

2. Stir in cinnamon, rum, and liqueur; mix well. Place bananas, cut side down, in sauce; cover with waxed paper, and microwave at HIGH for 45 seconds to 1 minute or until hot. Turn bananas, and baste well with sauce; cover with waxed paper, and microwave at HIGH an additional 45 seconds to 1 minute or until bananas are thoroughly heated.

3. Serve immediately over ice cream. Yield: 4 servings.

GERMAN SAUSAGE SUPPER

Smoked Sausage Reubens
Hot German Potato Salad
Gingerbread with
Cinnamon-Apple Topping

Serves 4

Make Ahead: Prepare gingerbread according to microwave directions on package, or bake gingerbread conventionally while preparing the rest of the dinner.

Prepare & Serve: Microwave potatoes. Make Reuben Sauce; assemble Smoked Sausage Reubens. While potatoes are cooling, prepare Hot German Potato Salad through step 4. Microwave sandwiches. Complete potato salad. At dessert time, make Cinnamon-Apple Topping.

Garnish sandwich plates with green pepper rings and carrot sticks or curls for crisp contrast and a wealth of vitamins A and C.

3. Preheat microwave browning dish at HIGH for 4 minutes.

4. Place sandwiches on browning dish, and microwave at HIGH for 1 minute. Turn sandwiches over; microwave at HIGH for 3 to 4 minutes or until lightly browned and thoroughly heated.

5. Serve warm. Yield: 4 sandwiches.

Note: Sandwiches may be heated without browning dish: Eliminate the butter, and toast bread in a toaster. Put sandwiches together, and place on a paper towel on a rack. Microwave sandwiches at HIGH for 3 to 4 minutes or until thoroughly heated.

Reuben Sauce:

⅓ cup commercial sour cream
3 tablespoons catsup
1 tablespoon sweet pickle relish, drained
1 teaspoon Worcestershire sauce
¼ teaspoon salt
Dash of hot sauce

1. Combine sour cream, catsup, relish, Worcestershire sauce, salt, and hot sauce in a small mixing bowl; stir well.

2. Cover and chill. Yield: ⅔ cup.

SMOKED SAUSAGE REUBENS

8 slices dark rye bread
Reuben Sauce
6 fully-cooked smoked sausage links, split lengthwise
1 (10-ounce) can sauerkraut, well drained
4 slices Swiss cheese
¼ cup butter or margarine, softened

1. Spread one side of each bread slice with Reuben Sauce.

2. Top each of 4 bread slices with 3 sausage halves, one-fourth of sauerkraut, and 1 slice cheese. Top with remaining bread. Butter both sides of sandwich.

HOT GERMAN POTATO SALAD

3 medium potatoes (1½ pounds)
3 slices bacon, diced
½ cup chopped onion
½ cup chopped celery
⅓ cup cider vinegar
2 tablespoons water
1 teaspoon sugar
1 teaspoon salt
¼ teaspoon caraway seeds
¼ teaspoon celery seeds
¼ teaspoon dried parsley flakes
Dash of hot sauce

1. Rinse potatoes, and pat dry; prick with a fork. Arrange potatoes in a circular pattern on a paper towel in microwave oven. Microwave at HIGH for 8 to 10 minutes, turning potatoes after 4 minutes. Cool potatoes; peel and slice. Set aside.

2. Place bacon in a 1½-quart casserole. Microwave at HIGH for 5 minutes or until crisp. Remove bacon using a slotted spoon; drain on paper towels.

3. Add onion and celery to bacon drippings. Cover with heavy-duty plastic wrap, and vent to allow steam to escape; microwave at HIGH for 3 to 4 minutes. Stir well.

4. Place remaining ingredients in a 2-cup glass measure; microwave at HIGH for 2 minutes or until mixture boils.

5. Add potatoes, bacon, and vinegar mixture to onion mixture; toss lightly. Microwave at HIGH for 2 minutes or until thoroughly heated.

6. Serve salad immediately. Yield: 4 servings.

GINGERBREAD WITH CINNAMON-APPLE TOPPING

    1 (14½-ounce) package gingerbread
       mix
    2 medium-size cooking apples,
       peeled, cored, and sliced
    ½ cup light corn syrup
    ¼ cup sugar
    ¼ cup butter or margarine
    ½ teaspoon ground cinnamon
    ½ teaspoon cornstarch

1. Prepare gingerbread mix according to microwave directions on package, using a 9-inch square baking dish.

2. Place apples, corn syrup, sugar, butter, and cinnamon in a 4-cup glass measure; microwave at HIGH for 3 to 4 minutes or until apples are tender.

3. Add cornstarch to apple mixture; stir until smooth. Microwave at HIGH for 2 to 3 minutes or until thickened and bubbly.

4. Cut gingerbread into 3-inch squares; spoon apple mixture over gingerbread. Yield: 9 servings.

EL PASO CHICKEN SUPPER

El Paso Chicken
Spanish Rice
Zucchini-Carrot Salad

Serves 4

Prepare & Serve: Prepare and cook Spanish Rice; keep covered until ready to serve. Make El Paso Chicken. Arrange Zucchini-Carrot Salad on individual salad plates.

Sliced ripe avocado and lime wedges would garnish the chicken and rice deliciously. Add sprigs of fresh coriander, if available. Coriander can also be chopped and stirred into the cooked Spanish Rice.

EL PASO CHICKEN

    3   cups corn chips, finely crushed
    1½ teaspoons chili powder
    ½   teaspoon onion powder
    ¼   teaspoon garlic powder
    4   chicken thighs, skinned
    4   chicken legs, skinned
    3   tablespoons mayonnaise

1. Combine crushed corn chips, chili powder, onion powder, and garlic powder; mix well. Rub chicken with mayonnaise; dredge in corn chip mixture.

2. Place chicken in a 13- x 9- x 2-inch baking dish. Cover with waxed paper, and microwave at HIGH for 18 minutes, rotating dish a half-turn after 9 minutes. Let chicken stand, covered with aluminum foil, 5 minutes.

3. Serve warm. Yield: 4 servings.

Note: To save time, substitute a 1.25-ounce package Taco Seasoning Mix for the spices, if desired.

SPANISH RICE

½ cup chopped green pepper
¼ cup chopped onion
1 clove garlic, minced
½ teaspoon dried whole basil
1 tablespoon vegetable oil
¾ cup uncooked regular rice
1½ cups water
1 large tomato, peeled and
    chopped
1 teaspoon salt
¼ teaspoon ground cumin
⅛ teaspoon chili powder

1. Place green pepper, onion, garlic, basil, and oil in a 2-quart casserole. Cover with heavy-duty plastic wrap, and vent to allow steam to escape; microwave at HIGH for 2 minutes or until vegetables are tender, stirring after 1 minute.

2. Stir in rice, water, tomato, salt, cumin, and chili powder. Cover and microwave at HIGH for 4 to 5 minutes or until boiling. Microwave at MEDIUM (50% power) for 12 to 14 minutes. Let stand 5 minutes or until liquid is absorbed.

3. Serve warm. Yield: 4 servings.

Note: Try sprinkling ¾ cup (3 ounces) shredded sharp Cheddar cheese over rice for a heartier side dish.

ZUCCHINI-CARROT SALAD

4 large lettuce leaves
1 medium zucchini, shredded
1 medium carrot, shredded
1 medium tomato, diced
4 small fresh mushrooms, sliced
½ cup alfalfa sprouts
  Commercial creamy Italian salad
    dressing

1. Place lettuce leaves on individual salad plates. Arrange zucchini, carrot, tomato, mushrooms, and sprouts on top.

2. Serve Zucchini-Carrot Salad with creamy salad dressing. Yield: 4 servings.

CURRIED CHICKEN

*Chicken and Vegetables
with Curry Sauce
Orange-Almond Salad
Pita Crisps
Lemon Squares*

Serves 4

Make Ahead: Prepare dressing for salad, and chill. Bake Lemon Squares.
Prepare & Serve: Microwave Chicken and Vegetables with Curry Sauce. Prepare Pita Crisps. Finish making salad.

CHICKEN AND VEGETABLES WITH CURRY SAUCE

1 pound chicken breasts, skinless
    and boneless, cubed
½ teaspoon curry powder
½ cup chicken broth
2 medium carrots, scraped and cut
    into julienne strips
2 medium-size baking potatoes
    (about 1 pound), cut into
    julienne strips
½ pound fresh broccoli, cut into
    spears
¾ cup plain yogurt
3 tablespoons Dijon mustard
1 teaspoon dried whole dillweed
½ teaspoon ground cumin
¼ teaspoon ground allspice
  Dash of red pepper
  Salt to taste

1. Arrange chicken in a 3-quart casserole; sprinkle with curry powder. Pour broth over chicken. Cover with heavy-duty plastic wrap, and vent to allow steam to escape; microwave at HIGH for 6 to 8 minutes or until chicken is tender, rotating dish a half-turn and turning chicken pieces over after 4 minutes. Remove chicken to a serving platter. Reserve broth in casserole.

2. Add carrots to broth. Cover with heavy-duty plastic wrap, and vent to allow steam to escape; microwave at HIGH for 2 minutes. Stir in potatoes; cover and microwave at HIGH for 5 minutes, stirring after 2 minutes. Add broccoli; cover and microwave at HIGH for 6 to 8 minutes, or until vegetables are tender. Remove vegetables, using a slotted spoon; place on platter with reserved chicken. Cover to keep warm. Reserve broth in casserole.

3. Whisk yogurt, mustard, dillweed, cumin, allspice, red pepper, and salt into reserved broth. Microwave, uncovered, at HIGH for 1 minute.

4. Serve immediately. Yield: 4 servings.

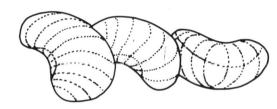

♠ ORANGE-ALMOND SALAD

⅓ **cup vegetable oil**
3 **tablespoons vinegar**
1 **tablespoon sugar**
¼ **teaspoon salt**
4 **cups torn romaine lettuce (about ½ pound)**
1 **(11-ounce) can mandarin oranges, drained**
⅓ **cup raisins (optional)**
¼ **cup sliced green onions**
¼ **cup slivered almonds, toasted**

1. Combine oil, vinegar, sugar, and salt in a jar. Cover tightly, and shake vigorously. Chill thoroughly.

2. Combine remaining ingredients in a large salad bowl; add dressing, and toss lightly.

3. Serve salad immediately. Yield: 4 to 6 servings.

PITA CRISPS

2 **(6-inch) whole wheat pita bread rounds**
2 **tablespoons butter or margarine, melted**

1. Split each whole wheat pita bread round to yield 2 flat discs. Cut each disc into 4 triangles. Brush each triangle with melted butter.

2. Place triangles on paper towels in microwave. Microwave at HIGH for 30 to 45 seconds, or until edges curl.

3. Let stand to cool. Yield: 4 servings.

LEMON SQUARES

1 **cup plus 2 tablespoons flour, divided**
1¼ **cups sugar, divided**
½ **cup butter or margarine, softened**
½ **teaspoon baking powder**
  Dash of salt
2 **eggs**
½ **teaspoon grated lemon rind**
¼ **cup lemon juice**
  Sifted powdered sugar

1. Combine 1 cup flour and ¼ cup sugar. Cut in butter with a pastry blender until mixture resembles coarse meal.

2. Spoon flour mixture into a 9-inch square baking pan; press into pan evenly and firmly, using fingertips. Bake at 350° for 15 to 20 minutes or until lightly browned.

3. Combine remaining 2 tablespoons flour, baking powder, and salt. Combine remaining 1 cup sugar, eggs, lemon rind, and lemon juice; beat well. Stir dry ingredients into egg mixture and pour over baked crust.

4. Bake at 350° for 20 to 25 minutes or until lightly browned and set. Cool on a wire rack.

5. Sprinkle powdered sugar over top, and cut into 3-inch squares to serve. Yield: 9 servings.

LEMON FISH BAKE

Perch with Lemon
Raspberry Tart Squares

Serves 4

Make Ahead: Microwave Raspberry Tart Squares and let stand.
Prepare & Serve: Microwave Perch with Lemon. For a tasty side dish, try steamed broccoli seasoned with butter, Parmesan cheese, garlic salt, and pepper.

PERCH WITH LEMON

1⅓ **pounds perch fillets**
¼ **cup butter or margarine, melted**
¼ **cup chopped onion**
2 **tablespoons lemon juice**
1½ **teaspoons Worcestershire sauce**
¼ **teaspoon salt**
¼ **teaspoon dried parsley flakes**
Lemon wedges

1. Arrange fish in a single layer in a 10- x 6- x 2-inch baking dish.
2. Combine next 6 ingredients in a 1-quart glass bowl. Pour over fish.
3. Cover with heavy-duty plastic wrap, and vent to allow steam to escape; microwave at HIGH for 4 minutes or until fish flakes easily when tested with a fork.
4. Garnish with lemon wedges. Serve hot. Yield: 4 servings.

RASPBERRY TART SQUARES

¼ **cup plus 2 tablespoons butter or margarine**
½ **cup firmly packed brown sugar**
¾ **cup quick-cooking oats, uncooked**
¾ **cup all-purpose flour**
½ **teaspoon baking powder**
¼ **teaspoon salt**
½ **cup finely chopped pecans**
½ **(12-ounce) jar raspberry preserves**

1. Place butter in an 8-inch square baking dish. Microwave at HIGH for 1 minute or until butter melts. Stir in brown sugar, oats, flour, baking powder, salt, and pecans; mix well.
2. Reserve ⅓ cup crumb mixture; pat remaining mixture evenly over bottom of baking dish.
3. Spread preserves over crumb layer. Sprinkle reserved crumbs over top. Shield corners with aluminum foil. Place baking dish on an inverted pieplate in microwave oven. Microwave at HIGH for 5 to 6 minutes or until preserves are thickened and bubbly, rotating dish a quarter-turn every two minutes.
4. Let stand 15 to 20 minutes. Cut into 2-inch squares. Yield: 16 squares.

Note: A dollop of thawed non-dairy whipped topping may be added on squares as a garnish.

Right: *Brownie Alaska from the Pork with Panache menu (page 110) is not only fantastic to look at and scrumptious to taste, it can also be frozen, if there's any left.*

Page 104: *Pork Medallions with Mediterranean Orzo is the impressive entrée in the Pork with Panache menu (page 110) with buttered green beans and Oranges Delphi as side dishes.*

Fast but Fancier

Menu of Menus

What's the difference between a fast meal for a special occasion and something-on-the-table-in-a-hurry? Basically, it's a matter of keeping one step ahead. So that's the way these menus are organized. There are some marvelous desserts, such as Mud Pie with Chocolate Sauce and Cold Lime Soufflé, that will hold overnight. There are many marinated dishes that don't take much time but become more flavorful if left overnight, such as Caribbean Flank Steak and Barbecued Turkey Kabobs. And then there are a few side dishes, such as Cheese-Stuffed Mushrooms and Sour Cream Potato Salad, that will reward a very small amount of advance preparation with festive tastes.

Popular flavors play a major role in these menus. Seafood-lovers will be delighted by Spicy Broiled Shrimp or Shrimp-Crab Casserole. Steaks are mated with Grilled Potato Slices in the Steak Celebration menu and with a bacon-dressed spinach salad in Everyone's Favorites. Chicken rises to special-event status in Paella or Chicken with Blue Cheese Sauce. Vegetables take on a party-pretty look in such combinations as Tomatoes Stuffed wth Herbed Peas and Marinated Artichoke Salad.

You'll be more than ready when the doorbell rings if you keep a few greetings on hand that require no cooking at all, such as assorted nuts, olives, smoked oysters, hard salami, cheeses . . . and a big bottle of sparkling wine! For other relaxed welcomes, see the snacks and dip recipes in the Appetizers chapter.

Some other hints for impromptu entertaining: Keep one or two sets of place mats and napkins that don't need ironing in the linen closet. Improvise a centerpiece from whatever is readily available, whether flowers from the garden, a bowl of fruits and nuts, or a small potted plant. Don't let the simplicity of a meal inhibit you from lighting candles—after all, the mood is yours to create! If you don't have time to make a dessert, treat everyone to a special box of chocolates. For a delicious alternative to coffee, offer a choice of Indian, Chinese, green, and herb teas.

STEAK CELEBRATION

Caribbean Flank Steak
Grilled Potato Slices
Tomatoes Stuffed with Herbed Peas
Mud Pie with Chocolate Sauce

Serves 6

Make Ahead: Make Mud Pie. Marinate flank steak.
Prepare & Serve: Get grill ready to cook. Prepare Grilled Potato Slices. Make Tomatoes Stuffed with Herbed Peas. Grill Caribbean Flank Steak. Make Chocolate Sauce at dessert time to accompany Mud Pie.

This celebration deserves a toast! Kir Aperitifs are easy and festive. For each serving, pour ½ to 1 teaspoon raspberry-flavored liqueur, crème de cassis, or blackberry-flavored liqueur into each glass. Fill with white wine or champagne.

◆ CARIBBEAN FLANK STEAK

1 teaspoon grated lime rind
⅓ cup fresh lime juice (about 3
　　medium limes)
¼ cup vegetable oil
¼ cup molasses
2 tablespoons prepared mustard
1 teaspoon garlic powder
½ teaspoon salt
½ teaspoon pepper
2 pounds flank steak
　Lime slices

1. Combine lime rind, juice, oil, molasses, mustard, garlic powder, salt, and pepper in 12- x 8- x 2-inch baking dish. Score steak across top surface; place in dish, turning to coat all sides.
2. Cover and refrigerate 4 hours or overnight, turning steak once or twice.

3. Remove steak from marinade; place on grill 4 inches from hot coals. Cover and grill 10 minutes. Turn; baste and grill, covered, 10 minutes or until desired degree of doneness.
4. Slice steak diagonally across the grain into thin slices. Garnish with lime slices. Yield: 6 servings.

GRILLED POTATO SLICES

3 to 4 tablespoons melted butter or
　　margarine
⅛ teaspoon soy sauce
⅛ teaspoon garlic powder
4 medium-size baking potatoes

1. Combine butter, soy sauce, and garlic powder, stirring well; set aside.
2. Scrub potatoes. Cut each potato into ⅛- to ¼-inch-thick lengthwise slices.
3. Place slices on grill, and brush with butter mixture. Cook over medium coals 15 to 20 minutes, turning and basting with butter mixture every 5 minutes.
4. Remove slices to a serving platter, and serve warm. Yield: 6 servings.

▭ TOMATOES STUFFED WITH HERBED PEAS

6 large ripe tomatoes
1 (16-ounce) package frozen English
　　peas
½ cup water
3 tablespoons chopped onion
¼ cup plus 2 tablespoons whipping
　　cream
½ teaspoon dried whole marjoram
　　leaves
½ teaspoon salt
¼ teaspoon pepper
¼ cup plus 2 tablespoons
　　herb-flavored stuffing

1. Cut a ¼-inch slice from the top of each tomato; scoop out pulp, reserving for other uses. Drain tomatoes on paper towels.

2. Combine peas and water in a medium saucepan. Cover and cook over medium heat until tender. Drain. Combine peas, onion, whipping cream, marjoram, salt, and pepper, stirring well.

3. Spoon 1 tablespoon stuffing into each tomato; fill tomatoes with pea mixture. Arrange tomatoes in a shallow baking dish. Bake at 325° for 15 to 20 minutes or until tomatoes are thoroughly heated.

4. Serve warm. Yield: 6 servings.

MicroMethod

1. Same as step 1.

2. Combine peas, onion, and water in a 1½-quart casserole; cover and microwave at HIGH for 8 minutes or until tender. Drain. Combine pea mixture, whipping cream, marjoram, salt, and pepper, stirring well.

3. Spoon 1 tablespoon stuffing into each tomato; fill tomatoes with pea mixture. Arrange tomatoes in a circle on a baking dish. Microwave at MEDIUM HIGH (70% power) for 5 to 6 minutes or until tomatoes are thoroughly heated.

4. Same as step 4.

◆▢ MUD PIE WITH CHOCOLATE SAUCE

20 chocolate sandwich cookies
¼ cup butter or margarine
1 quart coffee-flavored ice cream, softened
8 chocolate sandwich cookies (optional)
Chocolate Sauce

1. Place 20 cookies in bowl of food processor; pulse until cookies are fine crumbs. Add butter; pulse until mixture resembles coarse meal. Press cookie mixture into a 9-inch pieplate.

2. Spoon softened ice cream into cookie-mixture pie shell. Arrange 8 cookies an equal distance apart over ice cream, if desired. Freeze pie until ice cream mixture is firm.

3. Top pie with Chocolate Sauce. Yield: one 9-inch pie.

MicroNote: To soften ice cream, open ice cream carton, and microwave at MEDIUM (50% power) for 30 to 40 seconds or until softened.

Chocolate Sauce:

4 (1-ounce) squares unsweetened chocolate, grated
1 cup water
½ cup sugar
¼ teaspoon ground cinnamon
½ cup whipping cream
2 tablespoons Kahlúa or other coffee-flavored liqueur

1. Combine grated chocolate, 1 cup water, and ½ cup sugar in a medium-size heavy saucepan. Gradually bring mixture to a boil over medium heat, stirring constantly with a wire whisk. Remove saucepan from heat.

2. Add cinnamon, whipping cream, and liqueur to mixture in saucepan; stir well with a wire whisk.

3. Serve Chocolate Sauce hot or cold over Mud Pie. Yield: 2 cups.

MicroMethod

1. Combine grated chocolate, 1 cup water, and ½ cup sugar in a 1-quart glass measure. Microwave at MEDIUM (50% power) for 2 to 3 minutes or just until boiling, stirring mixture with a wire whisk after each minute of cooking.

2. Same as step 2.

3. Same as step 3.

EVERYONE'S FAVORITES

Marinated Flank Steak
Cheese-Stuffed Mushrooms
Corn-on-the-Cob (page 48)
Wilted Spinach Salad
Flaming Peaches

Serves 6

Make Ahead: Marinate steak. Stuff mushrooms, and refrigerate.
Prepare & Serve: Peel peaches; sprinkle with lemon juice and refrigerate. Bake Cheese-Stuffed Mushrooms. Make Wilted Spinach Salad. Broil Marinated Flank Steak, or grill as directed for Caribbean Flank Steak (page 106). After dinner, complete Flaming Peaches.

If you aren't in the mood for Flaming Peaches, try serving Peaches in Champagne. Peel peaches as directed in Flaming Peaches recipe. Slice peaches, and spoon into stemmed glasses. Pour in chilled sec or demi-sec (slightly sweet, rather than very dry) champagne to fill glasses.

MARINATED FLANK STEAK

    1 cup chopped green onions
  ⅓ cup soy sauce
  ¼ cup water
  ¼ cup red wine vinegar
    2 tablespoons vegetable oil
    2 tablespoons catsup
  ½ teaspoon hot sauce
    1 (1½-pound) flank steak
       Green onion fans

1. Combine chopped green onions, soy sauce, water, vinegar, oil, catsup, and hot sauce in a 12- x 8- x 2-inch baking dish.

Add steak, turning to coat. Cover and refrigerate 2 hours or overnight.
2. Remove steak from marinade, reserving marinade. Place on rack of a broiler pan. Brush with reserved marinade. Broil 3 to 4 inches from heating element for 5 minutes. Turn; brush with marinade. Broil an additional 4 or 5 minutes or until desired degree of doneness.
3. Place steak on a serving platter. Slice diagonally across the grain into thin slices. Garnish with green onion fans. Yield: 6 servings.

CHEESE-STUFFED MUSHROOMS

  18 medium-size fresh mushrooms
       (about 1½ pounds)
  ½ cup (2 ounces) shredded
       mozzarella cheese
  ¼ cup finely chopped fresh parsley
  ¼ cup commercial reduced-calorie
       Italian salad dressing

1. Remove mushroom stems, and finely chop; set mushroom caps aside.
2. Combine chopped mushroom stems, cheese, parsley, and salad dressing. Fill reserved caps with mixture.
3. Place stuffed mushrooms in a 13- x 9- x 2-inch baking dish. Cover and refrigerate overnight.
4. Uncover and bake at 350° for 30 minutes or until tender.
5. Serve warm. Yield: 6 servings.

MicroNote: To microwave step 4, arrange stuffed mushrooms on a large round plate. Microwave at HIGH for 1½ to 3 minutes or until thoroughly heated, rotating dish once every minute.

⊙⌨ WILTED SPINACH SALAD

3 slices bacon
¼ cup vinegar
2 teaspoons sugar
¼ teaspoon salt
⅛ teaspoon pepper
⅛ teaspoon dried whole tarragon,
    crushed
¼ cup chopped celery
1 tablespoon sliced green onions
1 (10-ounce) package fresh spinach
    leaves, torn
1 (11-ounce) can Mandarin oranges,
    drained

1. Cook bacon in a large skillet until crisp; remove bacon, reserving drippings in skillet. Crumble bacon, and set aside.

2. Stir vinegar, sugar, salt, pepper, and tarragon into drippings in skillet. Cook over high heat 2 minutes or until boiling. Remove from heat.

3. Stir in celery and green onions. Gradually add spinach to hot dressing, tossing to coat each piece and until slightly wilted.

4. Add oranges and reserved bacon; toss lightly, and serve. Yield: 6 servings.

MicroMethod

1. Cut bacon into 1-inch pieces. Place in a 3-quart dish. Microwave at HIGH 5 to 5½ minutes or until bacon is crisp. With a slotted spoon, remove bacon to paper towels to drain, reserving drippings.

2. Add vinegar, sugar, salt, pepper, and tarragon to drippings. Microwave at HIGH for 2 to 3 minutes.

3. Same as step 3.

4. Same as step 4.

⊙ FLAMING PEACHES

3 fresh peaches
2 tablespoons raspberry jelly
2 tablespoons finely chopped
    walnuts
2 tablespoons dark rum
    Vanilla ice cream

1. Blanch peaches in boiling water 30 seconds. Dip peaches immediately into cold water. Remove skins. Halve peaches, and remove pits.

2. In a skillet or chafing dish, melt jelly over medium heat. Add peaches. Stir gently to coat each peach half. Sprinkle with walnuts.

3. Warm rum over low heat; pour over peaches. Ignite rum with a long match. When flames die down, serve with ice cream. Yield: 6 servings.

SIMPLE AND SATISFYING

A cup of coffee, rich enough to invite slow sipping, may be all you need to end a company meal on a convivial note. A platter of fancy packaged cookies turns the cupful into a complete dessert. Borrow from the whole world's brewing enjoyment to serve these coffees:

• Cardamom Coffee. Serve coffee Swedish-style by brewing coffee with several cardamom pods. (Moroccans brew tea this way, also.)

• Cinnamon Coffee. Brew coffee with broken cinnamon sticks or ground cinnamon to make Persian-style coffee.

• Orange and Spice Coffee. Brew coffee with 1 strip orange rind, 1 strip lemon rind, and 10 whole cloves; sweeten with brown sugar. Or serve over ice and top with scoops of coffee ice cream.

• "Blanco y negro." This Spanish cooler is nothing more—or less—than espresso or extra strong coffee poured over ice and topped with a scoop of vanilla ice cream.

QUICK-SERVE HORS D'OEUVRES

Count on prepared foods that keep well to have these hors d'oeuvres ready to make when you need them.

● Honey-Mustard Smoked Sausage. Slice smoked sausage, and arrange on aluminum foil-lined baking sheet. Bake at 400° until thoroughly heated . Serve with wooden picks and dishes of brown mustard and honey for dipping.

● Almond-Glazed Brie Cheese. Cut rind from top of cheese and place on aluminum foil-lined baking sheet. Sift powdered sugar lightly over cheese. Press whole almonds in any pattern you desire into top of cheese. Bake at 300° until cheese melts.

● Spiced Chick Peas. Rinse canned chick peas, and drain well. Toss with ground cumin, lots of freshly ground pepper, and salt to taste. Or toss chick peas with chopped fresh parsley, crumbled feta cheese, and dried whole thyme.

● Smoked Salmon Canapes. Butter party pumpernickel rounds, or use large slices of pumpernickel bread cut into wedges or fingers. Sprinkle with chopped fresh dillweed. Top with thin slices of smoked salmon. Serve with lemon wedges.

● Ham-and-Cheesewiches. Cut a (16-ounce) loaf of French bread in half lengthwise. Spread one half of bread with butter, the other with Dijon mustard. Sandwich thin layers of boiled ham and provolone or mozzarella cheese between bread halves. Place sandwich on aluminum foil-lined baking sheet in 350° oven until cheese melts and bread is slightly toasted. Cut sandwich into 1-inch slices. Spear each slice with an olive-topped wooden pick.

PORK WITH PANACHE

*Pork Medallions
with Mediterranean Orzo
Buttered Green Beans
Oranges Delphi
Brownie Alaskas*

Serves 4

Make Ahead: Bake brownies for Brownie Alaskas; top with ice cream, and freeze. Assemble Pork Medallions.
Prepare & Serve: Cook orzo. Make Oranges Delphi. Boil water for green beans. Finish Mediterranean Orzo; broil Pork Medallions. Cook green beans. Complete Brownie Alaskas, and broil.

There's a very nice harmony in the flavors of this menu, but if you would like to simplify things, omit Oranges Delphi, and serve Baked Apples with Pecan Sauce (page 251) or Cream Cheese Tarts (page 256) instead of Brownie Alaskas.

PORK MEDALLIONS WITH MEDITERRANEAN ORZO
(pictured on page 104)

2 (1¼-pound) pork tenderloins
¼ cup chopped fresh basil
2 tablespoons chopped fresh parsley
2 tablespoons grated Parmesan cheese
1 tablespoon lemon juice
1 clove garlic, minced
¼ teaspoon salt
Dash of pepper
2 teaspoons olive oil

1. Cut both tenderloins lengthwise; open and lay flat. Set aside.

2. To prepare pesto, position knife blade in food processor bowl; add basil, parsley, cheese, lemon juice, garlic, salt, and pepper. Process until smooth and blended. Remove and reserve 1 tablespoon pesto for Mediterranean Orzo. Spread remaining pesto on cut side of tenderloins.

3. Roll tenderloins together; tie with string at 1-inch intervals. Slice tenderloin roll into 8 medallions. Place cut side up on rack in a broiler pan.

4. Broil tenderloins 3 to 4 inches from heating element 12 to 14 minutes, turning once. Baste with oil several times during broiling.

5. Serve with Mediterranean Orzo. Yield: 4 servings.

Mediterranean Orzo:

½ cup thinly sliced sweet red
      pepper
¼ cup chopped onion
2 tablespoons white wine
2 cups hot cooked orzo or fettucine
1 (2¼-ounce) can diced ripe olives,
      drained
¼ teaspoon salt
1 tablespoon pesto

1. Combine red pepper, onion, and wine in a medium saucepan. Cook mixture over medium heat 2 minutes, stirring constantly.

2. Add orzo, olives, salt, and pesto. Stir to combine.

3. Transfer Mediterranean Orzo to a serving bowl; serve hot. Yield: 4 servings.

☺ ORANGES DELPHI
(pictured on page 104)

4 medium oranges
2 green onions, sliced
3 pitted ripe olives, sliced (optional)
1 tablespoon olive oil
½ teaspoon dried whole oregano
½ teaspoon salt
      Lettuce leaves

1. Peel and section or slice oranges.

2. Combine oranges, onions, and olives, if desired, in a medium mixing bowl.

3. Add oil, oregano, and salt; toss lightly.

4. Serve Oranges Delphi on lettuce-lined salad plates. Yield: 4 servings.

◆ BROWNIE ALASKAS
(pictured on page 103)

1 (14.1 ounce) package brownie mix
½ gallon peppermint, strawberry, or
      coffee ice cream
5 egg whites
½ cup sugar

1. Make brownie mix according to package directions, using a 9-inch square pan; let cool completely. Cut brownies into 3-inch squares.

2. Arrange brownies on a cookie sheet; top each brownie with a scoop of ice cream. Freeze at least 1 hour.

3. Beat egg whites (at room temperature) until frothy. Gradually add sugar, 1 tablespoon at a time, beating until stiff peaks form.

4. Remove ice cream-topped brownies from freezer. Spread meringue over ice cream, sealing to edge of brownie. Bake at 500° for 2 to 3 minutes or until meringue is lightly browned.

5. Serve Brownie Alaskas immediately. Yield: 9 servings.

Note: Substitute your favorite flavor of ice cream. Freeze leftovers for later use.

PAELLA,
INDOORS OR OUT

Paella
Broccoli Salad
Cold Lime Soufflé

Serves 6

Make Ahead: Prepare and refrigerate Cold Lime Soufflé at least 3 hours ahead or overnight.
Prepare & Serve: Prepare and refrigerate Broccoli Salad. Cook Paella. Toasted Pumpkin Seeds (page 164) or Spicy Nuts (page 164) would be nice for nibbling before the meal. Serve them with a glass of sherry or bottled sangria poured over ice and garnished with fresh fruit.

PAELLA
(pictured on page 121)

1 medium-size green pepper, seeded and chopped
1 medium onion, chopped
1 clove garlic, minced
3 tablespoons olive oil
1 (28-ounce) can whole tomatoes, undrained and chopped
1 (10¾-ounce) can chicken broth, undiluted
1 (7-ounce) package paella rice mix
1 cup cubed cooked ham
1 bay leaf
½ teaspoon paprika
¼ teaspoon hot sauce
1 (3- to 3½-pound) broiler-fryer, cut up and skinned
½ pound medium shrimp, uncooked, peeled and deveined
1 (10-ounce) package frozen English peas

1. Sauté green pepper, onion, and garlic in oil in a Dutch oven 5 minutes or until tender. Add tomatoes, broth, rice mix, ham, bay leaf, paprika, and hot sauce, stirring well. Arrange chicken pieces over mixture; cover and simmer 40 minutes or until chicken is done, stirring occasionally.
2. Add shrimp and peas, stirring well; cover and simmer an additional 5 minutes or until shrimp are done. Remove and discard bay leaf.
3. Transfer Paella to a large serving dish, and serve warm or piping hot. Yield: 6 to 8 servings.

Note: In its native Spain, Paella is prepared with rice and whatever other ingredients cooks have on hand. So feel free to make substitutions or additions. You might try spicy sausage or boneless pork instead of ham, scallops or oysters instead of shrimp, and artichoke hearts instead of peas. Paella does not have to be served piping hot. So you may want to bring it outdoors on a nice evening. Or do as the Spanish do, and cook it outdoors in a pot or special paella pan set over the grill.

BROCCOLI SALAD
(pictured on page 121)

1 (1 pound) bunch fresh broccoli
¼ cup onion, chopped
1 (2¼-ounce) can sliced ripe olives, drained
¾ cup commercial ranch-style salad dressing
Purple cabbage leaves

1. Finely chop broccoli flowerets, reserving stems for other uses.
2. Combine broccoli, onion, olives, and dressing. Cover salad, and refrigerate.
3. Line serving bowl with purple cabbage leaves. Spoon broccoli mixture into center of bowl. Yield: 6 servings.

Note: Three medium zucchini, shredded, may be substituted for the broccoli.

COLD LIME SOUFFLÉ

(pictured on page 121)

4 eggs, separated
1 envelope unflavored gelatin
¾ cup sugar, divided
¼ cup water
¾ cup freshly squeezed lime juice
3 to 4 drops green food coloring
2 cups frozen whipped topping,
    thawed
    Lime slices
    Raspberry Puree

1. Cut a piece of aluminum foil long enough to fit around a 1-quart soufflé dish, allowing a 1-inch overlap; fold lengthwise into thirds. Lightly oil one side of foil; wrap around outside of dish, oiled side against dish, allowing it to extend 3 inches above rim to form a collar. Secure foil with tape.

2. Beat egg yolks in top of a double boiler; add gelatin, ¼ cup sugar, and water, beating well. Cook over simmering water 15 minutes, stirring constantly, until thickened and bubbly. Remove from heat. Stir in lime juice and food coloring. Set in bowl of ice water until cooled and thickened, stirring occasionally.

3. Beat egg whites (at room temperature) until foamy. Gradually add remaining ½ cup sugar, 1 tablespoon at a time, beating until stiff peaks form; fold with whipped topping into lime mixture. Spoon into dish; chill 3 hours or overnight.

4. Remove collar from dish; garnish with lime slices. Serve with Raspberry Puree. Yield: 6 servings.

Raspberry Puree:

1 (10-ounce) package frozen
    raspberries in light syrup,
    thawed

1. Position knife blade in food processor bowl; add raspberries. Process until smooth.

2. Strain raspberries, discarding seeds. Refrigerate until serving time.

3. Serve chilled. Yield: about ⅔ cup.

ADD A SALAD BAR

Start with a head of lettuce and a choice of bottled or homemade salad dressings, and you can set up a salad bar on a kitchen counter or dining table in minutes that will rival the most abundant restaurant salad bar. It's a good way to take the edge off appetites while a one-pot meal is simmering, and it contributes vitamins, minerals, and contrasting texture to the meal. Use a salad spinner to make cleaning the lettuce, spinach, or other greens much easier. Set the greens out in a big bowl, and offer a choice of topping ingredients along with them. A lazy Susan dish, especially one that comes with a cover, makes it easy to refrigerate a variety of salad toppings from one day to the next. Draw on all the resources in your supermarket to offer one or more toppings (none of which need to be pre-cooked) from each of the following groups:

● **Fresh vegetables:** sliced or diced cucumber, zucchini, peppers, mushrooms, celery, avocado, or tomato; thinly sliced purple onion, asparagus, or cauliflower; bean or alfalfa sprouts; sliced or shredded carrots or radishes; chopped fresh parsley, dillweed or coriander.

● **Canned vegetables:** green or ripe olives, artichoke hearts, pimientos, hot peppers, chick peas, sliced or diced beets, asparagus spears or cuts.

● **Frozen vegetables:** peas, corn kernels, baby lima beans, broccoli flowerets, cauliflowerets, snow peas, or chopped peppers. Rinse under cold water to separate; let vegetables finish thawing in serving bowl.

● **Packaged products:** croutons, shredded cheese, French-fried onion rings, sunflower seeds, grated Parmesan cheese, or chow mein noodles.

NATURALLY, A GARNISH . . .

Draw on the natural colors and shapes of vegetables and fruits to brighten serving platters. Here are some of the simplest ways to do so:

● Carrots, Zucchini, and Cucumber Ribbons. Use a vegetable peeler to pare lengthwise strips of carrot, zucchini or cucumbers. Heap the orange and green ribbons in the center or to one side of hors d'oeuvre and meat platters.

● Carrot or Radish Confetti. Shred carrots or radishes to add a splash of color to salads or any dish that needs an artful twist.

● Pepper Rings. Try the variety of bell peppers available now—red, yellow, or black. Use thin rings of two or three colors to garnish creamy salads and platters of fish, chicken, poultry, or pork.

● Scalloped Citrus Slices. Score citrus with a lemon zester, removing strips of rind at ¼-inch intervals around circumference of fruit. Slice to make attractive lemon, lime, or orange slices to serve with fish, chicken, or vegetables.

● Onion Pizzazz. Sprinkle finely chopped or thinly sliced purple onion over grilled and barbecued meats—it adds color, crispness, and zingy flavor. Thinly sliced green onions are milder in taste—perfect for creamy soups, salads, broiled chicken, corn, mushrooms, and hard-cooked eggs.

● A Chiffonade of Greens. Stack spinach, Romaine, chard, or other green leaves; roll up, and thinly slice. This is what chefs call a "chiffonade"—a little bundle of green strips to sprinkle atop soups, rice, or light-colored vegetables.

CHICKEN WITH SAUCE-APPEAL!

Chicken with Blue Cheese Sauce
Buttered Noodles
Julienne Vegetables
Chocolate Snap Squares

Serves 6

Make Ahead: Bake Chocolate Snap Squares.
Prepare & Serve: Bake Chicken with Blue Cheese Sauce. Julienne vegetables, and sauté. Cook noodles. Top each Chocolate Snap Square with a dollop of whipped topping at serving time.

Set out a serving platter of thin melon wedges, paper-thin slices of ham, and lime wedges for guests to arrange their own appetizer combinations. When melon is not in season, substitute thin wedges of ripe pears or figs — or try other fruit combinations.

CHICKEN WITH BLUE CHEESE SAUCE

6 boneless and skinless chicken breast halves
¼ cup butter or margarine, melted
1 (8-ounce) carton commercial sour cream
1 (4-ounce) package blue cheese, crumbled
1½ teaspoons Worcestershire sauce
1 large clove garlic, crushed
Chopped fresh parsley

1. Brown chicken in butter on all sides in a large skillet. Transfer chicken to a greased 13- x 9- x 2-inch baking pan.

2. Combine sour cream, blue cheese, Worcestershire sauce, and garlic in a small mixing bowl; mix well. Spoon mixture evenly over chicken.

3. Bake, uncovered, at 350° for 50 minutes or until tender.

4. Remove Chicken with Blue Cheese Sauce to individual serving plates. Sprinkle with fresh parsley. Serve warm. Yield: 6 servings.

MicroMethod

1. Place chicken breast halves in a greased 13- x 9- x 2-inch baking pan. Omit ¼ cup butter.

2. Same as step 2.

3. Cover with plastic wrap, and vent to allow steam to escape. Microwave at MEDIUM (50% power) for 9 to 14 minutes or until chicken is tender and no longer pink, rearranging once.

4. Same as step 4.

☺🔲 JULIENNE VEGETABLES

  1 **(1-pound) bunch broccoli, stems**
      and flowerets separated
  3 **medium-size yellow squash**
  3 **stalks celery**
  2 **medium carrots, scraped**
  2 **tablespoons vegetable oil**
  1 **tablespoon lemon juice**
  ½ **teaspoon dried whole thyme**
  ¼ **teaspoon salt**
  ⅛ **teaspoon pepper**
  1 **tablespoon minced fresh parsley**

1. Cut broccoli stems, yellow squash, celery, and carrots into 3- x ¼-inch strips. Sauté vegetables in oil in a large skillet 6 minutes or until crisp-tender. Add broccoli flowerets during last 3 minutes of cooking.

2. Sprinkle vegetables with lemon juice, thyme, salt, and pepper; toss well.

3. Transfer to a serving bowl; garnish with minced parsley. Yield: 6 servings.

MicroNote: To microwave step 1, place vegetables and oil in a 3-quart casserole. Cover with heavy-duty plastic wrap, and vent to allow steam to escape; microwave at HIGH for 6 minutes or until crisp-tender.

CHOCOLATE SNAP SQUARES

  3 **egg whites**
  ⅓ **cup sugar**
  1 **teaspoon vanilla extract**
  1 **(8½-ounce) package chocolate**
      wafers, finely crushed
  1 **cup chopped pecans**
  ½ **cup sugar**
  1 **teaspoon baking powder**
    Dash of salt
    Frozen whipped topping, thawed

1. Beat egg whites (at room temperature) in a large bowl until soft peaks form. Gradually add ⅓ cup sugar, 1 tablespoon at a time, beating until stiff peaks form. Fold in vanilla.

2. Combine chocolate wafer crumbs, pecans, ½ cup sugar, baking powder, and salt in a medium mixing bowl; mix well, and fold into egg white mixture. Spoon into a greased 9-inch square baking dish.

3. Bake at 350° for 20 minutes. Cool; cut into 3-inch squares.

4. Transfer to dessert plates; dollop with whipped topping. Yield: 9 squares.

Note: What to do with the leftover egg yolks from Chocolate Snap Squares? Mix the 3 yolks with 1 tablespoon water, and substitute for 2 whole eggs in scrambled eggs, pancakes, or cakes.

SCALLOPINI AND LINGUINE

Chicken Thighs Scallopini
Linguine Parmesan
Ratatouille
Grape Finale

Serves 6

Make Ahead: Flatten chicken and refrigerate. Prepare vegetables for Ratatouille, and refrigerate.
Prepare & Serve: Cook Ratatouille and linguine. Spoon grapes into dessert dishes, and refrigerate. Prepare Chicken Thighs Scallopini. Complete Linguine Parmesan; top with Chicken Thighs Scallopini. Complete Grape Finale just before serving.

Here's a time-saving alternative to Ratatouille: Sauté 2 sliced large zucchini and 2 tablespoons olive oil until zucchini begins to brown. Stir in 2 tablespoons dried tarragon leaves and salt to taste. Cover and cook over medium heat 5 to 8 minutes or just until tender, stirring occasionally.

 ### CHICKEN THIGHS SCALLOPINI

12 chicken thighs, skinned and
    boned
½ teaspoon salt
2 tablespoons butter or margarine
1 tablespoon lemon juice
2 tablespoons chopped fresh
    parsley
½ teaspoon dried whole marjoram
12 thin lemon slices
    Linguine Parmesan

1. Place chicken thighs on a sheet of waxed paper; flatten to ¼-inch thickness,

using a meat mallet or rolling pin. Cover tightly, and refrigerate overnight.
2. Remove chicken from refrigerator, and sprinkle with salt. Melt butter in a large skillet; add chicken and brown on all sides.
3. Sprinkle chicken with lemon juice, parsley, and marjoram; top each piece of chicken with a lemon slice. Cover and cook 10 minutes or until chicken is tender.
4. Place Linguine Parmesan on a serving platter; arrange Chicken Thighs Scallopini over pasta. Pour pan drippings over top. Serve warm. Yield: 6 servings.

LINGUINE PARMESAN

1 (12-ounce) package linguine
¼ cup butter or margarine, melted
¼ cup grated Parmesan cheese
2 tablespoons finely chopped fresh
    parsley

1. Cook linguine according to package directions. Rinse and drain.
2. Toss linguine with butter, cheese, and parsley. Place on a warm platter.
3. Serve warm. Yield: 6 servings.

RATATOUILLE

1 large onion, coarsely chopped
2 cloves garlic, finely chopped
¼ cup vegetable oil
1 medium-size sweet red pepper,
    seeded and cut into thin strips
1 medium eggplant, peeled and cut
    into ½-inch cubes (about 1
    pound)
4 small zucchini, thinly sliced
½ teaspoon dried whole basil leaves
½ teaspoon dried whole oregano
½ teaspoon dried whole rosemary
1 teaspoon salt
½ teaspoon pepper
4 medium tomatoes, peeled and
    quartered

1. Sauté onion and garlic in oil in a medium Dutch oven until tender. Add red pepper, eggplant, zucchini, basil, oregano, rosemary, salt, and pepper. Cover and cook 15 minutes. Stir gently; add tomatoes. Cover and cook an additional 5 minutes or until vegetables are cooked to desired degree of doneness.

2. Spoon Ratatouille into a large serving bowl. Serve immediately. Yield: 6 servings.

MicroMethod

1. Combine onion, garlic, oil, red pepper, and eggplant in a 4-quart casserole. Cover with heavy-duty plastic wrap, and vent to allow steam to escape; microwave at HIGH for 4 to 5 minutes.

2. Add zucchini, basil, oregano, rosemary, salt, and pepper to mixture. Cover with heavy-duty plastic wrap, and vent to allow steam to escape; microwave at HIGH for 5 minutes.

3. Stir mixture gently; add tomatoes. Cover and microwave at HIGH for 5 minutes. Let stand 5 minutes.

4. Same as step 2.

GRAPE FINALE

3 cups seedless green grapes
3 cups seedless red grapes
  Fresh galax leaves or fresh
    grape leaves
¼ cup commercial sour
    cream
¼ cup plain low-fat yogurt
2 tablespoons firmly packed
    brown sugar

1. Combine grapes in a large mixing bowl. Line 6 stemmed glasses with leaves. Spoon 1 cup grapes into each glass, and refrigerate.

2. Combine sour cream, yogurt, and sugar in a small mixing bowl, stirring well. Spoon mixture evenly over grapes. Serve chilled. Yield: 6 servings.

EASY ELEGANCE

Herbed Cornish Hens
Broccoli with Sicilian Sauce
Mushroom Wild Rice
Lemon Mousse with
Blueberry Sauce

Serves 6

Make Ahead: Prepare and refrigerate Lemon Mousse.
Prepare & Serve: While Herbed Cornish Hens are baking, prepare Mushroom Wild Rice. Cook broccoli; prepare Sicilian Sauce. At dessert time, cook Blueberry Sauce, and serve warm.

Something to munch on before dinner? Mix equal amounts of unsalted peanuts or mixed nuts and raisins.

HERBED CORNISH HENS

6 (1- to 1½- pound) Cornish hens
6 small onions
1 tablespoon dried whole tarragon
¾ cup butter or margarine, melted
¾ cup Chablis or other dry white
    wine
½ teaspoon salt
¼ teaspoon pepper

1. Remove giblets from hens; reserve for other uses. Rinse hens with cold water, and pat dry. Place an onion in the cavity of each hen; sprinkle hens with tarragon.

2. Combine butter, wine, salt, and pepper in a small mixing bowl, stirring well.

3. Place hens in a large flour-coated oven-cooking bag; pour butter mixture into bag. Follow manufacturer's directions for use of bag.

4. Bake at 350° for 1 hour and 15 minutes. Yield: 6 servings.

BROCCOLI WITH SICILIAN SAUCE

2 (10-ounce) packages frozen
    broccoli spears
1 medium onion, chopped
1 clove garlic, minced
2 tablespoons olive oil
1 tablespoon flour
1 teaspoon chicken-flavored bouillon
    granules
1 cup water
1 (3-ounce) jar grated Romano
    cheese
    Ripe olive slices

1. Cook broccoli according to package directions. Keep broccoli warm while preparing sauce.
2. Sauté onion and garlic in olive oil in a small saucepan. Add flour, stirring well.
3. Combine bouillon granules and water. Add to onion mixture, stirring well. Cook over medium heat, stirring constantly, until mixture is thickened and bubbly. Add cheese to onion mixture, stirring until cheese melts.
4. Arrange broccoli in a serving dish. Pour sauce over broccoli; garnish with olive slices. Serve immediately. Yield: 6 servings.

MUSHROOM WILD RICE

1 (6¼-ounce) package long grain
    and wild rice mix
1 (4-ounce) can mushroom stems
    and pieces, drained
1 cup chopped celery
2 tablespoons butter or margarine,
    melted

1. Cook rice mix according to package directions.
2. Sauté mushrooms and celery in butter in a small skillet until tender.
3. Add vegetables to rice, stirring well.
4. Spoon Mushroom Wild Rice into a serving bowl; serve immediately. Yield: 6 servings.

LEMON MOUSSE WITH BLUEBERRY SAUCE

½ (16-ounce) commercial pound
    cake, cut into ¼-inch slices
1 envelope unflavored gelatin
¾ cup water
1 (14-ounce) can sweetened
    condensed milk
1 teaspoon grated lemon rind
½ cup lemon juice
1 (8-ounce) container frozen
    whipped topping
    Blueberry Sauce

1. Line bottom and sides of an 8-inch springform pan with cake slices; set aside.
2. Sprinkle gelatin over water in a small saucepan; let stand 1 minute. Cook over low heat, stirring constantly, 1 minute or until gelatin dissolves; set aside.
3. Combine milk, lemon rind, and lemon juice, stirring well. Add reserved gelatin mixture, stirring well. Fold in whipped topping.
4. Pour mixture into prepared springform pan. Cover and refrigerate overnight or until set.
5. Remove sides of springform pan; place mousse on a serving platter. Serve with warm Blueberry Sauce. Yield: one 8-inch mousse.

Blueberry Sauce:

¼ cup sugar
2 teaspoons cornstarch
¼ teaspoon ground cinnamon
⅛ teaspoon ground nutmeg
½ cup water
1¼ cups fresh or frozen
    blueberries

1. Combine sugar, cornstarch, cinnamon, and nutmeg in a small saucepan, mixing well; gradually add water, stirring well. Cook over low heat, stirring constantly, until thickened and bubbly.
2. Add blueberries. Cook, stirring occasionally, 5 minutes.
3. Serve warm over Lemon Mousse. Yield: 1½ cups.

TURKEY ON THE GRILL

Barbecued Turkey Kabobs
Sour Cream Potato Salad
Melon Berry Baskets

Serves 4

Make Ahead: Marinate turkey. Cook potatoes, and refrigerate overnight.
Prepare & Serve: Complete salad. Make Melon Berry Baskets; chill. Assemble and grill Barbecued Turkey Kabobs.

BARBECUED TURKEY KABOBS

⅓ cup chili sauce
2 tablespoons lemon juice
1 tablespoon sugar
2 bay leaves
1 pound turkey breast (about one-half of a small breast), cut into eight 1½-inch cubes
8 medium cherry tomatoes
8 medium-size fresh mushrooms
2 small onions, quartered
1 large green pepper, seeded and cut into eighths
1 medium zucchini, cut into ½-inch slices
2 tablespoons vegetable oil

1. Combine chili sauce, lemon juice, sugar, and bay leaves in a medium mixing bowl; stir well. Add turkey, stirring to coat well. Cover and refrigerate overnight.
2. Alternately thread turkey and vegetables on 4 skewers. Reserve turkey marinade. Brush vegetables with oil.
3. Grill 5 to 6 inches from medium coals 10 to 12 minutes or until done; turn often. Baste with marinade.
4. Serve warm. Yield: 4 servings.

SOUR CREAM POTATO SALAD

1 small onion, finely chopped
¼ cup chopped celery
¼ cup chopped green pepper
2 hard-cooked eggs, chopped
1 tablespoon minced fresh parsley
1½ teaspoons minced fresh dillweed
½ teaspoon chopped capers
1 teaspoon salt
¼ teaspoon pepper
1 tablespoon lemon juice
½ cup commercial sour cream
4 cups sliced cooked potatoes (about 4 large)
Fresh dillweed sprig (optional)

1. Combine onion, celery, green pepper, eggs, parsley, minced dillweed, capers, salt, and pepper in a medium mixing bowl, stirring well.
2. Combine lemon juice and sour cream in a small mixing bowl, stirring well; add to vegetable mixture, mixing well.
3. Add potatoes slices, tossing to coat well. Cover and chill thoroughly.
4. Garnish with dillweed sprig, if desired. Yield: 4 servings.

MELON BERRY BASKETS

2 small canteloupe or honeydew melons
1 pint fresh blueberries
1 to 2 tablespoons Grand Marnier
1 cup lemon yogurt

1. Cut melons in half; remove and discard seeds. Scoop out melons with a melon baller.
2. Combine melon balls and berries. Spoon fruit into melon shells; chill.
3. Stir Grand Marnier into yogurt.
4. Dollop yogurt mixture over fruit, and serve. Yield: 4 servings.

Note: Raspberries may be substituted for the blueberries.

CREAMY SEAFOOD

Shrimp-Crab Casserole
Asparagus Salad
Italian Crescent Rolls

Serves 6

Prepare & Serve: While Shrimp-Crab Casserole is baking, make Asparagus Salad. Prepare Italian Crescent Rolls. Remove casserole from oven. Turn up oven setting; bake rolls.

SHRIMP-CRAB CASSEROLE

⅓ cup chopped onion
¼ cup butter or margarine, melted
¼ cup all-purpose flour
1 teaspoon salt
½ teaspoon white pepper
1 cup half-and-half
1 cup milk
3 cups cooked, peeled, and deveined shrimp
1 (6-ounce) package frozen crabmeat, thawed and flaked
1 (5-ounce) can sliced water chestnuts, drained
2 cups cooked rice
2 tablespoons lemon juice
2 tablespoons chopped pimiento
1 cup (4 ounces) shredded Cheddar cheese, divided

1. Sauté onion in butter in a large skillet until tender.
2. Add flour, salt, and pepper. Cook 2 minutes, stirring constantly.
3. Gradually add half-and-half and milk; cook over medium heat, stirring constantly, until thickened and bubbly. Remove from heat.
4. Stir in shrimp, crabmeat, water chestnuts, rice, lemon juice, pimiento, and ½ cup cheese. Spoon into a lightly greased 2-quart casserole. Bake at 325° for 25 minutes. Top with remaining ½ cup cheese; bake 5 minutes or until cheese melts.
5. Serve warm. Yield: 6 servings.

☺ ASPARAGUS SALAD

3 tablespoons vegetable oil
2 tablespoons lemon juice
1 tablespoon sugar
½ teaspoon Dijon mustard
¼ teaspoon salt
4 slices bacon, cooked and crumbled
1 (15-ounce) can asparagus spears, chilled and drained
Fresh spinach leaves
1 hard-cooked egg, finely chopped

1. Combine oil, lemon juice, sugar, mustard, and salt in a small mixing bowl, stirring well; add bacon, stirring well.
2. Arrange asparagus spears on spinach-lined salad plates. Spoon dressing over asparagus; sprinkle with hard-cooked egg. Yield: 6 servings.

☺ ITALIAN CRESCENT ROLLS

1 (8-ounce) package refrigerator crescent rolls
1 tablespoon butter, melted
½ teaspoon Italian seasoning

1. Unroll crescent roll dough. Separate into 8 triangles. Brush with melted butter; sprinkle with Italian seasoning.
2. Roll dough up, following package directions. Bake at 375° for 10 minutes or until golden brown. Yield: 8 rolls.

A no-fuss menu for entertaining, Paella Indoors and Out (page 112) includes Broccoli Salad and Cold Lime Soufflé.

SPICY SHRIMP

Spicy Broiled Shrimp
Corn-on-the-Cob (page 48)
Marinated Artichoke Salad
Lemon and Orange Coconut Cake

Serves 4

Make Ahead: Bake Lemon and Orange Coconut Cake. Marinate shrimp.
Prepare & Serve: Prepare salad. Boil corn. Broil the shrimp.

◆ SPICY BROILED SHRIMP
(pictured at left)

¼ cup lemon juice
¼ cup vegetable oil
2 tablespoons soy sauce
2 tablespoons finely chopped onion
1 clove garlic, pressed
¼ teaspoon salt
¼ teaspoon pepper
2 pounds large shrimp, uncooked, peeled, and deveined
Commercial cocktail sauce

1. Combine first 7 ingredients in a shallow dish; stir well to blend. Stir in shrimp; cover with plastic wrap, and refrigerate 45 minutes or overnight.
2. Remove shrimp from marinade, reserving marinade. Arrange shrimp in a single layer on rack of a broiler pan.
3. Broil 6 inches from heating element 1 minute. Brush shrimp with marinade. Cook an additional 1 minute or until shrimp are pink. Serve with cocktail sauce. Yield: 4 servings.

The Spicy Shrimp menu (above) makes the ideal summer supper.

MARINATED ARTICHOKE SALAD
(pictured at left)

1 (6-ounce) jar marinated artichoke hearts, undrained
1 (4-ounce) can sliced mushrooms, drained
1 (4-ounce) can sliced pitted and ripe olives, drained
½ cup chopped onion
2 stalks celery, sliced
1 medium tomato, peeled and cut into wedges
Bibb lettuce leaves

1. Combine all ingredients except lettuce leaves in a large mixing bowl, stirring well. Cover with plastic wrap, and chill thoroughly.
2. Spoon salad over a lettuce-lined serving platter. Yield: 4 servings.

LEMON AND ORANGE COCONUT CAKE
(pictured at left)

¼ cup butter or margarine
1 (10-ounce) jar orange marmalade
½ cup flaked coconut
1 (18.5-ounce) package lemon cake mix with pudding

1. Melt butter over low heat in a small saucepan. Remove from heat, and stir in marmalade and coconut. Pour evenly into bottom of a heavily greased 10-inch Bundt pan. Set aside.
2. Prepare cake mix according to package directions. Pour batter into Bundt pan over marmalade mixture.
3. Bake at 350° for 40 minutes or until a wooden pick inserted in center comes out clean.
4. Cool cake in pan 10 minutes. Invert cake onto a serving platter. Remove pan, and cool completely.
5. Slice cake and serve. Yield: one 10-inch cake.

SCALLOP SAUTÉ

Bay Scallops with Vegetables
Green Salad with Tart French
Dressing
Yogurt-Apricot Pie

Serves 4

Make Ahead: Prepare Tart French Dressing and chill.
Prepare & Serve: Prepare Yogurt-Apricot Pie. While pie is baking, prepare Bay Scallops with Vegetables. Complete salad.

BAY SCALLOPS WITH VEGETABLES

½ cup water
½ cup dry white wine
½ teaspoon salt
1½ pounds fresh bay scallops
½ pound fresh mushrooms, sliced
½ cup sliced green onions
½ cup sliced celery
3 tablespoons butter or margarine
1 (6-ounce) package frozen Chinese pea pods, thawed and drained
1 tablespoon soy sauce
2 teaspoons lemon juice
2 teaspoons cornstarch
¼ teaspoon white pepper
3 dashes of hot sauce
1 (2-ounce) jar diced pimiento, drained
Hot cooked rice

1. Combine water, wine, and salt in a large saucepan; bring to a boil. Add scallops; reduce heat and simmer 2 minutes, stirring occasionally, or until done. Drain scallops, reserving ½ cup liquid; set aside.
2. Sauté mushrooms, onions, and celery in butter until tender; stir in pea pods.
3. Combine reserved liquid, soy sauce, lemon juice, cornstarch, pepper, and hot sauce; mix well, and stir into vegetables. Cook over medium heat, stirring constantly, until smoothed and thickened.
4. Stir in scallops and pimiento; cook just until thoroughly heated.
5. Serve Bay Scallops with Vegetables over rice. Yield: 4 servings.

◆ GREEN SALAD WITH TART FRENCH DRESSING

¼ cup olive oil
1 clove garlic, finely chopped
1 tablespoon white wine vinegar
1 tablespoon lemon juice
½ teaspoon salt
¼ teaspoon pepper
5 cups torn mixed salad greens

1. Combine olive oil, garlic, vinegar, lemon juice, salt, and pepper in a jar. Cover tightly, and shake vigorously. Chill several hours.
2. To serve, pour dressing over salad greens; toss. Yield: 4 servings.

YOGURT-APRICOT PIE

2 eggs, beaten
1 cup sugar
2 tablespoons all-purpose flour
1 teaspoon almond extract
1 (8-ounce) carton plain low-fat yogurt
1 (6-ounce) package dried apricots, chopped
1 cup flaked coconut
1 unbaked 9-inch pastry shell
2 tablespoons flaked coconut, toasted

1. Combine eggs, sugar, flour, and almond extract, mixing well. Stir in yogurt, apricots, and 1 cup coconut.
2. Pour mixture into pastry shell. Bake at 350° for 35 minutes or until filling is set.
3. Sprinkle with toasted coconut and serve. Yield: one 9-inch pie.

A GREAT CATCH!

Broiled Fish with Deviled Cheese
Mixed Vegetable Stir-Fry
Almond Rice
Spiced Angel Food Cake with
Orange Custard Sauce

Serves 6

Make Ahead: Bake Spiced Angel Food Cake. Make Orange Custard Sauce. Chill sauce thoroughly.
Prepare & Serve: Make cheese topping for fish. Cook Almond Rice. Prepare ingredients for Mixed Vegetable Stir-Fry. Cook Broiled Fish with Deviled Cheese. Stir-fry vegetables.

If you have no time to make dessert ahead, cook Orange Custard Sauce, and refrigerate before you begin other dinner preparations. Serve the sauce over sliced bananas, blueberries, strawberries, vanilla ice cream, or packaged chocolate or yellow pound cake.

BROILED FISH WITH DEVILED CHEESE

1 cup (4 ounces) shredded Cheddar cheese
2 tablespoons chili sauce
1 tablespoon prepared mustard
1½ teaspoons prepared horseradish
   Vegetable cooking spray
2 pounds fresh grouper fillets, cut into serving-size portions
1 tablespoon butter or margarine, melted

1. Combine cheese, chili sauce, mustard, and horseradish in a small mixing bowl; mix well. Refrigerate until needed.

2. Line a shallow broiler pan with aluminum foil. Spray broiler rack with cooking spray. Place fillets on rack, and brush lightly with butter. Broil 6 inches from heating element 10 minutes or until fish flakes easily when tested with a fork.
3. Spread reserved cheese mixture evenly over fillets. Broil 2 minutes or until cheese melts.
4. Transfer fillets to a serving platter, and serve warm. Yield: 6 servings.

MIXED VEGETABLE STIR-FRY

1 tablespoon peanut oil
1 clove garlic, minced
1½ teaspoons chicken-flavored bouillon granules
¾ cup water
1 tablespoon cornstarch
1 tablespoon sherry
1 teaspoon soy sauce
½ pound fresh mushrooms, quartered
1 medium-size green pepper, seeded and cut into 1-inch pieces
1 medium-size sweet red pepper, seeded and cut into 1-inch pieces
1 (8-ounce) can sliced water chestnuts, drained
1 (6-ounce) package frozen snow peas, thawed

1. Heat oil in a wok or large skillet; add garlic, and sauté 1 minute.
2. Combine bouillon granules and water in a measuring cup, stirring well. Add cornstarch, sherry, and soy sauce to bouillon mixture, stirring well.
3. Add bouillon mixture, mushrooms, peppers, and water chestnuts to wok. Cook over medium heat, stirring frequently, 6 to 8 minutes or until peppers are crisp-tender. Add pea pods; cook, stirring constantly, 1 minute.
4. Serve warm. Yield: 6 servings.

ALMOND RICE

2 tablespoons butter or margarine
¼ cup slivered almonds
1½ cups uncooked regular rice
¼ teaspoon ground cardamom
¼ teaspoon salt (optional)
2¾ cups chicken broth or water

1. Melt butter in a medium saucepan over medium heat. Stir in almonds; sauté 5 minutes or until almonds begin to brown. Stir in rice; sauté 3 minutes. Add cardamom and salt, if desired.

2. Stir chicken broth into rice. Cover and simmer over low heat 18 minutes or until broth is absorbed. Yield: 6 servings.

SPICED ANGEL FOOD CAKE

1 (14.5-ounce) package angel food cake mix
1 teaspoon ground cinnamon
¼ teaspoon ground nutmeg

1. Prepare and bake cake according to package directions, adding cinnamon and nutmeg to batter; invert pan onto funnel or bottle 2 hours or until cake is completely cooled.

2. Loosen cooled cake from sides of pan, using a small metal spatula. Remove cake from pan.

3. Slice cake and serve with Orange-Custard Sauce. Yield: one 10-inch cake.

Note: There are all kinds of ways to vary Spiced Angel Food Cake. Here are a few: Substitute pumpkin pie spice for the cinnamon and ground cloves for the nutmeg; use ginger instead of cinnamon with the nutmeg, and add ¼ teaspoon ground cloves; add 1 tablespoon grated orange rind with any of the spice combinations.

ORANGE CUSTARD SAUCE

3 tablespoons sugar
1 tablespoon cornstarch
Dash of salt
1 cup orange juice
3 egg yolks, beaten
1 tablespoon Triple Sec or Cointreau
1 cup fresh orange sections, well-drained

1. Combine sugar, cornstarch, and salt in top of a double boiler; stir in orange juice. Cook over simmering water, stirring constantly, until mixture is thickened and bubbly.

2. Gradually stir one-fourth of hot mixture into yolks; add to remaining hot mixture, stirring constantly. Cook, stirring constantly, 2 minutes or until mixture thickens.

3. Remove from heat; stir in Triple Sec. Chill thoroughly.

4. Just before serving, stir in orange sections. Yield: 2 cups.

MicroMethod

1. Combine first 3 ingredients in a 2-quart glass measure; stir in orange juice. Microwave at HIGH 4 to 5 minutes or until thickened and bubbly, stirring twice.

2. Gradually stir one-fourth of hot mixture into yolks; add to remaining hot mixture, stirring constantly with a wire whisk. Microwave at MEDIUM (50% power) for 1½ to 2 minutes, stirring twice.

3. Same as step 3.

4. Same as step 4.

Time Out for Lunch

Everyone looks forward to lunch, and for very good reasons. The food energy prevents mid-afternoon droop. Other nutrients are essential for a balanced diet, since it's unlikely that you will consume recommended daily allowances of fruits and vegetables at breakfast and dinner alone. And, not least important, the mental and social break revives enthusiasm for the rest of the day's activities.

Lunch can also provide some fun for the cook. This is the time to improvise with leftovers stowed in the 'fridge, with glorious salad ingredients, and with all kinds of quick and packaged breads. It's the time to play creatively with bulging sandwiches, souped-up soups, and whole-meal salads. And it's the time to treat yourself to tastes that other family members may not share.

So enjoy! There aren't many pleasures greater than a big platter of Oriental Chicken Salad or garden-bright Classic Greek Salad. The ham and melted cheese stuffed into Cordon Bleu Croissants make every bite seem a treat. A hot bowl of Ham and Corn Chowder with Easy Cheese Bread creates instant coziness.

All of the recipes in this chapter are ripe for adaptation to whatever you have on hand. You could, for example, toss leftover poultry with Spinach-Beet Salad, or substitute tuna in Chicken Salad Niçoise. Chilled Shrimp and Fruit Curry can be made with fresh pineapple, papaya, or other summer fruit instead of nectarines and plums. The Greek salad would remain true to its Mediterranean origins with the addition of any kind of canned fish. The Oriental Chicken Salad would be luscious with pork substituted for the chicken.

If you wish to make a salad ahead, refrigerate the dressing and other ingredients separately. Pack them in separate containers to take to school or work, mix at lunchtime, and you can look forward to a noon-hour freshness break. Sandwiches taste better, too, if you pack moist ingredients in containers and wrap the bread separately. Be sure to pack utensils, if they will be needed. And don't hesitate to add a few crunchy garnishes, like zucchini slices, radishes, or small broccoli flowerets.

Menu of Menus

SPINACH-BEET SALAD

Spinach-Beet Salad
Soft Caraway Breadsticks
Chocolate Bar Pie

Serves 4

Make Ahead: Marinate beets. Hard-cook eggs, and refrigerate. Prepare Chocolate Bar Pie, and chill.
Prepare & Serve: Clean spinach. Make Soft Caraway Breadsticks. Assemble salad.

If you haven't prepared the Chocolate Bar Pie, complete this not-too-rich lunch by preparing Caramel Sauce (page 271) and serving with ice cream.

◆ SPINACH-BEET SALAD

- 1 (16-ounce) can sliced beets, drained
- ½ cup commercial Italian salad dressing
- ¼ pound fresh spinach, cleaned and torn into bite-size pieces
- 4 green onions, chopped
- 2 stalks celery, sliced
  Additional fresh spinach leaves
- 2 slices bacon, cooked and crumbled
- 2 hard-cooked eggs

1. Combine beets and dressing in a medium mixing bowl; cover with plastic wrap, and marinate overnight.
2. Drain beet mixture. Add torn spinach, green onions, and celery to beet mixture; toss gently. Arrange beet mixture on additional spinach leaves; sprinkle bacon over top.
3. Finely chop hard-cooked eggs, and sprinkle over top of salad before serving. Yield: 4 servings.

◖ SOFT CARAWAY BREADSTICKS

- 1 (4.5-ounce) can refrigerated biscuits
- 2 tablespoons milk
- 3 to 4 tablespoons caraway seeds

1. Cut biscuits in half. Roll each half into a 4-inch long stick. Dip sticks into milk; roll in seeds.
2. Place sticks on a lightly greased baking sheet. Bake at 450° for 8 to 10 minutes or until lightly browned.
3. Serve warm. Yield: 1 dozen.

Note: For variety, try poppy or sesame seeds instead of caraway seeds.

◆ ▢ CHOCOLATE BAR PIE

- 10 large marshmallows
- ¼ cup milk
- 1 (4-ounce) milk chocolate candy bar
- 1 teaspoon instant coffee powder
- 1 (4-ounce) container frozen whipped topping, thawed
- 1 (9-inch) chocolate cookie crust
- ¼ cup chopped almonds, toasted

1. Combine marshmallows and milk in top of a double boiler; cook over simmering water until marshmallows are just melted. Remove from heat; add chocolate bar and coffee powder, stirring until chocolate melts. Let mixture cool to room temperature.
2. Fold whipped topping into chocolate mixture. Pour into crust, and sprinkle almonds over top of pie. Chill 4 hours.
3. Slice and serve. Yield: one 9-inch pie.

MicroNote: To microwave step 1, place marshmallows, milk, chocolate, and coffee in a large mixing bowl. Microwave at HIGH for 2 to 3 minutes or until marshmallows and chocolate melt, stirring every minute. Cool to room temperature.

CLASSIC GREEK SALAD

*Classic Greek Salad
Pita Wedges with Herb Butter*

Serves 6

Prepare & Serve: Assemble salad. Bake Pita Wedges with Herb Butter.

The only standard ingredients of Classic Greek Salad are olives and feta cheese. All the rest can be varied according to taste. Try substituting 1 small head romaine lettuce for the iceberg and endive. For a Mediterranean-style salad, substitute 1 large can tuna in water, drained and flaked, for the feta cheese.

Serve Garbanzo and Sesame Dip (page 159) with crackers and a glass of roditis wine before the salad to make this meal festive enough for guests. Make Creamy Rice Pudding (page 258) for dessert.

1. Combine lettuce, endive, green pepper, tomato, onion, and cheese in a large mixing bowl. Place on a large platter. Garnish with olives and green onion; arrange cucumber slices around outer edge of platter. Refrigerate.

2. Combine olive oil, vinegar, oregano, salt, and pepper in a jar. Cover tightly, and shake well.

3. Pour dressing over salad just before serving. Yield: 6 servings.

Note: Because it is stored in brine, feta cheese can be quite often salty. To reduce saltiness, rinse the cheese in a colander under cold water, and pat dry before you crumble it.

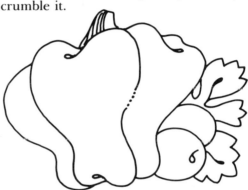

CLASSIC GREEK SALAD

½ medium head iceberg lettuce, shredded
½ head curly endive, torn
1 medium-size green pepper, seeded and coarsely chopped
1 medium tomato, coarsely chopped
½ medium-size red onion, sliced and separated into rings
8 ounces crumbled feta cheese
6 large green olives
6 large ripe olives
1 (2¼-ounce) can sliced ripe olives
¼ cup sliced green onion
1 medium cucumber, sliced
⅔ cup olive oil
⅓ cup white wine vinegar
½ teaspoon dried whole oregano
½ teaspoon salt
⅛ teaspoon pepper

PITA WEDGES WITH HERB BUTTER

⅓ cup butter or margarine, softened
1 tablespoon finely chopped fresh parsley
1 teaspoon lemon juice
1 clove garlic, crushed
⅛ teaspoon salt
⅛ teaspoon pepper
2 (6-inch) pita bread rounds

1. Combine butter, parsley, lemon juice, garlic, salt, and pepper in a small mixing bowl, stirring well.

2. Split pita bread rounds in half to form 4 flat discs; spread each half with herb butter. Cut each half into 6 wedges on a baking sheet. Bake at 350° for 3 minutes or until crisp.

3. Serve warm. Yield: 2 dozen.

CLASSY CROISSANTS

Cordon Bleu Croissants
Marinated Asparagus

Serves 8

Make Ahead: Make Marinated Asparagus, and refrigerate 3 hours or overnight.
Prepare & Serve: Make Cordon Bleu Croissants, and place Marinated Asparagus in serving dish.

For dessert, try Double Fudge Brownies (page 269).

If there's a microwave oven where you work, you might want to assemble the Cordon Bleu Croissants, wrap them in waxed paper, and take them with you to heat at lunchtime. Individual servings of the Marinated Asparagus will travel well in zip-top plastic bags.

CORDON BLEU CROISSANTS

  2 (6-ounce) packages frozen
      croissants
  8 thin slices cooked ham
  2 tablespoons plus 2 teaspoons
      prepared horseradish
  8 thin slices cooked turkey breast
  1 (8-ounce) package sandwich-size
      sliced Swiss cheese

1. Heat croissants according to package directions. Wrap in aluminum foil, and keep warm.

2. Spread each slice of ham with 1 teaspoon horseradish; top each with a slice of turkey and a slice of Swiss cheese. Roll up ham jellyroll fashion, and secure with wooden picks.

3. Place rolls in a 12- x 8- x 2-inch baking dish; bake at 400° for 8 minutes or until cheese melts. Discard wooden picks.

4. Split each croissant; place a ham roll in each, and serve. Yield: 8 sandwiches.

MicroNote: To microwave step 3, place ham rolls in a 12- x 8- x 2-inch baking dish. Cover with heavy-duty plastic wrap, and vent to allow steam to escape; microwave at HIGH for 3 to 4 minutes or until cheese melts. Remove wooden picks, and discard.

MARINATED ASPARAGUS

  2 pounds fresh asparagus, cleaned
  2 teaspoons lemon juice
  1 teaspoon Dijon mustard
  ¼ teaspoon salt
  ⅛ teaspoon pepper
  1 clove garlic, crushed
  ⅓ cup olive oil
1½ teaspoons red wine vinegar
      Pimiento strips

1. Arrange asparagus in a steaming basket. Cover and cook over boiling water 5 minutes or until crisp-tender. Drain.

2. Combine lemon juice, mustard, salt, pepper, and garlic, stirring well; gradually add oil and vinegar, whisking well.

3. Place asparagus in a 12- x 8- x 2-inch baking dish; add marinade. Cover and refrigerate 3 hours or overnight.

4. Drain asparagus. Arrange on a serving platter; garnish with pimiento strips. Yield: 8 servings.

MicroNote: To microwave step 1, place asparagus in a 12- x 8- x 2-inch baking dish with buds toward center. Cover with heavy-duty plastic wrap, and vent to allow steam to escape; microwave at HIGH for 10 to 12 minutes or until crisp-tender. Let stand 2 minutes; drain.

HOT SOUP AND HOMEMADE BREAD

Ham and Corn Chowder
Easy Cheese Bread

Serves 4 to 6

Prepare & Serve: Bake Easy Cheese Bread. Make Ham and Corn Chowder.

HAM AND CORN CHOWDER

2 cups diced cooked ham
1 cup chopped celery
½ cup chopped onion
¼ cup butter or margarine
2 (16-ounce) cans cream-style
    corn
1 cup milk
½ teaspoon celery salt
½ teaspoon garlic powder
½ teaspoon pepper

1. Sauté ham, celery, and onion in butter in a large saucepan until tender.
2. Add remaining ingredients; bring to a boil. Reduce heat; cover and simmer 20 minutes.
3. Serve hot. Yield: 7 cups.

EASY CHEESE BREAD

3¾ cups biscuit mix
2 cups (8 ounces) shredded sharp
    Cheddar cheese
2 tablespoons poppy seeds
⅛ teaspoon ground red
    pepper
1¼ cups milk
1 egg, beaten

1. Combine first 4 ingredients; stir well. Combine milk and egg; add to cheese mixture, and stir 2 minutes.
2. Pour batter into a greased 9- x 5- x 3-inch loafpan. Bake at 350° for 55 to 60 minutes. Remove from pan.
3. Cool slightly. Yield: 1 loaf.

SOUPED-UP SOUPS

Canned soups freshened with additional seasonings and garnishes can give any supper or lunch menu a fast warm-up. Here are some options:

● Stir sliced smoked sausage or diced ham into minestrone soup. Top with sliced celery or grated Parmesan cheese.

● Stir curry powder into cream of celery soup reconstituted with skim milk or water. Swirl yogurt into each serving, and sprinkle with dillweed.

● Heat chicken broth with soy sauce and minced fresh gingerroot. Garnish with green onions and mushrooms.

● Heat nacho cheese soup with frozen corn kernels, ground cumin, and dried oregano leaves. Garnish with chopped green pepper and crumbled corn chips.

● Perk up French onion soup by stirring in Dijon mustard. Top French bread rounds with grated Parmesan cheese; toast and serve in hot soup.

● Whip up a hearty chowder by adding frozen chopped spinach and a can of minced clams to cream of shrimp soup. Garnish with sliced green onions.

● Reconstitute cream of potato soup with half-and-half. Add a dash of sherry and top with fresh chopped chives.

CHICKEN SALAD NIÇOISE

Chicken Salad Niçoise
Breadstick Bowknots

Serves 4

Make Ahead: Prepare and chill Chicken Salad Niçoise.

Prepare & Serve: Bake Breadstick Bowknots. Turn this attractive French salad into a menu for guests by preparing Easy Chocolate Mousse (page 254), in advance, for dessert. Serve Kir Aperitifs—white wine with a half teaspoon crème de cassis per glass.

◆ CHICKEN SALAD NIÇOISE

1 medium-size baking potato, cooked, drained, and cooled
½ pound fresh green beans, blanched and rinsed in cold water
¾ cup vegetable oil
¼ cup red wine vinegar
1 tablespoon chopped fresh parsley
2 cloves garlic, crushed
¼ teaspoon salt
⅛ teaspoon pepper
    Romaine lettuce leaves
2 medium tomatoes, peeled and cut into wedges
1 medium-size red onion, sliced and separated into rings
1 medium-size green pepper, seeded and cut into thin strips
1 pound boneless and skinless chicken breasts, cooked and sliced into strips
    Capers

1. Peel and slice potato; arrange slices in a shallow dish. Drain green beans, and

trim ends. Place beans over potatoes in dish. Set aside.

2. Combine oil, vinegar, parsley, garlic, salt, and pepper in a jar. Cover tightly, and shake until well blended.

3. Drizzle half of dressing over potato-bean mixture. Cover mixture with plastic wrap, and chill 30 minutes. Set remaining dressing aside.

4. Arrange lettuce leaves on 4 dinner plates. Spoon potato-bean mixture on lettuce leaves. Divide tomatoes, red onion, green pepper, and chicken evenly on potato-bean mixture. Pour remaining dressing over top. Garnish salad with capers. Cover each salad with plastic wrap, and chill at least 2 hours.

5. Serve chilled. Yield: 4 servings.

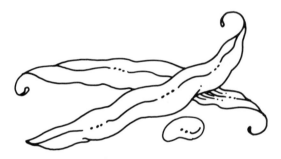

BREADSTICK BOWKNOTS

1 (11-ounce) package refrigerated breadsticks
2 tablespoons butter or margarine, melted
1 teaspoon dried parsley flakes
    Additional butter or margarine

1. Separate breadsticks into ropes. Tie each rope into a loose knot, leaving 2 long ends. Tuck one end under knot. Bring other end up, and tuck into center of knot.

2. Brush each bowknot with butter; sprinkle top with parsley. Place bowknots 3 inches apart on a lightly greased baking sheet. Bake at 350° for 15 minutes or until golden brown.

3. Serve warm with additional butter. Yield: 8 bowknots.

ORIENTAL CHICKEN SALAD

Oriental Chicken Salad
Assorted Crackers
Pineapple-Orange Surprise

Serves 4

Make ahead: Prepare Oriental Chicken Salad and Pineapple-Orange Surprise, and chill at least 2 hours.
Prepare and Serve: Arrange salad on serving platter; spoon dessert into individual dishes.

This lunch is just as easy to pack to take along as it is to serve at home. Spoon drained Oriental Chicken Salad into pita pockets, and wrap in heavy-duty aluminum foil. Pack Pineapple-Orange Surprise in a small insulated jug, or substitute tangerines for dessert.

1. Combine orange juice, oil, sherry, soy sauce, salt, ginger, and garlic powder in a small mixing bowl, stirring well; set aside.
2. Combine mushrooms, chicken, rice, green pepper, almonds, and green onion in a large mixing bowl; add marinade mixture, tossing to mix well. Cover and chill.
3. Cook snow peas in boiling water 1 minute. Drain and chill thoroughly. Set snow peas aside.
4. Place chicken mixture in the center of a lettuce-lined serving platter, using a slotted spoon; discard marinade. Arrange snow peas and red pepper strips around chicken salad. Yield: 4 servings.

MicroNote: To microwave chicken for any recipe calling for diced cooked chicken, arrange 1 pound chicken pieces in glass baking dish with thicker parts of chicken toward edge of dish. Cover with heavy-duty plastic wrap, and vent to allow steam to escape. Microwave at HIGH for 7 minutes, turning chicken and rearranging after 4 minutes. One pound of chicken pieces with bones will yield about 1 cup diced cooked chicken; you'll get more meat if you use chicken breasts only.

ORIENTAL CHICKEN SALAD

⅔ cup orange juice
⅓ cup vegetable oil
1 tablespoon dry sherry
1 tablespoon soy sauce
½ teaspoon salt
¼ teaspoon ground ginger
¼ teaspoon garlic powder
½ pound fresh mushrooms, sliced
1 cup diced cooked chicken
1 cup cooked rice
⅓ cup diced green pepper
¼ cup toasted slivered almonds
2 tablespoons chopped green onion
¼ pound fresh snow peas, trimmed
    Bibb lettuce leaves
½ medium-size sweet red pepper, seeded and cut into strips

PINEAPPLE-ORANGE SURPRISE

1 (20-ounce) can pineapple chunks, drained
1 (11-ounce) can Mandarin oranges, drained
1 tablespoon Triple Sec or other orange-flavored liqueur
    Fresh mint leaves

1. Combine pineapple, Mandarin oranges, and liqueur in a small serving bowl, stirring gently. Chill thoroughly.
2. Garnish with mint leaves before serving. Yield: 4 servings.

Note: For variety, substitute 3 nectarines and ½ pint blueberries for the pineapple and oranges.

CHILLED SHRIMP CURRY

Chilled Shrimp and Fruit Curry
Spoon Rolls

Serves 6

Make Ahead: Cook and peel shrimp; chill. Prepare Curry Dressing, and refrigerate. **Prepare & Serve:** Bake Spoon Rolls, and assemble fruit.

Colorful Chilled Shrimp and Fruit Curry would also be a refreshing supper entrée on a hot summer day. Serve it with toasted French bread if you don't feel like baking. Serve a crisp chocolate wafer or vanilla cookie with coffee ice cream and a splash of Kahlúa for dessert.

⌨️🖥️ CHILLED SHRIMP AND FRUIT CURRY

- ½ medium head iceberg lettuce, shredded
- 2 pounds medium shrimp, cooked, peeled, deveined, and chilled
- 2 medium nectarines, peeled, seeded, and coarsely chopped
- 5 medium plums, seeded and sliced
- 2 medium nectarines, seeded and sliced
- 1 (20-ounce) can unsweetened pineapple chunks, drained
- 2 green onions, sliced
  Curry Dressing

1. Place lettuce on a large platter.
2. Combine shrimp, chopped nectarines, and plums in a large mixing bowl. Spoon shrimp mixture onto center of lettuce. Arrange nectarine slices and pineapple around edge of platter. Sprinkle green onions on top.

3. Serve with Curry Dressing. Yield: 6 servings.

MicroNote: To cook 2 pounds of shrimp for use in any recipe, arrange peeled and deveined shrimp in a single layer in a baking dish. Cover with heavy-duty plastic wrap and vent to allow steam to escape. Microwave at HIGH for 5 to 7 minutes, stirring halfway through cooking time. Let stand, covered, 1 to 2 minutes.

Curry Dressing:

- 1 (8-ounce) carton commercial sour cream
- 2 tablespoons lemon juice
- 2 teaspoons sugar
- 1¼ teaspoons curry powder
- ¼ teaspoon salt

1. Combine all ingredients in a small mixing bowl, stirring well. Cover and chill until ready to serve.
2. Serve with Chilled Shrimp and Fruit Curry. Yield: 1 cup.

SPOON ROLLS

- 1 package dry yeast
- 2 cups warm water (105° to 115°)
- ¾ cup butter or margarine, melted
- ¼ cup sugar
- 1 egg
- 4 cups self-rising flour

1. Dissolve yeast in warm water; set yeast mixture aside.
2. Combine butter, sugar, and egg; beat until well blended. Add yeast mixture; mix well. Stir in flour to make a soft dough.
3. Spoon batter into well-greased muffin pans, filling two-thirds full. Bake at 350° for 25 minutes or until lightly browned.
4. Serve warm. Yield: 2 dozen.

Note: Batter may be refrigerated for several days in an airtight container.

Brunch
or
Breakfast

Menu of Menus

No doubt the greatest luxury for time-pressed cooks is time itself. And time in the morning seems most luxurious, for the freshness of the air, the sounds of the birds, and a chance to read the newspaper can make anyone feel pampered. But there is no recipe for this indulgence. There are only such early wake-up incentives as the fragrance of Wheat-Pumpkin Muffins, the heartiness of Brunch Scramble, the Mexican flavors of Huevos Rancheros, the sweet crunchiness of a Honey-Pecan Roll . . . and many other great breakfast sensations.

Each of the menus here is presented in two ways, because not only is breakfast or brunch a pleasant time to sit with the family, but it's also the most casual meal you can share with friends. No fancy preparations or table settings are needed. A home-made bread or coffee cake is enough to supplement the ease of fruit and eggs. The full menus provide these brunch options, but the accompanying notes also suggest streamlining tactics for any-day breakfasts.

The egg dishes on these menus also translate quickly into lunch or supper fare. They go as well with salads, soups, and potatoes as they do with juice and toast. For easiest egg cookery, set aside one skillet for eggs only. You'll find that the repeated heating of butter in the pan will "season it," giving it a naturally oiled finish that prevents eggs from sticking. Don't scrub the pan or put it in the dishwasher; just wash it gently and dry well. A pan with a nonstick finish offers the same benefit when given the same careful treatment.

The quickest possible breakfast treat is a change-of-pace fruit juice. Try equal parts of grapefruit, pineapple, and orange juice, or a combination of apple, cranberry, and orange juice. When it's cold outside, think tropical with a tall glass of passion fruit juice or papaya nectar. When it's hot and muggy, enjoy the cool refreshment of apricot or pear nectar poured over ice, diluted to taste with water, and garnished with a spear of fresh melon or pineapple. For a real eye-opener, buy a juicer—simple or elaborate—and let the fragrance of fresh oranges rouse you to the day.

MAKE-AHEAD STRATA

Fresh Strawberries with Melon Balls
Cheese Strata
Fried Ham Slices
Wheat-Pumpkin Muffins

Serves 6

Make Ahead: Prepare and refrigerate Cheese Strata several hours ahead of time or overnight.
For Brunch: While Cheese Strata is baking, prepare fruit, fry ham, and mix Wheat-Pumpkin Muffins. Bake muffins after strata is removed from oven, or microwave in batches.
For Breakfast: Add bacon, sausage, or ham to the Cheese Strata, so that you can pop it in the oven when you wake up, pour some juice, make the coffee, and sit down to an all-in-one meal.

CHEESE STRATA

10 slices white bread, cubed
¼ cup butter or margarine, melted
3 cups (12 ounces) shredded sharp Cheddar cheese
3 eggs
2 cups milk
½ teaspoon salt
½ teaspoon red pepper
½ teaspoon dry mustard
½ teaspoon Worcestershire sauce
   Celery leaves

1. Toss together bread cubes and melted butter. Place half in a lightly greased 12- x 8- x 2-inch baking dish. Sprinkle half of cheese over bread cubes. Repeat procedure with remaining bread cubes and cheese.

2. Combine remaining ingredients except celery leaves; beat well. Pour over cheese layers. Cover and refrigerate 3 hours or overnight.
3. Uncover and bake at 350° for 30 to 40 minutes.
4. Garnish with celery leaves; serve warm. Yield: 6 servings.

Note: Cooked and crumbled sausage, bacon, or fully-cooked cubed ham may be layered with bread and cheese, if desired.

WHEAT-PUMPKIN MUFFINS

1½ cups whole wheat flour
1 teaspoon pumpkin pie spice
¾ teaspoon baking powder
½ teaspoon baking soda
½ teaspoon salt
2 eggs
¾ cup mashed cooked pumpkin
½ cup firmly packed brown sugar
½ cup chopped walnuts
½ cup raisins
½ cup vegetable oil
½ cup honey

1. Combine flour, pumpkin pie spice, baking powder, soda, and salt in a large mixing bowl.
2. Combine remaining ingredients in a medium mixing bowl; stir well. Add to dry ingredients; stir just until dry ingredients are moistened.
3. Spoon batter into paper-lined muffin cups, filling two-thirds full. Bake at 400° for 18 to 20 minutes.
4. Serve muffins hot. Yield: 1½ dozen.

MicroNote: To microwave step 3, spoon batter into double paper-lined muffin cups, filling half full. Microwave at HIGH for 2 to 3 minutes, rotating muffin ring a half-turn after half the cooking time. Repeat with additional batter.

MADE-TO-ORDER OMELETS

Fresh Fruit Juice
Classic Omelet and Variations
Whole Wheat Toast
Prune-Nut Bars

Serves 6

For Brunch: Make Prune-Nut Bars. Prepare filling for omelets. Invite guests to combine fillings any way they wish—such as bacon, cheese, onion, and pepper, or shrimp and chopped fresh dill. Cook omelets to order. If time allows, make Prune-Nut Bars the night before; bake and serve Double Quick Wheat Rolls (page 76) instead of toast.

For Breakfast: Made-to-order omelets are a great way to use up leftovers. Try a spoonful of crumbled blue cheese with bacon or ham, a couple of spoonfuls of spaghetti sauce, or leftover chopped broccoli or asparagus with a sprinkling of Parmesan cheese.

☺ CLASSIC OMELET AND VARIATIONS

2 eggs, lightly beaten
2 tablespoons water
  Dash of salt
  Dash of pepper
1 tablespoon butter or margarine

1. Combine eggs, water, salt, and pepper in a small mixing bowl; mix just until blended.

2. Heat butter in an 8-inch omelet pan or heavy skillet over medium heat. Pour egg mixture into skillet all at once. As mixture starts to cook, gently lift edges of omelet with a spatula; tilt pan to allow uncooked portion to flow underneath. Cook until set, but not dry.

3. Fold omelet in half; gently slide omelet onto a warm serving plate.

4. Serve warm. Yield: 1 serving.

Variations: Cheese: Sprinkle ⅓ cup shredded or sliced Cheddar, Swiss, mozzarella, gouda, provolone, or Muenster cheese over omelet before folding in half.
Meat: Sprinkle ⅓ cup cooked, drained, and crumbled sausage, bacon, or ground beef over omelet before folding in half.
Seafood: Sprinkle ⅓ cup cooked shrimp, crab, scallops, canned fish, or cooked fish over omelet before folding in half.
Vegetable: Sprinkle ⅓ cup sautéed and drained chopped onion, green pepper, or other vegetables over omelet before folding in half.
Jelly: Spread 1 tablespoon jam or jelly over omelet before folding in half. Transfer omelet to a warm serving plate, and sprinkle with sifted powdered sugar.

PRUNE-NUT BARS

1 cup all-purpose flour
1 cup sugar
½ teaspoon salt
¼ teaspoon baking powder
½ cup vegetable oil
¼ cup milk
2 eggs, beaten
1 teaspoon grated orange rind
½ teaspoon vanilla extract
1 cup finely chopped prunes
¾ cup chopped walnuts

1. Combine flour, sugar, salt, and baking powder in a medium mixing bowl, stirring well. Add oil, milk, eggs, orange rind, and vanilla, stirring until smooth. Stir in prunes and walnuts.

2. Pour batter into a lightly greased 13- x 9- x 2-inch baking pan. Bake at 350° for 35 minutes or until lightly browned. Cool in pan.

3. Cut into 2- x 1½-inch bars. Yield: about 3 dozen.

MORNING FIESTA

Golden Fruit Compote
Fiesta Scrambled Eggs
with Quick Spanish Sauce
Fried Smoked Sausage Links

Serves 6

For Brunch: Make Golden Fruit Compote ahead, and serve chilled or make it before you fry the sausage, and serve the compote warm. While Fiesta Scrambled Eggs are in the oven, pan-fry sausage and make Quick Spanish Sauce. Serve toasted buttered Italian rolls or French bread with the eggs.
For Breakfast: Cook sausage and make sauce while the eggs are in the oven.

☺ GOLDEN FRUIT COMPOTE

1 (17-ounce) can apricot halves, drained
1 (15¼-ounce) can unsweetened pineapple chunks, undrained
¼ cup raisins
1 tablespoon lemon juice
4 whole cloves
2 (2½-inch) sticks cinnamon
2 Red or Golden Delicious apples, cored and sliced

1. Combine first 6 ingredients in a medium saucepan. Bring mixture to a boil. Reduce heat; cover and simmer for 5 minutes.
2. Stir in apples. Cook 3 to 4 minutes or until apples are heated, but not soft.
3. Serve compote warm or chilled. Yield: 6 servings.

Note: Golden Fruit Compote may be stored in refrigerator for up to 1 week.

FIESTA SCRAMBLED EGGS WITH QUICK SPANISH SAUCE

2 tablespoons butter or margarine
12 eggs
¾ cup milk
¾ teaspoon salt
¼ teaspoon pepper
Quick Spanish Sauce

1. Place butter in a 13- x 9- x 2-inch baking dish; place in oven 5 minutes or until butter melts. Tilt dish slightly to coat bottom of dish.
2. Combine eggs, milk, salt, and pepper in a medium mixing bowl; beat until well blended. Pour egg mixture into baking dish. Bake at 325° for 18 minutes, stirring every 4 minutes. Bake an additional 4 minutes, stirring after 2 minutes.
3. Cut into squares, and transfer to a serving platter. Pour Quick Spanish Sauce over squares, and serve immediately. Yield: 6 servings.

Quick Spanish Sauce:

1 tablespoon butter or margarine
½ cup chopped green pepper
1 (8-ounce) can tomato sauce with onions
¼ cup chili sauce
3 tablespoons water
¼ to ½ teaspoon chili powder

1. Melt butter in a medium skillet over low heat; add green pepper, and sauté until tender. Add tomato sauce, chili sauce, water, and chili powder, and continue to cook over low heat until thoroughly heated, stirring frequently.
2. Serve warm over Fiesta Scrambled Eggs. Yield: about 1½ cups.

Quick breads start the day (clockwise from top): Cranberry Surprise Muffins, and Blueberry Muffins (page 168), Orange-Nut Loaf (page 170), Sour Cream-Praline Biscuits, and Irish Soda Bread (page 166).

A FESTIVE FRITTATA

Spinach Frittata
Baked Tomato Halves
Cinnamon Swirl Loaves
Pineapple Freeze

Serves 4

Make Ahead: Keep pineapple chunks and juice in the freezer, ready to finish making Pineapple Freeze in a matter of minutes.
For Brunch: Make Cinnamon Swirl Loaves dough. While dough is rising, prepare vegetables for Spinach Frittata. Prepare Baked Tomato Halves. Bake Cinnamon Swirl Loaves; cook Spinach Frittata. Make Pineapple Freeze at dessert time for a refreshing conclusion to this satisfying brunch.
For Breakfast: Substitute 2 cups of any chopped leftover or frozen vegetables for the spinach, mushrooms, and onion in the frittata. Reheat or sauté in butter in skillet before adding eggs.

You can make up all kinds of delicious combinations, such as diced potatoes mixed with drained chopped olives and spiced with chili powder and cumin, or frozen corn kernels mixed with diced green pepper and chopped chilies. Use a different kind of cheese on top, if you wish, such as shredded Cheddar or Swiss.

Serve with Quick Spanish Sauce (page 138) or another tomato sauce, if you wish.

Greet the morning with this bright and sunny Mexican Brunch menu (page 144). Huevos Rancheros get top billing and are served with Peach Sangría, Sliced Mango and Papaya, and Spice Cookies. For breakfast, serve 2 Huevos Rancheros per person with fresh fruit or papaya nectar.

SPINACH FRITTATA

1 (10-ounce) package frozen chopped spinach
½ pound fresh mushrooms, sliced
¼ cup finely chopped onion
1 tablespoon butter or margarine, melted
8 eggs
½ teaspoon seasoned salt
⅛ teaspoon pepper
⅓ cup grated Parmesan cheese
Fresh parsley sprigs
Sweet red pepper rings

1. Cook spinach according to package directions. Drain well, pressing out excess liquid.
2. Sauté mushrooms and onion in butter in a large skillet until tender.
3. Beat eggs in a medium mixing bowl. Add salt, pepper, and spinach, stirring well. Pour over mushroom mixture. Cook over low to medium heat 7 minutes or until eggs are almost set.
4. Sprinkle with cheese. Broil 5 to 6 inches from heating element 3 minutes or until lightly browned.
5. Cut into wedges. Garnish with parsley and pepper rings. Yield: 4 servings.

MicroMethod

1. Remove outer waxed paper covering from spinach container. Pierce container several times with meat fork. Place container on paper plate. Microwave at HIGH for 5 minutes. Drain well, pressing to remove excess liquid.
2. Microwave mushrooms and onion in butter in a 10-inch pieplate at HIGH for 1 minute or until vegetables are tender.
3. Beat eggs in a medium mixing bowl. Add salt, pepper, and spinach, stirring well. Pour over mushroom mixture. Microwave at MEDIUM (50% power) for 3 to 5 minutes, or until partially set. Lift edges to allow uncooked portion to spread evenly over dish. Sprinkle with cheese. Microwave at MEDIUM 3 to 5 minutes, or until center is almost set.
4. Same as step 5.

☺ BAKED TOMATO HALVES

½ cup finely chopped onion
2 tablespoons butter or margarine, melted
2 teaspoons prepared mustard
1 teaspoon Worcestershire sauce
2 medium tomatoes, cut in half crosswise
1 cup soft breadcrumbs
1 tablespoon chopped fresh parsley
2 tablespoons butter or margarine, melted

1. Sauté onion in 2 tablespoons butter in a small skillet until tender. Remove from heat; stir in mustard and Worcestershire sauce. Spread over cut sides of tomatoes.
2. Combine remaining ingredients, tossing lightly. Sprinkle evenly over tomatoes.
3. Place tomato halves in a 12- x 8- x 2-inch baking dish. Bake at 350° for 10 to 12 minutes.
4. Serve warm. Yield: 4 servings.

CINNAMON SWIRL LOAVES

2 tablespoons sugar
1 teaspoon ground cinnamon
½ cup raisins
1 (16-ounce) package hot roll mix
1 cup very warm water (120° to 130°)
2 tablespoons butter or margarine, softened
1 egg

1. Combine sugar, cinnamon, and raisins in a small mixing bowl; set aside.
2. Combine flour mixture and yeast from hot roll mix in a large mixing bowl, mixing well. Add water, butter, and egg; stir well.
3. Turn dough out onto a lightly floured surface; knead 5 minutes or until smooth and elastic. Cover and let rest 5 minutes.
4. Divide dough in half. Roll each half into a 13- x 8-inch rectangle. Sprinkle each rectangle with half of the reserved sugar mixture. Beginning at narrow edge, roll up dough; press firmly to eliminate air pockets. Pinch edges to seal. Place loaves, seam side down, in 2 greased 8½- x 4½- x 3-inch loafpans. Cover and let rise in a warm place (85°), free from drafts, 20 minutes or until doubled in bulk.
5. Bake at 350° for 35 minutes or until loaves sound hollow when tapped. Remove from pans, and let cool on wire racks.
6. Slice loaves, and serve. Yield: 2 loaves.

◆ PINEAPPLE FREEZE

1 (20-ounce) can pineapple chunks, undrained
8 teaspoons Amaretto or raspberry liqueur

1. Pour pineapple and juice into an 8-inch square baking pan. Freeze 2 hours or overnight.
2. Position knife blade in food processor bowl; spoon frozen mixture into processor bowl. Process until mixture is smooth and slushy.
3. Pour mixture into 4 individual dessert dishes. Spoon 2 teaspoons liqueur over each portion. Serve immediately. Yield: 4 servings.

Note: Garnish with fresh raspberries when using raspberry liqueur, if desired.

BRUNCH SCRAMBLE

Grapefruit in Champagne
Brunch Scramble
Fried Cheese Grits
Honey-Pecan Roll

Serves 8

Make Ahead: Cook grits and prepare according to Fried Cheese Grits recipe, refrigerating overnight as directed.

For Brunch: Prepare Grapefruit in Champagne ahead of time. Make Brunch Scramble, and while it is baking, assemble Honey-Pecan Roll. Complete Fried Cheese Grits. Bake Honey-Pecan Roll while Brunch Scramble and Fried Cheese Grits are being served.

For Breakfast: Serve Fried Grits with poached, fried, or scrambled eggs topped with warm taco sauce. Instead of the traditional glass of orange juice for breakfast, try this tasty vitamin C packed alternative: Brush pink or white grapefruit halves lightly with honey, and sprinkle with chopped pecans; place under broiler to heat honey and toast pecans.

GRAPEFRUIT IN CHAMPAGNE

3 large pink grapefruit, peeled and
   sectioned
1 cup pink champagne
   Fresh mint leaves (optional)

1. Combine grapefruit sections and champagne. Refrigerate grapefruit mixture several hours or overnight.

2. Spoon grapefruit mixture evenly into 8 stemmed glasses; garnish with mint leaves, if desired. Yield: 8 servings.

BRUNCH SCRAMBLE

5 eggs, beaten
1 cup milk
5 slices white bread, cubed
1 cup cubed cooked ham, chicken,
   or turkey (about 4 ounces)
1 cup (4 ounces) shredded sharp
   Cheddar cheese
1 (4-ounce) can sliced mushrooms,
   drained
¼ cup chopped onion
2 tablespoons chopped green pepper
2 tablespoons chopped pimiento
½ teaspoon salt
¼ teaspoon pepper

1. Combine eggs and milk in a large mixing bowl, beating well; add remaining ingredients, stirring well. Pour mixture into a lightly greased 1½-quart baking dish. Let stand 10 minutes.

2. Bake at 325° for 45 to 50 minutes or until set.

3. Serve immediately. Yield: 8 servings.

MicroMethod

1. Combine all ingredients in a greased 1½-quart casserole, mixing well. Let stand 10 minutes.

2. Cover casserole with waxed paper. Microwave at HIGH for 10 minutes, rotating casserole a quarter-turn and stirring every 3 minutes. Let stand, covered, 10 minutes before serving.

3. Same as step 3.

⬥ FRIED CHEESE GRITS

1 cup quick-cooking grits, uncooked
½ cup (2 ounces) shredded Swiss
  cheese (optional)
2 tablespoons crumbled, cooked
  bacon
¼ cup plus 1 tablespoon butter or
  margarine, divided

1. Cook grits according to package directions. Add Swiss cheese, if desired, bacon, and 1 tablespoon butter; stir until butter melts.
2. Pour grits into a greased 8½- x 4½- x 3-inch loafpan. Cool; cover and refrigerate overnight.
3. Remove grits by inverting pan; cut loaf into ½-inch slices. Fry slices in remaining ¼ cup butter in a large skillet over medium heat 5 to 7 minutes or until lightly browned, turning once.
4. Serve hot. Yield: about 8 servings.

HONEY-PECAN ROLL

1 (8-ounce) package refrigerated
  crescent rolls
1 cup finely chopped pecans,
  divided
¼ cup firmly packed brown sugar
2 tablespoons butter or margarine,
  softened
  Honey

1. Open crescent rolls, and spread out to a rectangle on a lightly floured surface. Roll dough to a 14- x 9-inch rectangle, pressing perforations together.
2. Combine ½ cup pecans, sugar, and butter in a small bowl; stir well. Spread over dough. Beginning at long end, roll up jellyroll fashion; pinch ends to seal. Place seam side down in a crescent shape on a greased baking sheet. Brush with honey; sprinkle with remaining pecans.
3. Bake at 350° for 20 minutes or until golden brown; cool 10 minutes.
4. Transfer to a wooden board. Slice and serve warm. Yield: one 14-inch roll.

MEXICAN BRUNCH

Peach Sangría
Huevos Rancheros
Zesty Refried Beans
Sliced Mango and Papaya
Spice Cookies

Serves 8

For Brunch: Freeze sangría base, and bake Spice Cookies ahead of time. Take sangría base out of the freezer 2 hours before serving time. Slice mango and papaya, and refrigerate. Fry tortillas; heat taco sauce, and peel avocado for Huevos Rancheros. Prepare Zesty Refried Beans, and complete Huevos Rancheros just before serving. Try topping Huevos Rancheros with Monterey Jack cheese and sliced ripe olives for extra pizzazz.
For Breakfast: Serve 2 Huevos Rancheros per person with fresh fruit or papaya nectar—you really don't need anything more!

⬥ PEACH SANGRÍA
(pictured on page 140)

1 (12-ounce) can frozen lemonade
  concentrate, thawed
1½ cups water
2 pounds (about 4 large) fresh
  peaches, peeled and sliced
2 cups fresh strawberries
1 medium orange, thinly sliced
1 medium lime, thinly sliced
1 (750 ml) bottle Burgundy or other
  dry red wine, chilled
1 (10-ounce) bottle club soda,
  chilled

1. Combine lemonade concentrate and water in a 3-quart container, stirring well;

add peaches, strawberries, orange, and lime. Freeze.

2. Remove fruit mixture from freezer 2 hours before serving.

3. To serve, place fruit mixture in a punch bowl; add wine and club soda, stirring gently to mix. Serve immediately. Yield: about 2½ quarts.

HUEVOS RANCHEROS
(pictured on page 140)

8 corn tortillas
2 tablespoons vegetable oil
½ cup commercial taco sauce
8 eggs
3 tablespoons butter or margarine, melted
½ cup (2 ounces) shredded Cheddar cheese
1 medium-size ripe avocado, peeled and cut into 16 slices

1. Fry tortillas in hot oil until crisp but not browned; drain on paper towels.

2. Place taco sauce in a small saucepan. Cook over low heat until thoroughly heated; keep warm.

3. Fry eggs in butter to desired degree of doneness.

4. Top each tortilla with a fried egg; spoon 1 tablespoon taco sauce over top. Sprinkle each egg with 1 tablespoon cheese; top each with 2 avocado slices.

5. Transfer to a serving platter, and serve warm. Yield: 8 servings.

☻ ZESTY REFRIED BEANS
(pictured on page 140)

2 (16-ounce) cans refried beans
½ teaspoon chili powder
¼ teaspoon ground cumin
1 (8-ounce) carton commercial sour cream

1. Combine refried beans, chili powder, and cumin in a medium saucepan; cook over low heat until thoroughly heated.

2. Top each serving wtih a dollop of sour cream. Yield: 8 servings.

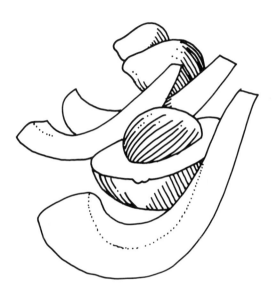

SPICE COOKIES
(pictured on page 140)

¼ cup butter or margarine, softened
¼ cup firmly packed brown sugar
1 egg
¼ teaspoon vanilla extract
½ cup all-purpose flour
½ teaspoon ground ginger
¼ teaspoon ground allspice
¼ teaspoon ground cinnamon
⅛ teaspoon ground cloves

1. Cream butter; add sugar, beating until light and fluffy. Add egg and vanilla, beating well. Add flour, ginger, allspice, cinnamon, and cloves, stirring well.

2. Drop batter by teaspoonfuls 3 inches apart onto lightly greased cookie sheets. Bake at 375° for 5 to 7 minutes or until lightly browned.

3. Remove from cookie sheets; cool on wire racks.

4. Serve on a platter. Yield: 2½ dozen.

QUICHE ANYTIME!

Quiche Lorraine
Sautéed Cherry Tomatoes
Fruit Fantasy

Serves 6

Make Ahead: Prepare and refrigerate dressing for Fruit Fantasy.
For Brunch: Bake Quiche Lorraine. Cut up fruit for Fruit Fantasy, and refrigerate. Prepare Sautéed Cherry Tomatoes.
For Breakfast: Quiche is easy if it starts with a purchased pastry shell.

QUICHE LORRAINE

  1 **unbaked (9-inch) pastry shell**
10 **slices bacon, cooked and crumbled**
  1 **cup (4 ounces) shredded Swiss cheese**
⅓ **cup sliced green onions**
  5 **eggs, beaten**
  1 **cup half-and-half**
    Dash of pepper
    Dash of nutmeg

1. Bake pastry shell at 450° for 5 minutes. Remove from oven, and let cool.
2. Sprinkle bacon, cheese, and green onions in pastry shell. Combine eggs, half-and-half, pepper, and nutmeg in a large bowl; beat well. Pour into shell.
3. Bake at 350° for 35 minutes or until set. Remove from oven; let stand 10 minutes before serving.
4. Serve warm. Yield: 6 servings.

MicroMethod

1. Microwave pastry at HIGH for 3½ to 4 minutes, turning once.

2. Sprinkle bacon, cheese, and green onions in pastry shell. Reduce number of eggs to 4, and combine with half-and-half, pepper, and nutmeg in a large mixing bowl; beat well. Pour into pastry shell.
3. Microwave at MEDIUM (50% power) for 20 minutes or until set, turning every 5 minutes. Let stand on flat surface 5 minutes before serving.
4. Same as step 4.

SAUTÉED CHERRY TOMATOES

  2 **tablespoons butter or margarine, melted**
1½ **pints cherry tomatoes, stems removed**
  1 **teaspoon dried whole basil leaves**
  1 **teaspoon dried whole tarragon leaves**
    Salt and pepper

1. Combine first 4 ingredients. Sauté 3 to 5 minutes or until thoroughly heated.
2. Add salt and pepper to taste. Serve immediately. Yield: 6 servings.

FRUIT FANTASY

½ **cup plain low-fat yogurt**
¼ **cup commercial sour cream**
  1 **teaspoon grated lime rind**
  1 **tablespoon lime juice**
  1 **tablespoon honey**
  3 **large nectarines**
  2 **large peaches**
  2 **large plums**
  2 **tablespoons lemon juice**

1. Combine first 5 ingredients in a small bowl; stir well. Cover and chill.
2. Peel and slice fruit; sprinkle with lemon juice. Cover tightly, and chill.
3. To serve, spoon chilled fruit into stemmed dessert dishes. Top with yogurt mixture. Yield: 6 to 8 servings.

Recipes to COOK Quick

A quick recipe that never fails to please is something that every cook cherishes. It's what you cook when you don't really feel like cooking, what you serve when an out-of-town cousin arrives by surprise. It's the boost you can count on to lift spirits when everyone's weary from a busy day. And it's the reassurance that somehow things do turn out all right. No cook ever gets enough of such recipes. Take time to browse the hundreds presented in this section for those that appeal most to your tastes. Here are some ways to maximize their convenience and give them greater versatility in your repertoire.

APPETIZERS

Any food that's not too sweet to blunt appetites can be served as an appetizer in small portions. In many cuisines, the most popular first courses are egg, vegetable, and seafood dishes, as these tend to be light. So you'll find recipes that can be divided into appetizer-size servings in almost every chapter in this book. Generally speaking, the portion size for an appetizer is half that for a main course. But an appetizer doesn't have to be something added to a menu. Serve a simple part of the meal, such as a salad or vegetable, and sit down to enjoy it before you get involved in preparing anything else!

BREADS

There's a built-in rhythm to baking bread that makes it ideal for informal suppers or company brunches. Whether there are only two steps involved, mixing and baking, or three, with the addition of kneading and rising, the waiting periods can be coordinated with the time needed to simmer a quick soup, assemble a main course salad, or prepare a filled omelet. The flavors and textures will harmonize beautifully, and the whole meal needn't take more than an hour to make.

ENTRÉES

Today's nutrition news points to the wisdom of eating smaller amounts of protein and fat and more complex carbohydrates. This is very good news for time-pressed cooks, since it encourages the practice of preparing one dish and serving it twice in half-size portions. Increase and vary accompanying grains, vegetables, salads, and breads to keep meals tempting. Remember that a new garnish can do wonders to pick up second-time around flavor. Some easy ones to add include pea pods, shredded carrots, and toasted bread crumbs.

SALADS

Salads can be the quickest appetite appeasers because they don't require any cooking. Plan ahead for everyday salads by making a selection of dressings when you have time. Prepare enough vegetables for several days of salads, if you wish, as soon as you unpack the groceries. Wash leafy greens, spin them dry, and refrigerate in plastic bags for two or three days. Keep crisper greens, such as iceberg and romaine lettuce, wrapped in plastic, without washing, for five or six days. Keep carrot and celery sticks, sliced radishes, and cucumber sticks wrapped in damp paper toweling and refrigerated in plastic bags for several days. But don't slice tomatoes, peppers, and other good sources of vitamin C until you're ready to eat them, as this vitamin is lost quickly when cut surfaces are exposed to air.

SOUPS AND SANDWICHES

The simplicity and hominess of soups and sandwiches can be deceptive, for they also make excellent party fare. To turn any soup, whether a light gazpacho or vichyssoise, into a buffet centerpiece, surround it with assorted garnishes, and invite guests to add their own combinations. The toppings might include croutons, chopped olives or chilies, crumbled blue cheese or bacon, toasted nuts or sunflower seeds, grated Parmesan cheese—there are scores of possibilities. Set out a carafe or two of sherry, Port, or an herb vinegar for extra seasoning power. To turn sandwiches into festive morsels, cut them into bite-size pieces. Remove bread crusts first, if you wish, and garnish serving platters with any bright fruits or vegetables.

VEGETABLES AND SIDE DISHES

It's not quite accurate to call vegetables and grains "side dishes," for balanced nutrition requires that these be mainstays of your diet. At least three one-half cup portions of vegetables and four servings of grains, including bread and cereal, are the recommended daily amounts. Protect the nutrient content and flavor of vegetables by being careful not to overcook them. Steam, blanch, stir-fry, or microwave them until they're crisp-tender. Turn Cook Quick sauces for vegetables into an infinite repertoire by varying the seasonings. To a basic cheese sauce, for example, add nutmeg to flatter broccoli, dillweed to enhance green beans, curry powder to top cauliflower, and chopped walnuts to turn baked or steamed potatoes into a whole meal.

DESSERTS

What everyone knows instinctively is that the best dessert is the one you can taste in your mind—and dig into soon after! So keep baking mixes, other pantry staples, and frozen fruits in good supply, because many Cook Quick dessert recipes rely on these for pleasures that come together almost as quickly as wishes. Easygoing, but elegant dinner hosts favor fruit desserts, including sherbets and pies, because fruit harmonizes most easily with the flavors and pace of a party menu. They also give priority to whichever type of fruit is at peak harvest, because its flavor will be a treat with just the simplest preparation. Chocolate-lovers rely on the intrinsic convenience of their favorite food, secure in the knowledge that even a pan of brownies will be fit for a connoisseur if the chocolate is of highest quality.

Appetizers

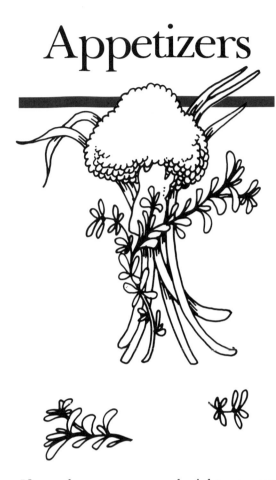

If you choose your morsels right, you can make many complete meals from the recipes in this chapter. Set out a bowl of creamy Caraway Vegetable Dip or Hot Artichoke Dip with an assortment of crisp vegetable dippers and call it a dip-your-own salad. Follow with the protein of Almond Chicken Sticks or Chile Rellenos Squares. Add a side dish of Parmesan Potato Wedges or Stuffed Mushrooms. Finish with a juicy apple or melon wedge, and all taste buds will be sated. If this sounds like a party, it's because it is—an informal gathering you can invite your family to anytime you'd like to set out some snacks, put up your feet, and call time-out for the day! Multiply the morsels to include, say, Baked Camembert in Puff Pastry or Chicken Liver Pâté, and all you need is more guests to change your lazy-day buffet into all-out entertainment.

BEEFED-UP MINI TOSTADAS

1 pound ground beef
1½ cups (6 ounces) shredded Cheddar cheese
½ cup tomato salsa
1 (16-ounce) bag round tortilla chips (about 48 chips)
Avocado Sauce

1. Cook ground beef in a large skillet over medium heat until browned, stirring to crumble. Drain off drippings. Add cheese and salsa to ground beef; stir well.
2. Arrange tortilla chips on a baking sheet; spoon about 1 tablespoon beef mixture on each tortilla chip. Bake at 350° for 5 minutes or until hot.
3. Serve immediately with Avocado Sauce. Yield: about 4 dozen appetizers.

Avocado Sauce:

1 medium avocado, peeled and coarsely chopped
¼ cup commercial sour cream
¼ teaspoon lemon juice

1. Combine all ingredients in container of an electric blender or food processor; process until smooth.
2. Spoon mixture into a small serving bowl; chill thoroughly. Yield: about 1 cup.

MicroMethod

1. Place ground beef in a colander; place colander in a 3-quart casserole. Microwave at HIGH for 4 minutes or until browned, stirring after 2 minutes to crumble meat.
2. Combine ground beef, cheese, and salsa in a small mixing bowl, stirring well.
3. Arrange 12 tortilla chips in a circle on a platter; spoon 1 tablespoon beef mixture on each tortilla chip. Microwave at HIGH for 30 seconds or until hot. Repeat procedure with remaining tortilla chips and beef mixture.
4. Serve immediately with Avocado Sauce.

BACON-CHEESE APPETIZERS

4 ounces sharp Cheddar cheese
½ cup coarsely chopped onion
½ pound lean bacon slices
   Shredded whole wheat crackers or party rye bread

1. Position shredding disk in food processor bowl, and top with cover. Cut cheese to fit food chute, if necessary. Place cheese in food chute; shred, applying firm pressure with food pusher.
2. Place onion in food chute; grate, applying firm pressure with food pusher. Remove shredded cheese and onion from processor bowl; set aside.
3. Cut bacon into 1-inch pieces. Add to cheese mixture. Position knife blade in processor bowl. Spoon mixture into processor bowl; process until smooth.
4. Spread mixture evenly over crackers or bread; place in a 15- x 10- x 1-inch jellyroll pan. Place pan 5 to 6 inches from heating element. Broil 5 minutes or until brown and bubbly.
5. Serve hot on a serving plate. Yield: about 6 dozen appetizers.

BACON-DATE WRAPS

13 slices bacon (about 1 pound)
1 (8-ounce) package pitted dates

1. Cut each slice of bacon into thirds. Wrap each third around a date, and secure with a wooden pick. Transfer to a lightly greased rack of a broiler pan.
2. Bake at 400° for 15 minutes or until crisp. Remove from rack; drain on paper towels, if necessary.
3. Arrange Bacon-Date Wraps on a serving platter, and serve hot. Yield: 39 appetizers.

Note: Keep bacon in the freezer, thaw it in the microwave just long enough to separate slices, and you'll be ready to wrap up

an appetizer anytime. Follow the method given for Bacon-Date Wraps and try wrapping up the following: drained marinated whole mushrooms or artichoke hearts; slices of deli smoked turkey, rolled up tightly; smoked oysters; partially thawed frozen cooked shrimp.

BACON-WRAPPED WATER CHESTNUT BALLS

24 whole water chestnuts
   Soy sauce
12 slices bacon, cut in half crosswise
¾ cup firmly packed brown sugar

1. Cover water chestnuts with soy sauce, and soak at least 30 minutes. Drain.
2. Cook bacon, in several batches, in a large skillet just until limp. Drain well.
3. Roll each water chestnut in brown sugar; wrap with a bacon piece. Secure with a wooden pick.
4. Place water chestnuts on lightly greased rack of a broiler pan. Bake at 400° for 20 minutes or until crisp.
5. Drain water chestnuts on paper towels, if necessary. Arrange on a serving platter, and serve hot. Yield: 2 dozen appetizers.

MicroMethod

1. Same as step 1.
2. Place half of bacon pieces on a roasting rack in a 12- x 8- x 2-inch baking dish; cover with a paper towel. Microwave at HIGH for 4 minutes, rotating rack one-half turn every 2 minutes. Drain on paper towels. Repeat with remaining bacon.
3. Same as step 3.
4. Arrange half of bacon-wrapped chestnuts in a circular pattern on rack in a baking dish. Cover with waxed paper. Microwave at HIGH for 4 to 5 minutes, rotating dish one-half turn every 2½ minutes. Repeat with remaining chestnuts.
5. Same as step 5.

CHICKEN NUGGETS

½ cup all-purpose flour
2 teaspoons sesame seeds
1 teaspoon salt
⅓ cup water
1 egg, beaten
2 boneless and skinless chicken
    breasts (about 1 pound), cut into
    1-inch pieces
2 cups corn oil
    Nippy Pineapple Sauce
    (optional)
    Royalty Sauce (optional)
    Ginger Soy Sauce (optional)

1. Combine flour, sesame seeds, and salt in a shallow bowl; stir until well blended. Add water and egg; mix well.
2. Dip chicken pieces into batter; drain off excess.
3. Heat oil to 375° in a large skillet. Fry chicken in hot oil, a few pieces at a time, until golden brown. Drain chicken on paper towels.
3. Serve with Nippy Pineapple Sauce, Royalty Sauce, or Ginger Soy Sauce, if desired. Yield: 6 appetizer servings.

Nippy Pineapple Sauce:

1 (16-ounce) jar pineapple preserves
¼ cup prepared mustard
¼ cup prepared horseradish

1. Combine all ingredients in a medium saucepan. Cook over low heat 5 minutes or until mixture is thoroughly blended and heated; stir frequently.
2. Serve hot with chicken, or refrigerate and serve over softened cream cheese as a spread for crackers. Yield: 2½ cups.

Royalty Sauce:

1 cup catsup
¼ cup plus 2 tablespoons butter or
    margarine
2 tablespoons vinegar
1 tablespoon firmly packed brown
    sugar
½ teaspoon dry mustard

1. Combine all ingredients in a small saucepan. Cook over low heat 5 minutes or until mixture is thoroughly blended and heated; stir frequently.
2. Serve hot with chicken or other meats. Yield: about 1¼ cups.

Ginger Soy Sauce:

½ cup soy sauce
¼ cup water
1 tablespoon cider vinegar
2 cloves garlic, minced
1 tablespoon minced fresh ginger or
    1 teaspoon ground ginger

1. Combine all ingredients in a small saucepan. Cook over low heat 5 minutes or just until thoroughly heated.
2. Serve warm with chicken, or use as a marinade and basting sauce for broiled chicken or fish. Yield: ¾ cup.

ALMOND CHICKEN STICKS

1 egg, beaten
1 tablespoon water
⅔ cup finely chopped toasted
    almonds
2 tablespoons all-purpose flour
½ teaspoon salt
¼ teaspoon ground ginger
1½ pounds chicken drummettes
    (about 20 drummettes)
¼ cup butter or margarine, melted

1. Combine egg and water in a small bowl; set aside.
2. Combine almonds, flour, salt, and ginger in a small mixing bowl, stirring well.
3. Dip each drummette in egg mixture; roll in almond mixture.
4. Place drummettes in a 13- x 9- x 2-inch baking dish; drizzle butter over chicken. Bake at 375° for 50 minutes or until lightly browned. Drain drummettes on paper towels.
5. Serve drummettes immediately. Yield: 20 appetizers.

SHRIMP-STUFFED SHELLS

1½ cups medium pasta shells
1 pound medium shrimp, cooked, peeled, and deveined
2 tablespoons lemon juice
1 tablespoons Dijon mustard
1 tablespoon plus 1½ teaspoons finely chopped fresh dillweed
Lettuce leaves
Lime wedges

1. Cook pasta according to package directions. Drain and rinse in cold water.
2. Combine shrimp, lemon juice, mustard, and dillweed; chill thoroughly.
3. Place 1 shrimp in each pasta shell.
4. Arrange pasta shells on a lettuce-lined plate; garnish with lime wedges. Serve with wooden picks. Yield: about 6½ dozen appetizers.

PICKLED EGGS ABLUSH

6 hard-cooked eggs
1 cup vinegar
1 cup beet juice
3 tablespoons finely chopped onion
3 whole cloves

1. Peel eggs, and place loosely in a jar; set aside.
2. Combine remaining ingredients in a small mixing bowl. Pour mixture over eggs. Seal with airtight lid. Refrigerate 2 days before serving. Store in refrigerator up to one week.
3. Serve as an appetizer or with sandwiches. Yield: 6 servings.

SCOTCH EGGS

1 pound hot bulk pork sausage
6 hard-cooked eggs, peeled
1 egg, beaten
1 cup crushed corn flakes cereal
Vegetable oil

1. Allow sausage to reach room temperature, and divide into 6 equal portions. Press each portion around each peeled hard-cooked egg. Dip each coated egg in beaten egg, and roll in crushed corn flakes cereal.
2. Deep fry eggs, one at a time, in hot oil (350°) for 3 minutes or until sausage is done. Drain well on paper towels.
3. Serve eggs hot. Yield: 6 servings.

MicroNote: To microwave step 2, omit oil and arrange coated eggs in a circular pattern on a roasting rack; cover with waxed paper. Microwave at HIGH for 6 minutes or until sausage is done, turning eggs and rotating plate every 2 minutes. Drain eggs well on paper towels.

PECAN-STUFFED MUSHROOMS

12 large fresh mushrooms
2 tablespoons chopped onion
2 tablespoons butter or margarine
⅓ cup chopped pecans
¼ cup soft breadcrumbs
1 teaspoon lemon juice
¼ teaspoon salt

1. Clean mushrooms with damp paper towels. Remove mushroom stems; set caps aside. Chop stems.
2. Add onion to chopped stems; sauté in butter in a small skillet. Add remaining ingredients; stir well.
3. Spoon pecan mixture evenly into reserved mushroom caps, pressing mixture gently into caps. Place caps on a baking sheet.
4. Broil 4 inches from heating element 3 to 4 minutes. Yield: 12 appetizers.

MicroNote: To microwave step 4, arrange stuffed mushrooms in a circular pattern on a platter. Microwave at HIGH 2 to 3 minutes, rotating platter one-half turn after 1 minute.

STUFFED MUSHROOMS

12 large fresh mushrooms (1½ to 2 inches in diameter)
 3 tablespoons butter or margarine, melted and divided
 ¼ cup fine dry breadcrumbs
 1 tablespoon chopped fresh parsley
 ¼ teaspoon dried Italian seasoning
 ¼ teaspoon salt
 ⅛ teaspoon pepper
 1 tablespoon lemon juice

1. Clean mushrooms with damp paper towels. Remove mushroom stems; set caps aside. Chop stems.
2. Combine mushroom stems, 2 tablespoons butter, breadcrumbs, parsley, Italian seasoning, salt, and pepper in a small mixing bowl, stirring well.
3. Combine remaining 1 tablespoon butter and lemon juice. Brush mushroom caps with butter mixture. Spoon stuffing mixture into mushroom caps.
4. Place mushrooms in an 8-inch square baking pan. Bake at 450° for 8 minutes or until breadcrumbs are lightly browned.
5. Serve hot. Yield: 12 appetizers.

MicroNote: To microwave step 4, arrange stuffed mushrooms in a circular pattern on a platter. Microwave at HIGH for 2 to 3 minutes, rotating platter one-half turn after 1 minute.

Note: Recipe may be doubled.

TUNA-STUFFED MUSHROOMS

2 dozen large fresh mushrooms
1 (3½-ounce) can tuna, drained and flaked
½ cup mayonnaise
3 tablespoons grated Parmesan cheese
3 tablespoons fine dry breadcrumbs
1 teaspoon minced onion
1 teaspoon lemon juice
 Pimiento strips

1. Clean mushrooms with damp paper towels. Remove mushroom stems; set caps aside. Finely chop stems and place in a medium-size mixing bowl.
2. Add tuna, mayonnaise, Parmesan cheese, breadcrumbs, onion, and lemon juice to mushroom stems; stir until well blended. Spoon 2 teaspoons mixture into each mushroom cap.
3. Place stuffed mushrooms in a 13- x 9- x 2-inch baking dish. Bake at 450° for 8 minutes or until thoroughly heated.
4. Remove mushrooms to a platter, using a slotted spoon. Garnish tops of stuffed mushrooms with pimiento strips, and serve. Yield: 2 dozen appetizers.

MicroNote: To microwave step 3, arrange half of stuffed mushrooms in a circular pattern on a large platter; cover with waxed paper. Microwave at HIGH for 2 to 3 minutes, rotating platter one-half turn after every minute. Repeat procedure with remaining stuffed mushrooms.

PARMESAN POTATO WEDGES

1 (8-ounce) carton commercial sour cream
4 slices bacon, cooked and crumbled
1 (24-ounce) package frozen potato wedges
¼ cup butter or margarine, melted
¼ cup grated Parmesan cheese
⅛ teaspoon garlic salt
 Dash of red pepper

1. Combine sour cream and bacon, stirring well; chill thoroughly.
2. Place potatoes on a baking sheet; brush with butter. Bake at 450° for 20 minutes or until crisp.
3. Combine Parmesan cheese, garlic salt, and pepper, stirring well; sprinkle over potatoes. Bake 5 minutes.
4. Serve hot with sour cream mixture. Yield: about 3 dozen appetizers.

SAY "CHEESE" TO START

One of the world's oldest "convenience foods," cheese still offers the same no-cook nutrition and flavor that has made it a staple for thousands of years. Set out a block or platter of cheese while dinner's on the stove, and diners will enjoy not only a tasty appetizer, but a nutritious protein and calcium packed one as well. Here are some simple ways to make the presentation pretty enough for a party:

• Take advantage of the natural variety of cheese shapes, textures, and flavors. You needn't add anything more to a cheese board or platter if it features contrasting selections, such as a half-moon of Longhorn or Gouda, a block of Swiss or Muenster, and a small round of Camembert or Boursin; cubes of yellow Cheddar, wedges of Brie, and slices of Swiss or provolone; a large wedge of Cheddar, smoked Gruyère sliced into squares, and round crackers spread with an herbed cream cheese.

• Use the contours and colors of vegetables, fruits, and nuts to accent cheese platters. Some fast and easy ideas are zucchini and yellow squash, sliced on the diagonal; ruffles of green or red kale; cherry tomatoes; broccoli flowerets and cauliflowerets; green and red pepper rings; an assortment of hot peppers; miniature vegetables; black, red, and green grapes; apple and pear wedges; walnut and pecan halves.

• Round up an interesting assortment of breads at the supermarket. A basketful that takes no effort and looks terrific might include small pita breads, sesame breadsticks, Scandinavian flat bread, Armenian cracker bread, bagelettes, and soft pretzels. The large discs of Scandinavian flatbread make novel serving platters for cheese.

PARTY BRIE
(pictured on page 158)

 1 (8-ounce) round fully ripened
    Brie
¼ cup honey
 2 tablespoons sliced almonds,
    toasted
    Gingersnaps

1. Place cheese on an ungreased baking sheet. Bake at 300° for 8 to 10 minutes. Transfer cheese to a serving plate.
2. Pour honey over top of cheese; sprinkle with almonds.
3. Serve warm with gingersnaps. Yield: 10 to 12 appetizer servings.

Note: For a lighter glaze, remove rind from top of Brie. Sprinkle with sliced almonds, and sift powdered sugar over top. Bake at 300° for 8 to 10 minutes. Serve with toasted French bread.

BAKED CAMEMBERT
IN PUFF PASTRY

½ (17¼-ounce) package frozen puff
    pastry
 1 (8-ounce) round Camembert, cut
    into fourths
 2 apples, cored and sliced
 2 pears, cored and sliced

1. Thaw pastry according to package directions. Unfold pastry, and cut into 4 squares. Roll each portion into a 7-inch square on a lightly floured surface.
2. Place one portion of cheese just off center of pastry square. Brush edges of pastry with water. Fold pastry over cheese, forming a triangle; press edges together to seal. Repeat procedure with remaining pastry and cheese.
3. Place one triangle on a lightly greased baking sheet. Bake at 425° for 15 minutes or until golden brown. Repeat procedure with remaining triangles as needed.
4. Serve warm with apple and pear slices. Yield: 12 appetizer servings.

CHILE RELLENOS SQUARES
(pictured on page 157)

3 cups (12 ounces) shredded
    Monterey Jack cheese
1 (4-ounce) can diced green chiles,
    drained
4 eggs, beaten

1. Sprinkle cheese and chiles evenly into a well-greased 8-inch square baking pan. Pour eggs over top.

2. Bake at 350° for 35 minutes or until set. Let stand 10 minutes before cutting into 1¼-inch squares.

3. Place squares on a serving plate. Serve warm. Yield: 3 dozen appetizers.

OLIVE QUICHE
(pictured on page 157)

1 (11-ounce) package pastry mix
6 eggs, beaten
1 (16-ounce) carton commercial sour
    cream
1½ cups (6 ounces) shredded Swiss
    cheese
2 (2¼-ounce) cans sliced ripe olives,
    drained
2 tablespoons chopped fresh chives
1 teaspoon dried whole oregano
¾ teaspoon salt
⅛ teaspoon red pepper

1. Prepare pastry mix according to package directions. Press pastry into a 15- x 10- x 1-inch jellyroll pan. Set aside.

2. Combine remaining ingredients in a large mixing bowl, stirring well. Pour mixture into prepared pastry shell. Bake at 425° for 15 minutes; reduce heat to 375°, and bake an additional 25 minutes or until filling is set.

3. Cut into 2½- x 1½-inch bars. Serve warm. Yield: 40 appetizers.

CREAM CHEESE COCKTAIL SWIRLS
(pictured on page 157)

1 (3-ounce) package cream cheese,
    softened
2 tablespoons finely chopped onion
    or 1 teaspoon onion paste
1 teaspoon milk
5 slices bacon, cooked and
    crumbled
1 (8-ounce) package refrigerated
    crescent dinner rolls
Grated Parmesan cheese

1. Combine cream cheese, onion, and milk in a small mixing bowl; beat well. Stir in bacon.

2. Separate dough into 4 rectangles; press perforations to seal. Spread 1 tablespoon plus 1½ teaspoons cream cheese mixture on each rectangle. Starting at long side, roll up rectangles, and pinch edges to seal. Cut each roll into 8 pieces.

3. Place pieces cut side down on an ungreased baking sheet. Sprinkle lightly with Parmesan cheese. Bake at 375° for 12 minutes or until golden brown.

4. Serve warm on a serving plate. Yield: 32 appetizers.

Note: This recipe can be made earlier in the day and refrigerated. Two hours before baking, remove from refrigerator and let come to room temperature. Or bake swirls, wrap in foil, and freeze. To serve, thaw in aluminum foil. Loosen wrap; reheat at 350° for 8 to 10 minutes.

SAVORY CHEESE BITES

1 **cup water**
½ **cup butter or margarine**
⅛ **teaspoon salt**
1 **cup all-purpose flour**
4 **eggs**
1 **cup (4 ounces) shredded Swiss cheese**

1. Combine water, butter, and salt in a medium saucepan; bring to a boil, stirring until butter melts. Add flour; stir vigorously until mixture leaves sides of pan to form a smooth ball. Remove from heat.
2. Add eggs, one at a time, stirring until well blended. Return to heat, and beat mixture until smooth. Remove from heat; stir in cheese.
3. Drop batter by heaping teaspoonfuls onto lightly greased baking sheets. Bake at 400° for 20 minutes or until puffed and golden brown. Remove appetizers from baking sheets, and cool completely on wire racks.
4. Transfer Savory Cheese Bites to a serving platter. Yield: about 7 dozen.

◆ CHEESE-ONION WAFERS

4 **cups (16 ounces) shredded sharp Cheddar cheese**
2 **cups all-purpose flour**
1 **cup butter or margarine, softened**
1 **(1¼-ounce) package onion soup mix**
½ **teaspoon red pepper**

1. Combine all ingredients in a large mixing bowl; beat at high speed of an electric mixer until well blended.
2. Divide dough in half. Shape each portion into a roll 1½ inches in diameter. Cover and chill thoroughly.
3. Cut dough into ¼-inch slices; place on ungreased baking sheets. Bake at 375° for 10 minutes or until lightly browned. Remove from baking sheets, and cool completely on wire racks.

4. Transfer Cheese Onion Wafers to a serving platter. Yield: about 7½ dozen appetizers.

Note: Wafers can be stored in an airtight container or frozen until needed.

SALMON-CREAM CHEESE SANDWICHES

1 **(8-ounce) package cream cheese, softened**
1 **teaspoon dried whole dillweed**
1 **(8-ounce) loaf party rye bread**
½ **pound thinly sliced smoked salmon, cut into ½-inch strips**
1 **medium-size red onion, thinly sliced, and separated into rings**
  Fresh dillweed sprigs

1. Combine cream cheese and 1 teaspoon dillweed in a small mixing bowl. Beat at medium speed of an electric mixer until mixture is light and fluffy.
2. Spread cream cheese mixture on one side of each piece of bread. Top each with a strip of salmon, an onion ring, and a dillweed sprig.
3. Place Salmon-Cream Cheese Sandwiches on a serving platter. Yield: 3 dozen appetizers.

Put together a cocktail party in record time with these easily prepared appetizers (clockwise from right): Chile Rellenos Squares, Cream Cheese Cocktail Swirls, and Olive Quiche (recipes on page 155).

HOT ARTICHOKE DIP

1 (14-ounce) can artichoke hearts,
    drained and coarsely chopped
1 cup mayonnaise
1 cup grated Parmesan cheese

1. Combine all ingredients in a small mixing bowl, stirring well to blend. Spoon mixture into a 1-quart baking dish.

2. Bake at 350° for 20 minutes or until golden brown.

3. Serve hot with assorted crackers. Yield: about 2 cups.

GARBANZO AND SESAME DIP

1 (15-ounce) can garbanzo beans,
    undrained
2 cloves garlic
¼ cup lemon juice
½ teaspoon salt
½ cup tahini (sesame paste)
1 tablespoon chopped fresh
    parsley
    Toasted pita bread wedges

1. Drain garbanzo beans, reserving bean liquid.

2. Combine beans, garlic, lemon juice, salt, and ¼ cup plus 2 tablespoons reserved bean liquid in container of electric blender; process until smooth.

3. Add tahini; process until smooth and creamy. Spoon into a small serving bowl; cover, and refrigerate overnight.

4. Sprinkle Garbanzo and Sesame Dip with parsley, and serve with toasted pita wedges. Yield: 2 cups.

Surprise your guests with this unique presentation of Party Brie (page 154); soft, creamy Brie warmed in the oven, topped with honey and almonds, and served with ginger snaps.

MEXICAN-STYLE BEAN APPETIZER

¼ cup chopped onion
1 tablespoon vegetable oil
1 (29-ounce) can pinto beans, rinsed
    and drained
1 (1.25-ounce) package taco
    seasoning mix
1 cup water
1 (8-ounce) carton commercial sour
    cream, divided
    Guacamole
1 (12-ounce) bottle tomato salsa
1 cup (4 ounces) shredded sharp
    Cheddar cheese
    Tortilla chips

1. Sauté onion in oil in a saucepan until tender. Mash half of beans; add mashed beans, taco mix, and water to onion. Cook over medium heat, stirring frequently, 10 minutes or until thickened. Remove from heat; stir in ¼ cup sour cream and remaining beans. Cool.

2. Spread bean mixture on a large platter. Top with layers of Guacamole, salsa, remaining sour cream, and cheese, making each layer smaller in diameter.

3. Serve with tortilla chips. Yield: about 7 cups.

Guacamole:

2 medium-size ripe avocados, peeled
    and coarsely chopped
1 (3-ounce) package cream cheese,
    softened
¼ cup lime juice
¾ teaspoon seasoned salt
3 to 4 drops hot sauce

1. Combine all ingredients in container of electric mixer; process until smooth.

2. Use Guacamole in Mexican-Style Bean Appetizer, or serve with tortilla chips. Yield: about 2 cups.

Note: To make fresh tortilla chips, cut corn tortillas into wedges. Fry wedges in ½-inch hot vegetable oil for 1 to 2 minutes, turning chips over once. Drain well on paper towels.

CARAWAY VEGETABLE DIP

¾ cup cream-style cottage cheese
3 tablespoons mayonnaise
2 medium carrots, scraped and cut into ½-inch pieces
3 radishes, chopped
1 tablespoon caraway seeds
½ teaspoon salt
¼ teaspoon pepper
　Additional caraway seeds
　Fresh broccoli flowerets

1. Combine cottage cheese and mayonnaise in container of an electric blender or food processor bowl; process until smooth.

2. Add carrots, radishes, caraway seeds, salt, and pepper; process 30 seconds or until well blended. Spoon mixture into a serving bowl. Cover; chill thoroughly.

3. Sprinkle dip with additional caraway seeds, and serve with fresh broccoli flowerets. Yield: about 1½ cups.

FRESH HERB DIP

1 cup mayonnaise
1 (8-ounce) carton sour cream or low calorie sour cream dressing
3 tablespoons chopped fresh parsley
2 teaspoons onion juice
¼ teaspoon salt
⅛ teaspoon pepper

1. Combine mayonnaise, sour cream, parsley, and onion juice. Blend well. Add salt and pepper.

2. Cover tightly; chill thoroughly before serving. Yield: about 2 cups.

DILL DIP

⅔ cup mayonnaise
⅔ cup commercial sour cream
1 tablespoon dried whole dillweed
1 tablespoon dried parsley flakes
1 tablespoon dried shredded green onion flakes
1 teaspoon Beau Monde seasoning

1. Combine all ingredients in a small mixing bowl; mix well. Cover and chill at least one hour.

2. Spoon dip into a small serving bowl. Serve with assorted crackers or vegetables. Yield: about 1½ cups.

Note: Dip may be served in a large, round, hollowed-out loaf of pumpernickel bread. Tear center of bread into bite-size pieces; use for dipping.

EGGPLANT CAVIAR

1 medium eggplant, peeled and diced
1 medium tomato, diced
1 medium zucchini, diced
1 medium-size green pepper, seeded and chopped
1 medium onion, chopped
2 cloves garlic, minced
1 (8-ounce) can tomato sauce
1 tablespoon red wine vinegar
¼ teaspoon dried whole basil
¼ teaspoon dried whole thyme

1. Combine all ingredients in a small Dutch oven; bring to a boil. Reduce heat; simmer, uncovered, 40 minutes, or until thickened, stirring occasionally. Cover and refrigerate overnight.

2. Serve with assorted crackers. Yield: about 4 cups.

MicroNote: Combine all ingredients in a 3-quart baking dish; cover with heavy-duty plastic wrap, and vent to allow steam to escape. Microwave at HIGH for 12 to 15 minutes, stirring every 4 minutes.

◆ SALMON CUCUMBER DIP

½ cup finely chopped cucumber
1 (7¾-ounce) can salmon, drained
 and flaked
½ cup commercial sour cream
2 teaspoons grated onion
½ teaspoon lemon juice
1 clove garlic, crushed
⅛ teaspoon dried whole dillweed
⅛ teaspoon hot sauce
 Cucumber slice

1. Place cucumber on paper towel; squeeze gently to remove excess moisture.
2. Combine chopped cucumber and remaining ingredients in a small mixing bowl; stir well. Cover and chill thoroughly.
3. Garnish with a slice of cucumber. Serve with fresh vegetables, assorted crackers, or potato chips. Yield: 1½ cups.

◆ SPICY SOUR CREAM DIP WITH BROCCOLI

1 (8-ounce) carton commercial sour
 cream
1 teaspoon prepared mustard
1 teaspoon prepared horseradish
⅛ teaspoon pepper
2½ ounces pastrami, finely chopped
1 medium bunch broccoli, broken
 into flowerets

1. Combine first 5 ingredients in a medium mixing bowl, stirring well. Cover; chill overnight.
2. Spoon dip into a serving bowl. Place bowl on a tray, and arrange broccoli around bowl. Yield: about 1½ cups.

Note: For a pretty presentation, serve dip with a combination of broccoli flowerets, cauliflowerets, and small carrot sticks. If desired, blanch raw vegetables in boiling water 1 minute, or microwave with 2 tablespoons water, covered, at HIGH for 1 minute. Rinse vegetables under cold water, and drain well.

◆ SPINACH DIP

1 (10-ounce) package frozen
 chopped spinach, thawed and
 drained
1 (8-ounce) carton commercial sour
 cream
1 cup mayonnaise
1 (8-ounce) can sliced water
 chestnuts, drained and chopped
1 (1.8-ounce) package instant
 vegetable soup mix
¼ cup finely chopped onion

1. Combine all ingredients, stirring well. Cover and chill 2 hours.
2. Spoon dip into a serving bowl. Serve with assorted crackers or fresh vegetables. Yield: about 4 cups.

◆ PIMIENTO CHEESE SPREAD

2 cups (8 ounces) sharp Cheddar
 cheese
1 cup small curd cottage cheese
1 (4-ounce) jar diced pimiento,
 drained
¼ cup mayonnaise
3 drops hot sauce
½ teaspoon salt
⅛ teaspoon pepper

1. Position shredding disk in food processor bowl, and top with cover. Cut cheese to fit food chute, if necessary. Place cheese in food chute; shred, applying firm pressure with food pusher. Remove shredded cheese from processor bowl; set aside.
2. Position knife blade in food processor bowl; add cottage cheese, shredded cheese, and remaining ingredients. Process until smooth. Cover; chill thoroughly.
3. Serve with assorted crackers, or use to stuff celery stalks. Yield: 2½ cups.

Note: For a chunkier texture, combine shredded cheese and other ingredients in a large mixing bowl; mix with an electric mixer until blended.

SMOKY SALMON CHEESE SPREAD

1 (7¾-ounce) can salmon
1 (8-ounce) package cream cheese, softened
3 tablespoons chopped green onions
6 drops liquid smoke
  Paprika

1. Drain salmon, reserving 2 teaspoons liquid in a medium mixing bowl.
2. Flake salmon, and add to reserved liquid. Add cream cheese, green onions, and liquid smoke; beat on medium speed of electric mixer until well blended.
3. Transfer mixture to a serving bowl. Cover with plastic wrap, and refrigerate at least 2 hours.
4. Sprinkle paprika over top of spread to garnish. Serve with assorted crackers. Yield: about 1¾ cups.

Note: For an attractive presentation, spoon dip into seeded green peppers cut in half crosswise. Remove a thin slice from the bottom of each half to stabilize pepper cup, if necessary. Use a mixture of green, red, yellow, and black bell peppers for the most dramatic effect.

SPICY SHRIMP SPREAD

1 (8-ounce) package cream cheese, softened
¼ cup mayonnaise
1½ teaspoons dry mustard
½ teaspoon prepared horseradish
⅛ teaspoon garlic salt
⅓ cup chopped green onions
1 pound medium shrimp, cooked, peeled, deveined, and chopped
  Green onion fan (optional)

1. Combine cream cheese, mayonnaise, mustard, horseradish, and garlic salt in a medium mixing bowl; beat well. Stir in green onions and shrimp.
2. Cover and chill at least 3 hours.

3. Spoon spread into a serving bowl, and serve with assorted crackers. Garnish with green onion fan, if desired. Yield: about 2 cups.

Note: Dress up Spicy Shrimp Spread for a party by spooning spread into a serving bowl lined with red or green kale, alternating leaves of red and green cabbage, or Belgian endive leaves. Or try spooning the spread into hollowed pineapple or melon halves lined with leafy greens, serving the cut-up pineapple or melon on the side.

CHICKEN LIVER PÂTÉ

¼ cup butter or margarine
1 pound chicken livers, drained and rinsed
¼ cup finely chopped onion
½ teaspoon salt
⅛ teaspoon pepper
2 tablespoons brandy
1 hard-cooked egg, chopped
  Fresh parsley sprigs

1. Melt butter over low heat in a large skillet. Add chicken livers, onion, salt, and pepper. Cook over low heat 10 minutes or until livers are lightly browned and onion is tender.
2. Position knife blade in food processor bowl. Spoon liver mixture into processor bowl; cover and process 10 seconds or until mixture is smooth. Add brandy, and process an additional 5 seconds.
3. Line a 10-ounce custard cup with plastic wrap. Firmly pack chicken liver mixture into custard cup, using a wooden spoon. Cover with additional plastic wrap, and chill overnight.
4. Remove plastic wrap from top of custard cup; invert custard cup onto serving platter. Remove additional plastic wrap. Let stand at room temperature 15 minutes before serving.
5. Garnish pâté with chopped egg and parsley sprigs. Serve with assorted crackers. Yield: about 1½ cups.

VEGETARIAN PÂTÉ

2 tablespoons instant minced onion
2 tablespoons water
½ pound fresh mushrooms, finely
  chopped
½ teaspoon paprika
⅛ teaspoon dried whole thyme,
  crushed
⅛ teaspoon pepper
⅛ teaspoon garlic powder
2 teaspoons dry sherry
1 hard-cooked egg, chopped
2 tablespoons commercial sour
  cream or plain yogurt
2 teaspoons parsley flakes
  Chopped fresh parsley

1. Combine onion and water; let stand
10 minutes.
2. Combine mushrooms, paprika,
thyme, pepper, garlic powder, and onion
mixture in a large skillet. Cover and cook
over low heat 3 minutes. Uncover and
continue cooking 5 minutes or until liquid
evaporates. Stir in sherry; cook 1 minute.
Remove from heat and cool.
3. Position knife blade in food processor
bowl; add mushroom mixture, egg, sour
cream, and parsley flakes. Process until
smooth. Chill thoroughly.
4. Mound pâté onto a serving plate or
serve in a small serving bowl; garnish with
fresh parsley. Serve with assorted crackers.
Yield: 1 cup.

GOUDA CHEESE BALL

1 (8-ounce) package Gouda cheese,
  shredded
3 ounces blue cheese, crumbled
2 tablespoons Chablis or other dry
  white wine
2 tablespoons butter or margarine,
  softened
1 tablespoon Dijon mustard
1 teaspoon onion powder
1 teaspoon prepared horseradish
½ teaspoon Worcestershire sauce

1. Position knife blade in food processor
bowl. Place all ingredients in food processor bowl; process until smooth.
2. Spoon cheese mixture onto heavy-
duty plastic wrap; shape into a ball. Cover
cheese ball with plastic wrap and chill thoroughly.
3. Place cheese ball on a small serving
tray. Serve with assorted crackers, pear
slices, or apple slices. Yield: 1 cheese ball.

CURRY CHEESE LOGS

1 cup pecans or walnuts
1 (8-ounce) package cream
  cheese, cut into cubes and
  softened
2 cloves garlic, chopped
1 (8-ounce) package sharp
  Cheddar cheese, cut into
  cubes
1 tablespoon mayonnaise
1 tablespoon curry powder
1 tablespoon chili powder
  Fresh parsley sprigs

1. Position knife blade in food processor
bowl; add nuts. Cover and pulse 6 to 8
times or until nuts are chopped. Add
cream cheese and garlic; process about 20
seconds, scraping sides of processor bowl
once.
2. Drop cheese and mayonnaise
through food chute with processor running; process 20 seconds, scraping sides of
bowl once. Pulse 10 to 12 times or until
mixture is well blended, scraping sides of
bowl occasionally.
3. Remove mixture from bowl, and
shape into two 6-inch logs. Wrap in waxed
paper, and chill several hours.
4. About 1 hour before serving time,
unwrap logs. Combine curry powder and
chili powder, stirring until well blended.
Roll logs in curry powder mixture, and
transfer to serving platter.
5. Garnish platter with parsley. Serve
cheese logs at room temperature with assorted crackers. Yield: two 6-inch logs.

SPICY NUTS

½ **pound whole almonds with skins
   (about 2 cups)**
½ **pound whole salted cashews
   (about 2 cups)**
3 **tablespoons butter or margarine**
1 **tablespoon liquid smoke**
1 **teaspoon garlic salt**
1 **teaspoon curry powder**

1. Combine almonds and cashews in a 15- x 10- x 1-inch aluminum foil-lined jellyroll pan; mix well.
2. Melt butter over low heat in a small saucepan. Remove from heat; add liquid smoke, garlic salt, and curry powder, stirring until well blended.
3. Drizzle butter mixture over almonds and cashews, tossing nuts lightly to coat well. Spread nut mixture evenly in pan. Bake at 375° for 10 minutes or until nuts are lightly toasted, stirring after 5 minutes.
4. To serve, transfer nuts to a serving bowl. Serve warm or let cool. Store any leftover nuts in an airtight container. Yield: about 1 quart.

Note: For a Tex-Mex variation, try substituting 1 pound pecan halves (about 4 cups) for the almonds and cashews; spice them up by adding 1 teaspoon ground cumin, ½ teaspoon ground coriander, ½ teaspoon chili powder, and ¼ teaspoon salt instead of the liquid smoke, garlic salt, and curry powder.

MicroMethod

1. Combine almonds and cashews in a shallow 1½-quart dish, mixing well.
2. Place butter in a 1-cup glass measure; microwave at HIGH for 45 seconds or until butter melts. Stir in liquid smoke, garlic salt, and curry powder.
3. Drizzle butter mixture over almonds and cashews, tossing lightly to coat well. Spread nut mixture evenly in dish. Microwave at HIGH for 5 to 6 minutes, stirring after 2½ minutes. Drain well on paper towels.
4. Same as step 4.

TOASTED PUMPKIN SEEDS

2 **cups shelled roasted pumpkin
   seeds**
1 **teaspoon salt**
1½ **teaspoons vegetable oil**

1. Combine pumpkin seeds, salt, and vegetable oil in a 13- x 9- x 2-inch baking pan; stir until seeds are well coated. Spread in a thin layer over bottom of pan.
2. Bake at 350° for 10 minutes or until toasted, stirring after 5 minutes. Drain well on paper towels.
3. To serve, transfer seeds to a serving bowl. Yield: 2 cups.

MicroNote: To microwave step 2, place pumpkin seed mixture in a shallow 3-quart dish. Microwave at HIGH for 8 to 10 minutes, stirring every 3 minutes. Drain well on paper towels.

WHEAT SNACKS

⅓ **cup butter or margarine**
1 **teaspoon onion salt**
1 **teaspoon parsley flakes**
½ **teaspoon dried whole thyme**
⅛ **teaspoon pepper**
1 **bay leaf**
3 **cups bite-sized shredded whole
   wheat biscuits**

1. Combine butter, onion salt, parsley, thyme, pepper, and bay leaf in a small saucepan; cook over low heat 3 minutes, stirring frequently. Remove from heat. Remove bay leaf and discard. Set butter mixture aside.
2. Spread biscuits over bottom of a 13- x 9- x 2-inch baking pan; drizzle butter mixture over top, tossing lightly to coat well. Bake at 350° for 15 minutes or until lightly toasted.
3. Transfer Wheat Snacks to a serving bowl, or reserve as a garnish for soups and salads. Store any leftovers in an airtight container. Yield: 3 cups.

Breads

Too busy to bake bread? Not if you've got time to watch the morning news—because that's all the time it takes to bake a batch of Applesauce Muffins or Sour Cream-Praline Biscuits. Too sleepy to mix the batter? Keep pre-mixed Prune-Bran Muffins ready to pop into the oven and waken you with their fragrance. You can put a pan of Whole Wheat Batter Bread or Cheddar-Onion Cornbread into the oven in less than 10 minutes, and the loaves will be ready to slice by the time dinner is ready. When schedules reach a yuletide frenzy, turn to the spirit-raising speed of Holiday Tea Rings for brunchtime gatherings or gifts. And whenever you have just a minute or two, make a supply of Orange Cream Spread or herbed butter to slather on your homemade bread.

CHEDDAR-ONION CORNBREAD

½ cup chopped onion
2 tablespoons butter or margarine
1 (6-ounce) package cornbread mix
2 teaspoons caraway seeds (optional)
1 cup (4 ounces) shredded Cheddar cheese

1. Sauté onion in butter in a small skillet 5 minutes or until tender.
2. Prepare cornbread mix according to package directions; add caraway seeds, if desired, stirring well. Pour batter into a greased 8-inch round cake pan. Spoon sautéed onions over batter; sprinkle with cheese. Bake at 425° for 20 minutes or until golden brown.
3. Cut into wedges, and serve hot. Yield: 8 servings.

SESAME-CHEDDAR STICKS

1½ cups all-purpose flour
2 teaspoons sesame seeds
½ teaspoon salt
1 cup (4 ounces) shredded sharp Cheddar cheese
½ cup butter or margarine
3 tablespoons Worcestershire sauce
2 teaspoons hot water

1. Combine flour, sesame seeds, and salt in a medium mixing bowl; stir well. Cut in cheese and butter until mixture resembles coarse meal.
2. Combine Worcestershire sauce and water; sprinkle evenly over flour mixture, stirring with a fork just until moistened. Shape into a ball.
3. Roll dough to ¼-inch thickness on a lightly floured surface, and cut into 3- x ½ inch strips.
4. Place strips on ungreased baking sheets. Bake at 450° for 6 to 8 minutes or until golden brown. Place on wire racks to cool. Yield: about 6 dozen.

☺ HAM-CHEESE BISCUITS

2 cups biscuit mix
½ cup minced cooked ham
½ cup (2 ounces) shredded Cheddar
   cheese
⅔ cup milk

1. Combine biscuit mix, ham, and cheese in a medium mixing bowl, stirring well. Sprinkle milk over flour mixture, stirring just until moistened.
2. Pat dough out onto a floured surface to ½-inch thickness; cut with a 2-inch biscuit cutter.
3. Place biscuits on a greased baking sheet. Bake at 450° for 8 minutes or until lightly browned. Yield: 14 biscuits.

☺ WHIPPING CREAM BISCUITS

1¾ cups all-purpose flour
2½ teaspoons baking powder
½ teaspoon salt
1 cup whipping cream

1. Combine flour, baking powder, and salt in a medium bowl; stir until well blended. Add whipping cream; stir with a fork just until moistened.
2. Turn dough out onto a lightly floured surface, and knead 4 to 5 times. Roll dough to ½-inch thickness; cut with a 2-inch biscuit cutter.
3. Place biscuits 1-inch apart on an ungreased baking sheet. Bake at 450° for 10 minutes or until lightly browned.
4. Serve hot. Yield: 1 dozen.
Variations: Bacon Biscuits: Add ⅓ cup cooked crumbled bacon to dry ingredients. Continue with recipe as directed.
Cheese Biscuits: Add ½ cup (2 ounces) shredded sharp Cheddar cheese to dry ingredients. Continue with recipe as directed.
Herb Biscuits: Add 1¼ teaspoons caraway seeds, ½ teaspoon dried whole sage, and ¼ teaspoon dry mustard to dry ingredients. Continue with recipe as directed.

SOUR CREAM-PRALINE BISCUITS
(pictured on page 139)

⅓ cup plus 2 teaspoons butter or
   margarine, melted
½ cup firmly packed brown sugar
¾ cup chopped pecans
2 cups biscuit mix
1 (8-ounce) carton commercial sour
   cream

1. Spoon 1½ teaspoons butter and 2 teaspoons sugar into each cup of a muffin pan; sprinkle 1 tablespoon pecans in each cup. Set aside.
2. Combine biscuit mix and sour cream; beat 30 seconds, using a wooden spoon.
3. Turn dough out onto a lightly floured surface; knead 5 times. Roll dough to ¾-inch thickness; cut with a 2-inch biscuit cutter. Place one biscuit in each cup of the muffin pan. Bake at 425° for 10 minutes or until golden brown.
4. Invert pan onto a serving platter. Serve biscuits immediately. Yield: 1 dozen.

IRISH SODA BREAD
(pictured on page 139)

3 cups all-purpose flour
¼ cup sugar
1 teaspoon baking soda
½ teaspoon baking powder
¼ teaspoon cream of tartar
¼ teaspoon salt
⅓ cup butter or margarine
1¼ cups buttermilk
¼ cup currants
1 tablespoon caraway seeds

1. Sift flour, sugar, soda, baking powder, cream of tartar, and salt together into a large mixing bowl; cut in butter, using a pastry blender, until mixture resembles coarse meal.
2. Add buttermilk, currants, and caraway seeds; stir with a fork just until dry ingredients are moistened. Turn dough out onto a lightly floured surface, and

knead 8 to 10 times. Shape dough into a round loaf 6 inches in diameter and 1½ inches thick; transfer to a lightly greased baking sheet. Cut a cross-shaped slash 5 inches long and ¼ inch deep in top of loaf.

3. Bake at 350° for 45 to 50 minutes. Remove bread to a wire rack to cool.

4. Slice and serve warm. Yield: 1 loaf.

WHOLE WHEAT BATTER BREAD

¼ cup sugar
1 egg
½ cup molasses
1 tablespoon vegetable oil
1 teaspoon baking soda
1 cup buttermilk
1 cup whole wheat flour
⅔ cup all-purpose flour
½ teaspoon salt

1. Combine sugar and egg in a large mixing bowl, beating well. Add molasses and oil; beat until well blended.

2. Dissolve soda in buttermilk. Add flour, salt, and buttermilk mixture to molasses mixture; beat until well blended.

3. Pour batter into a well-greased 8½- x 4½- x 3-inch loafpan. Bake at 350° for 50 minutes or until a wooden pick inserted in center comes out clean.

4. Cool completely on a wire rack. Slice and serve. Yield: 1 loaf.

APPLE MUFFINS

1¾ cups all-purpose flour
½ cup sugar
½ teaspoon salt
½ teaspoon baking soda
½ teaspoon ground cinnamon
1½ cups finely chopped, peeled apple
1 (8-ounce) carton commercial sour cream
½ cup vegetable oil
1 egg
½ cup chopped pecans
1 teaspoon vanilla extract

1. Combine flour, sugar, salt, soda, cinnamon, and apple in a large mixing bowl. Combine sour cream, oil, egg, pecans, and vanilla; add to dry ingredients, stirring just until moistened. Spoon batter into greased or paper-lined muffin pans, filling three-fourths full.

2. Bake at 350° for 25 minutes or until lightly browned. Remove from pans, and cool slightly on wire racks.

3. Serve warm. Yield: 1½ dozen.

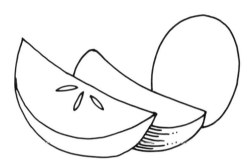

APPLESAUCE MUFFINS

2¼ cups biscuit mix
½ cup sugar, divided
2 teaspoons apple pie spice, divided
⅔ cup milk
½ cup applesauce
¼ cup butter or margarine, melted and divided
1 egg, beaten

1. Combine biscuit mix, ¼ cup sugar, and 1½ teaspoons apple pie spice in a large mixing bowl. Set aside.

2. Combine milk, applesauce, 2 tablespoons butter, and egg; add to dry ingredients, stirring just until moistened.

3. Spoon batter into greased or paper-lined muffin pans, filling three-fourths full. Bake at 400° for 20 minutes or until golden brown. Remove muffins from pan, and cool slightly on wire racks.

4. Combine remaining ¼ cup sugar and ½ teaspoon apple pie spice. Dip tops of muffins in remaining butter; dip in sugar mixture. Yield: 1 dozen.

BLUEBERRY MUFFINS
(pictured on page 139)

1¾ cups all-purpose flour
¼ cup sugar plus 2 tablespoons
    sugar, divided
2½ teaspoons baking powder
¾ teaspoon salt
¾ cup milk
⅓ cup vegetable oil
1 egg, beaten
1 cup fresh or frozen blueberries
    (thawed and well-drained)
1 teaspoon grated lemon rind

1. Combine flour, ¼ cup sugar, baking powder, and salt in a large mixing bowl. Set aside.
2. Combine milk, oil, and egg; add to dry ingredients, stirring just until moistened.
3. Combine blueberries, 2 tablespoons sugar, and lemon rind. Fold into batter.
4. Spoon batter into greased or paper-lined muffin pans, filling two-thirds full. Bake at 400° for 25 minutes or until lightly browned.
5. Remove from pan, and cool slightly on wire racks. Serve warm. Yield: 1 dozen.

BLUEBERRY-OATMEAL MUFFINS

3 cups biscuit mix
¾ cup quick-cooking oats, uncooked
½ cup firmly packed dark brown
    sugar
1 teaspoon ground cinnamon
2 eggs, well beaten
1½ cups milk
¼ cup butter or margarine, melted
2 cups fresh or frozen blueberries
    (thawed and well-drained)
Additional butter

1. Combine biscuit mix, oats, brown sugar, and cinnamon in a large mixing bowl; set aside.
2. Combine eggs, milk, and butter. Add to dry ingredients, stirring just until moistened. Fold in blueberries.

3. Spoon into greased or paper-lined muffin pans, filling two-thirds full. Bake at 400° for 15 to 20 minutes. Remove from pans, and cool slightly on wire racks.
4. Serve warm with additional butter. Yield: 2 dozen.

CHOCOLATE OATMEAL MUFFINS

¾ cup all-purpose flour
3 tablespoons cocoa
1 tablespoon baking powder
1 cup skim milk
¼ cup sugar
¼ cup butter or margarine, melted
1 egg, beaten
1 cup quick-cooking oats, uncooked
1 teaspoon grated orange rind

1. Sift together flour, cocoa, and baking powder.
2. Combine milk, sugar, butter, egg, oats, and orange rind in a large mixing bowl; stir well. Let stand 2 minutes. Stir in flour mixture.
3. Spoon batter into greased or paper-lined muffin pans, filling three-fourths full. Bake at 400° for 20 minutes or until muffins test done.
4. Remove from pan, and cool slightly on a wire rack. Yield: 1 dozen.

CRANBERRY SURPRISE MUFFINS
(pictured on page 139)

1 (3-ounce) package cream cheese
1 (16-ounce) package cranberry
    bread mix
1 cup milk
1 egg
1 tablespoon grated orange rind

1. Cut cream cheese into 12 equal cubes; set aside.

2. Combine cranberry mix, milk, egg, and orange rind; stir just until dry ingredients are moistened.

3. Spoon batter into greased or paper-lined muffin pans, filling three-fourths full. Press 1 cube of cream cheese into middle of each muffin cup, spreading batter to cover cream cheese.

4. Bake at 400° for 25 minutes or until golden brown. Remove from pan, and cool slightly on wire racks.

5. Serve warm. Yield: 1 dozen.

◆ PRUNE-BRAN MUFFINS

    1 cup boiling water
    3 cups shreds of wheat bran
        cereal, divided
2½ cups all-purpose flour
2½ teaspoons baking soda
    ½ teaspoon salt
    ½ cup butter or margarine,
        softened
1¼ cups sugar
    2 eggs
    2 cups buttermilk
    1 cup chopped pitted prunes

1. Pour boiling water over 1 cup cereal in a small mixing bowl; mix well, and set aside to cool.

2. Combine flour, soda, and salt in a small mixing bowl. Cream butter in a large mixing bowl; gradually add sugar, beating well. Add eggs, beating well.

3. Stir in reserved soaked cereal, remaining 2 cups cereal, buttermilk, and flour mixture. Stir just until dry ingredients are moistened. Fold in prunes.

4. Cover tightly with plastic wrap, and refrigerate overnight or up to 3 weeks.

5. Allow batter to stand at room temperature 5 minutes, stirring once or twice. Spoon into paper-lined or greased muffin pans, filling two-thirds full. Bake at 375° for 15 to 20 minutes.

6. Remove from pan, and cool slightly on wire racks. Serve warm. Yield: about 2½ dozen.

Mmm . . .Mmm. . . MUFFINS!

Fortunately, for all who love the flavor and aroma of hot-from-the-oven muffins, they are the easiest breads to bake. These simple steps will ensure picture-perfect results every time:

1. If your baking powder has been sitting on the shelf a long time, you might want to test its effectiveness before you begin baking. Mix 1 teaspoon baking powder with 1/3 cup warm water. If the mixture fizzes, the baking powder is still active. If not, buy a fresh supply to ensure optimum results.

2. Be lazy when you mix the batter. The dry ingredients should just be moistened, and the batter should not be perfectly smooth. If you overbeat the batter, gluten will develop in the flour, and the muffins will be tough.

3. Line the muffin pans with paper liners, or spray with vegetable cooking spray, or grease with a crumpled paper towel dipped into shortening. Don't grease any cups that won't be filled, or the grease will burn. Put a few tablespoons of water into unfilled cups to protect the pan from warping, and keep the muffins moist.

4. Fill muffin cups no more than three-fourths full.

5. To keep freshly baked muffins warm until ready to serve, tip each muffin slightly in its cup to lift it slightly away from the hot metal. Then leave the pan in the warm oven with the heat turned off.

6. To reheat leftover muffins, either wrap them loosely in aluminum foil and heat at 350° for 8 to 10 minutes, or microwave muffins at HIGH for 15 to 30 seconds per muffin, or until warm to the touch.

APPLE-DATE LOAF

1 (17-ounce) package date quick
    bread mix
½ cup milk
½ cup commercial sour cream
1 cup finely chopped, peeled apple
1 egg
½ teaspoon ground cinnamon
2 tablespoons granola cereal
    (optional)

1. Combine bread mix, milk, sour
cream, apple, egg, and cinnamon in a large
mixing bowl; stir just until dry ingredients
are moistened.
2. Pour batter into a greased and
floured 8½- x 4½- x 3-inch loafpan. Sprinkle with granola, if desired. Bake at 350°
for 1 hour and 10 minutes or until a
wooden pick inserted in center comes out
clean.
3. Cool in pan 10 minutes; remove from
pan. Cool completely on a wire rack.
4. Slice loaf, and serve. Yield: 1 loaf.

ORANGE-NUT LOAF
(pictured on page 139)

2½ cups buttermilk baking mix
⅔ cup sugar
3 eggs
2 tablespoons grated orange rind
¾ cup orange juice
¾ cup chopped pecans
    Orange Glaze
    Zest of 1 orange (optional)

1. Combine baking mix, sugar, eggs, orange rind, and juice in a large mixing
bowl; beat at medium speed of an electric
mixer 3 minutes. Fold in pecans.
2. Pour batter into a well-greased 9- x 5-
x 3-inch loafpan. Bake at 350° for 55 minutes or until a wooden pick inserted in
center comes out clean.
3. Cool in pan 10 minutes; remove from
pan, and cool completely on a wire rack.

4. Drizzle loaf with Orange Glaze, and
garnish with orange zest, if desired. Slice
loaf, and serve. Yield: 1 loaf.

Orange Glaze:

¾ cup sifted powdered sugar
3 tablespoons butter or margarine,
    melted
2 teaspoons grated orange rind
2 teaspoons orange juice

1. Combine all ingredients in a small
mixing bowl. Beat at medium speed of an
electric mixer until well blended.
2. Use immediately on Orange-Nut
Loaf or other quick breads. Yield: 1 cup.

PEANUT BUTTER BREAD

2 cups all-purpose flour
½ cup firmly packed dark brown
    sugar
1 tablespoon baking powder
½ teaspoon ground cinnamon
¼ teaspoon salt
⅛ teaspoon ground nutmeg
½ cup chopped pecans
½ cup golden raisins
1 cup applesauce
½ cup creamy peanut butter
2 eggs
    Jelly (optional)

1. Combine first 6 ingredients in a large
bowl, stirring well. Add pecans and raisins,
stirring well.
2. Combine applesauce, peanut butter,
and eggs in a small mixing bowl, beating
well; add to dry ingredients, stirring just
until moistened.
3. Pour batter into a greased 9- x 5- x
3-inch loafpan. Bake at 350° for 40 minutes or until a wooden pick inserted in
center comes out clean.
4. Cool bread in pan 10 minutes. Remove to a wire rack to cool completely.
5. Slice loaf, and serve toasted with jelly,
if desired. Yield: 1 loaf.

PUMPKIN-NUT BREAD

1 (15.4-ounce) package nut quick
   bread mix
1 cup mashed, cooked pumpkin
¾ cup milk
¾ cup chopped pecans or walnuts
1 egg
1 tablespoon pumpkin pie spice
   Sifted powdered sugar
   Cream cheese (optional)

1. Combine bread mix, pumpkin, milk, pecans, egg, and pumpkin pie spice in a large mixing bowl; stir until blended. Spoon batter into a greased and floured 8½- x 4½- x 3-inch loafpan.
2. Bake at 350° for 1 hour and 10 minutes or until a wooden pick inserted in center comes out clean.
3. Cool in pan 10 minutes; remove from pan, and cool completely on a wire rack.
4. Sprinkle with powdered sugar. Slice loaf, and serve with cream cheese, if desired. Yield: 1 loaf.

SOUTHERN
SWEET POTATO BREAD

¼ cup butter or margarine, softened
½ cup firmly packed brown sugar
1 cup mashed, cooked sweet
   potatoes
2 eggs, beaten
3 tablespoons milk
1 teaspoon grated orange rind
2 cups self-rising flour
¼ teaspoon ground nutmeg
¼ teaspoon ground allspice
½ cup chopped pecans
   Orange Cream Spread

1. Cream butter; gradually add sugar, beating well.
2. Add sweet potatoes, eggs, milk, and orange rind, mixing well.
3. Add flour, nutmeg, and allspice; mix well. Stir in pecans.

4. Pour mixture into a greased 9- x 5- x 3-inch loafpan, and bake at 350° for 55 minutes or until a wooden pick inserted in center comes out clean. Let bread cool in pan 10 minutes.
5. Remove bread from pan and cool completely on a wire rack. Yield: 1 loaf.

Orange Cream Spread:

1 (3-ounce) package cream cheese,
   softened
1 teaspoon grated orange rind
1 tablespoon orange juice
2 tablespoons sifted powdered sugar

1. Beat cream cheese; add orange rind and juice.
2. Add sugar, beating until light and fluffy. Serve spread with Southern Sweet Potato Bread. Yield: ½ cup.

ZUCCHINI BREAD

2⅓ cups buttermilk baking mix
¾ cup sugar
3 eggs
¼ cup commercial sour cream
¼ cup vegetable oil
   Grated rind of 1 orange
1½ teaspoons ground cinnamon
½ teaspoon ground nutmeg
1 teaspoon vanilla extract
½ pound zucchini, shredded
⅓ cup chopped pecans
   Softened cream cheese (optional)

1. Combine first 9 ingredients in a large mixing bowl; beat well. Fold in zucchini and pecans.
2. Pour batter into a greased 9- x 5- x 3-inch loafpan. Bake at 350° for 1 hour or until a wooden pick inserted in center comes out clean.
3. Cool in pan 10 minutes; remove from pan, and cool completely on a wire rack.
4. Slice loaf, and serve with cream cheese, if desired. Yield: 1 loaf.

EASY BUTTERMILK PAN ROLLS

3 to 3½ cups all-purpose flour,
    divided
2 tablespoons sugar
1 teaspoon salt
½ teaspoon baking soda
1 package rapid-rise yeast
1 cup buttermilk
¼ cup water
¼ cup shortening

1. Combine 1 cup flour, sugar, salt, soda, and yeast in a large mixing bowl, stirring well.

2. Combine buttermilk, water, and shortening in a small saucepan. Place over low heat until very warm (120° to 130°); add to flour mixture.

3. Blend at low speed of an electric mixer until moistened. Beat 2 minutes at medium speed. Stir in enough remaining flour to make a soft dough. Knead on a floured surface 2 minutes or until smooth.

4. Press dough evenly into a greased 9-inch square baking pan. (Sprinkle top of dough lightly with flour as you press dough into pan.)

5. Cut dough into 16 rolls with a dull knife or metal spatula, cutting almost to bottom of pan. Cover and let rise in a warm place (85°), free from drafts, 20 minutes or until doubled in bulk.

6. Bake at 400° for 12 to 15 minutes or until golden brown. Remove from pan; break apart into rolls.

7. Serve warm. Yield: 16 rolls.

Note: Use the food processor to make these rolls even easier, if you wish. Do step 1 in the food processor fitted with a plastic mixing blade, letting the machine run about 10 seconds. With processor running, pour buttermilk mixture through food chute; process until thoroughly mixed. Sprinkle 2 cups flour over batter; pulse 6 to 8 times or until flour is blended into mixture. Process 40 seconds. If dough is too wet, add additional flour, 1 tablespoon at a time, processing after each addition, until dough is soft and smooth. Proceed with recipe from step 4.

SPEEDY PECAN ROLLS

2 cups all-purpose flour, divided
1 package rapid-rise yeast
½ teaspoon salt
¼ cup plus 2 tablespoons water
¼ cup milk
¼ cup honey, divided
¼ cup plus 2 tablespoons butter or
    margarine, softened and divided
1 egg
3 tablespoons sugar
1½ teaspoons ground cinnamon
½ cup firmly packed brown sugar
½ cup chopped pecans

1. Combine 1 cup flour, yeast, and salt in a large mixing bowl, stirring well.

2. Combine water, milk, 1 tablespoon honey, and 1 tablespoon butter in a small saucepan; place over low heat until very warm (120° to 130°). Add warmed mixture and egg to flour mixture; beat at low speed of an electric mixer until dry ingredients are moistened. Beat at medium speed of electric mixer 3 minutes. Stir in enough remaining flour to make a soft dough.

3. Turn dough out onto a floured surface; knead 5 minutes or until smooth and elastic. Place dough in a greased bowl, turning to grease top. Cover and let rise in a warm place (85°), free from drafts, 20 minutes or until doubled in bulk.

4. Combine 3 tablespoons sugar and cinnamon in a small mixing bowl, stirring well; set aside. Sprinkle brown sugar evenly in a greased 13- x 9- x 2-inch baking pan; dot with ¼ cup butter. Drizzle with remaining honey; sprinkle with pecans.

5. Turn dough out onto a lightly floured surface; roll to a 12- x 8-inch rectangle. Spread remaining 1 tablespoon butter evenly over dough; sprinkle with reserved sugar-cinnamon mixture. Roll up jellyroll fashion, starting with the long side. Cut into 1-inch slices; place cut side down in pan. Let rise in a warm place (85°), free from drafts, 20 minutes or until doubled in bulk. Bake at 375° for 20 minutes or until golden brown. Invert rolls immediately onto a baking sheet.

6. Serve warm. Yield: 1 dozen.

☐ PRUNE-ORANGE ROLLS

1 (1-pound) loaf frozen bread
   dough
¾ cup pitted prunes, chopped
⅓ cup orange juice
¼ cup sugar
1 teaspoon grated orange rind
2 tablespoons butter or margarine,
   melted
   Orange Glaze

1. Thaw dough according to package directions; let thawed dough stand on a lightly floured surface 5 minutes.

2. Combine prunes and orange juice in a small saucepan; bring to a boil. Reduce heat, and simmer 5 minutes or until liquid is absorbed, stirring frequently. Remove from heat; add sugar and orange rind, stirring well.

3. Roll dough into a 12- x 6-inch rectangle; brush with 2 tablespoons melted butter. Spread prune mixture evenly over dough. Roll up jellyroll fashion, beginning at long side; pinch ends and seam to seal. Cut roll into 1-inch slices; place slices, cut side down, in a greased 9-inch round baking pan. Let rise in a warm place (85°), free from drafts, 45 minutes or until doubled in bulk.

4. Bake at 375° for 30 minutes or until rolls are golden brown. Spoon Orange Glaze over rolls.

5. Serve warm. Yield: 1 dozen.

Orange Glaze:

1 cup sifted powdered sugar
2 tablespoons orange juice

1. Combine all ingredients in a small mixing bowl, stirring well.

2. Spoon over warm Prune-Orange Rolls. Yield: about ½ cup.

MicroNote: To microwave step 3, place slices, cut side down, in a greased 9-inch round baking dish. Cover with a damp cloth. Microwave at LOW (10% power) for 10 to 15 minutes or until dough is doubled in bulk.

DON'T TOSS THAT BREAD!

Give bread that's going stale a second chance by transforming it in these ways:

● Fresh breadcrumbs. Tear slices of any kind of bread into pieces and process in the food processor or blender. Refrigerate crumbs in an airtight container up to 1 month. Use to make fine-textured stuffings for mushrooms and whole fish; as a binding for meatballs and meat loaves; and as a topping, mixed with melted butter and Parmesan cheese, for broiled tomatoes, baked eggplant, and casseroles.

● Croutons. Brush slices of day-old (or older) bread lightly with melted butter on both sides. Cut into cubes and place in a baking dish. Microwave at HIGH for 3 to 4 minutes or until lightly browned, stirring after 2 minutes. Or spread cubes in a 15- x 10- x 1-inch jellyroll pan, and bake at 300° 15 minutes; turn croutons over and bake an additional 10 to 15 minutes or until dry. Cool croutons completely; store in an airtight container up to 1 month or freeze for longer storage. Use in stuffings and to garnish soups and salads. Croutons made from raisin bread make a delicious bread pudding.

● French toast. Make French toast whenever you have a less-than-fresh loaf. Freeze leftover slices of French toast between sheets of waxed paper. To reheat one slice of French toast for a hot breakfast anytime, microwave at MEDIUM (50% power) for 30 seconds or until thoroughly heated, turning over halfway through cooking time.

● Bagel chips. Slice stale—but not rock-hard!—bagels, using the food processor. Spread slices in a 15- x 10- x 1-inch jellyroll pan, and sprinkle with seasoned salt, if desired. Toast them in a 350° oven, stirring occasionally.

HOLIDAY TEA RING

(pictured at right)

¼ cup firmly packed brown sugar
1 teaspoon ground cinnamon
1 (16-ounce) package hot roll mix
1 cup warm water (120° to 130°)
2 tablespoons butter or margarine, softened
1 egg
3 tablespoons butter or margarine, melted
¾ cup chopped walnuts
1 cup sifted powdered sugar
2 tablespoons water
  Green and red candied cherries, cut into fourths (optional)

1. Combine brown sugar and cinnamon; set aside.

2. Combine flour mixture and yeast from hot roll mix in a large mixing bowl; mix well. Add 1 cup warm water, softened butter, and egg; stir well.

3. Turn dough out onto a lightly floured surface; knead 5 minutes or until smooth and elastic. Cover dough; let rest 5 minutes.

4. Roll dough into a 17- x 10-inch rectangle on a lightly floured surface. Brush melted butter evenly over dough. Sprinkle walnuts and reserved brown sugar mixture evenly over dough.

5. Roll up dough jellyroll fashion, beginning at long side; pinch ends and seam to seal. Place roll on a greased baking sheet, seam side down; shape into a ring, and pinch ends together to seal.

6. Make cuts in dough with kitchen shears at 1-inch intervals around ring, cutting two-thirds of the way through roll with each cut. Gently turn each piece of dough on its side, overlapping slightly.

7. Cover and let ring rise in a warm place (85°), free from drafts, 20 minutes or until doubled in bulk. Bake at 350° for 20 minutes or until golden brown. Transfer to a wire rack.

8. Combine powdered sugar and water; drizzle over ring. Garnish with cherries, if desired. Slice ring, and serve warm. Yield: 1 tea ring.

APRICOT-CHEESE COFFEE CAKE

1 tablespoon graham cracker crumbs
¼ cup plus 2 tablespoons butter or margarine, divided
1 cup chopped pecans
½ cup sugar, divided
½ teaspoon ground cinnamon
2 (3-ounce) packages cream cheese, softened
2 eggs
½ cup apricot preserves
2 cups biscuit mix
⅔ cup milk

1. Lightly grease an 8-inch Bundt pan; coat with cracker crumbs. Melt 3 tablespoons butter in a small saucepan; pour into Bundt pan, tilting to coat.

2. Combine pecans, ¼ cup sugar, and cinnamon; sprinkle half of mixture over melted butter.

3. Combine cream cheese and 1 egg; beat until smooth. Set aside.

4. Place preserves in a small saucepan; cook over low heat, stirring constantly until melted. Set aside.

5. Combine biscuit mix and remaining ¼ cup sugar; cut in remaining 3 tablespoons butter with a pastry blender until mixture resembles coarse meal. Stir in milk and remaining egg. Spoon half of batter into Bundt pan; top with cream cheese mixture, ¼ cup apricot preserves, and remaining pecan mixture. Spoon remaining batter over pecans.

6. Bake at 400° for 20 to 25 minutes. Cool in pan 5 minutes.

7. Invert onto a serving plate; spoon remaining preserves over top. Yield: 1 (8-inch) coffee cake.

Right: *Decorated here for Christmas, this Holiday Tea Ring (above) could be prepared and decorated for any season.*

Page 176: *Put away your old meatloaf recipes; this Taco Meatloaf (page 177) is guaranteed to become a family favorite.*

Entrées

Pick an entrée according to your mood, your schedule, and the ingredients you have on hand. Choose the one-dish convenience of Beef-Asparagus Oriental. Or turn to such egg and cheese dishes as Ham-Spinach-Cheese Pie or Cheese Omelet Supreme when the larder is low. Cook Easy, Elegant Halibut or Grouper with Cheesy Herb Sauce in less than 15 minutes. Or guiltlessly quiet hunger pangs with the low-calorie pleasures of Chinese Chicken or Cornish Hens Ruby. Want something more romantic? Light the candles and pour the wine for Steak Diane. How 'bout something pure fun? Giant Stuffed Burger will make the kids smile. And something you can tuck in the oven and walk away from? Count on Taco Meatloaf, or hearty Corn-Stuffed Pork Chops.

TACO MEATLOAF
(pictured at left)

1½ pounds lean ground beef
1 (8-ounce) can tomato sauce
½ cup soft breadcrumbs
½ cup chopped onion
¼ cup chopped green pepper
2 tablespoons chopped green chiles
1 egg, beaten
1 (1.25-ounce) package taco seasoning mix
1 cup (4 ounces) shredded Cheddar cheese
1 (8-ounce) carton commercial sour cream
   Chili powder
   Jalapeño peppers (optional)
   Corn chips

1. Combine ground beef, tomato sauce, breadcrumbs, onion, green pepper, chiles, egg, and taco seasoning mix in a large mixing bowl; mix well. Press half of mixture into a 9- x 5- x 3-inch loafpan. Top with cheese; press remaining meat mixture over cheese.
2. Bake at 350° for 1 hour.
3. Drain meatloaf well, and invert onto a serving plate. Top with sour cream; sprinkle with chili powder. Garnish with jalapeño peppers, if desired. Serve with corn chips. Yield: 6 to 8 servings.

MicroMethod

1. Combine ground beef, tomato sauce, breadcrumbs, onion, green pepper, chiles, egg, and taco seasoning mix in a large mixing bowl; mix well. Press half of mixture into a 12-cup ring mold. Top with cheese; press remaining meat mixture over cheese.
2. Cover with heavy-duty plastic wrap, and vent to allow steam to escape. Microwave at HIGH for 15 minutes, rotating pan a half-turn after 7½ minutes.
3. Same as step 3.

Note: You may substitute ground turkey, pork, or a mixture of ground pork and lean hot sausage for the beef.

INDIVIDUAL CHILE MEATLOAVES

1 pound ground chuck
1 egg, beaten
1 tablespoon Worcestershire sauce
½ teaspoon garlic salt
¼ teaspoon pepper
1 tablespoon plus 1 teaspoon
   chopped onion
1 tablespoon plus 1 teaspoon diced
   green chiles
¼ cup (1 ounce) shredded Cheddar
   cheese, divided
   Tomato wedges

1. Combine first 5 ingredients; mix well.
2. Divide into 4 equal portions; shape each into a 5-inch patty. Spoon 1 teaspoon each of onion, green chiles, and cheese into center of each patty; fold edges over to form loaves. Seal edges.
3. Place on a rack in a shallow roasting pan. Bake at 350° for 25 minutes.
4. Arrange meatloaves on a serving plate; sprinkle with remaining cheese. Garnish with tomato wedges. Serve warm. Yield: 4 servings.

MicroNote: To microwave step 3, arrange loaves in a circle on a roasting rack; cover with waxed paper. Microwave at HIGH for 5 minutes, rotating pan one-half turn after 3 minutes. Let stand 10 minutes.

GIANT STUFFED BURGER

1¼ cups herb-seasoning stuffing mix
1 (4-ounce) can mushroom stems
   and pieces, drained
¼ cup chopped almonds, toasted
¼ cup chopped green onion
¼ cup chopped fresh parsley
⅓ cup beef broth
2 tablespoons butter or margarine,
   melted
1 teaspoon lemon juice
1 egg, beaten
2 pounds ground beef
1 teaspoon salt

1. Combine stuffing mix, mushrooms, almonds, onion, parsley, beef broth, butter, lemon juice, and egg in a medium mixing bowl; stir well. Set aside.
2. Combine ground beef and salt in a medium mixing bowl, stirring well. Divide mixture into 2 equal portions; shape each portion into an 8-inch circle. Spread stuffing mixture over one circle, leaving a 1-inch space around edge. Top with remaining circle of meat, and pinch edges to seal. Place burger in a lightly greased wire grilling basket.
3. Grill over medium coals 25 minutes or until desired degree of doneness, turning burger once.
4. Cut into wedges to serve. Yield: 6 to 8 servings.

BEEFY RICE

1 pound ground chuck
1 medium onion, chopped
1 medium-size green pepper, seeded
   and chopped
1 (16-ounce) can whole tomatoes,
   undrained and chopped
1 tablespoon chili powder
½ teaspoon garlic powder
1 teaspoon salt
4 cups shredded cabbage
3 cups cooked rice
½ cup commercial sour cream
1 cup (4 ounces) shredded Monterey
   Jack cheese

1. Sauté ground chuck, onion, and chopped green pepper in a Dutch oven until meat is lightly browned. Stir in tomatoes, chili powder, garlic powder, salt, shredded cabbage, and rice. Cover and cook over medium heat 10 minutes or until cabbage is crisp-tender.
2. Stir in sour cream. Cover and cook an additional 2 to 3 minutes. Spoon mixture into a large serving bowl. Sprinkle cheese on top of mixture.
3. Serve immediately. Yield: 8 to 10 servings.

GROUND BEEF STROGANOFF

1 **pound ground chuck**
½ **cup chopped onion**
½ **teaspoon beef-flavored bouillon
    granules**
½ **cup boiling water**
1 **(6-ounce) jar sliced mushrooms,
    drained**
½ **cup commercial sour cream**
½ **teaspoon salt**
¼ **teaspoon pepper**
3 **cups medium egg noodles (about
    6 ounces)**

1. Combine ground chuck and onion in a large skillet; cook over medium heat until beef is browned and onion is tender, stirring frequently. Drain well.

2. Dissolve bouillon granules in boiling water, stirring well. Add to skillet, and cook over high heat until liquid evaporates. Remove from heat, and stir in mushrooms, sour cream, salt, and pepper.

3. Cook noodles according to package directions, omitting salt. Drain well, and combine with beef mixture in a large serving bowl. Toss lightly to mix well. Serve immediately. Yield: 4 servings.

ROTELLE WITH BEEF SAUCE

1 **pound lean ground beef**
½ **cup chopped onion**
2 **cloves garlic, crushed**
1 **(28-ounce) can tomatoes,
    undrained and chopped**
3 **ounces prosciutto, chopped**
¾ **cup dry red wine**
¼ **teaspoon pepper**
¼ **teaspoon dried whole basil**
¼ **teaspoon fennel seeds**
¼ **teaspoon dried rosemary, crushed**
8 **ounces rotelle pasta**

1. Combine ground beef, onion, and garlic in a large skillet; cook until meat is browned, stirring to crumble. Drain well. Add remaining ingredients, except pasta.

2. Bring to a boil. Reduce heat, and simmer, uncovered, 1 hour or until thickened, stirring occasionally.

3. Cook pasta according to package directions; drain well.

4. Serve ground beef sauce over pasta. Yield: 6 servings.

▣ GROUND BEEF TERIYAKI

1 **pound ground chuck**
2 **teaspoons cornstarch**
⅓ **cup water**
⅓ **cup teriyaki sauce**
1 **(8-ounce) can bamboo shoots,
    drained**
1 **(4-ounce) can mushroom stems
    and pieces, drained**
4 **green onions, sliced**
1 **tablespoon sesame seeds**
1 **teaspoon ground ginger**
  Hot cooked rice

1. Brown ground chuck in a large skillet; drain well.

2. Combine cornstarch, water, and teriyaki sauce, stirring well. Add cornstarch mixture and remaining ingredients, except rice to meat, stirring well. Cover; cook 10 minutes, stirring occasionally.

3. Spoon over hot cooked rice. Yield: 4 servings.

MicroMethod

1. Place ground chuck in a 2-quart baking dish; cover with waxed paper. Microwave at HIGH for 5 minutes, stirring after 3 minutes. Drain well.

2. Combine cornstarch, water, and teriyaki sauce, stirring well. Add cornstarch mixture and remaining ingredients, except rice to meat, stirring well. Cover with heavy duty plastic wrap, and vent to allow steam to escape; microwave at HIGH for 4 to 5 minutes, stirring after 2 minutes. Let stand 5 minutes.

3. Same as step 3.

A CHOICE OF BEEF!

You can use various cuts of beef interchangeably if you know which ones have enough fat to cook using dry heat methods—grilling, broiling, panbroiling, and roasting—and which ones need to simmer with some liquid to make them tender.

For grilling, broiling, or panbroiling, choose: sirloin steak, rib steak, rib eye steak (also called Delmonico), loin steak (also called shell steak, strip steak), and club steak, T-bone steak, porterhouse steak, and tenderloin steak (also called filet mignon). Skirt and chuck filet steaks may be grilled or broiled if marinated first.

For roasting in the oven or on the grill, choose: rib roast, rib eye roast, and tenderloin roast. Round tip roast (also called sirloin tip), chuck blade roast or steak, chuck eye roast, rump roast, top round roast, and bottom round roast may also be cooked without added liquid, but they will not be as tender as other cuts of meat.

For pot roasts and other simmered dishes, choose: chuck arm pot-roast or steak, chuck shoulder pot-roast (also called English roast) or steak, chuck cross rib pot-roast (also called Boston or English cut roast), chuck blade roast or steak, chuck eye roast, brisket, rump roast, top round steak, bottom round roast or steak, eye of round roast, tip roast, and short ribs.

For hamburgers, choose: ground beef that has some fat in it, such as ground chuck or regular hamburger, to ensure juiciness. Leaner beef will taste dry when grilled or broiled.

For meatballs, meatloaves, and stuffings, choose: lean ground beef, such as ground round. For even leaner meat, mix equal parts of ground beef and ground veal or ground turkey.

PICCADILLO

1½ pounds ground chuck
1 medium onion, finely chopped
1 large tomato, peeled, seeded and finely chopped
1 large clove garlic, minced
½ cup chopped green pepper
⅓ cup raisins
1 bay leaf
¼ teaspoon dried whole oregano
¼ cup Burgundy or other dry red wine
¼ cup water
10 pimiento-stuffed olives, thinly sliced
3 tablespoons tomato sauce
3 to 5 drops hot sauce
½ teaspoon salt
⅛ teaspoon ground nutmeg
Hot cooked rice
Additional chopped tomato

1. Brown meat in a large skillet; drain well. Add onion, tomato, garlic, green pepper, raisins, bay leaf, and oregano. Cover and cook 10 minutes.

2. Add wine, water, olives, tomato sauce, hot sauce, salt, and nutmeg. Cover and simmer 30 minutes. Uncover and simmer until mixture thickens and liquid evaporates. Remove bay leaf; discard.

3. Serve sauce over hot cooked rice. Garnish with additional chopped tomato. Yield: 6 servings.

MicroMethod

1. Place meat in a 1½-quart casserole. Cover with waxed paper and microwave at HIGH for 3 to 4 minutes; stir well once to crumble meat. Drain well. Add onion, 1 tomato, garlic, green pepper, raisins, bay leaf, and oregano. Cover with heavy-duty plastic wrap, and vent to allow steam to escape; microwave at HIGH for 4 to 5 minutes.

2. Add wine, water, olives, tomato sauce, hot sauce, salt, and nutmeg, stirring well. Cover and microwave at HIGH 5 to 6 minutes. Remove bay leaf and discard.

3. Same as step 3.

STEAK DIANE

½ pound fresh mushrooms, sliced
1 medium onion, chopped
½ cup butter or margarine, melted
2 tablespoons Worcestershire sauce
2 (8-ounce) rib-eye steaks
¼ cup Dijon mustard
¼ cup brandy

1. Sauté mushrooms and onion in butter and Worcestershire sauce in a large skillet over low heat.

2. Flatten steaks slightly, using a meat mallet. Spread a thin layer of mustard on one side of each steak. Push mushrooms and onion to side of skillet; add steaks, mustard side down. Brown steaks 3 to 4 minutes, stirring mushrooms and onion occasionally. Spread a thin layer of mustard on top side of steak; turn and brown other side.

3. Lightly pierce steak in several places with a fork. Pour brandy over steaks; cover and simmer about 1 minute. Remove steaks to heated platter; spoon mushrooms and onion over top. Yield: 2 servings.

Note: Preparation time may be cut by substituting a 4-ounce can of sliced mushrooms, drained, for fresh ones.

CHEESE-MUSHROOM STEAK

1¼ pounds (½-inch-thick) sirloin steak
2 teaspoons Worcestershire sauce
1 teaspoon dried whole basil
8 ounces fresh mushrooms, sliced
½ cup Chablis or other dry white wine
¼ teaspoon salt
⅛ teaspoon pepper
2 tablespoons chopped fresh parsley, divided
1½ cups (6 ounces) shredded Monterey Jack cheese
1 tablespoon all-purpose flour

1. Cut steak into 4 portions. Brush both sides of each steak with Worcestershire sauce; sprinkle with basil. Place on a rack in a shallow roasting pan 2 inches from heating element. Broil 5 minutes on each side or until desired degree of doneness.

2. Combine pan drippings, mushrooms, wine, salt, pepper, and 1 tablespoon parsley in a medium saucepan. Cook over medium heat 5 minutes, stirring occasionally.

3. Spoon mushrooms over steak, using a slotted spoon; reserve liquid in saucepan. Sprinkle cheese over mushrooms. Broil an additional 5 minutes or until bubbly. Transfer to a warm serving platter; garnish with remaining 1 tablespoon parsley.

4. Add flour to cooking liquid; cook over medium heat, stirring constantly, 3 minutes or until thickened.

5. Serve steak immediately with sauce. Yield: 4 servings.

MicroMethod

1. Cut steak into 4 portions. Brush both sides of each steak with Worcestershire sauce; sprinkle with basil. Place steak in a 12- x 8- x 2-inch baking dish. Cover with heavy-duty plastic wrap, and vent to allow steam to escape; microwave at HIGH for 2 minutes. Turn steak, and rotate dish for a half-turn; microwave at HIGH 2 minutes.

2. Combine pan drippings, mushrooms, wine, salt, pepper, and 1 tablespoon parsley in a 4-cup glass measure. Microwave at HIGH for 4 minutes.

3. Spoon mushrooms over steak, using a slotted spoon; reserve liquid in glass measure. Sprinkle cheese over mushrooms. Cover and microwave at HIGH for 2 minutes or until cheese melts. Transfer to a warm serving platter; garnish with remaining parsley.

4. Add flour to cooking liquid, stirring well; microwave at HIGH for 2 minutes, stirring after 1 minute.

5. Same as step 5.

Note: To give the sauce an even richer flavor, substitute 2 tablespoons brandy for the wine. Mozzarella cheese may be substituted for the Monterey Jack.

STEAK AU POIVRE

1 (2 to 2½-pound) boneless sirloin
    steak (1½-inches-thick)
2 tablespoons cracked black pepper
¼ cup brandy

1. Rub steak on all sides with pepper; let stand at room temperature 30 minutes.

2. Place steak on grill 5 inches from medium coals. Cook 10 minutes on each side or until desired degree of doneness.

3. Transfer steak to a hot platter. Place brandy in a small saucepan; heat just until warm. Pour over steak, and ignite with a long match.

4. Serve immediately after flames die down. Yield: 8 servings.

BEEF STROGANOFF

¼ cup all-purpose flour
½ teaspoon salt
¼ teaspoon pepper
1 pound boneless sirloin steak, cut
    into ⅛-inch-thick strips
½ cup chopped onion
1 tablespoon butter or margarine
8 ounces fresh mushrooms, sliced
1¼ cups water
1½ teaspoons beef-flavored bouillon
    granules
1 tablespoon catsup
⅛ teaspoon garlic powder
½ cup commercial sour cream
1½ teaspoons lemon juice
2 tablespoons Chablis or other dry
    white wine
    Hot buttered noodles

1. Combine flour, salt, and pepper. Dredge steak in flour mixture; set aside.

2. Sauté onion in butter in a large skillet until tender. Add steak, mushrooms, water, bouillon granules, catsup, and garlic powder; stir well. Cover and cook over low heat 15 minutes, stirring occasionally.

3. Combine sour cream, lemon juice, and wine in a small mixing bowl; stir well.

Add to beef mixture, stirring well. Cook, stirring constantly, until mixture is thoroughly heated.

4. Serve immediately over hot buttered noodles. Yield: 4 to 6 servings.

MicroMethod

1. Same as step 1.

2. Combine onion and butter in a 2-quart baking dish. Microwave at HIGH for 3 minutes, stirring after 2 minutes. Add beef, mushrooms, water, bouillon granules, catsup, and garlic powder; stir well. Cover with heavy-duty plastic wrap, and vent to allow steam to escape; microwave at HIGH for 10 minutes, stirring after 5 minutes.

3. Combine sour cream, lemon juice, and wine in a small mixing bowl; stir well. Add to beef mixture, stirring well. Cover and microwave at HIGH for 4 minutes, stirring after 2 minutes. Let stand, covered, 5 minutes.

4. Same as step 4.

BEEF-ASPARAGUS ORIENTAL

1 (1-pound) flank steak
1 tablespoon vegetable oil
12 fresh spears asparagus (about ¼
    pound), cut diagonally into
    1-inch pieces
2 tablespoons Chablis or other dry
    white wine
2 tablespoons chicken broth
2 tablespoons soy sauce
1 tablespoon cornstarch
1 teaspoon sugar
    Hot cooked rice

1. Partially freeze steak, and slice diagonally across grain into thin pieces.

2. Pour oil around top of preheated wok, coating sides; allow to heat at high (350°) for 2 minutes. Add steak and asparagus, and stir-fry 2 minutes.

3. Combine wine, chicken broth, soy sauce, cornstarch, and sugar in a small mixing bowl; stir until well blended. Stir into steak. Continue to cook, stirring constantly, until thickened.

4. Spoon mixture over hot cooked rice on a serving platter. Serve immediately. Yield: 4 servings.

MicroMethod

1. Same as step 1.
2. Preheat microwave browning skillet at HIGH for 6 minutes. Immediately add steak, and stir until partially cooked.
3. Add oil and asparagus to skillet. Combine wine, chicken broth, soy sauce, cornstarch, and sugar in a small mixing bowl; stir until well blended. Add to skillet; cover and microwave at HIGH for 4 minutes, stirring after 2 minutes. Remove from microwave, and let stand, covered, 5 minutes.
4. Same as step 4.

FILET OF BEEF IN RED WINE-MUSHROOM SAUCE

      4 (6-ounce) tenderloin steaks
         (1¼-inches-thick)
         Salt
         Coarsely ground black pepper
         Vegetable cooking spray
      3 tablespoons finely chopped onion
     ¼   cup fresh mushrooms, sliced
         (about ¼ cup)
     ¾   cup Burgundy or other dry red
         wine
      1 tablespoon butter or margarine,
         softened

1. Trim any excess fat from steaks and pound, using a meat mallet, to ½-inch thickness. Sprinkle both sides of meat with salt and pepper to taste.
2. Coat a large skillet with cooking spray. Add meat, and cook over medium-high heat 9 minutes, turning every 3 minutes. Transfer meat to a warm serving platter, and keep warm. Reserve pan drippings in skillet.

3. Add onion and mushrooms to skillet; sauté in pan drippings until tender. Place mushroom mixture over top of steaks.
4. Add wine to skillet, stirring to loosen brown particles from bottom of skillet. Bring to a boil, and cook 2 minutes or until liquid is reduced to ⅓ cup. Add butter, stirring until melted and well blended.
5. Pour sauce over steaks, and serve immediately. Yield: 4 servings.

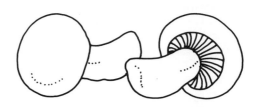

BARBECUED PORK BURGERS

    1¼ pounds ground pork
     ½   cup soft breadcrumbs
     ⅓   cup finely chopped water
         chestnuts
      2 tablespoons finely chopped green
         onions
     ½   teaspoon salt
     ⅛   teaspoon pepper
     ½   cup commercial barbecue sauce
      2 tablespoons firmly packed brown
         sugar
      2 teaspoons teriyaki sauce
      1 teaspoon lemon juice
      4 kaiser rolls, split and toasted

1. Combine ground pork, breadcrumbs, water chestnuts, green onions, salt, and pepper in a large mixing bowl; mix well. Shape into 4 patties.
2. Combine barbecue sauce, brown sugar, teriyaki sauce, and lemon juice; stir well, and set aside.
3. Place patties 4 to 5 inches from medium coals; grill 6 minutes on each side. Baste patties with sauce; grill an additional 3 to 4 minutes on each side, basting often.
4. Serve burgers on kaiser rolls with any remaining sauce. Yield: 4 servings.

Note: Burgers may be broiled in the oven.

▢ CREOLE CHOPS

4 (1-inch-thick) pork chops (about 1 pound)
1 medium onion, chopped
1 small green pepper, seeded and cut into strips
½ cup chopped celery
2 teaspoons parsley flakes
½ teaspoon salt
½ teaspoon pepper
⅛ teaspoon garlic powder
1 (14½-ounce) can stewed tomatoes
½ cup water
  Hot cooked rice

1. Brown pork chops on both sides in a large skillet. Add remaining ingredients except rice. Cover and cook over medium-low heat 35 minutes or until pork chops are tender.
2. Serve with rice. Yield: 4 servings.

MicroMethod

1. Arrange pork chops in a 12- x 8- x 2-inch baking dish. Add onion, green pepper, and celery. Cover with heavy-duty plastic wrap, and vent to allow steam to escape. Microwave at MEDIUM-HIGH (70% power) for 10 minutes, rotating dish a half-turn after 5 minutes.
2. Add remaining ingredients except rice. Cover and microwave at MEDIUM-HIGH for 16 minutes or until pork chops are tender. Let stand, covered, 10 minutes.
3. Same as step 2.

PORK CHOPS WITH FRUIT SAUCE

4 loin pork chops (about 1¾ pounds), trimmed
¼ teaspoon garlic powder
¼ teaspoon onion powder
1 tablespoon vegetable oil
½ cup apricot preserves
¼ cup water
⅛ teaspoon salt
  Fresh parsley sprigs

1. Sprinkle pork chops with garlic powder and onion powder.
2. Brown chops on both sides in hot oil in a large skillet. Add remaining ingredients except parsley. Cover and simmer 30 minutes or until pork chops are tender.
3. Remove pork chops to a warm serving platter. Cook sauce mixture over medium-high heat 3 minutes or until thickened.
4. Spoon sauce over pork chops. Garnish with parsley. Serve immediately. Yield: 4 servings.

Note: Peach preserves may be substituted for apricot preserves.

CORN-STUFFED PORK CHOPS

½ cup chopped celery
⅓ cup chopped onion
2 teaspoons butter or margarine
1 (7-ounce) can vacuum-packed corn, drained
1 cup herbed-seasoned stuffing mix
½ cup water
6 (1-inch-thick) loin pork chops (about 2 pounds), cut with pockets

1. Sauté celery and onion in butter until tender. Remove from heat, and stir in corn, stuffing mix, and water.
2. Spoon mixture into pockets of pork chops. Place pork chops in a lightly greased 13- x 9- x 2-inch baking dish. Bake, uncovered, at 350° for 1 hour or until pork chops are tender.
3. Transfer chops to a warmed serving platter, and serve immediately. Yield: 6 servings.

☐ SMOKED PORK CHOPS WITH CABBAGE SLAW

    3 cups shredded cabbage
 1⅓ cups grated carrots
    ⅓ cup chopped green or sweet red
         pepper
    ⅓ cup chopped onion
    2 tablespoons mayonnaise
    2 teaspoons prepared mustard
 1½ teaspoons Worcestershire sauce
    ¾ teaspoon sugar
    ¼ teaspoon salt
    ¼ teaspoon celery seeds
    4 smoked pork chops (about 1½
         pounds)

1. Combine all ingredients except pork chops; mix well. Place in a 10-inch square baking dish. Arrange pork chops on top of cabbage mixture.

2. Cover and bake at 350° for 30 minutes or until pork chops are tender and slaw is thoroughly heated.

3. Serve immediately. Yield: 4 servings.

MicroNote: To microwave step 2, assemble and microwave at HIGH for 6 to 8 minutes. Remove chops, and stir slaw. Return chops; cover and microwave at HIGH for 6 to 8 minutes or until slaw is thoroughly heated.

HAM-CHILI MAC

    1 (¾-pound) ham slice, cubed
    1 (16-ounce) can tomatoes,
         undrained and chopped
 1½ cups water
    1 large onion, chopped
    1 green pepper, seeded and
         chopped
    2 jalapeño peppers, seeded and
         chopped
    2 cloves garlic, minced
    1 teaspoon ground cumin
    ¼ teaspoon ground oregano
    1 (8-ounce) package elbow macaroni
    1 cup (4 ounces) shredded Cheddar
         cheese

1. Brown ham on all sides in a large skillet over medium heat. Drain off pan drippings, if necessary.

2. Add tomatoes, water, onion, green pepper, jalapeño peppers, garlic, cumin, and oregano to skillet. Cover and simmer 20 minutes.

3. Stir in macaroni; simmer, uncovered, 15 minutes, stirring often. Remove from heat; top with cheese.

4. Spoon Ham-Chili Mac into a large serving bowl, and serve immediately. Yield: 6 servings.

☐ HAM-RICE CASSEROLE

 2½ cups cubed, cooked ham
    2 cups cooked regular rice
    ½ cup finely chopped onion
    ½ cup chopped celery
    ½ cup chopped green or sweet red
         pepper
    1 (10¾-ounce) can cream of celery
         soup, undiluted
    1 cup milk
    1 egg, beaten
    ⅛ teaspoon pepper
    ½ cup (2 ounces) shredded sharp
         Cheddar cheese
    1 cup soft breadcrumbs
    2 tablespoons butter or margarine,
         melted

1. Combine ham, rice, onion, celery, green pepper, soup, milk, egg, and pepper in a large mixing bowl; stir just until blended. Pour into a lightly greased 10- x 6- x 2-inch baking dish. Sprinkle with cheese.

2. Combine breadcrumbs and butter, tossing lightly. Sprinkle over casserole. Bake at 375° for 30 minutes or until hot and bubbly.

3. Serve immediately. Yield: 6 servings.

MicroNote: To microwave step 2, microwave at HIGH for 5 to 7 minutes or until hot and bubbly.

HEARTY HAM AND BEAN SUPPER

¾ cup chopped onion
1 medium carrot, scraped and
    grated
1 clove garlic, minced
1½ teaspoons vegetable oil
½ teaspoon dried whole basil
2 (16-ounce) cans navy beans,
    drained and rinsed
1 pound cooked ham, cut into
    1-inch cubes (about 2 cups)
½ cup Chablis or other dry white
    wine
¼ cup water

1. Combine onion, carrot, garlic, oil, and basil in a large skillet; cook over medium heat until vegetables are tender.
2. Stir in remaining ingredients; bring to a boil. Reduce to medium heat; cover and cook 20 minutes, stirring occasionally. Remove cover, and cook an additional 5 minutes, stirring frequently, until mixture thickens.
3. Remove from heat, and serve immediately. Yield: 6 servings.

HAM-BROCCOLI ROLLS

8 large broccoli spears, steamed
1 (6-ounce) package sliced cooked
    ham (8 slices)
1 tablespoon butter or margarine
2 tablespoons all-purpose flour
2 teaspoons dry mustard
1½ cups milk
    Dash of salt
¼ teaspoon pepper
½ cup (2 ounces) shredded sharp
    Cheddar or Swiss cheese
    Paprika

1. Center 1 broccoli spear at short edge of each ham slice. Roll broccoli spear in ham slice tightly. Place rolls in a 12- x 8- x 2-inch baking dish, seam side down.
2. Melt butter in a heavy saucepan over low heat; add flour and dry mustard, stirring until smooth. Cook 1 minute, stirring

constantly. Gradually add milk; cook over medium heat, stirring constantly, until thickened and bubbly. Add salt, pepper, and cheese; stir until cheese melts.
3. Pour sauce over ham rolls; sprinkle with paprika. Bake at 450° for 10 minutes or until hot and bubbly.
4. Serve immediately. Yield: 4 servings.

GRILLED HAM SLICES

½ cup orange marmalade
¾ cup prepared mustard
1 teaspoon Worcestershire sauce
¾ cup plus 2 tablespoons water
6 (6- to 8-ounce) slices fully cooked
    ham (about 1 inch thick)

1. Combine marmalade, mustard, Worcestershire sauce, and water; mix well, and pour into a large baking dish. Add ham slices, turning to coat; marinate in refrigerator 1 hour.
2. Remove ham from marinade, reserving marinade for basting. Place ham 4 to 5 inches from slow to medium coals; grill 30 to 45 minutes, turning frequently and basting with marinade.
3. Serve on a warm platter. Yield: 6 servings.

HEARTY SAUSAGE SUPPER

1 pound bulk pork sausage
2 tablespoons chopped onion
2 tablespoons cracker meal
1 teaspoon steak sauce
1 (6-ounce) can unsweetened apple
    juice
1 tablespoon all-purpose flour
1 tablespoon sugar
1 teaspoon ground cinnamon
2 cooking apples, peeled, cored, and
    thinly sliced
1 tablespoon butter or margarine
2 (16-ounce) cans sweet potatoes,
    drained

1. Combine sausage, onion, cracker meal, and steak sauce in a large mixing bowl; mix well. Shape sausage mixture into 8 patties. Cook patties in a large skillet over medium heat until done, turning once. Drain patties on paper towels, and keep warm. Discard pan drippings, and wipe skillet with a paper towel.

2. Combine apple juice, flour, sugar, and cinnamon in a medium mixing bowl; stir well. Add apples; toss gently to coat.

3. Melt butter in skillet. Add apple mixture, and cook over medium heat until apples are tender and sauce has thickened. Add sweet potatoes; cover and heat thoroughly.

4. Transfer sausage patties to a warm serving platter; spoon apples and potatoes over patties. Serve immediately. Yield: 4 to 6 servings.

Note: Leftover baked sweet potatoes can be peeled, sliced, and used in place of canned sweet potatoes.

SHEPHERD'S PIE

1 cup chopped onion
½ cup chopped celery
1 tablespoon butter or margarine
1 (¾-ounce) package brown gravy
    mix
1 pound smoked sausage, quartered
    and sliced
1 (10-ounce) package frozen green
    peas, thawed
¼ teaspoon salt
⅛ teaspoon pepper
2 cups mashed potatoes, cooled
2 tablespoons chopped fresh parsley
    Paprika

1. Sauté onion and celery in butter in a large skillet until tender. Remove from heat. Prepare gravy according to package directions, and add to skillet. Stir in sausage, peas, salt, and pepper. Pour mixture into a lightly greased 10-inch deep-dish pieplate.

2. Combine mashed potatoes and parsley in a small mixing bowl; stir until well blended. Attractively spoon or pipe potato mixture around edges of dish. Sprinkle with paprika.

3. Bake at 350° for 35 minutes or until thoroughly heated.

4. Serve pie immediately. Yield: 6 to 8 servings.

Note: To speed preparation time, use instant mashed potatoes, following package directions.

LAYERED LAMB CASSEROLE

1 (17-ounce) can whole kernel corn,
    drained
1½ pounds ground lamb
1 tablespoon all-purpose flour
1 (8-ounce) can tomato sauce
1 teaspoon garlic salt
¼ teaspoon ground cinnamon
1 (12-ounce) carton small curd
    cottage cheese
2 eggs, beaten
1 tablespoon chopped fresh chives
1 (4-ounce) package shredded
    mozzarella cheese
¼ cup grated Parmesan cheese
2 tablespoons slivered almonds,
    toasted

1. Spread corn evenly in a 10- x 6- x 2-inch baking dish; set aside.

2. Brown meat in a large skillet over medium heat, stirring to crumble; drain off pan drippings. Add flour to meat; cook, stirring constantly, over medium heat 1 minute. Remove from heat. Add tomato sauce, garlic salt, and cinnamon, stirring well. Spoon mixture evenly over corn. Bake at 350° for 15 minutes.

3. Combine cottage cheese, eggs, and chives in a medium mixing bowl; mix well. Spoon mixture evenly over meat mixture. Sprinkle with cheese and almonds. Bake an additional 20 minutes or until bubbly and browned.

4. Serve hot. Yield: 6 to 8 servings.

☐ MIDDLE EASTERN LAMB AND EGGPLANT

(pictured on page 194)

1 pound ground lamb
1 medium eggplant, peeled and
   cubed
3 medium tomatoes, peeled, seeded,
   and chopped
1 tablespoon dried whole
   oregano
2 teaspoons curry powder
1½ teaspoons dried whole thyme
1 teaspoon ground cardamom
½ teaspoon rubbed sage
2 cloves garlic, crushed
1 medium-size green pepper, seeded
   and chopped
¼ cup chopped fresh parsley,
   divided
1 tablespoon lemon juice
   Hot cooked brown rice
2 tablespoons chopped walnuts

1. Brown meat in a skillet over medium heat, stirring to crumble; drain.
2. Add next 8 ingredients to meat in skillet; stir well. Cover and cook over medium heat 10 minutes, stirring occasionally. Add green pepper; cover and cook 5 minutes or until pepper is tender. Stir in 2 tablespoons parsley and lemon juice.
3. Serve over hot cooked brown rice. Garnish with remaining 2 tablespoons parsley and walnuts. Yield: 6 servings.

MicroMethod

1. Place meat in a 3-quart baking dish; cover with waxed paper, and microwave at HIGH for 5 minutes, stirring every 2 minutes. Drain off pan drippings.
2. Add eggplant, tomatoes, oregano, curry, thyme, cardamom, sage, and garlic; stir well. Cover with heavy-duty plastic wrap, venting to allow steam to escape, and microwave at HIGH for 5 minutes, stirring every 2 minutes. Add green pepper; cover and microwave at HIGH for 5 minutes. Stir in 2 tablespoons parsley and lemon juice.
3. Same as step 3.

◆ EPICUREAN LAMB RIB CHOPS

8 (1-inch-thick) lamb rib chops
½ cup Chablis or other dry white
   wine
½ cup olive oil
2 bay leaves, crumbled
1 tablespoon parsley flakes
1 teaspoon dried whole oregano
¼ teaspoon garlic powder
½ teaspoon salt

1. Trim any excess fat from chops. Place in a 12- x 8- x 2-inch baking dish. Combine remaining ingredients in a small mixing bowl; stir well. Pour marinade over chops; cover and refrigerate overnight.
2. Place chops on rack in a shallow roasting pan. Broil chops 4 to 5 inches from heating element 5 minutes. Turn and brush with marinade; broil an additional 5 minutes or until desired degree of doneness.
3. Serve hot. Yield: 4 servings.

Note: Epicurean Lamb Rib Chops may be grilled. Place chops on grill over medium coals. Grill chops 5 to 6 minutes on each side, or until desired degree of doneness, brushing occasionally with marinade.

LAMB LOIN CHOPS WITH HERB BUTTER

¼ cup butter or margarine, softened
½ teaspoon dried whole thyme
8 (1-inch-thick) lamb loin chops
   Salt and pepper to taste

1. Combine butter and thyme in a small mixing bowl; stir well. Set aside.
2. Place chops on grill over medium coals. Grill 8 minutes on each side or until desired degree of doneness.
3. Sprinkle with salt and pepper to taste, and brush with butter mixture. Serve immediately. Yield: 4 servings.

TERIYAKI LAMB SHOULDER CHOPS

4 (¾-inch-thick) lamb shoulder
  chops
½ cup soy sauce
¼ cup pineapple juice
2 tablespoons firmly packed brown
  sugar
½ teaspoon garlic powder
½ teaspoon ground ginger

1. Trim any excess fat from chops. Place
chops in a 13- x 9- x 2-inch baking dish.
Combine remaining ingredients in a small
mixing bowl; stir well. Pour marinade over
chops; cover and refrigerate overnight.
2. Place chops on rack in a shallow
roasting pan. Broil chops 4 to 5 inches
from heating element 5 minutes on each
side or until desired degree of doneness.
3. Serve hot. Yield: 4 servings.

COUNTRY CASSEROLE

½ pound lean ground veal
½ pound lean ground pork
½ teaspoon salt
¼ teaspoon onion powder
⅛ teaspoon ground nutmeg
1 (16-ounce) can sauerkraut, rinsed
  and drained
1 large cooking apple, peeled, cored
  and diced

1. Combine veal, pork, salt, onion powder, and nutmeg; mix well. Shape into 16
(1½-inch) balls. Brown meatballs on all
sides in a large skillet over high heat.
2. Combine sauerkraut and apple in a
10- x 6- x 2-inch baking dish. Arrange
meatballs on top. Bake at 375° for 20 minutes. Yield: 4 servings.

PASTA, PEPPERS 'N VEAL

2 cups coarsely chopped green
  pepper
½ cup chopped onion
2 cloves garlic, minced
1 tablespoon vegetable oil
1 (15-ounce) can tomato sauce
½ pound lean, boneless veal, cut
  into ½-inch cubes
½ teaspoon dried whole basil
½ teaspoon dried whole oregano
¼ teaspoon salt
8 ounces rigatoni, mostaccioli or
  other pasta

1. Sauté green pepper, onion, and garlic in oil in a large skillet until tender. Add
tomato sauce, veal, basil, oregano, and salt.
Bring to a boil. Reduce heat; cover and
simmer 20 minutes.
2. Cook rigatoni according to package
directions. Drain well. Serve veal sauce
over pasta. Yield: 4 servings.

MORE FLAVOR FROM LAMB AND VEAL

To get the most pleasure from lamb
and veal, follow these tips:

● Large cuts of lamb benefit from
standing in the refrigerator for 3 to 5
days before cooking. To enhance flavors,
rub herbs and grated lemon rind into
the meat, and marinate in red wine,
turning once a day.

● Rib and loin cuts of lamb are juicy
enough to broil; rib and loin veal chops
tend to dry out when broiled, but may
be pan-fried. Less-tender blade, arm,
and sirloin chops and steaks should be
marinated before broiling, or braised.

● Veal scallops will not be tender
enough to sauté unless cut across the
grain; check before you buy.

VEAL MARSALA

1 pound (⅜-inch-thick) veal cutlets
1 tablespoon all-purpose flour
¼ teaspoon salt
⅛ teaspoon pepper
¼ cup butter or margarine
8 ounces fresh mushrooms, sliced
1 medium onion, sliced
¼ cup Marsala wine
¼ cup chicken broth
   Lemon wedges (optional)

1. Pound veal cutlets to ¼-inch thickness, using a meat mallet. Combine flour, salt, and pepper. Dredge cutlets in flour mixture.

2. Melt butter in a large skillet over medium heat. Add veal; cook 1 minute on each side or until lightly browned. Remove veal from skillet; set aside. Reserve pan drippings.

3. Add mushrooms and onion to skillet; sauté 5 minutes or until tender. Add Marsala and chicken broth, stirring well. Arrange veal over mushroom mixture. Cover and simmer 5 minutes.

4. Remove cutlets to a serving platter; spoon mushroom mixture over cutlets. Garnish with lemon wedges, if desired. Serve immediately. Yield: 4 servings.

JULIENNE OF VEAL

1 pound (½-inch-thick) veal cutlets
½ teaspoon paprika
½ teaspoon salt
¼ teaspoon pepper
2 tablespoons butter or margarine
¼ pound fresh mushrooms, sliced
2 tablespoons chopped green onions
2 tablespoons all-purpose flour
½ cup whipping cream
¼ cup Chablis or other dry white
   wine
2 tablespoons brandy
   Hot cooked noodles

1. Flatten veal to ¼-inch thickness, using a meat mallet. Sprinkle both sides of cutlets with paprika, salt, and pepper. Cut meat into strips ¼-inch wide and 1½-inches long; set aside.

2. Melt butter in a large skillet over medium heat. Add mushrooms and green onions; sauté 5 minutes or until tender. Add veal strips, and cook, stirring occasionally, 5 minutes or until done. Remove veal and vegetables from skillet, using a slotted spoon; reserve pan drippings in skillet.

3. Add flour to drippings, stirring well. Stir in whipping cream and Chablis. Cook, stirring constantly, 5 minutes or until sauce is thickened.

4. Add reserved veal and vegetables and brandy to sauce, stirring well. Cook over medium heat until thoroughly heated.

5. Serve immediately over hot cooked noodles. Yield: 4 servings.

VEAL AND VEGETABLE SKILLET

6 (¾-inch-thick) loin veal chops
   (about 1½ pounds)
1 tablespoon vegetable oil
1 teaspoon salt
½ teaspoon pepper
½ teaspoon dried whole oregano
2 medium onions, peeled and sliced
1 (4-ounce) can sliced mushrooms,
   undrained
1 cup chicken broth
1 (4-ounce) jar sliced pimiento,
   drained
1 (9-ounce) package frozen green
   beans

1. Brown veal chops in hot oil in a large skillet over medium heat. Sprinkle chops with salt, pepper, and oregano. Add onion, mushrooms, and broth. Cover and simmer 20 minutes.

2. Add pimiento and green beans. Cover and simmer 10 minutes or until veal is tender. Yield: 6 servings.

Note: Pork chops may be substituted for veal chops.

CHINESE CHICKEN

1 (3-pound) broiler-fryer
¾ cup soy sauce
¼ cup sherry
¼ cup water
¼ cup chopped green onions
3 cloves garlic, minced
1 tablespoon sugar
1 teaspoon grated fresh gingerroot
  Commercial Chinese noodles,
    cooked

1. Place chicken, breast side down, in a large Dutch oven.
2. Combine remaining ingredients except noodles; pour mixture over chicken.
3. Cover and simmer 30 minutes. Turn chicken, and simmer an additional 30 minutes or until chicken is tender. Remove chicken from pot, discarding liquid.
4. Serve chicken on a serving platter with Chinese noodles. Yield: 4 servings.

Note: Hot cooked rice may be substituted for Chinese noodles.

TERRACE BARBECUED CHICKEN

1 (2- to 2½-pound) broiler-fryer, cut
  up
1 teaspoon garlic powder
1 teaspoon onion powder
1 teaspoon paprika
½ teaspoon pepper
2 tablespoons lime juice
½ cup commercial barbecue sauce
¼ cup Chablis or other dry white
    wine

1. Arrange chicken in a 13- x 9- x 2-inch baking dish; sprinkle with garlic powder, onion powder, paprika, and pepper. Pour lime juice over chicken.
2. Combine barbecue sauce and wine, stirring well; pour over chicken. Cover and refrigerate overnight.

3. Remove chicken from marinade, reserving marinade. Grill over medium coals 45 minutes or until tender, turning chicken frequently. Baste with marinade during last 15 minutes of cooking.
4. Remove chicken from grill, and transfer to a serving platter. Serve warm. Yield: 4 servings.

RANCHER'S CHICKEN
(pictured on page 193)

1 (8-ounce) can tomato sauce
¼ cup vinegar
¼ cup vegetable oil
¼ cup onion soup mix
2 tablespoons honey
2 teaspoons chili powder
⅛ teaspoon salt
1 (3- to 3½-pound) broiler-fryer,
    skinned and cut up

1. Combine tomato sauce, vinegar, vegetable oil, onion soup mix, honey, chili powder, and salt in a small saucepan; stir until well blended. Cover and bring to a boil; reduce heat, and simmer 15 minutes, stirring occasionally. Remove mixture from heat, and set aside.
2. Place chicken and water to cover in a large Dutch oven; bring to a boil. Reduce heat; cover and simmer 15 minutes. Drain chicken, and pat dry.
3. Transfer chicken to a grill. Grill over medium coals 30 minutes or until tender, turning chicken every 10 minutes. Brush chicken with sauce during last 20 minutes of cooking.
4. Remove chicken from grill, and transfer to a serving platter. Serve immediately. Yield: 4 to 6 servings.

MicroNote: To microwave step 2, arrange chicken pieces in a circular pattern on a platter. Cover with waxed paper; microwave at HIGH for 8 minutes, turning chicken and rotating platter after 4 minutes. Drain off drippings.

SPANISH RICE AND CHICKEN

1 teaspoon garlic salt
1 teaspoon celery salt
1 teaspoon paprika
1 (2½-pound) broiler-fryer, cut up
1 cup uncooked regular rice
¾ cup chopped onion
¾ cup chopped green pepper
¼ cup chopped fresh parsley
1½ cups chicken broth
1 (16-ounce) can tomatoes,
   undrained and chopped
1½ teaspoons chili powder
½ teaspoon salt

1. Combine garlic salt, celery salt, and paprika, mixing well; sprinkle over chicken. Arrange chicken pieces, skin side up, in a lightly greased 13- x 9- x 2-inch baking dish. Bake at 425° for 20 minutes.
2. Remove chicken from dish; set aside. Combine rice, onion, green pepper, and parsley in baking dish; stir well.
3. Combine chicken broth, tomatoes, chili powder, and salt in a small saucepan; bring to a boil. Pour over rice mixture, stirring well. Arrange chicken pieces over rice; cover and bake 20 to 25 minutes or until chicken and rice are tender.
4. Serve immediately in baking dish. Yield: 4 to 6 servings.

ORANGE-GLAZED CHICKEN THIGHS

8 broiler-fryer chicken thighs
½ teaspoon salt
⅛ teaspoon pepper
¼ cup orange juice
1 tablespoon honey
1 teaspoon Worcestershire sauce
¼ teaspoon dry mustard

1. Place chicken in a 12- x 8- x 2-inch baking dish, sprinkle with salt and pepper. Bake at 350° for 30 minutes.
2. Combine remaining ingredients in a small bowl; stir well. Pour orange juice mixture over chicken, and bake 30 minutes or until chicken is tender.
3. Arrange chicken on a serving platter and serve hot. Yield: 4 servings.

MUSHROOM CHICKEN

4 boneless and skinless chicken
   breast halves (about 1 pound)
1 tablespoon plus 1 teaspoon Dijon
   mustard
1 teaspoon dried whole tarragon
   leaves
   Salt and pepper to taste
¼ pound fresh mushrooms, sliced
   and divided
2 carrots, sliced diagonally
1 green pepper, seeded and cut into
   strips
1 sweet red pepper, seeded and cut
   into strips
2 tablespoons butter or margarine,
   divided
2 teaspoons lemon juice, divided

1. Place each chicken breast half between 2 sheets of waxed paper; flatten chicken to ¼-inch thickness, using a meat mallet or rolling pin.
2. Place each chicken breast half in the center of a 12-inch square of aluminum foil. Brush each with 1 teaspoon mustard; sprinkle each with ¼ teaspoon tarragon and salt and pepper to taste. Top each evenly with sliced mushrooms, carrots, green pepper, and sweet red pepper; dot each with 1½ teaspoons butter, and sprinkle with ½ teaspoon lemon juice.
3. Seal foil securely; place on a baking sheet. Bake at 450° for 15 minutes.
4. Serve warm in foil pouch, or remove and serve on individual serving plates. Yield: 4 servings.

Chili powder, onion soup mix and honey blended with tomato sauce lend a rich and hearty taste of the old Southwest to this Rancher's Chicken (page 191).

ORANGE CHICKEN

6 boneless and skinless chicken
    breast halves
¼ cup butter or margarine, melted
1 tablespoon orange-flavored liqueur
6 (1-ounce) slices fully cooked ham
1 teaspoon grated orange rind
1 cup orange juice
¼ teaspoon salt
¼ teaspoon dried whole tarragon
1 tablespoon cornstarch
    Orange slices
    Fresh parsley sprigs

1. Place each chicken breast half between 2 sheets of waxed paper. Flatten chicken to ¼-inch thickness, using a meat mallet or rolling pin. Combine melted butter and orange liqueur; brush over chicken.

2. Place a ham slice on each piece of chicken; roll up lengthwise, tucking edges of ham inside. Secure each roll of chicken with a wooden pick. Place in a 12- x 8- x 2-inch baking dish. Bake at 400° for 15 minutes. Remove from oven.

3. Combine orange rind, juice, salt, and tarragon; pour over chicken. Cover with aluminum foil; bake at 350° for 25 minutes or until tender. Remove wooden picks and discard. Transfer chicken to a warm serving platter. Pour remaining orange juice mixture into a small saucepan.

4. Combine cornstarch and a small amount of water to form a smooth paste. Stir into orange juice mixture. Cook over medium heat until thickened and bubbly.

5. Spoon sauce over chicken. Garnish with orange slices and parsley, and serve immediately. Yield: 6 servings.

Cooked conventionally or in the microwave, Middle Eastern Lamb and Eggplant (page 188) combines several tasty spices to make a quick and nutritious entrée.

HOW TO BONE CHICKEN BREASTS

To save some money at the supermarket, you might want to bone chicken breasts at home. It's easier to do if you start with a whole breast, without wings attached, rather than separate breast halves. Proceed in this way:

1. Start with a sharp boning knife or other sharp long bladed knife.

2. Place the chicken breast, skin-side down, on a cutting surface. Using the tip of the knife, cut and scrape the meat away from the center breastbone and cartilage. Cut under the cartilage to loosen meat completely.

3. Cut under the bottom ribs, on either side of the cartilage, with the tip of the knife. Reach underneath the ribs with your fingers, and pull them away from the chicken breast meat. Use the knife, if necessary, to slit the membrane around the ribs.

4. Pull the ribs and cartilage away from the chicken breast meat in one piece. Turn breast over and remove the skin, if desired. Cut chicken breast in half or slice into strips, according to desired cooking method.

5. Wrap chicken breast halves individually. Fresh cut-up chicken will keep in the refrigerator for 2 days. If you are not going to use the chicken within 2 days, the chicken breast halves can be frozen for up to 6 months. If you plan to stuff or grill breasts, you might want to flatten each piece between sheets of waxed paper with a meat mallet or rolling pin, before overwrapping and freezing. It's easier to slice or dice the chicken breasts for stir-frying or salads if you do so while the meat is still partially frozen. Frozen poultry should not be allowed to thaw on work surfaces where other foods are to be placed.

CHEESE-STUFFED CHICKEN BREASTS

4 boneless and skinless chicken
    breast halves
2 tablespoons butter or margarine,
    melted
¼ teaspoon garlic salt
¼ teaspoon pepper
½ cup (2 ounces) shredded sharp
    Cheddar cheese
2 tablespoons chopped green onions
1 tablespoon chopped fresh parsley

1. Place each chicken breast half between 2 sheets of waxed paper. Flatten chicken to ¼-inch thickness, using a meat mallet or rolling pin. Brush chicken with melted butter; sprinkle with garlic salt and pepper.
2. Combine cheese and green onions. Place ¼ cheese mixture in center of each piece of chicken; roll up lengthwise, tucking edges inside. Secure each roll with a wooden pick. Place in a lightly greased 10- x 6- x 2-inch baking dish.
3. Cover with aluminum foil; bake at 375° for 25 minutes or until tender.
4. Remove wooden picks. Top with parsley, and serve immediately. Yield: 4 servings.

OVEN-FRIED CHICKEN KIEV

¼ cup butter, softened
1 tablespoon chopped chives
1 clove garlic, minced
¼ teaspoon dried whole marjoram
¼ teaspoon dried whole thyme
4 boneless and skinless chicken
    breast halves
1 egg
1 tablespoon skim milk
⅓ cup fine dry breadcrumbs

1. Combine butter, chives, garlic, marjoram, and thyme in a small mixing bowl; mix well. Shape mixture into a roll about 8 inches long on waxed paper. Wrap in waxed paper, and freeze another 20 minutes until hard.
2. Place each piece of chicken between sheets of waxed paper; flatten chicken to ¼-inch thickness, using a meat mallet or rolling pin.
3. Divide butter mixture into four equal pieces. Place one piece of butter mixture in center of each piece of chicken; roll up lengthwise. Tuck edges inside, and secure with a wooden pick.
4. Beat egg and milk in a small bowl. Dip each roll in egg mixture, and dredge in breadcrumbs. Place rolls in a 12- x 8- x 2-inch baking dish. Bake at 400° for 30 to 35 minutes.
5. Remove wooden picks, and serve hot. Yield: 4 servings.

CHICKEN O'BRIEN

1 cup chopped onion
2 tablespoons butter or margarine
2 cups chicken broth
1 cup uncooked regular rice
½ teaspoon salt
½ teaspoon pepper
3 cups diced cooked chicken
1 medium-size green pepper, seeded
    and cut into strips
1 cup cooked green peas
1 (2-ounce) jar diced pimiento,
    drained

1. Sauté onion in butter in a large skillet 5 minutes or until tender. Add chicken broth, rice, salt, and pepper, stirring well. Bring to a boil. Reduce heat; cover and simmer 15 minutes.
2. Add remaining ingredients, stirring well. Cover and cook an additional 10 minutes or until rice is tender.
3. Serve warm. Yield: 8 servings.

CORNISH HENS RUBY

2 (1¼-pound) Cornish hens
2 tablespoons red currant jelly
2 tablespoons brandy
    Fresh parsley sprigs or watercress

1. Remove giblets from hens; reserve for other uses. Rinse hens with cold water, and pat dry. Place hens, breast side up, in a lightly greased shallow roasting pan. Bake at 375° for 30 minutes.

2. Combine jelly and brandy in a small saucepan. Cook over low heat, stirring constantly, until jelly melts and mixture is well blended.

3. Brush hens evenly with jelly mixture, and bake an additional 10 minutes.

4. Transfer to a serving platter, and garnish with parsley or watercress. To serve, cut each hen in half lengthwise. Yield: 4 servings.

TURKEY DIVAN CASSEROLE

1 (10-ounce) package frozen broccoli
    spears
2 cups cubed cooked turkey
1 (10¾-ounce) can cream of chicken
    soup, undiluted
1 (2.5-ounce) jar sliced mushrooms,
    undrained
¼ cup half-and-half
¼ teaspoon curry powder
1 cup (4 ounces) shredded sharp
    Cheddar cheese
1 cup cracker crumbs

1. Cook broccoli according to package directions; drain and coarsely chop. Place broccoli in bottom of a lightly greased 10- x 6- x 2-inch baking dish.

2. Combine next 5 ingredients; stir well. Pour over broccoli. Bake at 350° for 30 minutes or until hot and bubbly.

3. Sprinkle cheese and cracker crumbs over casserole. Return to oven and bake an additional 5 minutes or until cheese melts. Serve hot. Yield: 6 servings.

MicroNote: Microwave casserole at HIGH for 4 to 5 minutes. Sprinkle cheese and cracker crumbs over casserole. Microwave at HIGH for 1 to 1½ minutes, or until hot and bubbly.

Note: To reduce sodium content, substitute unsalted crackers for cracker crumbs.

CHICKEN LIVERS MARSALA

1 medium onion, sliced
2 tablespoons butter or margarine
1¼ pounds chicken livers
½ pound fresh mushrooms, sliced
½ teaspoon salt
⅛ teaspoon pepper
¼ cup Marsala
¼ cup water
1 tablespoon all-purpose flour
    Hot cooked rice

1. Sauté onion in butter in a large skillet until almost tender. Cut livers apart at membrane, if necessary. Stir in livers, mushrooms, salt, and pepper; cook over medium heat 5 minutes, stirring frequently, or until livers are tender but still pink inside.

2. Combine Marsala, water, and flour in a small mixing bowl; stir until well blended. Gradually stir into liver mixture in skillet; cook over medium heat, stirring constantly, 3 minutes or until mixture is slightly thickened. Remove the skillet from heat to serve.

3. Serve immediately over hot cooked rice. Yield: 4 servings.

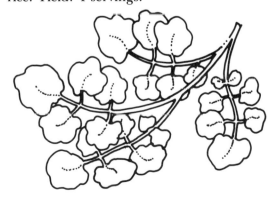

ROLLED FLOUNDER

4 (5⅓-ounce) flounder fillets
1 tablespoon butter or margarine, melted
1 tablespoon grated lemon rind
1 teaspoon onion powder
½ teaspoon salt
¼ teaspoon pepper
¼ teaspoon dried whole marjoram
½ cup shredded carrot
½ cup chopped fresh mushrooms
  Buttered breadcrumbs
  Lemon wedges

1. Brush one side of each fillet with butter; sprinkle with lemon rind, onion powder, salt, pepper, and marjoram. Spoon 2 tablespoons carrot and 2 tablespoons mushrooms over each fillet. Roll up fillets jellyroll fashion.

2. Place fillets seam side down in a greased 9-inch pan. Top with buttered breadcrumbs. Bake at 350° for 20 minutes or until fish flakes easily when tested with a fork.

3. Transfer rolls to a serving platter; garnish with lemon. Yield: 4 servings.

MicroNote: To microwave step 2, cover with waxed paper. Microwave at MEDIUM (50% power) for 6 to 8 minutes, rotating dish one-quarter turn every 2 minutes. Let stand 5 minutes.

FLOUNDER DIVAN

1 (10-ounce) package frozen broccoli spears
1⅓ pounds flounder or sole fillets
1 cup sliced fresh mushrooms
1 tablespoon butter or margarine
1 cup milk, divided
1 teaspoon chicken-flavored bouillon granules
1 tablespoon cornstarch
½ cup (2 ounces) shredded sharp Cheddar cheese
  Paprika

1. Cook broccoli according to package directions; drain well. Arrange in bottom of a lightly greased 10- x 6- x 2-inch baking dish. Place flounder over broccoli.

2. Sauté mushrooms in butter in a medium skillet until tender. Spoon mushrooms over flounder, reserving liquid in skillet.

3. Add ¾ cup milk and bouillon granules to skillet. Dissolve cornstarch in remaining ¼ cup milk; stir into skillet. Cook over medium heat, stirring constantly, until thickened and bubbly. Remove from heat. Stir in cheese. Pour mixture over mushrooms.

4. Bake at 400° for 15 minutes or until fish flakes easily when tested with a fork. Sprinkle with paprika. Serve immediately. Yield: 4 servings.

CRAB-STUFFED FLOUNDER

¼ cup chopped onion
¼ cup chopped green pepper
1 tablespoon butter or margarine
1 (6-ounce) can crabmeat, rinsed and drained
2 tablespoons soft breadcrumbs
½ teaspoon dried parsley flakes
½ teaspoon lemon-pepper seasoning
2 flounder fillets (about 1 pound)
  Lemon slices

1. Sauté onion and green pepper in butter in a large skillet until tender. Remove from heat. Add crabmeat, breadcrumbs, parsley flakes, and lemon-pepper seasoning, stirring well.

2. Place 1 fillet on a rack in a shallow roasting pan; spoon stuffing mixture evenly over fillet. Lay remaining fillet on a cutting board; slit lengthwise, beginning 1½ inches from one end and cutting down center of fillet to 1½ inches from other end. Place fillet on top of stuffing mixture.

3. Bake at 350° for 25 minutes or until fish flakes easily when tested with a fork.

4. Transfer to a serving platter. Garnish with lemon slices. Serve immediately. Yield: 4 servings.

MicroMethod

1. Place onion and green pepper in a 4-cup glass measure, omitting butter. Microwave at HIGH for 2 to 2½ minutes, or until tender, stirring after 1 minute. Add crabmeat, breadcrumbs, parsley flakes, and lemon-pepper seasoning, stirring well.
2. Place 1 fillet on a roasting rack in a baking dish. Spoon stuffing mixture evenly over fillet. Lay remaining fillet on a cutting board; slit lengthwise, beginning 1½ inches from one end and cutting down center of fillet to 1½ inches from other end. Place fillet on top of stuffing mixture. Cover with waxed paper.
3. Microwave at MEDIUM (50% power) for 8 to 10 minutes, or until bottom fillet flakes easily when tested with a fork.
4. Same as step 4.

▢ CHIPPER FILLETS

2 pounds grouper fillets
½ cup commercial creamy French salad dressing
1½ cups crushed bite-size Cheddar cheese crackers
2 tablespoons butter or margarine, melted
Paprika to taste

1. Rinse fish thoroughly in cold water; pat dry, and cut into 6 serving-size portions. Dip fish into dressing; dredge fish in cracker crumbs.
2. Place fish in a well-greased 13- x 9- x 2-inch baking dish. Drizzle butter over fish; sprinkle with paprika.

3. Bake at 500° for 12 minutes or until fish flakes easily when tested with a fork.
4. Serve hot. Yield: 6 servings.

MicroMethod

1. Same as step 1.
2. Place fish in a single layer with thicker portions to the outside of a large platter. (Do not drizzle with butter.) Sprinkle with paprika.
3. Microwave at HIGH for 8 to 10 minutes or until fish flakes easily when tested with a fork, giving dish a half-turn after 4 minutes.
4. Same as step 4.

GROUPER AU GRATIN

1 pound grouper fillets
½ teaspoon salt
¼ cup chopped green pepper
2 tablespoons finely chopped onion
½ cup Chablis or other dry white wine
½ cup (2 ounces) shredded Cheddar cheese
2 tablespoons fine dry breadcrumbs

1. Place fillets in a 9-inch square baking pan; sprinkle with salt. Top fillets with green pepper and onion. Pour wine into baking pan. Bake at 375° for 18 minutes or until fish flakes easily with a fork.
2. Pour off cooking liquid. Sprinkle fillets with cheese and breadcrumbs. Broil about 3 inches from heating element 2 minutes or until cheese melts and crumbs are lightly browned.
3. Transfer fish fillets to a warm serving platter, and serve. Yield: 3 servings.

Note: Any firm, white fish will work well in this simple recipe. Try red snapper, halibut, monkfish, or haddock. You may also use an equal weight of fish steaks. For a different topping, substitute 1 ounce grated Parmesan cheese for the 2 ounces of Cheddar; add ½ teaspoon crushed dried basil leaves.

GROUPER
WITH ORANGE RICE

½ cup chopped celery
¼ cup chopped onion
 2 tablespoons grated orange rind
¼ cup butter or margarine
¾ cup orange juice
¾ cup water
 2 tablespoons lemon juice
½ teaspoon salt
1½ cups uncooked instant rice
 2 (1-pound) grouper fillets
    Lemon and orange slices
    Fresh parsley sprigs

1. Sauté celery, onion, and orange rind in butter in a large skillet until vegetables are tender. Stir in orange juice, water, lemon juice, and salt. Cover and bring to a boil. Stir in rice, and remove from heat. Cover and let stand 5 minutes.

2. Spoon rice into a lightly greased 12- x 8- x 2-inch baking dish. Place fillets over rice, and cover with aluminum foil.

3. Bake at 400° for 15 minutes. Uncover and bake an additional 15 minutes or until fish flakes easily when tested with a fork.

4. Garnish with fresh lemon and orange slices and parsley sprigs. Serve immediately. Yield: 6 servings.

MicroMethod

1. Combine celery, onion, orange rind, and butter in a 4-cup glass measure; cover with waxed paper, and microwave at HIGH for 2 minutes.

2. Stir in orange juice, water, lemon juice, and salt. Cover with waxed paper, and microwave at HIGH for 7 minutes or until mixture boils. Remove from oven. Stir in rice; cover with waxed paper, and let stand 5 minutes.

3. Spoon rice into a lightly greased 12- x 8- x 2-inch baking dish. Place fillets over rice, and cover with waxed paper.

4. Microwave at HIGH for 10 to 11 minutes, turning dish every 3 minutes. Remove from oven, and let stand, covered, 5 minutes.

5. Same as step 4.

GROUPER
WITH CHEESY HERB SAUCE

 2 tablespoons chopped onion
 2 tablespoons chopped sweet red
    pepper
 2 tablespoons sliced celery
 1 tablespoon plus 1½ teaspoons
    butter or margarine
 1 tablespoon plus 1½ teaspoons
    all-purpose flour
⅛ teaspoon salt
    Dash of pepper
⅛ teaspoon dried tarragon, crushed
¾ cup milk
½ cup (2 ounces) shredded Monterey
    Jack cheese
1⅓ pounds grouper fillets, cut into 4
    serving-size pieces

1. Sauté onion, sweet red pepper, and celery in butter in a skillet until tender. Add flour, salt, pepper, and tarragon; stir well. Cook 1 minute, stirring constantly. Gradually add milk; cook over medium heat, stirring constantly, until thickened. Add cheese; stir until melted.

2. Place fish fillets in a 12- x 8- x 2-inch baking dish. Spoon sauce evenly over fish.

3. Bake at 425° for 8 to 10 minutes or until fish fillets flake easily when tested with a fork.

4. Serve immediately. Yield: 4 servings.

FETTUCCINE
WITH HADDOCK SAUCE

 1 (10¾-ounce) can cream of
    mushroom soup, undiluted
½ cup water
¼ cup chopped fresh parsley
 2 (2-ounce) jars sliced pimiento,
    drained
½ teaspoon salt
¼ teaspoon pepper
⅛ teaspoon dried whole dillweed
1⅓ pounds haddock fillets, cut into
    cubes
½ (16-ounce) package fettuccine
    noodles

1. Combine first 7 ingredients in a large skillet; stir until well blended. Cover and bring to a boil; reduce heat, and add haddock. Cover and simmer 10 minutes, stirring occasionally. Uncover and simmer an additional 5 minutes or until fish flakes easily when tested with a fork.

2. Cook fettuccine according to package directions; drain well, and transfer to a serving platter.

3. Pour haddock sauce over fettuccine, and toss lightly to mix. Serve immediately. Yield: 4 to 6 servings.

ELEGANT, EASY HALIBUT

4 (½-inch-thick) halibut steaks
    (about 1 pound)
    Salt to taste
1 (2½-ounce) jar sliced mushrooms, drained
1 tablespoon butter or margarine
½ cup commercial sour cream
1 tablespoon dry sherry
    Dash of paprika

1. Rinse halibut steaks thoroughly in cold water; pat dry. Sprinkle with salt; place in a lightly greased 13- x 9- x 2-inch baking dish. Bake at 425° for 5 minutes.

2. Sauté mushrooms in butter in a small skillet until thoroughly heated. Remove from heat. Stir in sour cream and sherry. Remove halibut steaks from oven; spoon mushroom mixture over steaks, and sprinkle with paprika.

3. Reduce oven temperature to 375°; return halibut steaks to oven, and continue baking 5 minutes or until fish flakes easily when tested with a fork.

4. Transfer halibut steaks to a warm serving platter. Serve immediately. Yield: 4 servings.

Note: Salmon or swordfish steaks may be substituted for the halibut. To vary sauce, substitute 2 green onions with tops, minced or sliced, for the mushrooms; stir in 1 tablespoon minced parsley.

FISHING AT THE MARKET

Most types of fish can be used interchangeably if you know how to prepare them. You can make oily fish more delicate by removing the dark part of the flesh; delicate fish firmer by marinating it with lemon juice before cooking. The following list has been designed to make things easier, by indicating which types of fish can be substituted without any additional preparation. Whenever possible, substitute the same cut of fish, whether fillets, steaks, or whole.

Bass: grouper, halibut, red snapper.

Catfish: orange roughy, walleye pike.

Cod: haddock, pollack, flounder.

Flounder: ocean perch, orange roughy, sole, turbot.

Haddock: cod, ocean catfish, flounder.

Halibut: sea bass, snapper, monkfish.

Mackerel: bluefish, lake trout.

Perch: walleye pike, orange roughy, flounder, turbot, sole.

Pompano: snapper, sea bass, yellow tail, redfish.

Redfish: snapper, grouper, halibut.

Salmon: swordfish, halibut, lake trout, yellowtail.

Sole: flounder, turbot, orange roughy, ocean perch.

Snapper: sea bass, grouper, redfish, pompano.

Swordfish: halibut, shark, marlin, tuna.

Trout, freshwater: walleye pike, salmon.

PERCH WITH GARLIC SAUCE

⅓ cup dry vermouth
⅓ cup white wine vinegar
2 cloves garlic, minced
1 cup water
2 tablespoons lemon or lime juice
2 tablespoons chopped green onions
1 teaspoon salt
½ teaspoon white pepper
2 pounds perch, turbot, or red snapper fillets, cut into serving-size pieces
3 tablespoons butter or margarine

1. Combine vermouth, vinegar, and garlic in a small saucepan. Bring to a boil; cook over medium heat until mixture is reduced to ¼ cup. Set aside.

2. Combine water, lemon juice, green onions, salt, and pepper in a large skillet. Bring to a boil. Reduce heat to low. Add fish; poach 5 minutes or until fish flakes easily when tested with a fork. Remove fish to a warm serving plate, reserving liquid in skillet.

3. Add butter to vinegar mixture. Bring to a boil; stir vigorously until butter melts and mixture is smooth.

4. Pour sauce over fish. Serve immediately. Yield: 6 servings.

POACHED SALMON WITH TARRAGON SAUCE

⅔ cup Chablis or other dry white wine
1 tablespoon dried whole tarragon leaves
1¼ teaspoons salt, divided
1 shallot, chopped
2 (1-inch-thick) salmon steaks
2 tablespoons butter or margarine
1 tablespoon all-purpose flour
½ cup whipping cream
1 egg yolk
⅛ teaspoon pepper
Fresh parsley sprigs
Lemon slices

1. Combine wine, tarragon, 1 teaspoon salt, and shallot in a large skillet; bring to a boil. Add salmon; reduce heat. Cover; simmer 10 minutes or until fish flakes easily when tested with a fork. Drain off poaching liquid, reserving ½ cup. Transfer salmon to a serving platter; keep warm.

2. Melt butter in a small saucepan; add flour, stirring until smooth. Cook 1 minute, stirring constantly. Gradually add reserved poaching liquid, and cook over medium heat, stirring constantly, until thickened and bubbly. Combine whipping cream and egg yolk; gradually add to sauce, stirring constantly. Add remaining ¼ teaspoon salt and pepper; cook, stirring constantly, until mixture thickens.

3. Spoon sauce over salmon. Garnish with parsley sprigs and lemon slices. Serve immediately. Yield: 4 servings.

MicroMethod

1. Combine wine, tarragon, 1 teaspoon salt, and shallot in a 12- x 8- x 2-inch baking dish; add salmon. Cover with heavy-duty plastic wrap, and vent to allow steam to escape; microwave at HIGH for 8 to 10 minutes or until fish flakes easily when tested with a fork, turning salmon steaks after 5 minutes. Drain off poaching liquid, reserving ½ cup. Transfer salmon to a serving platter; keep warm.

2. Place butter in a 2-cup glass measure. Microwave at HIGH for 45 seconds or until butter melts. Add flour, stirring until smooth; gradually stir in reserved poaching liquid. Microwave at MEDIUM-HIGH (70% power) for 1½ to 2 minutes or until thickened, stirring after 1 minute. Combine whipping cream and egg yolk; gradually stir into sauce. Add remaining salt and pepper. Microwave at MEDIUM-HIGH for 1½ to 2 minutes or until mixture thickens.

3. Same as step 3.

Note: To turn poaching liquid into a lighter sauce, follow recipe through step 1. Heat ½ cup poaching liquid to simmering; whisk in 2 tablespoons whipping cream, and simmer until slightly thickened.

BROILED SALMON
WITH
HERBED LEMON BUTTER

6 **salmon fillets (about 2 pounds)**
¼ **cup butter or margarine,**
     melted
2 **tablespoons chopped fresh**
     parsley
2 **tablespoons lemon juice**
¼ **teaspoon salt**
¼ **teaspoon dried whole dillweed**
⅛ **teaspoon pepper**
     Fresh dillweed sprigs (optional)
     Lemon wedges (optional)

1. Place salmon fillets on the rack of a broiler pan.
2. Combine remaining ingredients, except fresh dillweed sprigs and lemon wedges, in a small mixing bowl; stir well.
3. Brush salmon with butter mixture. Broil 4 inches from heating element for 8 minutes or until fish flakes easily when tested with a fork, basting frequently.
4. Arrange salmon on a serving platter; garnish with fresh dillweed sprigs and lemon wedges, if desired. Serve immediately. Yield: 6 servings.

JIFFY CRABMEAT
(pictured on page 211)

1 **cup sliced fresh mushrooms**
1 **small green pepper, seeded**
     and chopped
1 **tablespoon butter or margarine**
1 **(10¾-ounce) can cream of celery**
     soup, undiluted
1 **(6-ounce) package frozen**
     crabmeat, thawed and drained
1 **(2-ounce) jar diced pimiento,**
     drained
2 **tablespoons toasted slivered**
     almonds
1 **tablespoon chopped fresh parsley**
1 **tablespoon lemon juice**
¼ **teaspoon celery salt**
     Dash of hot sauce
     Hot cooked rice

1. Sauté mushrooms and green pepper in butter in a medium skillet until tender. Add remaining ingredients, except rice.
2. Cook over medium heat 5 minutes or until hot and bubbly, stirring occasionally.
3. Serve crabmeat mixture over rice. Yield: 4 servings.

MicroMethod

1. Combine mushrooms, green pepper, and butter in a 2-quart baking dish. Cover with heavy-duty plastic wrap, and vent to allow steam to escape; microwave at HIGH for 2 to 3 minutes.
2. Add remaining ingredients, except rice; stir well. Cover and microwave at HIGH for 6 minutes, stirring after 3 minutes. Let stand, covered, 3 minutes.
3. Same as step 3.

BUTTER-FRIED OYSTERS

1 **(12-ounce) container Select**
     oysters, drained and patted dry
¼ **teaspoon salt**
⅛ **teaspoon pepper**
1 **egg**
2 **tablespoons milk or whipping**
     cream
1½ **cups soft breadcrumbs**
½ **cup butter**
     Commercial cocktail sauce

1. Sprinkle oysters with salt and pepper.
2. Combine egg and milk, mixing well. Dip oysters in egg mixture; dredge in breadcrumbs.
3. Melt butter in a medium-size skillet. Cook over medium-high heat. Fry oysters until golden brown, turning once. Drain well on paper towels.
4. Serve hot with cocktail sauce. Yield: 2 to 4 servings.

Note: Butter-Fried Oysters may be served on a toasted bun for an oyster sandwich. For a quick cocktail sauce, mix catsup with prepared horseradish, Worcestershire sauce, and fresh lemon juice to taste.

BAKED OYSTERS

2 (12-ounce) containers Standard
    oysters, undrained
4 slices bacon
1 medium onion, chopped
4 cloves garlic, minced
1¼ cups Italian-style breadcrumbs
¼ cup grated Parmesan cheese
    Vegetable cooking spray
    Commercial sour cream,
      Horseradish Sauce, or Fresh
      Horseradish Sauce

1. Drain oysters; reserving liquid.
2. Cook bacon in a large skillet until crisp; remove bacon, reserving ¼ cup drippings in skillet. Crumble bacon.
3. Sauté onion and garlic in drippings until tender. Add oysters; cook over medium heat until edges begin to curl.
4. Remove from heat; stir in reserved oyster liquid, breadcrumbs, and cheese. Transfer mixture to a 1-quart casserole coated with cooking spray.
5. Bake at 350° for 15 minutes. Broil 2 minutes or until golden brown. Serve with sour cream, Horseradish Sauce, or Fresh Horseradish Sauce. Yield: 4 servings.

Horseradish Sauce:

1 (8-ounce) carton commercial sour
    cream
¼ cup prepared horseradish

1. Combine ingredients in a small mixing bowl; mix well, and chill.
2. Serve with oysters, shrimp, or roast beef. Yield: 1¼ cups.

Fresh Horseradish Sauce:

½ cup whipping cream
2 to 3 tablespoons grated fresh
    horseradish
    Salt and pepper to taste

1. Beat whipping cream until soft peaks form. Stir in remaining ingredients.
2. Serve sauce immediately with oysters, shrimp, or roast beef. Yield: 1 cup.

SCALLOPED OYSTERS WITH PECANS

1 (12-ounce) container Standard
    oysters, drained and patted dry
½ cup butter or margarine, melted
    and divided
1 teaspoon grated onion
¼ teaspoon salt
¼ teaspoon pepper
¼ teaspoon dried thyme, crumbled
3 cups soft breadcrumbs
⅔ cups chopped pecans
    Fresh parsley sprigs

1. Dip oysters in 3 tablespoons butter to coat; arrange in a single layer in a 9-inch pieplate. Sprinkle with onion, salt, pepper, and thyme.
2. Toss breadcrumbs with 3 tablespoons butter; sprinkle over oysters. Bake at 350° for 25 minutes or until oysters are done.
3. Sauté pecans in remaining 2 tablespoons butter in a small skillet until lightly toasted; sprinkle over breadcrumbs.
4. Garnish with parsley. Serve hot. Yield: 4 servings.

SCALLOP KABOBS
(pictured on page 211)

2 pounds sea scallops
1 (6-ounce) package sliced Canadian
    bacon, cut in half
5 limes, cut into wedges
⅓ cup butter or margarine, melted
¼ cup grated Parmesan cheese

1. Alternate scallops, bacon, and lime on 12 (12-inch) skewers. Squeeze several wedges of lime over scallops.
2. Brush scallops with butter, reserving remaining butter to baste scallops during grilling. Sprinkle kabobs with cheese.
3. Grill kabobs 4 inches from hot coals 10 minutes, turning and basting once with remaining butter.
4. Serve immediately. Yield: 6 servings.

Note: Kabobs may also be broiled.

SAUTÉED SHRIMP

(pictured on page 211)

1 clove garlic, minced
1 tablespoon unsalted margarine,
   melted
1¼ pounds medium shrimp, peeled
   and deveined
¼ pound fresh snow peas
⅓ cup sherry
1 teaspoon paprika
½ teaspoon salt
¼ teaspoon pepper
   Toast points

1. Sauté garlic in margarine until lightly browned.

2. Add shrimp, snow peas, sherry, paprika, salt, and pepper. Cover and bring to a boil. Reduce heat, and simmer, uncovered, 3 minutes, stirring constantly.

3. Serve immediately over toast points. Yield: 4 servings.

Note: Sautéed Shrimp can also be served over rice, brown rice, thin egg noodles, buckwheat noodles, or chow mein noodles. Stir some chopped water chestnuts into the rice, if you wish, to make the combination wonderfully crunchy.

SHRIMP PASTRY LOG

1 (14-ounce) can artichoke hearts,
   drained and quartered
½ pound fresh mushrooms,
   halved
1 tablespoon parsley flakes
3 tablespoons butter or margarine,
   melted
½ teaspoon salt
½ (15-ounce) package frozen puff
   pastry, thawed
2 (6-ounce) packages sliced Swiss
   cheese
1 pound medium shrimp, peeled,
   deveined, and cooked
1 egg, beaten

1. Sauté artichoke hearts, mushrooms, and parsley flakes in butter in a large skillet 3 minutes or until mushrooms are tender; drain well. Sprinkle with salt, and set aside.

2. Roll pastry into a 15- x 10-inch rectangle on a lightly greased baking sheet. Arrange cheese slices on half of pastry along long edge, leaving a 1-inch border. Spoon reserved vegetable mixture evenly over cheese; arrange shrimp over vegetable mixture. Brush edges of pastry with egg; fold opposite side of dough over filling, pressing edges with the tines of a fork to seal. Brush pastry with egg. Bake at 375° for 15 minutes or until golden brown.

3. Serve hot. Yield: 4 to 6 servings.

SHRIMP QUICKY

1 green onion, chopped
2 tablespoons finely chopped green
   pepper
1 tablespoon butter or margarine
1 (8-ounce) can whole tomatoes,
   undrained and chopped
1 (3-ounce) can sliced mushrooms,
   drained
2 tablespoons Chablis or other dry
   white wine
1 tablespoon parsley flakes
½ teaspoon garlic powder
½ teaspoon chili powder
¼ teaspoon salt
¼ teaspoon dried whole thyme
¾ pound medium shrimp, peeled
   and deveined
   Hot cooked rice

1. Sauté onion and green pepper in butter in a large skillet until tender.

2. Add tomatoes, mushrooms, wine, parsley flakes, garlic powder, chili powder, salt, and thyme; stir well. Bring to a boil. Reduce heat; cover and simmer 10 minutes, stirring occasionally. Add shrimp, and simmer, covered, an additional 3 to 5 minutes or until tender.

3. Serve over hot cooked rice. Yield: 2 servings.

⬛ SHRIMP CHOW MEIN

1 medium onion, chopped
1 medium-size green pepper, seeded
    and cut into strips
1 cup sliced celery
2 tablespoons butter or margarine
12 ounces fresh bean sprouts
1 (8-ounce) can sliced water
    chestnuts, drained
1 (2-ounce) jar diced pimiento,
    drained
½ cup sliced fresh mushrooms
3 tablespoons soy sauce
3 tablespoons cornstarch
1 cup water
2 teaspoons chicken-flavored
    bouillon granules
1 pound medium shrimp, peeled
    and deveined
    Chow mein noodles

1. Sauté onion, green pepper, and celery in butter in a large skillet or wok; add bean sprouts, water chestnuts, pimiento, and mushrooms.
2. Combine soy sauce and cornstarch; add to skillet with water and bouillon granules. Cook, stirring constantly, until mixture is thickened. Add shrimp; cook 3 minutes or until shrimp are tender, stirring constantly.
3. Serve over chow mein noodles. Yield: 4 servings.

MicroMethod

1. Combine onion, green pepper, celery, and butter in a 3-quart baking dish; cover with heavy-duty plastic wrap, and vent to allow steam to escape; microwave at HIGH for 5 to 6 minutes or until tender. Add bean sprouts, water chestnuts, pimiento, and mushrooms; stir to combine.
2. Combine soy sauce and cornstarch; mix well. Add soy sauce mixture, water, and bouillon granules to vegetable mixture; stir well. Cover and microwave at HIGH for 8 to 9 minutes or until mixture is thickened, stirring every 3 minutes. Add shrimp; cover and let stand 10 minutes.
3. Same as step 3.

⬛ SHRIMP AND WILD RICE

1 small onion, chopped
1 small green pepper, seeded and
    sliced into thin strips
1 (4-ounce) can sliced mushrooms,
    drained
¼ cup butter or margarine
2 tablespoons all-purpose flour
1 cup whipping cream
1 cup milk
1 tablespoon Worcestershire
    sauce
4 drops hot sauce
¼ teaspoon pepper
1 (6¼-ounce) package long grain
    and wild rice mix, cooked
    according to package directions
1 pound medium shrimp, cooked,
    peeled, and deveined

1. Sauté onion, green pepper, and mushrooms in butter in a large skillet over low heat until tender.
2. Stir in flour, cream, and milk; bring to a boil. Reduce heat and cook, stirring constantly, until mixture begins to thicken. Remove from heat.
3. Combine cream sauce, Worcestershire sauce, hot sauce, pepper, rice, and shrimp in a lightly greased 12- x 8- x 2-inch baking dish, stirring well. Bake at 350° for 10 to 15 minutes.
4. Serve hot. Yield: 6 to 8 servings.

MicroMethod

1. Combine onion, green pepper, mushrooms, and butter in a 2-quart glass measure. Cover with heavy-duty plastic wrap, and vent to allow steam to escape; microwave at HIGH for 2 to 3 minutes.
2. Stir in flour, cream, and milk. Cover and microwave at HIGH for 3 to 4 minutes or until slightly thickened, stirring once every minute.
3. Stir in Worcestershire sauce, hot sauce, pepper, rice, and shrimp. Cover and microwave at MEDIUM (50% power) for 12 to 15 minutes, rotating dish after 6 minutes.
4. Same as step 4.

⌨ SEAFOOD THERMIDOR

1 pound cod fillets (fresh or frozen, thawed), cut into 1-inch pieces
1 cup water
1 small onion, quartered
1 lemon, quartered
1 (10¾-ounce) can cream of shrimp soup, undiluted
2 tablespoons all-purpose flour
½ cup milk
½ cup (2 ounces) shredded Monterey Jack cheese
1 (6-ounce) package frozen cooked shrimp, thawed and drained
¼ cup sherry
   Toast points, baked patty shells, or hot cooked rice
2 tablespoons chopped fresh parsley
1 teaspoon paprika

1. Place fish, water, onion, and lemon in a large skillet; bring to a boil. Reduce heat; cover and simmer 5 minutes. Drain well, and set aside.

2. Combine soup and flour in skillet; stir in milk. Cook over medium heat until hot and bubbly.

3. Add cheese, stirring until cheese melts. Stir in reserved fish, shrimp, and sherry. Cook over low heat until thoroughly heated.

4. Serve over toast points. Sprinkle with parsley and paprika. Yield: 6 servings.

MicroMethod

1. Place fish, water, onion, and lemon in a 2-quart baking dish. Cover with heavy-duty plastic wrap, and vent to allow steam to escape; microwave at HIGH for 5 minutes. Drain well, and set fish aside.

2. Combine soup and flour in a 2-quart mixing bowl; stir in milk. Cover and microwave at HIGH for 4 minutes, stirring after 2 minutes.

3. Add cheese to hot mixture, and stir until cheese melts. Add reserved fish, shrimp, and sherry. Microwave at MEDIUM-HIGH (70% power) for 6 minutes or until thoroughly heated.

4. Same as step 4.

◷ SCRAMBLED EGGS WITH TOMATOES

4 eggs, beaten
1 medium tomato, peeled and chopped
¼ teaspoon salt
¼ teaspoon pepper
⅛ to ¼ teaspoon dried whole basil
1 tablespoon butter or margarine
   Fresh parsley sprigs

1. Combine eggs, tomato, salt, pepper, and basil in a medium mixing bowl, stirring well.

2. Melt butter in a large skillet over medium heat; add egg mixture. Cook, stirring occasionally, until eggs are set.

3. Serve immediately. Garnish each serving with a fresh parsley sprig. Yield: 4 servings.

POACHED EGGS IN HASH

1 (7½-ounce) can corned beef hash
2 tablespoons chili sauce
3 eggs
1 tablespoon butter or margarine
¼ cup vinegar
¼ cup water
2 tablespoons sugar
1 tablespoon dry mustard
¼ teaspoon salt
   Dash of ground nutmeg

1. Combine corned beef hash and chili sauce in a small mixing bowl; stir until well blended. Press mixture evenly into two 10-ounce custard cups, forming an indention in center of mixture in each cup. Break and slip an egg into each indentation. Bake at 350° for 25 minutes or until eggs reach desired doneness.

2. Melt butter in a small saucepan over low heat. Add remaining ingredients, beating with a wire whisk until well blended. Cook over medium-high heat, stirring constantly, until mixture thickens.

3. Top hash with mustard sauce, and serve immediately. Yield: 2 servings.

MEXICAN EGGS

1 (15-ounce) can chili with beans
1 cup (4 ounces) shredded Monterey
   Jack cheese, divided
¼ cup chopped green pepper
4 eggs
   Corn chips

1. Combine chili with beans, ½ cup cheese, and green pepper in a small mixing bowl; stir until well blended.

2. Press mixture evenly into bottom and sides of four lightly greased 6-ounce custard cups, forming an indention in center of mixture in each cup. Break and slip an egg into each indention.

3. Bake at 350° for 25 minutes or until eggs reach desired doneness. Remove from oven, and sprinkle with remaining ½ cup cheese. Cover with aluminum foil, and let stand 3 minutes.

4. Uncover and serve immediately with corn chips. Yield: 4 servings.

MicroNote: To microwave step 3, pierce each egg yolk with a wooden pick. Cover with heavy-duty plastic wrap, and vent to allow steam to escape; microwave at MEDIUM (50% power) for 6 to 8 minutes, rotating custard cups every 3 minutes. Sprinkle with remaining ½ cup cheese. Cover with heavy-duty plastic wrap, and let stand 3 minutes. Yield: 4 servings.

ASPARAGUS AND TARRAGON OMELET

4 spears cooked asparagus
½ teaspoon butter or margarine
½ teaspoon tarragon leaves
2 eggs, lightly beaten
2 tablespoons water
   Dash of salt
   Dash of pepper
1 tablespoon butter or margarine

1. Sauté asparagus spears in ½ teaspoon butter until thoroughly heated; sprinkle with tarragon. Set asparagus aside.

2. Combine eggs, water, salt, and pepper in a small mixing bowl; stir just until blended. Set aside.

3. Melt 1 tablespoon butter in an 8-inch omelet pan or heavy skillet over medium heat. Pour egg mixture into skillet. As mixture starts to cook, gently lift edges of omelet with a spatula, tilting pan to allow uncooked portion to flow underneath. Cook until eggs are set but not dry.

4. Spoon asparagus mixture over half of omelet; fold omelet in half. Gently slide omelet onto a warm serving plate.

5. Serve immediately. Yield: 1 serving.

MUSHROOM OMELET

1 cup sliced fresh mushrooms
1 green onion, sliced
1 tablespoon butter or margarine
4 eggs
¼ cup water, divided
½ teaspoon tarragon leaves, divided
   Dash of salt
   Dash of pepper
2 tablespoons butter or margarine, divided

1. Sauté mushrooms and green onion in 1 tablespoon butter in a small skillet until tender; set aside.

2. Combine 2 eggs, 2 tablespoons water, ¼ teaspoon tarragon, salt, and pepper in a small mixing bowl; mix just until blended.

3. Heat 1 tablespoon butter in an 8-inch omelet pan or heavy skillet over medium heat. Pour egg mixture into skillet. As mixture starts to cook, gently lift edges of omelet with spatula, tilting pan to allow uncooked portion to flow underneath. Cook until eggs are set but not dry.

4. Spoon half of reserved mushroom mixture over half of omelet, and fold omelet in half. Gently slide omelet onto a warm serving plate.

5. Repeat procedure with remaining ingredients.

6. Serve immediately. Yield: 2 servings.

▢ CHEESE OMELET SUPREME

¼ cup chopped green pepper
¼ cup chopped onion
1 tablespoon butter or margarine
4 eggs, separated
¼ cup milk
¼ teaspoon salt
  Dash of pepper
3 slices bacon, cooked and
    crumbled
1 tablespoon butter or margarine
¾ cup (3 ounces) shredded sharp
    Cheddar cheese, divided
  Fresh parsley sprigs

1. Sauté green pepper and onion in 1 tablespoon butter in a small saucepan over low heat until tender. Set aside.

2. Beat egg yolks, milk, salt, and pepper in a small mixing bowl until thick and lemon colored. Stir in bacon and sautéed vegetables. Beat egg whites (at room temperature) in a large mixing bowl until stiff peaks form. Gradually fold in egg yolk mixture.

3. Melt 1 tablespoon butter in a 10-inch omelet pan or heavy skillet over medium heat until bubbly. Pour egg mixture into pan. As mixture starts to cook, gently lift edges of omelet with a spatula, tilting pan so uncooked portion flows underneath. Continue to cook over medium heat 3 minutes or until eggs are set and top is still moist and creamy.

4. Sprinkle ½ cup cheese over half of omelet. Let stand 2 to 3 minutes before folding omelet in half.

5. Gently slide omelet onto a warm serving platter; sprinkle remaining ¼ cup cheese over top. Garnish with parsley sprigs, and serve immediately. Yield: 2 servings.

MicroMethod

1. Place green pepper, onion, and 1 tablespoon butter in a 9-inch pieplate. Cover with waxed paper, and microwave at HIGH for 2 minutes, stirring after 1 minute. Remove from pieplate to a small bowl; set aside.

2. Same as step 2.

3. Place 1 tablespoon butter in pieplate. Microwave at HIGH for 35 seconds or until butter melts. Tip pieplate to coat with butter. Pour egg mixture into pieplate. Microwave at MEDIUM (50% power) for 8 minutes or until center is almost set, rotating pieplate every 2 minutes.

4. Same as step 4.

5. Same as step 5.

BROCCOLI-CARROT FRITTATA

1 (10-ounce) package frozen
    chopped broccoli
1 medium carrot, scraped and
    chopped
¼ cup water
8 eggs
½ cup milk
1 tablespoon instant minced onion
2 teaspoons prepared mustard
1 teaspoon seasoned salt
⅛ teaspoon pepper
¾ cup (3 ounces) shredded sharp
    Cheddar cheese
1 tablespoon butter or margarine

1. Place broccoli, carrot, and water in a 10-inch skillet. Cover; cook over medium-high heat 10 minutes or until carrot is tender. Drain; set aside.

2. Combine eggs, milk, onion, mustard, salt, and pepper; beat well. Stir in cheese and broccoli-carrot mixture.

3. Melt butter in a 10-inch ovenproof skillet. Pour egg mixture into skillet. Cook over medium-low heat 10 minutes or until eggs are almost set.

4. Place skillet in oven; broil 6 inches from heating element 3 minutes or until top is lightly browned and eggs are set.

5. Cut frittata into wedges, and serve immediately. Yield: 6 servings.

Note: To make any skillet ovenproof, wrap handle securely in heavy-duty aluminum foil.

TACO FRITTATA

1 tablespoon butter or margarine
6 eggs
2 tablespoons chopped green chiles
2 tablespoons water
½ teaspoon Worcestershire sauce
¼ teaspoon salt
  Dash of pepper
  Dash of ground cumin
⅓ cup commercial taco sauce
  Chopped fresh parsley

1. Melt butter in an 8-inch ovenproof skillet over low heat. Combine eggs, chiles, water, Worcestershire sauce, salt, pepper, and cumin in a medium mixing bowl; beat until well blended. Pour into skillet.

2. Cook over medium-low heat 6 minutes, gently lifting edges of frittata with a spatula and tilting pan so that uncooked portion flows underneath.

3. Transfer skillet to oven, and broil 6 inches from heating element 2 to 3 minutes.

4. Top frittata with taco sauce, and garnish with parsley. Cut into wedges, and serve immediately. Yield: 4 servings.

SALMON-VEGETABLE FRITTATA

¼ cup chopped green onion
¼ cup chopped green pepper
1 clove garlic, minced
2 teaspoons vegetable oil
½ (7¾-ounce) can salmon, drained
   and flaked
8 eggs
2 tablespoons grated Parmesan
   cheese
2 tablespoons water
½ teaspoon whole oregano
½ teaspoon dried parsley flakes
¼ teaspoon salt
¼ teaspoon pepper

1. Sauté green onion, green pepper, and garlic in oil in a large ovenproof skillet until tender. Remove from heat. Sprinkle salmon evenly over vegetables in skillet.

2. Combine eggs, Parmesan cheese, water, oregano, parsley flakes, salt, and pepper in a small mixing bowl; beat until well blended. Pour over vegetables and salmon in skillet.

3. Cook over medium-low heat 6 minutes or until eggs are set.

4. Transfer skillet to oven; broil 6 inches from heating element 2 to 3 minutes or until lightly browned.

5. Cut frittata into wedges, and serve immediately. Yield: 6 servings.

HAM-SPINACH-CHEESE PIE

  Pastry for a 9-inch pie
1 (10-ounce) package frozen
   chopped spinach, thawed and
   well-drained
1 cup chopped cooked ham
1 pound ricotta cheese
½ cup grated Parmesan or Romano
   cheese
¼ cup half-and-half
3 eggs
¼ teaspoon salt
⅛ teaspoon pepper

1. Line a pieplate or quiche dish with pastry; trim excess pastry around edges. Flute edges, if desired. Prick the bottom and sides of pastry shell with a fork. Bake at 425° for 6 to 8 minutes. Remove from oven, and cool on a wire rack.

2. Combine spinach and remaining ingredients; mix well. Pour into pastry shell.

3. Bake at 350° for 40 minutes or until pie is set.

4. Cut into wedges, and serve warm. Yield: 6 servings.

When cooking time is short, think "shellfish." Three entrées bound to please are (from top) Sautéed Shrimp (page 205), Jiffy Crabmeat (page 203), and Scallop Kabobs (page 204).

TURKEY-VEGETABLE STRATA

1 (6-ounce) package seasoned
     croutons, divided
1 (10-ounce) package frozen
     chopped broccoli, thawed and
     drained
1 cup diced cooked turkey or
     chicken
1 cup (4 ounces) shredded Cheddar
     cheese
3 tablespoons chopped green onions
6 eggs
1½ cups milk
2 tablespoons sliced blanched
     almonds

1. Sprinkle half the croutons in bottom
of a greased 8-inch square baking dish.
Layer broccoli, turkey, cheese, and green
onion over croutons; sprinkle with remaining croutons.
2. Combine eggs and milk, beating well.
Pour over crouton mixture. Sprinkle with
almonds. Cover and refrigerate at least 3
hours or overnight.
3. Remove cover; bake at 350° for 45
minutes or until mixture is hot and bubbly.
4. Cut into squares, and serve immediately. Yield: 8 servings.

TORTILLA TURNOVERS

4 wheat tortillas
2 cups shredded Cheddar or
     Monterey Jack cheese, divided
1 medium-size green pepper,
     seeded, chopped, and divided
     (optional)
Chili powder

1. Heat a skillet over medium-high until
very hot; place 1 tortilla in skillet, cooking

*Fusilli Salad (page 222) served with
breadsticks makes a quick and easy lunch.*

until lightly browned on bottom. Sprinkle
with one-fourth of cheese and green pepper, if desired; add chili powder to taste.
Heat 1 minute or just until cheese melts.
Fold in half, pressing lightly to seal.
2. Repeat procedure with remaining ingredients. Serve Tortilla Turnovers immediately. Yield: 4 servings.

VEGETABLE STRATA

4 medium zucchini, cut into ½-inch
     slices
½ medium onion, sliced
¼ cup water
4 eggs
2 cups (8 ounces) shredded Cheddar
     cheese
2 slices bread, cut into ½-inch
     cubes
1 tomato, peeled and diced
½ teaspoon salt
⅛ teaspoon red pepper

1. Cook zucchini and onion in water in a
medium saucepan until crisp-tender.
Drain well on paper towels. Set aside.
2. Beat eggs; stir in drained vegetables
and remaining ingredients.
3. Pour mixture into a greased 10- x 6- x
2-inch baking dish. Bake at 350° for 30
minutes or until set.
4. Serve warm. Yield: 6 to 8 servings.

MicroMethod

1. Combine zucchini, onion, and water
in a 10- x 6- x 2-inch baking dish. Cover
with heavy-duty plastic wrap, and vent to
allow steam to escape; microwave at HIGH
for 8 minutes or until crisp-tender. Drain
well on paper towels. Set aside.
2. Same as step 2.
3. Pour mixture into a greased 10- x 6- x
2-inch baking dish. Cover with waxed
paper. Microwave at MEDIUM (50%
power) for 8 minutes. Remove waxed
paper; stir and microwave at MEDIUM for
8 to 10 minutes or until set.
4. Same as step 4.

EGG-SPINACH BAKE

2 eggs, beaten
1½ cups commercial sour cream
2 tablespoons all-purpose flour
3 tablespoons grated Parmesan cheese
1 tablespoon finely chopped onion
½ teaspoon salt
⅛ teaspoon pepper
1 (10-ounce) package frozen chopped spinach, thawed and drained
4 hard-cooked eggs, chopped

1. Combine 2 beaten eggs, sour cream, flour, cheese, onion, salt, and pepper in a medium mixing bowl, stirring until well blended. Fold in spinach and chopped eggs. Spoon mixture into six greased 6-ounce custard cups or ramekins.

2. Place cups in a 13- x 9- x 2-inch baking dish; pour hot water into dish to a depth of ½ inch. Bake at 350° for 25 minutes or until knife inserted in center comes out clean.

3. Serve immediately. Yield: 6 servings.

MicroNote: To microwave step 2, place cups in microwave in a circular pattern. Microwave at HIGH for 2 minutes. Microwave at MEDIUM (50% power) for 15 to 18 minutes or until a knife inserted in center comes out clean, rotating cups half-turn every 3 minutes. Cover with waxed paper 1 minute, and let stand.

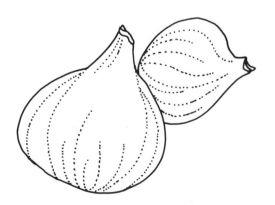

WAFFLE-CHEESE BAKE

1 (10-ounce) package frozen waffles
6 slices bacon, cooked, drained, and crumbled
1 cup (4 ounces) shredded Cheddar cheese
4 eggs, beaten
1½ cups milk
½ teaspoon salt

1. Place 4 waffles in the bottom of a lightly greased 8-inch square baking dish; sprinkle with bacon and cheese. Cut remaining waffles in half diagonally, and arrange waffles in 2 rows over cheese, overlapping rows slightly.

2. Combine eggs, milk, and salt in a medium mixing bowl, mixing well; pour mixture evenly over waffles. Cover and refrigerate 1 hour.

3. Bake, uncovered, at 375° for 35 minutes or until set.

4. Serve hot. Yield: 6 to 8 servings.

WELSH RAREBIT

1 (10½-ounce) can Cheddar cheese soup, undiluted
½ cup beer
1 tablespoon Worcestershire sauce
½ teaspoon dry mustard
8 slices (½-inch thick) French bread, toasted
16 rings red onion
8 slices bacon, cooked and halved
Paprika

1. Combine soup, beer, Worcestershire sauce, and mustard in a medium saucepan, stirring well. Cook over low heat until thoroughly heated. Do not boil.

2. Place 2 slices bread on each plate. Arrange 2 onion rings and 2 half slices of bacon on each bread slice.

3. Pour cheese sauce over toast; sprinkle with paprika. Serve immediately. Yield: 4 servings.

Salads and Salad Dressings

You'll find salads for all seasons in this chapter. The cellared vegetables of winter yield such favorites as Cabbage-Pineapple Slaw and Orange Carrot Salad. Come Spring, the fresh tastes of Potato-Egg Salad and Asparagus Vinaigrette await. Summer's bounty stars in great-for-a-picnic Fusilli Salad and Cucumbers in Dill-Yogurt Dressing. Autumn brings the vitamin-packed enjoyment of Wilted Kale Salad and the crispness of Classic Waldorf Salad. For busy seasons year-round, there is the whole-meal convenience of warm Beef Taco Salad, luscious Turkey and Rice Salad, and party-pretty Chicken Salad in Pineapple Boats. And for the spontaneous supermarket harvest of any season, there is the flavor enhancement of Creamy Walnut Dressing, olive and caper-flecked Mustard-Caper Dressing, or subtly sweet Mint Dressing.

◆ CLASSIC WALDORF SALAD

    3 medium-size tart red apples (about
        1½ pounds)
 1½ cups sliced celery
  ½ cup chopped walnuts
  ¼ cup mayonnaise or salad dressing
    1 tablespoon lemon juice
    1 teaspoon sugar
  ¼ teaspoon salt
      Dash of ground allspice
      Additional apple slices

1. Core and dice apples. Place in a medium mixing bowl; add celery and walnuts.
2. Combine mayonnaise, lemon juice, sugar, salt, and allspice, stirring well. Pour over apple mixture, tossing lightly to coat.
3. Cover and chill 3 hours or overnight. Garnish with apple slices. Yield: 6 servings.

Note: To turn this classic into a light main course, add 1½ cups diced cooked chicken or turkey, and double the amounts of mayonnaise, lemon juice, sugar, and salt. For another variation, substitute firm pears for apples, halved seedless red grapes for the celery, and pecans for the walnuts; substitute vanilla yogurt for the mayonnaise, and omit or reduce lemon juice and sugar.

◆ FROZEN CRANBERRY SALAD

    1 (16-ounce) can whole berry
        cranberry sauce
    1 (8¼-ounce) can crushed
        pineapple, drained
    1 (8-ounce) carton commercial sour
        cream
  ½ cup chopped pecans
      Lettuce leaves

1. Combine first 4 ingredients; stir well. Spoon mixture into 12 paper-lined muffin cups. Freeze overnight.
2. Remove from pan; peel off paper liners, and serve immediately on lettuce-lined salad plates. Yield: 12 servings.

CRANBERRY SALAD

2 (3-ounce) packages raspberry
    gelatin
2 cups boiling water
1 (15¼-ounce) can unsweetened
    crushed pineapple, undrained
1 (16-ounce) can whole berry
    cranberry sauce
1 cup port
½ cup chopped walnuts
    Lettuce leaves

1. Dissolve gelatin in boiling water. Add pineapple, cranberry sauce, port, and walnuts; mix well.
2. Pour into an 8-cup mold. Chill 4 hours or overnight.
3. Unmold onto a lettuce-lined serving platter. Yield: 12 servings.

JEWELED ORANGE SALAD

1 envelope unflavored gelatin
1¼ cups orange juice, divided
¾ cup lemon-lime carbonated
    beverage
1 (11-ounce) can mandarin oranges,
    drained
½ cup halved seedless green grapes
    Lettuce leaves

1. Soften gelatin in ¼ cup orange juice; set aside.
2. Combine remaining 1 cup orange juice and lemon-lime beverage in a medium non-metal saucepan; bring to a boil. Remove from heat.
3. Add reserved gelatin mixture, stirring until gelatin is dissolved. Chill until mixture reaches the consistency of unbeaten egg white.
4. Add oranges and grape halves to chilled mixture, stirring well. Spoon mixture into a lightly oiled 3-cup mold; chill 2 hours or until set.
5. Unmold salad onto a lettuce-lined serving plate; serve immediately. Yield: 4 to 6 servings.

ORANGE CARROT SALAD

2 cups shredded cabbage
1½ cups shredded carrot
1 (11-ounce) can mandarin
    oranges, drained
½ cup raisins
½ cup chopped pecans or
    walnuts
¾ cup mayonnaise
    Cabbage leaves (optional)

1. Combine shredded cabbage, carrot, oranges, raisins, pecans, and mayonnaise in a large mixing bowl; toss gently to coat. Cover and chill thoroughly.
2. Serve Orange Carrot Salad in a cabbage lined serving bowl, if desired. Yield: 6 servings.

LIME-PINEAPPLE SALAD

1 (3-ounce) package lime-flavored
    gelatin
1 cup boiling water
1 (15¼-ounce) can crushed
    pineapple, undrained
½ cup mayonnaise
½ cup small-curd cottage
    cheese
½ cup chopped celery
½ cup chopped pecans
    Lettuce leaves
    Pecan halves

1. Dissolve gelatin in boiling water in a large mixing bowl; stir until gelatin is dissolved. Chill until consistency of unbeaten egg white.
2. Fold in pineapple, mayonnaise, cottage cheese, celery, and ½ cup chopped pecans; pour into a lightly oiled 3½-cup ring mold. Cover with plastic wrap, and chill overnight.
3. Unmold salad on a lettuce-lined serving platter, and garnish with pecan halves. Slice and serve immediately. Yield: 8 to 10 servings.

◆ WINTER FRUIT SALAD WITH CREAMY DRESSING

1 cup grapefruit sections
1 cup orange sections or 1 (11-ounce) can Mandarin oranges, drained
1 cup pineapple chunks
1 cup sliced peaches
1 cup chopped pecans
    Lettuce leaves
1 (3-ounce) package cream cheese, softened
2 tablespoons honey
    Juice of ½ lemon
½ cup whipping cream, whipped

1. Combine fruit in a large colander; drain well. Add pecans to fruit mixture.
2. Spoon fruit evenly onto 6 lettuce-lined serving plates. Refrigerate.
3. Combine cream cheese, honey, and lemon juice in a small mixing bowl. Beat with an electric mixer until smooth. Fold in whipped cream.
4. Spoon 1 tablespoon dressing over each serving. Refrigerate any remaining dressing. Yield: 6 servings.

ARTICHOKES VINAIGRETTE

6 medium artichokes (about 2¼ pounds)
1 tablespoon plus 1 teaspoon vegetable oil
1 tablespoon lemon juice
1 clove garlic, halved
⅔ cup tomato juice
2 tablespoons red wine vinegar
2 teaspoons garlic salt
¼ teaspoon pepper

1. Wash artichokes by plunging up and down in cold water. Cut off stem end, and trim ½ inch from top of each artichoke. Remove any loose bottom leaves from artichoke. With scissors, trim away one-fourth of each outer leaf.
2. Place artichokes in a large Dutch oven in water to cover by 2 inches. Bring to a boil. Add oil, lemon juice, and garlic. Reduce heat; cover and simmer 30 minutes or until leaves pull away easily from base. Remove artichokes from liquid. Invert onto paper towels, and drain well. Cool and refrigerate until serving time.
3. Combine tomato juice, vinegar, garlic salt, and pepper. Serve with artichokes as a dipping sauce. Yield: 6 servings.

▢ ASPARAGUS VINAIGRETTE

1½ pounds asparagus
⅓ cup vegetable oil
⅓ cup olive or vegetable oil
2 tablespoons tarragon or raspberry vinegar
1 tablespoon fresh lemon or lime juice
2 cloves garlic, minced
2 teaspoons dried whole tarragon leaves
¼ teaspoon ground cardamom
    Salt and pepper to taste

1. Break off stem ends from asparagus. Steam asparagus or cook in ½ inch simmering water in a shallow saucepan 6 to 8 minutes or just until crisp-tender. Cool quickly under cold running water, and drain well. Refrigerate until serving time.
2. Divide asparagus among serving plates. Whisk remaining ingredients in small bowl or shake in covered jar to blend.
3. Spoon vinaigrette over asparagus. Yield: 6 servings.

MicroNote: To microwave step 1, place ¼ cup water in a 12- x 8- x 2-inch dish. Arrange spears in dish with buds toward the center. Cover with heavy-duty plastic wrap, and vent to allow steam to escape; microwave at HIGH for 7 to 10 minutes, or until crisp-tender.

Salads 217

NEXT-DAY VEGETABLE SALAD

1 small head iceberg lettuce, torn into bite-size pieces
½ pound fresh spinach, torn into bite-size pieces
½ pound bacon, cooked and crumbled
1 bunch green onions, chopped
1 (10-ounce) package frozen English peas, thawed
1 (8-ounce) can sliced water chestnuts, drained
1 cup (4 ounces) shredded sharp Cheddar cheese, shredded
1½ cups mayonnaise
Green onion fan

1. Layer first 7 ingredients in order listed in a large salad bowl.
2. Spread mayonnaise over top of salad, sealing to edge of bowl. Cover salad tightly with plastic wrap, and refrigerate overnight. Garnish with green onion fan.
3. Serve salad in a large salad bowl, or spoon onto individual salad plates. Yield: 12 servings.

HOT BEAN SALAD

4 slices bacon
⅔ cup vinegar
½ cup sugar
1 tablespoon cornstarch
½ teaspoon salt
¼ teaspoon pepper
1 (16-ounce) can cut green beans, drained
1 (16-ounce) can cut wax beans, drained
1 (16-ounce) can red kidney beans, drained and rinsed
1 medium onion, sliced

1. Cook bacon in a large Dutch oven until crisp; remove to paper towels to drain, reserving drippings in Dutch oven. Crumble bacon, and set aside.
2. Add vinegar, sugar, cornstarch, salt, and pepper to bacon drippings; stir well to blend. Cover and bring to a boil; reduce heat, and cook, stirring constantly, until thickened.
3. Add drained beans and onion slices to vinegar sauce, stirring well. Cover and cook over medium heat 10 minutes or until onion is tender; stir occasionally.
4. Transfer to a serving bowl, and sprinkle bacon over top just before serving. Serve hot. Yield: 8 servings.

MicroMethod

1. Cut bacon strips into small pieces, and place in a 2-quart baking dish. Cover with heavy-duty plastic wrap, and vent to allow steam to escape; microwave at HIGH for 3 to 4 minutes, stirring after 2 minutes. Remove cooked bacon pieces using a slotted spoon to paper towels; drain, reserving bacon drippings in baking dish. Set bacon pieces aside.
2. Add vinegar, sugar, cornstarch, salt, and pepper to bacon drippings. Beat well with a wire whisk to blend. Microwave at HIGH for 3 to 4 minutes or until mixture is thickened.
3. Add drained beans and onion slices to vinegar sauce, stirring well. Cover with heavy-duty plastic wrap, and vent to allow steam to escape; microwave at HIGH for 6 to 7 minutes, stirring after 3 minutes. Let mixture stand 10 minutes before serving.
4. Same as step 4 above.

CABBAGE-PINEAPPLE SLAW

1 small cabbage (about 1½ pounds), shredded
1 (8¼-ounce) can pineapple chunks, drained
1 medium orange, peeled, seeded, and diced
¼ cup chopped green pepper
⅔ cup commercial Russian salad dressing

1. Combine all ingredients; toss lightly. Chill thoroughly.

2. Serve in a large serving bowl. Yield: 4 to 6 servings.

◆ CAULI-SLAW

1 small cauliflower (about 1¼ pounds)
¼ cup commercial French reduced-calorie salad dressing
¼ cup sliced green onions
½ teaspoon caraway seeds
½ teaspoon celery salt
½ cup low-fat plain yogurt

1. Wash cauliflower; break into flowerets, and thinly slice. Combine cauliflower and dressing in a small mixing bowl. Cover and chill several hours.

2. Combine onions, caraway seeds, celery salt, and yogurt in a small bowl; set aside.

3. Drain cauliflower; combine cauliflower and yogurt mixture. Spoon into a serving bowl. Yield: 6 servings.

GRATED SQUASH SLAW

1 pound zucchini, coarsely grated
1 pound yellow squash, coarsely grated
1 medium-size sweet red pepper, coarsely chopped
1 bunch green onions, chopped
¼ cup vegetable oil
¼ cup cider vinegar
2 tablespoons mayonnaise
1 teaspoon sugar
½ teaspoon salt
¼ teaspoon celery salt
⅛ teaspoon pepper

1. Combine zucchini, squash, red pepper, and green onions; toss lightly.

2. Combine remaining ingredients; stir well using a wire whisk. Pour over vegetables; toss lightly.

3. Cover and chill 30 minutes before serving. Yield: 6 servings.

◆ TOMATO ASPIC

1 package unflavored gelatin
1¾ cups tomato juice, divided
2 tablespoons lemon juice
½ teaspoon Worcestershire sauce
Dash of hot sauce
Lettuce leaves
Mayonnaise

1. Soften gelatin in ¾ cup tomato juice in a medium saucepan. Place over medium heat, stirring constantly, 3 minutes or until gelatin dissolves. Remove from heat.

2. Add remaining 1 cup tomato juice, lemon juice, Worcestershire sauce, and hot sauce; stir well. Pour into 6 lightly oiled ⅓-cup ring molds; chill until set.

3. Turn molds out onto 6 individual lettuce-lined salad plates; dollop with mayonnaise. Yield: 6 servings.

◆ CUCUMBERS IN DILL-YOGURT DRESSING

1 (8-ounce) carton plain low-fat yogurt
1 teaspoon lemon juice
¼ teaspoon salt
¼ teaspoon dried whole dillweed
2 medium cucumbers, scored and thinly sliced
Bibb lettuce

1. Combine yogurt, lemon juice, salt, and dillweed in a medium mixing bowl; stir well.

2. Add cucumbers, and gently fold into yogurt mixture. Cover with plastic wrap, and chill at least 2 hours.

3. Spoon cucumber mixture into a lettuce-lined serving bowl, and serve immediately. Yield: 4 servings.

Note: To slice a cucumber in the food processor, cut into lengths that will fit the food chute. Cut each piece in half lengthwise, if necessary. Stand cucumber in the food chute, and slice with thick or thin slicing disc, applying firm pressure.

BEEF TACO SALAD

1 pound lean ground beef
1 medium onion, chopped
1 cup commercial taco sauce
1 cup water
1 tablespoon plus 1 teaspoon chili
  powder
6 cups shredded lettuce
1 cup (4 ounces) shredded Cheddar
  cheese
1 avocado, peeled and cut into
  wedges
1 medium tomato, coarsely chopped
½ cup commercial sour cream
¼ cup sliced ripe olives
  Tortilla chips

1. Combine beef and onion in a large skillet; cook over medium heat until beef is browned, stirring to crumble; drain. Add taco sauce, water, and chili powder. Cook, uncovered, over medium heat 5 minutes.

2. Divide lettuce equally among 4 large salad plates. Top evenly with beef mixture, cheese, avocado, and tomato. Top each salad with a dollop of sour cream; sprinkle evenly with olives.

3. Serve salads immediately with tortilla chips. Yield: 4 servings.

◆ BEEF SALAD PAISANO

3 stalks celery, cleaned and sliced
  diagonally
3 carrots, scraped and sliced
  diagonally
1 (8-ounce) can green beans,
  drained
¾ cup chopped green pepper
1 (4-ounce) jar diced pimiento,
  drained
¾ cup commercial Italian
  reduced-calorie salad dressing
1 medium head iceberg lettuce
3 cups thinly sliced cooked beef
1 medium-size red onion, sliced and
  separated into rings

1. Cook celery and carrots in boiling water in a medium saucepan 5 minutes or until crisp-tender. Drain.

2. Combine drained celery-carrot mixture, green beans, chopped green pepper, pimiento, and salad dressing in a medium mixing bowl, stirring well. Cover and chill mixture thoroughly.

3. Remove outer leaves of lettuce; set aside. Cut remaining lettuce into 1-inch pieces. Combine chopped lettuce, beef, onion, and celery-carrot mixture in a large mixing bowl, tossing well.

4. Line a large serving bowl with reserved lettuce leaves; spoon lettuce mixture into prepared bowl.

5. Serve chilled. Yield: 6 to 8 servings.

HOT CHICKEN SALAD

2 cups diced cooked chicken
1 cup chopped celery
⅓ cup chopped green pepper
¼ cup sliced almonds, toasted
2 tablespoons chopped onion
1 (2-ounce) jar diced pimiento,
  drained
¾ cup mayonnaise
2 teaspoons lemon juice
½ teaspoon salt
¾ cup (3 ounces) cubed Cheddar
  cheese
½ cup crushed potato chips

1. Combine chicken, celery, green pepper, almonds, onion, pimiento, mayonnaise, lemon juice, and salt in a large mixing bowl, stirring well.

2. Spoon mixture into a lightly greased 1-quart baking dish. Bake at 350° for 20 minutes or until bubbly.

3. Stir in cheese; sprinkle with potato chips. Bake an additional 5 minutes or until cheese melts.

4. Serve warm. Yield: 4 servings.

Note: Tuna, cooked turkey, or shrimp may be substituted for chicken.

♠ CHICKEN DE-LITE SALAD

3 cups cubed cooked chicken
1 cup chopped celery
1 cup sliced fresh mushrooms
1 medium-size green pepper,
    chopped
2 tablespoons chopped green onions
¼ teaspoon salt
⅛ teaspoon pepper
1 cup commercial buttermilk salad
    dressing
8 medium tomatoes, cored
    Lettuce leaves

1. Combine first 8 ingredients; toss lightly. Chill thoroughly.

2. Cut tomatoes almost completely through into wedges; spread apart. Spoon salad mixture into center of tomatoes.

3. Place tomatoes on lettuce leaves, and serve immediately. Yield: 8 servings.

♠ CHICKEN SALAD IN PINEAPPLE BOATS

2 boneless and skinless chicken
    breasts (about ¾ pound)
1 medium pineapple
½ cup mayonnaise
¼ cup commercial sour cream
1 tablespoon lime juice
¾ teaspoon salt
1¼ cups chopped pecans, divided
1 cup seedless green grapes, halved

1. Place chicken in boiling water. Reduce heat; cover and cook 15 minutes or until tender. Remove from heat; drain and cool. Cut chicken into ½-inch cubes.

2. Cut pineapple in half lengthwise. Scoop out pulp, leaving a ½-inch-thick shell; set aside. Chop 1 cup of pineapple pulp, and set aside.

3. Combine mayonnaise, sour cream, lime juice, and salt in a large mixing bowl; mix well. Fold in chicken, pineapple, 1 cup pecans, and grapes. Cover with plastic wrap, and chill 2 hours.

4. Spoon salad into reserved pineapple shells. Garnish tops with remaining ¼ cup pecans. Yield: 4 servings.

♠ CALIFORNIA CLUB SALAD
(pictured on page 230)

½ cup mayonnaise
½ cup commercial French salad
    dressing
2 ounces blue cheese, crumbled
6 cups shredded lettuce
1½ cups chopped cooked chicken
2 medium tomatoes, cut into wedges
1 medium avocado, peeled and
    sliced
4 slices bacon, cooked and
    crumbled
1 hard-cooked egg, chopped

1. Combine first 3 ingredients; stir well. Cover; chill thoroughly.

2. Place shredded lettuce on a large serving platter; arrange chicken, tomatoes, avocado, bacon, and egg over lettuce.

3. Spoon chilled dressing over salad just before serving. Yield: 6 servings.

♠ TURKEY AND RICE SALAD

½ cup commercial Russian salad
    dressing
½ cup plain low-fat yogurt
1½ teaspoons chili powder
3 cups cubed cooked turkey
2 cups regular cooked rice, chilled
1 medium-size green pepper, seeded
    and chopped
1 medium tomato, chopped
1 cup sliced celery
    Lettuce leaves

1. Combine dressing, yogurt, and chili powder; stir well. Add remaining ingredients except lettuce; toss lightly. Cover and chill thoroughly.

2. Serve salad on lettuce-lined serving plates. Yield: 6 servings.

CRAB SALAD

1 pound lump or flake crabmeat
½ cup mayonnaise
½ cup chopped celery
2 hard-cooked eggs, chopped
2 tablespoons capers
1 tablespoon lemon juice
¼ teaspoon salt
⅛ teaspoon pepper
  Dash of red pepper
  Tomato cups, lettuce cups, or
    cooked artichokes
  Pimiento strips

1. Combine crabmeat, mayonnaise, celery, eggs, capers, lemon juice, salt, pepper, and red pepper; mix well. Cover with plastic wrap, and chill thoroughly.

2. Spoon salad mixture into tomato cups, lettuce cups, or artichokes. Garnish with pimiento strips. Serve chilled. Yield: 4 servings.

OLIVE EGG SALAD

1 (3-ounce) package cream cheese,
    softened
¼ cup mayonnaise
¾ teaspoon dried whole dillweed
½ teaspoon salt
½ teaspoon dry mustard
6 hard-cooked eggs, chopped
½ cup sliced ripe olives
½ cup chopped celery
2 tablespoons chopped onion
1 tablespoon chopped pimiento
  Lettuce leaves or pita bread
    rounds

1. Combine cream cheese, mayonnaise, dillweed, salt, and mustard in a medium mixing bowl; beat at medium speed of an electric mixer until well blended.

2. Stir in remaining ingredients except lettuce leaves. Cover with plastic wrap, and chill until serving time. Serve on lettuce leaves or in pita bread rounds. Yield: about 3 cups.

FUSILLI SALAD
(pictured on page 212)

1 (8-ounce) package corkscrew
    pasta, uncooked
1 large zucchini, thinly sliced (about
    2 cups)
1½ cups large, pitted ripe olives
½ pound cooked ham, cut into
    ½-inch cubes
1 medium-size yellow sweet pepper,
    seeded and cut into strips
1 medium tomato, peeled and cut
    into wedges
½ cup chopped fresh parsley
½ teaspoon pepper
1 (8-ounce) bottle commercial
    Italian reduced-calorie dressing
  Lettuce leaves

1. Cook pasta according to package directions; drain. Rinse under cold running water to cool quickly; drain well. Place pasta in a large bowl.

2. Add remaining ingredients except lettuce to pasta; toss lightly. Cover and chill thoroughly.

3. Transfer salad to a lettuce-lined serving platter. Yield: 8 to 10 servings.

ORZO SALAD

1¼ cups (8 ounces) orzo, uncooked
2 cups thinly sliced zucchini (about
    2 medium)
1 medium-size green pepper, seeded
    and chopped
¼ cup sliced green onions
½ cup mayonnaise
½ cup commercial sour cream
1 teaspoon dried whole dillweed
½ teaspoon salt
⅛ teaspoon pepper
  Tomato wedges

1. Cook orzo according to package directions; drain. Rinse under cold running water to cool quickly. Drain.

2. Combine cooked orzo, zucchini,

green pepper, green onions, mayonnaise, sour cream, dillweed, salt, and pepper in a large mixing bowl, stirring well. Cover and chill thoroughly.

3. Spoon mixture into a serving bowl; garnish with tomato wedges. Serve chilled. Yield: 8 servings.

◆ POTATO-EGG SALAD

2 **pounds new potatoes, cooked and sliced**
4 **hard-cooked eggs, chopped**
¾ **cup mayonnaise**
⅓ **cup chopped sweet pickle**
⅓ **cup chopped celery**
¼ **cup chopped onion**
¼ **cup chopped green pepper**
1 **tablespoon prepared mustard**
½ **teaspoon salt**
¼ **teaspoon pepper**
¼ **teaspoon dried whole dillweed**

1. Combine all ingredients in a large mixing bowl, stirring well. Cover and chill thoroughly.

2. Transfer to a large serving bowl, and serve chilled. Yield: 6 to 8 servings.

WILTED KALE SALAD

1 **pound fresh kale, washed, stems removed, and torn into pieces**
6 **slices bacon**
1 **medium-size sweet red pepper, seeded and cut into 1-inch pieces**
1 **medium onion, coarsely chopped**
½ **cup red wine vinegar**

1. Drop kale into boiling salted water; blanch 1 minute. Drain well, and transfer to a large salad bowl. Set aside.

2. Cook bacon in a large skillet over medium-high heat until crisp. Transfer bacon to paper towels to drain; reserve 2 tablespoons bacon drippings in skillet. Crumble bacon, and set aside.

3. Add sweet red pepper and onion to bacon drippings in skillet; sauté until tender. Stir in vinegar and reserved bacon.

4. Remove from heat, and pour mixture over reserved kale in salad bowl; toss lightly to coat well.

5. Serve Wilted Kale Salad immediately. Yield: 4 to 6 servings.

THE GREENING OF SALADS

Make every day a salad day, and you'll benefit from the fiber, vitamins, and minerals that abound in salad greens. Mix several greens in one salad for greatest taste harmony and most tempting appearance. Here is a glossary of some of the less common greens that mix well with the more familiar varieties:

Arugula. An herb that's leafy enough to use as a green. Arugula (also called rocket) adds a spicy note to salads made with milder lettuces. It's high in calcium and delicious with vinaigrette dressings.

Dandelion Greens. The young tender leaves are a sign of spring and an excellent source of vitamin A. Toss with olive oil, lemon juice, and black pepper, or combine with other greens.

Mache. Also called corn salad, field lettuce, and lamb's lettuce—delicate yet flavorful. Combine with other greens, and toss with a light vinaigrette.

Mustard Greens. These very spicy, curled leaves add a great peppery bite to iceberg salads served with avocado or blue cheese dressings.

Radicchio. Small, firm-textured heads with a glorious red wine color. This sturdy, slightly bitter tasting green makes pale lettuces look festive.

ITALIAN SALAD DRESSING

½ cup vegetable oil
2 tablespoons vinegar
2 tablespoons lemon juice
2 tablespoons water
1 teaspoon sugar
½ teaspoon dry mustard
½ teaspoon paprika
¼ teaspoon salt
¼ teaspoon seasoned salt
¼ teaspoon dried Italian seasoning
⅛ teaspoon red pepper

1. Combine all ingredients in a jar. Cover tightly; shake vigorously. Chill.
2. Shake before serving. Serve over salad greens. Yield: 1 cup.

MUSTARD-CAPER DRESSING

½ cup mayonnaise
2 tablespoons minced fresh parsley
2 tablespoons minced green olives
1 tablespoon minced celery
1 tablespoon minced onion
1 tablespoon minced capers
1 tablespoon lemon juice
1 tablespoon white wine vinegar
1 tablespoon Dijon mustard
½ teaspoon pepper

1. Combine all ingredients; stir well. Cover and chill 1 hour or overnight.
2. Serve dressing over lettuce wedges. Yield: 1 cup.

MUSTARD VINAIGRETTE

1 cup vegetable oil
⅓ cup white wine vinegar or lemon juice
1½ teaspoons dry mustard
½ teaspoon salt
⅛ teaspoon paprika
Dash of hot sauce or red pepper

1. Combine all ingredients in a jar. Cover tightly, and shake vigorously. Chill several hours.
2. Shake vinaigrette well before serving. Serve dressing over salad greens. Yield: 1⅓ cups.

Note: Add a spicy note to this dressing, if you wish, with one or a combination of the following spices: ¼ teaspoon ground cinnamon, ¼ teaspoon pumpkin pie spice, ¼ teaspoon ground cardamom, or ⅛ teaspoon ground nutmeg.

CREAMY WALNUT DRESSING

1 (3-ounce) package cream cheese, softened
½ cup mayonnaise
½ cup whipping cream
1 cup chopped walnuts, toasted

1. Combine cream cheese and mayonnaise in a small mixing bowl; beat on medium speed of electric mixer until well blended.
2. Beat whipping cream until soft peaks form; fold whipped cream and walnuts into cream cheese mixture.
3. Cover with plastic wrap, and chill thoroughly. Serve with fresh fruit salads. Yield: about 2 cups.

MINT DRESSING

⅔ cup plain low-fat yogurt
½ cup evaporated skimmed milk
1 tablespoon finely chopped fresh mint
2 tablespoons honey
¼ teaspoon poppy seeds

1. Combine all ingredients in a small mixing bowl. Stir until well blended. Cover with plastic wrap, and chill at least 3 hours.
2. Spoon chilled dressing over fresh fruit combinations of your choice at serving time. Yield: about 1½ cups.

Soups and Sandwiches

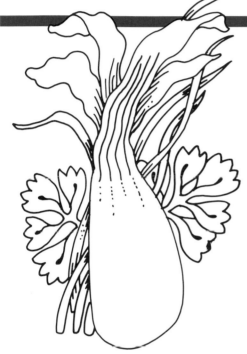

Soups and sandwiches can inspire you to be a clever matchmaker, a creative party host—or just a very smart cook! Take the cues for successful matchmaking from contrasting textures, as in creamy Corn Chowder with Zesty Beef and Bagel Sandwiches, or from seasoning affinities, as in Curried Carrot Soup with Lamb-Stuffed Pita Pockets. Keynote an elegant party with chilled goblets of Easy Vichyssoise. Invite the whole gang over for a kettleful of Tempting Meatball Stew or Savory Beef Goulash. And make it all very easy on yourself by keeping the pantry stocked with the fixings for these simple recipes, which need nothing more than a tossed salad to make a satisfying meal.

WINE BROTH

1 quart water
4 beef-flavored bouillon cubes
1 teaspoon Worcestershire sauce
1 teaspoon lime juice
½ cup Burgundy or other dry red wine
Lime slices

1. Combine water, bouillon cubes, Worcestershire sauce, and lime juice in a medium saucepan; bring to a boil, stirring occasionally. Add wine, stirring well; cook over medium heat until thoroughly heated.

2. Ladle into individual serving bowls; garnish each serving with a lime slice. Yield: 4 cups.

BEER CHEESE SOUP

¼ cup butter or margarine
⅓ cup all-purpose flour
3 cups chicken broth
2 cups milk
¼ teaspoon white pepper
1 cup beer
1 teaspoon Worcestershire sauce
¼ teaspoon hot sauce
3½ cups (14 ounces) shredded sharp Cheddar cheese
Croutons (optional)

1. Melt butter in a small Dutch oven over low heat; add flour, stirring until smooth. Cook 1 minute, stirring constantly. Gradually add broth and milk; cook over medium heat, stirring constantly, until thickened and bubbly. Stir in pepper.

2. Add beer, Worcestershire sauce, and hot sauce; bring to a boil, stirring frequently. Remove from heat; add cheese, and stir until melted.

3. Ladle soup into individual bowls. Garnish each serving with croutons, if desired. Serve Beer Cheese Soup immediately. Yield: 8 cups.

VEGETABLE-CHEESE CHOWDER

    2 cups water
    1 (10¾-ounce) can chicken broth,
         undiluted
    1 cup sliced carrots
    ½ cup chopped onion
    1 small clove garlic, minced
    ⅛ teaspoon pepper
    2 cups coarsely chopped fresh
         broccoli
    2 tablespoons all-purpose flour
    1½ cups milk
    1½ cups (6 ounces) shredded Swiss
         cheese

  1. Combine first 6 ingredients in a large
saucepan. Bring to a boil. Reduce heat;
cover and simmer 10 minutes.
  2. Add broccoli; cook 1 minute.
  3. Combine flour and milk, stirring well.
Add milk mixture to vegetable mixture.
Cook over medium heat 10 minutes or
until thickened and bubbly. Stir in cheese.
Serve immediately. Yield: 6 cups.

BROCCOLI SOUP
(pictured on page 229)

    1 (10-ounce) package frozen
         chopped broccoli
    2 tablespoons butter or margarine
    ¼ cup plus 1½ teaspoons
         all-purpose flour
    3 cups milk, divided
    ½ teaspoon salt
    ¼ teaspoon celery salt
    ⅛ teaspoon red pepper
       Fresh parsley sprigs

  1. Cook broccoli in a medium saucepan
according to package directions; drain,
and set aside.
  2. Melt butter in a medium saucepan
over low heat; add flour, stirring until
smooth. Cook 1 minute, stirring constantly. Gradually add 2 cups milk; cook
over medium heat, stirring constantly,
until thickened and bubbly. Stir in salt,
celery salt, and red pepper.

  3. Add reserved broccoli and remaining
1 cup milk; cook, stirring constantly, until
thickened. Process 2 cups broccoli mixture
in container of an electric blender until
smooth; repeat procedure with remaining
broccoli mixture.
  4. Return pureed mixture to saucepan;
cook over medium heat until thoroughly
heated.
  5. Ladle soup into individual serving
bowls; garnish each serving with fresh
parsley sprigs. Serve hot. Yield: 4 cups.

MicroMethod

  1. Microwave broccoli according to
package directions; drain and set aside.
  2. Place butter in a 2-quart glass measure; microwave at HIGH for 20 seconds
or until butter melts. Add flour, stirring
well; add 2 cups milk, stirring well. Microwave at HIGH for 4 minutes or until thickened and bubbly, stirring every minute.
Stir in salt, celery salt, and red pepper.
  3. Add reserved broccoli and remaining
1 cup milk, stirring well; microwave at
MEDIUM-HIGH (70% power) for 5 minutes or until thickened, stirring every minute. Process 2 cups broccoli mixture in
container of an electric blender until
smooth; repeat procedure with remaining
mixture.
  4. Return pureed mixture to a 2-quart
glass measure; microwave at MEDIUM-
HIGH (70% power) for 3 to 5 minutes or
until thoroughly heated.
  5. Same as step 5.

CORN CHOWDER

    6 slices bacon
    1 medium onion, coarsely chopped
    2 medium potatoes, peeled and
         cubed
    ½ cup water
    2 cups milk
    1 (17-ounce) can cream-style corn
    ½ teaspoon salt
       Dash of pepper

1. Cook bacon in a Dutch oven until crisp; remove bacon, reserving 2 table-spoons drippings in Dutch oven. Crumble bacon, and set aside.

2. Sauté onion in reserved drippings until tender; add potatoes and water. Cover and simmer 15 to 20 minutes or until potatoes are tender. Stir in milk, corn, salt, and pepper; cook over medium heat, stirring frequently, until thoroughly heated.

3. Sprinkle each serving with reserved bacon. Yield: about 5 cups.

Note: This soup can be easily varied by adding ½ (10-ounce) package of frozen green peas, lima beans, green beans, or broccoli cuts. Add to soup during last 5 minutes of simmering.

CURRIED CARROT SOUP
(pictured on page 229)

1 medium onion, chopped
1 teaspoon dried whole thyme
1 bay leaf
2 teaspoons vegetable oil
4 medium carrots, scraped and cut into ½-inch pieces
3 (14½-ounce) cans chicken broth, undiluted
2 teaspoons curry powder
½ (8-ounce) package Neufchâtel cheese
3 tablespoons chopped fresh parsley
Dash of red pepper

1. Sauté onion, thyme, and bay leaf in oil in a medium Dutch oven until onion is tender. Add carrots, chicken broth, and curry powder; cover and cook over medium heat 25 minutes or until carrots are tender. Remove from heat.

2. Remove bay leaf and discard. Combine carrot mixture and cheese in container of an electric blender; process until smooth. Strain mixture through a sieve into a Dutch oven, discarding pulp. Stir in parsley and pepper. Heat thoroughly.

3. Serve warm. Yield: 6½ cups.

EASY VICHYSSOISE

4 medium leeks, cleaned and sliced
1 tablespoon butter or margarine
4 medium potatoes (about 1½ pounds), peeled and diced
1 quart water
4 chicken-flavored bouillon cubes
¼ teaspoon pepper
1 cup whipping cream
Chopped fresh chives

1. Sauté leeks in butter in a small Dutch oven 10 minutes or until tender. Add potatoes, water, bouillon cubes, and pepper; bring to a boil. Reduce heat; cover and simmer 30 minutes, stirring occasionally.

2. Process 2 cups mixture in container of an electric blender until smooth; repeat procedure with remaining mixture.

3. Return pureed mixture to Dutch oven; add whipping cream, stirring well. Cook over low heat, stirring constantly, until thoroughly heated.

4. Ladle into individual serving bowls; garnish each serving with chopped chives. Serve warm. Yield: about 8 cups.

RICH ONION SOUP

1½ cups thinly sliced onion
3 tablespoons butter or margarine
1 quart water
4 beef-flavored bouillon cubes
¼ teaspoon pepper
5 (½-inch-thick) slices French bread, toasted
1¼ cups (5 ounces) shredded Swiss cheese, divided

1. Sauté onion in butter in a large sauce-pan 10 minutes or until tender. Add water, bouillon cubes, and pepper, stirring well; bring to a boil. Reduce heat; cover and simmer 25 minutes, stirring occasionally.

2. Ladle into ovenproof bowls; top each with a slice of bread and ¼ cup cheese. Place bowls on a baking sheet. Bake at 425° for 5 minutes or until cheese melts.

3. Serve immediately. Yield: 5 servings.

SPANISH GAZPACHO

2 medium tomatoes, coarsely
   chopped
1 cup chopped celery
¼ cup chopped onion
1 clove garlic, halved
1 quart tomato juice
2 tablespoons lemon juice
2 tablespoons olive oil
1 teaspoon salt
¼ teaspoon pepper
¼ teaspoon hot sauce
1 medium-size green pepper,
   seeded and finely chopped
1 medium cucumber, peeled and
   finely chopped
1 cup seasoned croutons

1. Position knife blade in food processor bowl; add tomatoes, celery, onion, and garlic. Pulse processor on and off to finely chop vegetables. Place vegetables in a large mixing bowl.

2. Add tomato juice, lemon juice, olive oil, salt, pepper, and hot sauce to vegetable mixture, stirring to combine. Cover mixture, and chill thoroughly. (May be refrigerated up to 7 days.)

3. Stir well before serving; garnish with green pepper, cucumber, and croutons. Yield: 7 cups.

EASY GAZPACHO

1 (28-ounce) can tomatoes,
   undrained
1 cup tomato juice
1 cup buttermilk
1 small onion, coarsely chopped
1 small cucumber, peeled and
   coarsely chopped
1 small green pepper, seeded and
   coarsely chopped
1 clove garlic
2 tablespoons olive oil
½ to 1 teaspoon chili powder
½ teaspoon salt
½ teaspoon cumin seeds
½ teaspoon hot sauce

1. Combine all ingredients in a large mixing bowl. Place half of mixture in container of an electric blender; process until smooth. Repeat procedure with remaining mixture.

2. Cover and chill thoroughly before serving. Yield: about 7½ cups.

CHICKEN-VEGETABLE SOUP

3½ cups water
1 tablespoon chicken-flavored
   bouillon granules
4 cups diced, peeled tomatoes
¼ cup dried minced onion
1 teaspoon dried whole basil
1 teaspoon paprika
¾ teaspoon instant minced garlic
¼ teaspoon salt
1 cup sliced carrots
1½ cups sliced fresh mushrooms
1 cup diced zucchini
1 cup diced, cooked chicken
2 tablespoons Burgundy or other
   red wine

1. Combine water, bouillon granules, tomatoes, onion, basil, paprika, garlic, and salt in a large saucepan. Bring to a boil. Reduce heat; cover and simmer 10 minutes. Add carrots; cover and simmer 10 minutes.

2. Add mushrooms, zucchini, chicken, and wine; simmer, uncovered, 8 minutes.

3. Serve hot. Yield: 8 cups.

Serve either one of the soups as a delicious appetizer for dinner or with a sandwich for lunch: Broccoli Soup or Curried Carrot Soup (page 226).

Above: *Topped with melted cheese and tomatoes, Cheesy Ham and Spinach Sandwich (page 234) is a meal in itself.*

Right: *Crumbled blue cheese in the dressing adds a rich tangy flavor to California Club Salad (page 221).*

CALIFORNIA-STYLE CHICKEN-VEGETABLE SOUP

1½ quarts chicken broth
2 cups diced cooked chicken
1 cup uncooked quick-cooking rice
1 (16-ounce) package frozen California-style vegetables
1 small yellow squash, coarsely chopped
1 small onion, chopped
½ teaspoon dried whole tarragon
¼ teaspoon hot sauce

1. Bring chicken broth to a boil in a large Dutch oven. Add chicken, rice, California-style vegetables, squash, onion, tarragon, and hot sauce to chicken broth; bring to a boil. Reduce heat; cover, and simmer 5 minutes.

2. Remove from heat; let stand, covered, 5 minutes.

3. Serve hot. Yield: 8 cups.

TEMPTING MEATBALL STEW

1½ pounds lean ground beef
¼ cup finely chopped or grated onion
½ teaspoon salt
¼ teaspoon pepper
¼ teaspoon dried whole basil, crumbled
⅓ cup all-purpose flour
3 (10½-ounce) cans beef consommé or beef bouillon, undiluted
4 medium carrots, scraped and quartered
4 medium potatoes, peeled and cut into 1-inch cubes
1 (16-ounce) package frozen cut green beans
½ pound fresh mushrooms, sliced
1 clove garlic, crushed
1 bay leaf

1. Combine first 5 ingredients; mix well. Pat meat mixture out into a rectangle about 1½ inches thick; cut into 1½-inch

squares. Shape each meat square into a meatball.

2. Brown meatballs in a large Dutch oven over medium heat. Remove meatballs, and set aside.

3. Combine flour and consommé; stir into skillet drippings. Cook over medium heat until mixture is thickened and bubbly. Add meatballs, carrots, potatoes, green beans, mushrooms, garlic, and bay leaf. Cover and simmer 30 minutes or until vegetables are tender. Remove bay leaf, and discard.

4. Serve stew warm. Yield: about 10 cups.

SAVORY BEEF GOULASH

1 pound lean beef for stewing, cut into ½-inch cubes
2 medium potatoes, peeled and cut into ½-inch cubes
1 large onion, chopped
1 (10½-ounce) can beef broth, undiluted
1 cup water
⅓ cup tomato paste
1½ teaspoons paprika
½ teaspoons dried whole marjoram
⅛ teaspoon pepper
1 clove garlic, minced
Cornbread croutons

1. Brown beef on all sides in a large Dutch oven over medium-high heat. Add remaining ingredients except croutons. Bring to a boil.

2. Reduce heat; cover and simmer 1 hour or until beef is tender.

3. Serve with croutons. Yield: 6 cups.

MicroMethod

1. Combine all ingredients except croutons in a 3-quart casserole. Cover with heavy-duty plastic wrap, and vent to allow steam to escape; microwave at MEDIUM HIGH (70% power) for 40 minutes, stirring every 10 minutes.

2. Same as step 3.

THE FLAVOR OF THE BROTH

The better the broth, the more flavorful a soup or stew will be. So use the best broth you can, depending on how much time and what kinds of ingredients you have on hand. If you don't have time to make a rich, tasty stock from scratch, here are some possibilities for improving convenience products without much fuss:

● A quick way to perk up the flavor of broth made from flavored chicken or beef bouillon granules or canned broth is to heat them to boiling with some vinegar or lemon juice, and a few sprigs of fresh parsley. Strain, if desired. The acid of the vinegar or lemon juice plus the slight bitterness of parsley will balance some of the saltiness of the broth. Add a grated carrot, if you have time, for the touch of sweetness it will contribute to the broth.

● Save bones, scraps of meat, and juices from roast beef, ham, or chicken. Store in the freezer up to 4 months. When you have time, simmer them with commercial broth for 2 hours. Strain; refrigerate broth up to 5 days, or freeze up to 6 months.

● Dried mushrooms provide a wonderful way to "beef-up" commercial beef broth. Soak the mushrooms in red wine or water until softened, 20 to 30 minutes. Add the soaking liquid and the mushrooms to the broth. You can use this base for any kind of hearty meat or bean soup.

● To make a quick broth that will make any fish soup or stew taste much better, simmer equal amounts of clam juice and water with some white wine, chopped green onions, dillweed, parsley, and thyme for 30 minutes. Strain; refrigerate broth up to 3 days, or freeze up to 3 months.

☻ OYSTER STEW

1 (12-ounce) container Standard oysters, undrained
½ cup whipping cream
½ teaspoon celery salt
½ teaspoon Worcestershire sauce
Dash of pepper
Paprika

1. Combine oysters, whipping cream, celery salt, Worcestershire sauce, and pepper in a medium saucepan; stir well. Cook over medium heat until mixture is thoroughly heated, and oyster edges curl.
2. Ladle into individual soup bowls, and garnish each serving with paprika. Serve hot. Yield: about 2 cups.

WESTERN ROAST BEEF SANDWICHES

1 (12-ounce) jar chili sauce
1 medium-size green pepper, seeded and chopped
1 pound cooked roast beef, cut into 1-inch strips
6 hamburger buns, toasted

1. Combine chili sauce and green pepper in a medium saucepan; cover and cook over medium heat 10 minutes, stirring occasionally. Add beef, stirring well; cover and cook an additional 5 minutes or until beef is thoroughly heated.
2. Serve beef mixture hot on toasted buns. Yield: 6 servings.

MicroNote: To microwave step 1, combine chili sauce and green pepper in a 1½-quart baking dish. Cover with heavy-duty plastic wrap, and vent to allow steam to escape; microwave at MEDIUM-HIGH (70% power) for 5 minutes. Add beef, stirring well. Cover and microwave at MEDIUM-HIGH for 4 minutes or until beef is thoroughly heated.

⊙ ZESTY BEEF AND BAGEL SANDWICHES

1 (12-ounce) can corned beef,
     coarsely chopped
1 cup (4 ounces) shredded Swiss
     cheese
1 medium-sized green pepper,
     seeded and chopped
1 medium onion, chopped
¼ cup mayonnaise
2 tablespoons sweet pickle relish
1 tablespoon horseradish
6 bagels, split

1. Combine all ingredients except bagels in a medium bowl, stirring well.
2. Place bagel halves on a baking sheet; spoon corned beef mixture evenly onto each half.
3. Broil 5 inches from heating element 5 minutes or until cheese melts and bagel is toasted.
4. Serve warm. Yield: 12 open-face sandwiches.

Note: Enhance the hearty flavor of these sandwiches by making them with pumpernickel, rye, onion, or garlic bagels. You may substitute ham, roast beef, or smoked turkey for the corned beef, and Muenster, Monterey Jack or provolone cheese for the Swiss cheese.

PERSONAL PIZZAS

1 (7.5-ounce) package refrigerated
     biscuits
½ (15½-ounce) jar quick pizza sauce
2 cups (8 ounces) shredded
     mozzarella cheese
   Sliced pepperoni
   Sliced fresh mushrooms
   Sliced pimiento-stuffed olives
   Chopped green pepper

1. Separate biscuits. Place biscuits on ungreased baking sheets; pat into 4-inch circles.

2. Spoon 2 tablespoons pizza sauce over each biscuit; sprinkle cheese evenly over each biscuit. Top each biscuit with pepperoni, mushrooms, olives, and green pepper. Bake at 425° for 10 minutes or until crust is golden brown.
3. Serve hot. Yield: 10 pizzas.

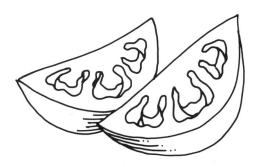

▭ SAUSAGE PIZZA SANDWICHES

4 hot dog buns, split
4 precooked bratwurst sausages
½ cup chopped onion
⅓ cup chopped green pepper
1 tablespoon vegetable oil
½ cup chopped tomato
1 (4-ounce) can mushroom stems
     and pieces, drained
1 (15-ounce) jar pizza sauce
1½ cups (6 ounces) shredded
     mozzarella cheese

1. Open buns flat, and place on a baking sheet. Split sausages in half lengthwise, and place on buns; set aside.
2. Sauté onion and green pepper in oil in a small skillet 5 minutes or until tender. Combine sautéed vegetables, tomato, mushrooms, and pizza sauce in a medium mixing bowl, stirring well.
3. Spoon mixture over sausage; top with cheese. Bake at 400° for 10 minutes or until thoroughly heated.
4. Serve immediately. Yield: 4 servings.

MicroNote: To microwave step 3, assemble sandwiches, and microwave sandwiches at HIGH for 3 minutes or until thoroughly heated, rotating platter after 1½ minutes.

LAMB-STUFFED PITA POCKETS

1 **pound lean ground lamb**
½ **medium-size green pepper, seeded and coarsely chopped**
¼ **cup chopped green onions**
1 **medium tomato, coarsely chopped**
1 **(2¼-ounce) can sliced ripe olives, drained**
½ **teaspoon seasoned salt**
¼ **cup commercial French salad dressing**
6 **pita bread rounds, halved and warmed**
1 **cup alfalfa sprouts**
  Plain yogurt

1. Combine lamb, green pepper, and green onions in a large skillet. Cook over medium heat, stirring frequently, until meat is browned. Drain.

2. Combine meat mixture, tomato, olives, salt, and French dressing; stir well.

3. Spoon mixture into pita halves; garnish with alfalfa sprouts, and serve with yogurt. Yield: 6 servings.

BAKED HAM AND ASPARAGUS SANDWICHES

24 **spears fresh asparagus (about ½ pound)**
6 **English muffins, split and toasted**
12 **(1-ounce) slices fully-cooked ham**
¾ **cup mayonnaise**
2 **tablespoons Dijon mustard**
¾ **cup (3 ounces) shredded Monterey Jack cheese**

1. Wash asparagus spears. Find the point at the end of each stalk where it breaks easily, and snap off. Line up tips; cut off ends even with broken stalk; break or cut each spear in half. Remove scales from spears, if desired. Set aside.

2. Place muffin halves on a baking sheet, cut side up. Top each with a slice of ham and 4 pieces of asparagus.

3. Combine mayonnaise and mustard in a small mixing bowl; stir until well blended. Spoon mixture evenly over top of each sandwich.

4. Broil 6 inches from heating element 3 minutes. Sprinkle cheese over top, and broil just until cheese melts.

5. Serve sandwiches immediately. Yield: 1 dozen open-face sandwiches.

CHEESY HAM AND SPINACH SANDWICH
(pictured on page 230)

1 **(16-ounce) loaf Italian or Vienna bread**
3 **tablespoons all-purpose flour**
¼ **cup beer or white wine**
3 **cups (12 ounces) shredded Swiss or Cheddar cheese**
3 **eggs, beaten**
1 **teaspoon Worcestershire sauce**
½ **teaspoon hot sauce**
½ **cup butter or margarine, softened**
½ **tablespoon prepared mustard**
½ **pound fresh spinach, chopped**
1 **pound thinly sliced cooked ham**
3 **medium tomatoes, sliced**

1. Cut bread into 3 equal horizontal slices (about ¾-inch thick). Place slices on a baking sheet; bake at 350° for 30 minutes or until lightly browned and dry.

2. Combine flour, beer, cheese, eggs, Worcestershire sauce, and hot sauce; stir well, and set aside.

3. Combine softened butter and mustard. Spread evenly over 3 slices of bread. Top each slice evenly with chopped spinach, ham slices, and tomato slices. Spoon cheese mixture evenly over tomatoes, spreading to edges.

4. Bake at 450° for 15 minutes or until puffed and browned.

5. Slice sandwich, and serve warm. Yield: 12 servings.

Vegetables and Side Dishes

How do vitamins and minerals taste? As rich and spicy as vitamin A laden Sweet Potato-Pear Bake. As crunchy as vitamin B loaded Pecan Brown Rice. As delicious as vitamin C stocked Carnival Broccoli. Calcium, potassium, and iron, by other names, are as tempting as Saucy Potato Casserole, Green Beans Provençal, and Baked Acorn Squash. If you're concerned about eating more carbohydrates and less fat, you'll be happy to taste this resolution fulfilled in Fettuccine with Vegetables or Vermicelli with Hot Sauce. But if all you really had in mind was wonderful flavor, then dig into a plateful of Cheesy Spinach Stuffed Manicotti, and be assured of a quick meal full of wise nutrition.

GLAZED CARROTS

- 1 pound carrots, scraped and diagonally sliced
- ½ cup water
- 2 tablespoons butter or margarine
- ¾ cup apricot preserves

1. Place carrots and water in a medium saucepan. Bring to a boil. Reduce heat; cover and simmer 8 minutes or just until tender. Remove from heat; drain.

2. Combine butter and preserves in a saucepan; cook over low heat, stirring constantly, until preserves melt. Stir in carrots; cook until thoroughly heated.

3. Serve warm. Yield: 4 servings.

SWISS CAULIFLOWER BAKE

- 1 large head cauliflower (about 2 pounds)
- ½ cup chopped celery
- ⅓ cup chopped green pepper
- ⅓ cup chopped onion
- 3 tablespoons butter or margarine, melted
- 1 cup milk
- 2 teaspoons cornstarch
- ¾ teaspoon salt
- ⅛ teaspoon pepper
- ¼ teaspoon paprika
- 1 cup (4 ounces) shredded Swiss cheese

1. Separate cauliflower into flowerets. Arrange in a steaming rack. Place over boiling water; cover and steam 10 minutes or until crisp-tender. Arrange in a 10- x 6- x 2-inch baking dish.

2. Sauté celery, green pepper, and onion in butter in a large skillet until tender. Combine milk and cornstarch, stirring well; add to vegetable mixture. Stir in seasonings. Cook over medium heat, stirring constantly, until thickened and bubbly. Add cheese; stir until melted.

3. Pour sauce over cauliflower. Bake at 475° for 8 to 10 minutes.

4. Serve warm. Yield: 6 servings.

CARNIVAL BROCCOLI

2 pounds fresh broccoli
½ cup sliced green onions
2 tablespoons butter or margarine, melted
2 tablespoons chopped pimiento
1 teaspoon grated lemon rind
2 tablespoons lemon juice
1 teaspoon salt
⅛ teaspoon pepper

1. Arrange broccoli in a steaming rack with stalks to center of rack. Place over boiling water; cover and steam 10 to 15 minutes. Place in a serving dish.
2. Sauté onions in butter until tender. Remove from heat, and stir in remaining ingredients. Pour mixture over broccoli.
3. Serve warm. Yield: 6 servings.

CABBAGE IN MUSTARD SAUCE

1 medium cabbage, cleaned
1 tablespoon butter or margarine
2 tablespoons all-purpose flour
1 cup milk
2 teaspoons prepared mustard
1 teaspoon dry mustard
½ teaspoon onion juice
¼ teaspoon salt
⅛ teaspoon garlic powder
Fresh parsley sprigs (optional)

1. Cut cabbage into 6 wedges. Cover and cook in a small amount of boiling salted water 15 minutes or until tender; drain well. Set aside; keep warm.
2. Melt butter in a heavy saucepan over low heat; add flour, stirring constantly. Gradually add milk; cook over medium heat, stirring constantly, until sauce is thickened and bubbly. Add remaining ingredients except parsley, stirring well.
3. Place cabbage wedges on a serving platter using a slotted spoon. Spoon sauce over cabbage. Garnish with parsley sprigs, if desired. Yield: 6 servings.

MicroMethod

1. Cut cabbage into six wedges. Place wedges in a 12- x 8- x 2-inch baking dish; add ¼ cup water. Cover with heavy-duty plastic wrap, and vent to allow steam to escape; microwave at HIGH for 8 minutes. Let stand 2 minutes.
2. Place butter in a 2-cup glass measure; microwave at HIGH for 35 seconds or until butter is melted. Add flour, stirring until smooth. Add remaining ingredients except parsley, stirring well. Microwave at HIGH for 1½ minutes; stir well. Microwave at HIGH an additional 1½ minutes, and stir.
3. Same as step 3.

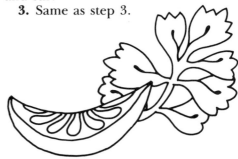

BRUSSELS SPROUTS IN WALNUT BUTTER
(pictured on page 248)

1 pound fresh brussels sprouts
1 cup water
½ teaspoon salt
¼ cup butter or margarine
½ cup coarsely chopped walnuts
⅛ teaspoon pepper

1. Wash brussels sprouts thoroughly, and remove discolored leaves. Cut off stem ends, and slash bottom of each sprout with a shallow X. Place sprouts in a large saucepan; add water and salt, and bring to a boil. Cover; reduce heat and simmer.
2. Melt butter in small saucepan until lightly browned. Add walnuts and cook until lightly browned, stirring constantly.
3. Place reserved brussels sprouts in a serving bowl; pour walnut butter over top. Sprinkle with pepper. Serve immediately. Yield: 4 servings.

BRAISED CELERY

(pictured on page 248)

1 bunch celery
1 chicken-flavored bouillon cube
¾ cup boiling water
½ teaspoon dried whole oregano
1 tablespoon diced pimiento
   (optional)

1. Cut off base of celery, and separate stalks. Wash under cold water; remove strings. Slice celery diagonally into 3-inch pieces.

2. Combine bouillon cube, water, and oregano in a medium saucepan, stirring until bouillon cube dissolves. Add celery; bring to a boil. Reduce heat; cover and simmer 15 minutes or until celery is tender.

3. Spoon celery into serving bowl; garnish with pimiento, if desired. Serve immediately. Yield: 4 servings.

EGGPLANT ITALIANO

3 small eggplant (about ¾ pound
   each)
¼ cup sliced green onions
½ cup chopped green pepper
1 small yellow squash, chopped
1 (16-ounce) can whole tomatocs,
   drained and chopped
1 cup seasoned croutons
3 tablespoons butter or margarine,
   melted
1 teaspoon dried Italian seasoning
½ teaspoon salt
¼ teaspoon pepper
2 tablespoons grated Parmesan
   cheese

1. Prick each eggplant 3 times with a fork. Place in a Dutch oven; cover with hot water, and bring to a boil. Reduce heat; cover and simmer 20 minutes or until tender. Drain well.

2. Cut eggplant in half lengthwise. Scoop out pulp, reserving pulp and shells. Chop pulp; combine pulp, onions, green pepper, squash, tomatoes, croutons, butter, Italian seasoning, salt, and pepper in a large mixing bowl. Divide mixture evenly among eggplant shells.

3. Arrange eggplant shells in a 13- x 9- x 2-inch baking dish. Bake at 375° for 15 minutes. Sprinkle cheese on top of eggplant, and continue baking 5 minutes.

4. Serve hot. Yield: 6 servings.

GREEN BEANS PROVENÇAL

3 tablespoons chopped onion
1 tablespoon vegetable oil
1 pound fresh green beans, trimmed
   and cut into 1½-inch pieces
⅓ cup water
1 teaspoon paprika
½ teaspoon salt
½ teaspoon garlic powder
½ teaspoon ground thyme
1 cup chopped tomato (about 1
   large)

1. Sauté onion in oil in a medium saucepan. Add remaining ingredients except chopped tomato. Bring to a boil. Reduce heat; cover and simmer 20 minutes, stirring occasionally.

2. Add tomato; cover and cook 1 minute or until beans are tender.

3. Transfer to a serving bowl; serve warm. Yield: 4 servings.

MicroMethod

1. Place onion and oil in a 1-quart shallow baking dish. Microwave at HIGH for 1 minute or until tender. Add beans and water; cover with heavy-duty plastic wrap, and vent to allow steam to escape. Microwave at HIGH for 12 to 14 minutes or until beans are tender, stirring every 4 minutes.

2. Add paprika, salt, garlic powder, thyme, and chopped tomato to beans, stirring well. Cover and microwave at HIGH for 1 minute.

3. Same as step 3.

☐ ONIONS WITH SAUSAGE STUFFING

3 medium-size sweet Spanish onions, peeled and halved crosswise
4 ounces bulk pork sausage
¼ cup fine Italian-style breadcrumbs
2 tablespoons chopped fresh parsley

1. Cook onions in boiling water 8 minutes or until just tender; drain. Scoop out center of onions, leaving ½-inch shells. Chop scooped-out onion. Arrange shells in a greased 12- x 8- x 2-inch baking dish.
2. Sauté chopped onion and sausage, until sausage is browned; stir to crumble sausage. Stir in remaining ingredients.
3. Stuff onion shells with sausage mixture. Cover with aluminum foil; bake at 350° for 25 minutes or until tender.
4. Serve immediately. Yield: 6 servings.

MicroMethod

1. Place onions, cut side up, in a 12- x 8- x 2-inch baking dish; cover with heavy-duty plastic wrap, and vent to allow steam to escape. Microwave at HIGH for 5 minutes or just until tender. Scoop out center of onions, leaving ½-inch shells. Chop scooped-out onion.
2. Place sausage and chopped onion in a 1-quart casserole. Cover and microwave at HIGH for 1 to 2 minutes; stir to crumble. Stir in remaining ingredients.
3. Stuff onion shells with sausage mixture. Cover and microwave at HIGH for 4 to 5 minutes.
4. Same as step 4.

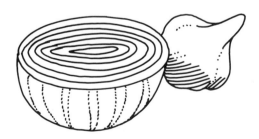

◆ POTATO ROSETTES

2 medium potatoes (about 1 pound), peeled and cooked
1 egg
2 tablespoons commercial sour cream
½ cup (2 ounces) shredded sharp Cheddar cheese
1 teaspoon minced chives
½ teaspoon salt
Paprika

1. Position knife blade in food processor bowl; add potatoes. Process until well-mashed. Scrape sides of bowl with a rubber spatula. Add egg, sour cream, cheese, chives, and salt. Process 3 to 5 seconds.
2. Spoon mixture into a pastry bag fitted with a large star tip. Pipe mixture into 2½-inch rosettes on paper-lined baking sheet; sprinkle with paprika.
3. Freeze 3 hours or until firm. Transfer to freezer bags, or bake.
4. Place rosettes on a lightly greased baking sheet; bake at 350° for 15 minutes or until rosettes are set.
5. Serve warm. Yield: 1 dozen rosettes (6 servings).

LEMON-BUTTERED NEW POTATOES

2 pounds new potatoes
2 teaspoons sugar
1 teaspoon salt
1 clove garlic, crushed
¼ cup butter or margarine, melted
2 tablespoons lemon juice
½ teaspoon paprika

1. Wash potatoes, and pare a 1-inch strip around center of each one. Place potatoes, sugar, salt, and garlic in a large saucepan; cover with water, and bring to a boil. Reduce heat; cover and simmer 15 to 20 minutes or until tender. Drain well.
2. Combine remaining ingredients; drizzle over potatoes. Toss gently. Transfer to a serving bowl. Yield: 6 to 8 servings.

SAUCY POTATO CASSEROLE

8 medium potatoes, peeled and
　　cubed
1 (10¾-ounce) can cream of
　　mushroom soup, undiluted
1 (8-ounce) carton commercial sour
　　cream
1 (8-ounce) jar process cheese
　　spread
1 (3-ounce) package cream cheese
⅛ teaspoon seasoned salt
　Breadcrumbs (optional)

1. Cook potatoes in boiling water to
cover 15 to 20 minutes or until tender.
Drain and set aside.

2. Combine next 5 ingredients in a
saucepan; cook over low heat until mixture
is thoroughly heated, stirring often. Pour
over potatoes; mix well.

3. Spoon into a greased 2½-quart casserole. Sprinkle with breadcrumbs, if desired. Bake at 350° for 20 to 25 minutes or
until bubbly. Serve hot. Yield: 10 servings.

SWEET POTATO-PEAR BAKE

2 (17-ounce) cans sweet potatoes,
　　drained
2 eggs
¼ cup whipping cream
¼ cup butter or margarine, melted
3 tablespoons brown sugar
½ teaspoon ground cinnamon
½ teaspoon ground ginger
¼ teaspoon salt
¼ teaspoon ground nutmeg
2 medium pears, peeled, cored, and
　　cut into cubes (about 2 cups)

1. Beat sweet potatoes in a large mixing
bowl until smooth. Add eggs, whipping
cream, butter, brown sugar, cinnamon,
ginger, salt, and nutmeg, beating until well
blended. Fold in pears.

2. Pour into a lightly greased 10- x 6- x
2-inch baking dish. Bake, uncovered, at
350° for 40 minutes or until hot.

3. Serve immediately. Yield: 8 servings.

SPINACH ROLL

4 eggs, separated
¼ teaspoon cream of tartar
¼ cup all-purpose flour
¼ teaspoon salt
1 (10-ounce) package frozen
　　chopped spinach, thawed
　　and drained
1 (10¾-ounce) can cream of
　　chicken soup, undiluted
　　and divided
¼ cup commercial sour
　　cream
1 tablespoon finely chopped
　　fresh parsley
　Fresh parsley sprigs (optional)

1. Lightly grease a 15- x 10- x 1-inch
jellyroll pan. Line jellyroll pan with waxed
paper, and grease waxed paper. Set prepared pan aside.

2. Beat egg yolks in a large mixing bowl
until thick and lemon colored. Beat egg
whites (at room temperature) in a medium
mixing bowl until foamy; add cream of
tartar, and continue beating until stiff
peaks form.

3. Sprinkle flour and salt over beaten
egg yolks; gently fold in beaten egg whites.
Spread egg mixture evenly into prepared
pan. Bake at 400° for 8 minutes. Immediately loosen roll from sides of pan, and
turn out onto a linen towel. Peel off waxed
paper, and carefully trim ⅛ inch from
edges of roll.

4. Combine spinach and half of soup in
a small saucepan. Cook over medium heat
2 to 3 minutes, stirring frequently. Spread
roll evenly with cooked spinach mixture.
Roll up, jellyroll fashion, beginning at
short side. Place seam side down on a serving platter.

5. Combine remaining half of soup,
sour cream, and 1 tablespoon chopped
parsley in a small saucepan. Cook over low
heat until thoroughly heated, stirring frequently. Remove from heat.

6. Slice Spinach Roll, using a serrated
knife, and serve immediately with sour
cream sauce. Garnish with parsley sprigs,
if desired. Yield: 6 servings.

BAKED ACORN SQUASH

(pictured on page 248)

2 small acorn squash, cleaned and
    cut in half lengthwise
3 medium carrots, scraped and
    diced
¼ cup plus 2 tablespoons raisins
2 tablespoons butter or margarine,
    melted
3 tablespoons maple syrup
⅛ teaspoon salt

1. Place squash, cut side down in a shallow baking dish. Add ½-inch of boiling water. Cover and bake at 375° for 30 minutes. Turn cut side up.
2. Combine remaining ingredients; stir well. Spoon into squash; cover. Bake at 375° for 30 minutes or until tender.
3. Serve immediately. Yield: 4 servings.

⊙ ZUCCHINI WITH HERB-LEMON SAUCE

2 medium zucchini, cut into 3-inch
    strips (about 1 pound)
1 medium onion, sliced
2 tablespoons vegetable oil
1 tablespoon cornstarch
1 cup cold milk
2 tablespoons butter or margarine
2 tablespoons lemon juice
1 tablespoon chopped fresh parsley
¾ teaspoon dried whole dillweed
¼ teaspoon salt
⅛ teaspoon pepper

1. Sauté zucchini and onion in oil in a large skillet 5 minutes or until crisp-tender. Set aside.
2. Combine cornstarch and milk in a small saucepan; beat, using a wire whisk, until well blended. Add butter; cover and bring to a boil. Uncover and boil 1 minute, stirring constantly. Remove from heat, and stir in remaining ingredients.
3. Transfer zucchini mixture to a serving bowl. Pour sauce over top; toss lightly. Serve immediately. Yield: 4 servings.

▣ YELLOW SQUASH WITH VEGETABLE STUFFING

6 medium-size yellow squash
1 medium tomato, peeled and finely
    chopped (about 1 cup)
⅓ cup finely chopped onion
½ cup finely chopped green pepper
½ cup (2 ounces) shredded sharp
    Cheddar cheese, divided
1 teaspoon bacon bits
¼ teaspoon salt
    Dash of pepper

1. Place squash in a medium saucepan with boiling water to cover. Cook 10 minutes or until squash is tender. Drain well; cool slightly.
2. Cut a lengthwise slice from the top of each squash; remove and reserve pulp. Chop pulp, and set aside. Drain shells well on paper towels.
3. Combine reserved chopped pulp, tomato, onion, green pepper, ¼ cup cheese, bacon bits, salt, and pepper in a small mixing bowl. Mix well, and spoon into squash shells.
4. Transfer squash to a lightly greased 12- x 8- x 2-inch baking dish. Bake at 400° for 15 minutes. Sprinkle with remaining ¼ cup cheese, and bake an additional 5 minutes. Serve immediately. Yield: 6 servings.

MicroMethod

1. Pierce squash at random, using tines of fork. Arrange squash on a platter in a spoke fashion with necks of squash pointing toward center. Cover with waxed paper, and microwave at HIGH for 8 minutes, giving platter a quarter-turn every 2 minutes. Set aside to cool slightly.
2. Cut a thin slice from top of each squash; remove and reserve pulp. Chop pulp, and set aside.
3. Combine reserved chopped pulp, tomato, onion, green pepper, ¼ cup cheese, bacon bits, salt, and pepper in a small mixing bowl; stir well. Cover with waxed paper, and microwave at HIGH for 1 minute. Spoon into squash shells; return to platter.

4. Cover with waxed paper, and microwave at MEDIUM (50% power) for 5 to 6 minutes, sprinkling remaining ¼ cup cheese over tops of squash during last 30 seconds. Serve immediately.

🖳 SUMMER SQUASH DUO
(pictured on page 248)

1 **pound zucchini, sliced**
1 **pound yellow squash, sliced**
1 **(2-ounce) jar sliced pimiento, drained**
1 **clove garlic, crushed**
2 **tablespoons butter or margarine, melted**
1 **teaspoon salt**

1. Sauté zucchini, yellow squash, pimiento, and garlic in butter in a large skillet 2 minutes.

2. Cover and cook over medium heat 8 minutes or until squash is crisp-tender.

3. Sprinkle with salt. Serve immediately. Yield: 6 to 8 servings.

MicroMethod

1. Combine first 4 ingredients in a 2-quart casserole; dot with butter.

2. Cover with heavy-duty plastic wrap, and vent to allow steam to escape; microwave at HIGH for 12 to 15 minutes. Let stand, covered, 5 minutes or until vegetables are crisp-tender.

3. Same as step 3.

Note: Dish can be refrigerated ahead; microwave just prior to serving.

🖳 HERBED SQUASH CASSEROLE

1 **pound small yellow squash, sliced**
1 **small onion, chopped**
1 **medium carrot, shredded**
1 **cup water**
1 **(10¾-ounce) can cream of chicken soup, undiluted**
½ **cup commercial sour cream**
1½ **cups herb-seasoned stuffing mix**
¼ **cup butter or margarine, melted**

1. Combine squash, onion, carrot, and 1 cup water in a medium saucepan. Bring to a boil. Reduce heat; cover and simmer 5 minutes or until vegetables are tender. Drain well.

2. Combine squash mixture, soup, and sour cream in a medium bowl.

3. Combine stuffing mix and melted butter in a small mixing bowl; stir well. Spread half the stuffing mixture in bottom of a lightly greased 10- x 6- x 2-inch baking dish. Pour squash mixture evenly over stuffing mixture.

4. Sprinkle remaining stuffing mixture on top. Bake at 350° for 25 minutes or until hot and bubbly.

5. Serve Herbed Squash Casserole immediately. Yield: 6 servings.

MicroMethod

1. Combine squash, onion, carrot, and 1 tablespoon water in a 10- x 6- x 2-inch baking dish. Cover with heavy-duty plastic wrap, and vent to allow steam to escape. Microwave at HIGH for 6 to 7 minutes or until tender. Drain well.

2. Same as step 2.

3. Same as step 3.

4. Cover and microwave at HIGH for 4 minutes. Sprinkle remaining stuffing mixture on top. Cover with a paper towel. Microwave at HIGH for 2 to 3 minutes or until hot and bubbly. Let stand, covered, for 5 minutes.

5. Same as step 5.

ZUCCHINI AND GREEN BEANS PIQUANT

1 medium onion, chopped
1 tablespoon vegetable oil
1 pound fresh green beans, snapped
3 medium tomatoes, seeded and
    coarsely chopped
¾ teaspoon salt
1 pound medium zucchini, sliced
½ (4-ounce) can chopped green
    chiles

1. Sauté onion in oil in a large saucepan 2 minutes.
2. Add snapped green beans, tomatoes, and salt; cover and cook over medium heat 20 to 25 minutes or until beans are tender, stirring often.
3. Add zucchini and chiles; cover and continue cooking 10 minutes.
4. Transfer to a serving bowl. Serve immediately. Yield: 8 servings.

SWEET TURNIPS

1 cup water
1 teaspoon chicken-flavored bouillon
    granules
3 tablespoons instant minced onion
2 tablespoons brown sugar
1 tablespoon plus 1½ teaspoons
    lemon juice
½ teaspoon salt
¼ teaspoon ground cinnamon
3 medium turnips, peeled and cut
    into ½-inch cubes (about 1
    pound)

1. Bring water to a boil in a medium saucepan. Add bouillon granules, onion, brown sugar, lemon juice, salt, and cinnamon; stir until granules dissolve. Stir in turnips.
2. Reduce heat; cover and simmer 25 minutes or until turnips are tender, stirring occasionally.
3. Transfer turnips to a serving bowl. Serve immediately. Yield: 4 servings.

BASIC WHITE SAUCE WITH VARIATIONS

2 tablespoons butter or margarine
2 tablespoons all-purpose flour
1 cup milk
¼ teaspoon salt

1. Melt butter in a heavy saucepan over low heat; add flour, stirring until smooth. Cook 1 minute, stirring constantly. Gradually add milk; cook over medium heat, stirring constantly, until thickened and bubbly. Stir in salt.
2. Serve warm over cooked vegetables. Yield: about 1 cup.
Variations: Dill Sauce: Add 1½ teaspoons dried whole dillweed and 1 teaspoon lemon juice to Basic White Sauce when salt is added.
Cheese Sauce: Add 1 cup (4 ounces) shredded sharp Cheddar cheese to hot Basic White Sauce, stirring until cheese melts. Yield: about 1½ cups.

MUSHROOM-CHEESE SAUCE

1 tablespoon cornstarch
1 cup milk
¼ cup butter or margarine,
    divided
½ teaspoon dried whole basil
¼ teaspoon salt
⅛ teaspoon pepper
½ cup commercial sour cream
½ cup (2 ounces) shredded process
    American cheese
½ pound fresh mushrooms, sliced

1. Combine cornstarch and milk in a saucepan; beat until smooth. Add 2 tablespoons butter, basil, salt, and pepper; cover and bring to a boil. Uncover; boil 1 minute, stirring constantly.
2. Reduce heat to low, and add sour cream and cheese. Stir constantly until cheese melts and mixture is well blended. Remove from heat.

3. Sauté mushrooms in remaining 2 tablespoons butter in a small saucepan. Stir mushrooms into cheese sauce.

4. Serve immediately over cooked vegetables. Yield: 2¼ cups.

CHEESE SAUCE

½ cup milk
1 (4-ounce) package sharp Cheddar cheese, cubed
1 tablespoon butter or margarine, softened
1 tablespoon all-purpose flour
⅛ teaspoon salt
⅛ teaspoon dry mustard

1. Position knife blade in food processor bowl; add all ingredients. Top with cover and process until smooth.
2. Pour into a saucepan. Cook over medium heat 5 minutes, stirring constantly, until thickened and bubbly.
3. Serve Cheese Sauce immediately over vegetables. Yield: ¾ cup.

MicroNote: To microwave step 2, pour mixture into a 2-cup glass measure. Microwave at MEDIUM-HIGH (70% power) for 2½ minutes, stirring after 1½ minutes. Let stand 5 minutes.

CURRY SAUCE
(pictured on page 248)

3 tablespoons minced onion
2 tablespoons butter or margarine, melted
2 tablespoons all-purpose flour
1 cup milk
1½ teaspoons curry powder
¼ teaspoon salt
⅛ teaspoon ground ginger
1 teaspoon lemon juice

1. Sauté onion in butter in a heavy saucepan over low heat until tender. Add

flour, stirring until smooth. Cook 1 minute, stirring constantly. Gradually add milk; cook over medium heat, stirring constantly, until mixture is thickened and bubbly. Stir in curry powder, salt, ginger, and lemon juice.
2. Serve warm over vegetables. Yield: about 1 cup.

MOCK HOLLANDAISE SAUCE

1 (8-ounce) carton plain low-fat yogurt, divided
1 egg, beaten
2 tablespoons lemon juice
¼ teaspoon salt
⅛ teaspoon dry mustard

1. Combine ¼ cup yogurt, egg, lemon juice, salt, and dry mustard in a small saucepan. Cook over low heat, stirring constantly, until mixture is smooth and thickened. Remove from heat, and stir in remaining yogurt.
2. Serve immediately over cooked vegetables. Yield: about 1 cup.

SOUR CREAM SAUCE

¾ cup commercial sour cream
2 egg yolks
2 teaspoons tarragon wine vinegar
½ teaspoon pepper

1. Combine all ingredients in top of a double boiler; beat with a wire whisk until smooth. Place over simmering water, and cook 5 minutes or until thoroughly heated, stirring frequently.
2. Serve hot over cooked vegetables, such as broccoli, cauliflower, carrots, or green beans. Yield: about 1 cup.

Note: Substitute ¼ to ½ teaspoon white pepper for black pepper, if desired.

PASTA PERFECT

The popularity of pasta may be attributed to its economy, ease of preparation, or its terrific taste! Whatever your reason for serving pasta, be aware of the fact that although pasta comes in dozens of shapes and sizes, there are only three basic catagories for cooking purposes—spaghetti and other long, round noodles; fettuccine and other long, flat noodles; and elbows and other macaroni. Many shapes can be used interchangeably, but the following combinations work especially well:

• For spaghetti that will be served with a meat sauce, substitute mostaccioli, rigatoni, or rotini.

• Cream sauces taste better with flat noodles, such as fettuccine or linguine, because the cream sauce has more surface area to cling to.

• The delicacy of clam and other seafood sauces is best matched by thin pasta, such as linguine, thin spaghetti, capellini, or vermicelli.

• For salads that have vegetables or other chunky ingredients, be sure to choose a pasta that will "catch" the other pieces of food, such as shells, rotini, elbows, wagon wheels, or rigatoni. Choose the size of the pasta according to the size pieces of the other ingredients. With broccoli flowerettes, for example, use rigatoni or mostaccioli; with peas, use small shells, elbows, or a short tube shape macaroni.

• When you need pasta in the fastest possible cooking time, choose orzo, pastina tubettini, or the little squares and stars sold as soup pasta. Any of these pastas can be tossed with butter and Parmesan cheese for a quick change of pace from rice or potatoes.

CURRIED RICE

½ cup chopped onion
1 tablespoon butter or margarine, melted
1¼ cups chicken broth
1 cup orange juice
½ cup raisins
⅓ cup slivered almonds, toasted
½ teaspoon curry powder
½ teaspoon salt
⅛ teaspoon pepper
1 cup uncooked regular rice
2 tablespoons chopped fresh parsley

1. Sauté onion in butter in a small skillet until tender.
2. Combine sautéed onion, chicken broth, orange juice, raisins, almonds, curry powder, salt, and pepper in a large saucepan; bring to a boil. Add rice, stirring well; return to a boil. Reduce heat; cover and simmer 20 minutes or until liquid is absorbed. Stir in parsley.
3. Serve warm. Yield: 4 to 6 servings.

FIESTA RICE

½ cup chopped onion
½ cup chopped green pepper
2 tablespoons butter or margarine, melted
1 cup water
1 (16-ounce) can whole tomatoes, undrained and chopped
1½ teaspoons garlic salt
Dash of red pepper
1 cup uncooked regular rice
½ cup (2 ounces) shredded Cheddar cheese

1. Sauté onion and green pepper in butter in a medium skillet until tender.
2. Combine sautéed vegetables, water, tomatoes, and seasonings in a saucepan; bring to a boil. Stir in rice; return to a boil. Reduce heat; cover and simmer 20 minutes or until liquid is absorbed.
3. Spoon rice into a serving dish; sprinkle with cheese. Yield: 4 to 6 servings.

PECAN BROWN RICE
(pictured on page 248)

2 cups chopped celery
½ cup chopped onion
¼ cup butter or margarine, melted
1 cup uncooked brown rice
½ teaspoon salt
½ teaspoon poultry seasoning
1 (10¾-ounce) can chicken broth, undiluted
1¼ cups water
1 cup coarsely chopped pecans, toasted

1. Sauté celery and onion in butter in a large skillet until tender.

2. Stir in rice, salt, poultry seasoning, chicken broth, and water. Bring to a boil. Reduce heat; cover and simmer 40 to 45 minutes or until liquid is absorbed.

3. Stir in pecans, and serve immediately. Yield: 6 servings.

VEGETABLE COUSCOUS
(pictured on page 248)

1½ cups water
1 (.9-ounce) package vegetable soup mix
1 cup couscous

1. Bring water to a boil; add vegetable soup mix. Reduce heat; cover and simmer 10 minutes.

2. Stir in couscous. Remove from heat. Let stand, covered, 5 minutes.

3. Serve warm. Yield: 4 to 6 servings.

PARMESAN NOODLES

1 (8-ounce) package medium egg noodles
3 tablespoons butter or margarine, melted
⅛ teaspoon garlic powder
2 tablespoons chopped fresh parsley
2 tablespoons grated Parmesan cheese

1. Cook noodles according to package directions; drain well.

2. Toss noodles with melted butter, garlic powder, and chopped parsley. Spoon noodles into a serving bowl, and sprinkle with Parmesan cheese.

3. Serve Parmesan Noodles immediately. Yield: 4 servings.

STRAW AND HAY
(pictured on page 247)

1½ cups medium egg noodles
1½ cups medium spinach egg noodles
1 (10-ounce) package frozen English peas, thawed
½ cup whipping cream
¼ cup grated Parmesan cheese
2 tablespoons butter or margarine, melted
¼ teaspoon salt
Dash of pepper
¼ pound prosciutto or country ham, chopped

1. Cook noodles and peas according to package directions, omitting salt. Drain thoroughly.

2. Combine cooked noodles, peas, whipping cream, Parmesan cheese, butter, salt, and pepper in a large serving bowl. Toss lightly to coat well. Stir in chopped prosciutto or ham.

3. Serve Straw and Hay immediately. Yield: 6 to 8 servings.

NOODLE-EGGPLANT CASSEROLE

½ (12-ounce) package medium egg
    noodles
1 (12-ounce) eggplant, peeled and
    cut into ¼-inch slices
2 eggs, beaten
1 cup fine dry breadcrumbs
¼ cup vegetable oil
1 (16-ounce) can tomatoes,
    undrained and chopped
1 (8-ounce) can tomato sauce
½ teaspoon dried whole oregano
⅛ teaspoon pepper
⅓ cup grated Parmesan cheese,
    divided
2 cups (8 ounces) shredded
    mozzarella cheese, divided

1. Cook noodles according to package directions; drain and set aside.
2. Dip eggplant slices in eggs; coat with breadcrumbs. Brown eggplant slices in oil in a large skillet. Drain eggplant on paper towels.
3. Combine tomatoes, tomato sauce, oregano, and pepper in a medium mixing bowl, stirring well.
4. Layer half of eggplant, noodles, tomato mixture, Parmesan cheese, and mozzarella in a lightly greased 13- x 9- x 2-inch baking dish. Repeat layers. Cover and bake at 375° for 30 minutes; uncover and bake an additional 15 minutes.
5. Serve hot. Yield: 10 to 12 servings.

FETTUCCINE WITH VEGETABLES

¾ (16-ounce) package fettuccine
1 cup chopped onion
1 cup chopped green pepper
¼ cup butter or margarine, melted
2 (10-ounce) packages frozen
    spinach, thawed and drained
1 cup shredded carrot
½ teaspoon salt
½ teaspoon garlic powder
½ teaspoon dried whole basil
½ cup grated Parmesan cheese

1. Cook fettuccine according to package directions; drain and set aside.
2. Sauté onion and green pepper in butter in a large skillet until tender; add remaining ingredients except cheese; stir well. Cook over medium heat 8 minutes or until tender, stirring occasionally.
3. Combine reserved fettuccine, spinach mixture, and Parmesan cheese in a large mixing bowl; toss well. Serve immediately. Yield: 10 to 12 servings.

LASAGNA ROLL-UPS

8 lasagna noodles, uncooked
2 cups sliced fresh mushrooms
½ cup chopped onion
1 clove garlic, crushed
1 tablespoon olive oil
1 (15½-ounce) jar commercial
    marinara sauce
1 (16-ounce) carton ricotta cheese
1 cup grated Parmesan cheese
1 (10-ounce) package frozen
    chopped spinach, thawed and
    drained
1½ cups (6 ounces) shredded
    mozzarella cheese, divided
1 egg, beaten
½ teaspoon salt
¼ teaspoon pepper

1. Cook lasagna according to package directions; drain and set aside.
2. Sauté mushrooms, onion, and garlic in oil in a large skillet until tender. Add marinara sauce, and cook until thoroughly heated. Remove from heat; set aside.
3. Combine ricotta, Parmesan, spinach, 1 cup mozzarella, egg, salt, and pepper in a large mixing bowl; mix well. Spread ½ cup cheese mixture on each cooked lasagna noodle. Roll up from short end. Place rolled noodles seam side down in a lightly greased 12- x 8- x 2-inch baking dish.
4. Pour reserved sauce over noodles. Bake at 350° for 25 minutes. Top with remaining ½ cup mozzarella cheese, and bake an additional 5 minutes.
5. Serve hot. Yield: 8 servings.

*Made with proscuitto ham, cheese, pasta, and vegetables, Straw and Hay (page 245)
could easily serve as a main dish salad. Team with French Breadsticks (page 82) and
Melon Ice (page 63) for a light, satisfying lunch.*

Right: Serve vegetables in a new way (clockwise from lower right): Braised Celery (page 237), Summer Squash Duo (page 241), Baked Acorn Squash (page 240), Brussels Sprouts in Walnut Butter (page 236), Curry Sauce (page 243).
Below: Complement any entrée with a carbohydrate-rich side dish, such as (clockwise from top): Pecan Brown Rice (page 245), Vegetable Couscous (page 245), or Linguine with Spinach Pesto (at right).

LINGUINE WITH SPINACH PESTO
(pictured at left)

½ pound fresh spinach, cleaned and
   trimmed
¼ cup chopped fresh parsley
¼ to ½ cup grated Parmesan cheese
 2 cloves garlic, halved
 2 tablespoons walnut pieces
 2 tablespoons olive oil
½ teaspoon salt
⅛ teaspoon pepper
½ (16-ounce) package linguine

1. Position knife blade in food processor
bowl; add first 8 ingredients. Process until
smooth. Set aside.
2. Cook linguine according to package
directions.
3. Toss linguine with pesto sauce; serve
immediately. Yield: 6 to 8 servings.

Note: The more traditional version of
pesto features fresh basil and pine nuts. So
if summer provides you with a bumper
basil crop, you may want to substitute 2
cups of fresh basil leaves for the spinach in
this recipe and use pine nuts instead of
walnuts. Pesto made with basil can be refrigerated in a covered container up to 1
week or frozen up to 6 months. Spinach
Pesto, however, should be made close to
serving time.

TOMATO-TOPPED MACARONI
AND CHEESE

 1 (8-ounce) package elbow macaroni
¼ cup butter or margarine
¼ cup all-purpose flour
 2 cups milk
½ teaspoon salt
¼ teaspoon pepper
 3 cups (12 ounces) shredded
   Cheddar cheese, divided
 3 medium tomatoes, peeled and
   sliced

1. Cook macaroni according to package
directions; drain and set aside.

2. Melt butter in a heavy saucepan over
low heat; add flour, stirring until smooth.
Cook 1 minute, stirring constantly. Gradually add milk, salt, and pepper; cook over
medium heat, stirring constantly, until
thickened and bubbly. Remove from heat;
add 2½ cups cheese, stirring until cheese
melts.
3. Combine macaroni and cheese sauce
in a large mixing bowl, stirring well. Spoon
mixture into a lightly greased 2½-quart
shallow baking dish; top with tomato slices.
Bake at 375° for 15 minutes or until thickened and thoroughly heated.
4. Sprinkle with remaining ½ cup
cheese, and bake an additional 5 minutes.
Serve hot. Yield: 8 to 10 servings.

CHEESY SPINACH STUFFED
MANICOTTI

 1 (8-ounce) package manicotti shells
 1 (10-ounce) package frozen
   chopped spinach, thawed and
   drained
 1 (16-ounce) carton small-curd
   cottage cheese
 2 cups (8 ounces) shredded
   mozzarella cheese
 1 egg, beaten
½ teaspoon garlic powder
¼ teaspoon pepper
 1 (32-ounce) jar commercial
   spaghetti sauce
 Parmesan cheese

1. Cook manicotti shells according to
package directions; drain and set aside.
2. Combine spinach, cottage cheese,
mozzarella, egg, garlic powder, and pepper in a medium mixing bowl, stirring
well. Stuff manicotti shells with spinach
mixture.
3. Spread ½ cup spaghetti sauce in a
lightly greased 13- x 9- x 2-inch baking
pan. Arrange stuffed manicotti in a single
layer over sauce; spoon remaining sauce
over manicotti. Cover and bake at 375° for
35 minutes or until hot and bubbly.
4. Sprinkle with Parmesan cheese; serve
hot. Yield: 6 to 8 servings.

ORZO-CAULIFLOWER CASSEROLE

½ (16-ounce) package orzo
4 cups cauliflower flowerets,
  coarsely chopped
2 cups milk
2 eggs, beaten
2 cups (8 ounces) shredded Cheddar
  cheese
½ teaspoon onion powder
½ teaspoon salt
¼ teaspoon white pepper

1. Cook orzo according to package directions; drain and set aside.
2. Cook cauliflower in boiling water 8 minutes or until tender; drain cauliflower, and set aside.
3. Combine milk, eggs, cheese, onion powder, salt, and white pepper in a large mixing bowl, stirring well. Add reserved orzo and cauliflower, stirring well. Spoon mixture into a lightly greased 13- x 9- x 2-inch baking dish. Bake at 375° for 35 minutes or until set.
4. Serve immediately. Yield: 10 to 12 servings.

VERMICELLI WITH HOT SAUCE

3 cloves garlic, minced
2 tablespoons olive oil
1 (2-ounce) can anchovy fillets,
  drained and rinsed
1 (28-ounce) can Italian-style
  tomatoes, pureed
½ cup sliced pimiento-stuffed olives
½ cup sliced pitted ripe olives
2 tablespoons capers
¼ teaspoon crushed red pepper
¼ cup chopped fresh parsley
1 (16-ounce) package vermicelli

1. Sauté garlic in olive oil in a large heavy skillet until lightly browned. Add anchovies, and stir, breaking them apart with the back of a wooden spoon. Continue to stir until mixture is well blended.
2. Add tomato puree to skillet, and bring to a boil. Reduce heat, and simmer, uncovered, 10 minutes, stirring mixture occasionally.
3. Stir in olives, capers, and red pepper. Continue to simmer, uncovered, 15 minutes, stirring occasionally. Remove from heat, and stir in parsley.
4. Prepare vermicelli according to package directions, omitting salt. Drain well. Combine vermicelli and sauce in a large serving bowl; toss lightly to coat well.
5. Serve immediately. Yield: 8 main-dish servings or 16 side-dish servings.

Note: Hot sauce may be made ahead and refrigerated until 20 minutes before serving time. As the vermicelli cooks, the sauce can be reheated. It can then be combined and tossed with the vermicelli.

LEMON VERMICELLI

⅓ cup milk
3 tablespoons butter or margarine
1 (7-ounce) package vermicelli
¼ cup lemon juice
⅓ cup grated Parmesan cheese
  Chopped fresh parsley
  Lemon twists

1. Combine milk and butter in a saucepan; cook over low heat until butter melts. Set aside, and keep warm.
2. Cook vermicelli according to package directions; drain. Rinse with warm water, and drain again. Place vermicelli in a serving bowl, and toss with lemon juice; let stand 1 minute.
3. Add Parmesan cheese and warm milk mixture, tossing well. Garnish with parsley and lemon twists. Yield: 6 servings.

Desserts

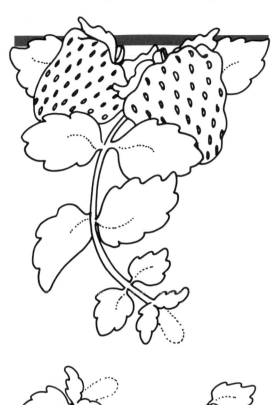

These days, busy cooks have no time for old-fashioned desserts—unless they mix Creamy Rice Pudding in a hurry, turn on the blender for Pots de Créme, or pour all the ingredients into one bowl for made-from-scratch Chocolate Cupcakes. After all, it's silly to invest hours in elaborate sweets—when you could make No-Bake Peanut Butter Pie, Easy Chocolate Mousse, or Devil's Food Cookies in minutes! Of course, if you feel a certain nostalgia for the smells of grandma's kitchen, you might want to devote a half hour or so to Mandarin Orange Cake or Lemon Pudding Cake. But if you really don't have even a minute to think about dessert—at least, not until you crave it!—you'll truly appreciate the instant satisfaction of Cherries Jubilee or Peach Melba.

BAKED APPLES WITH PECAN SAUCE

6 medium-size baking apples
1 cup hot water
2 tablespoons sugar
¼ cup butter or margarine
1 (14-ounce) can sweetened condensed milk
1 cup chopped pecans
1 tablespoon dark rum
Dash of salt

1. Core apples; peel top third of each. Place in a shallow baking dish. Combine water and sugar; pour over apples. Bake at 350° for 45 minutes or until tender.
2. Melt butter in a medium saucepan. Stir in remaining ingredients. Cook over medium heat 10 to 12 minutes, stirring constantly. Remove from heat, and cool.
3. Spoon sauce over baked apples. Yield: 6 servings.

APPLE ROLLUPS

2 cooking apples, peeled and cored
1 (8-ounce) package refrigerated crescent rolls
½ cup sugar
½ teaspoon ground cinnamon
⅛ teaspoon ground allspice
½ cup water or orange juice
2 tablespoons butter or margarine
Vanilla ice cream

1. Cut each apple into 8 wedges.
2. Separate crescent rolls into 4 rectangles; roll to ⅛-inch thickness on a lightly floured surface. Cut each into 4 portions.
3. Place one apple wedge on each crescent roll portion. Roll up, and place in a 10- x 6- x 2-inch baking dish.
4. Combine sugar, cinnamon, and allspice; sprinkle over apple rollups. Pour water over rollups; dot with butter.
5. Bake at 400° for 20 minutes or until rollups are browned. Serve hot with ice cream. Yield: 8 servings.

HOT APPLE PUFF

3 medium-size cooking apples,
    peeled, cored, and chopped
¼ cup water
¼ cup sugar, divided
½ teaspoon almond extract
5 egg whites
    Sifted powdered sugar

1. Combine apples and water in a medium saucepan. Bring to a boil. Reduce heat; cover and simmer 8 minutes or until apples are tender, stirring occasionally.

2. Stir in 3 tablespoons sugar and almond extract. Remove from heat. Cool in refrigerator 10 minutes. (Mixture may be covered and refrigerated up to 12 hours.)

3. Beat egg whites (at room temperature) until soft peaks form. Add remaining 1 tablespoon sugar, beating until stiff peaks form. Fold in apple mixture.

4. Spoon mixture gently into a 1½-quart soufflé dish. Bake at 400° for 15 minutes or until puffed and browned.

5. Sprinkle powdered sugar over puff; serve immediately. Yield: 6 servings.

APPLE CLAFOUTI

2 medium-size cooking apples,
    peeled, cored, and sliced
2 tablespoons butter or margarine
2 tablespoons brandy
1 tablespoon lemon juice
½ cup all-purpose flour
½ teaspoon baking powder
¼ teaspoon salt
¼ cup half-and-half
¼ cup honey
2 eggs
    Sifted powdered sugar

1. Combine apples, butter, brandy, and lemon juice in a small skillet. Cook over medium heat 5 minutes; set aside.

2. Combine flour, baking powder, and salt in a small mixing bowl, stirring well; add half-and-half, honey, and eggs, stirring until smooth.

3. Pour ⅓ cup batter into a lightly greased 9-inch pieplate. Bake at 400° for 4 minutes or until set. Spoon apple mixture over crust; pour remaining batter over apples. Bake an additional 20 minutes or until lightly browned.

4. Sprinkle with powdered sugar; serve warm. Yield: 6 servings.

EASY APPLE CRUMB DESSERT

1 (20-ounce) can apple slices,
    undrained
½ cup sugar
1 teaspoon lemon juice
½ teaspoon ground cinnamon
1 (9-ounce) package white cake mix
    without pudding
¼ cup plus 2 tablespoons butter or
    margarine

1. Place apples in bottom of a 10- x 6- x 2-inch baking dish. Sprinkle with sugar, lemon juice, and cinnamon.

2. Pour cake mix evenly over filling; dot with butter. Bake at 350° for 45 minutes or until browned and bubbly.

3. Serve warm. Yield: 8 servings.

APRICOT CRISP

2 (17-ounce) cans apricot halves,
    drained
½ cup sugar
⅓ (16-ounce) package round buttery
    crackers, crushed
½ cup butter or margarine, melted
    Whipped cream (optional)

1. Place apricots in a 12- x 8- x 2-inch baking dish; sprinkle sugar evenly over apricots. Cover with cracker crumbs. Pour butter over top.

2. Bake at 350° for 25 to 30 minutes.

3. Serve warm with whipped cream, if desired. Yield: 8 servings.

BAKED WINTER PEARS

¼ **cup raisins or chopped**
   dates
¼ **cup chopped pecans**
3 **pears, peeled, cored, and halved**
½ **cup water**
½ **cup firmly packed brown**
   sugar
1 **tablespoon butter or margarine**
½ **teaspoon ground cinnamon**

1. Combine raisins or dates and pecans in a small mixing bowl; set aside.

2. Place pear halves, cut side up, in a 10- x 6- x 2-inch baking dish. Spoon reserved filling into center of each pear.

3. Combine remaining ingredients in a small saucepan; bring to a boil. Pour over filled pears. Bake at 350° for 45 minutes or until pears are tender, basting frequently.

4. Serve warm. Yield: 6 servings.

LEMON-POACHED PEARS

4 **ripe pears**
1½ **cups water**
1 **cup apple juice**
1 **tablespoon grated lemon rind**
2 **tablespoons lemon juice**
6 **(3-inch) sticks cinnamon**
6 **whole cloves**
1 **cup vanilla ice cream**
   Additional grated lemon rind

1. Peel pears; remove core, leaving stem end intact.

2. Combine water, apple juice, 1 tablespoon lemon rind, juice, cinnamon sticks, and cloves in a large saucepan. Bring to a boil. Add pears, turning to coat well.

3. Reduce heat; cover and simmer 15 minutes or until pears are tender. Remove from heat; chill thoroughly.

4. Spoon a scoop of ice cream into chilled dessert dishes. Top each serving with a pear and additional grated lemon rind. Serve immediately. Yield: 4 servings.

MicroMethod

1. Same as step 1.

2. Combine water, apple juice, lemon rind, juice, cinnamon sticks, and cloves in an 8-inch square baking dish. Microwave at HIGH for 4 minutes or just until boiling. Add pears, turning to coat well.

3. Cover with heavy-duty plastic wrap, and vent to allow steam to escape. Microwave at HIGH for 10 minutes or until pears are tender. Chill thoroughly.

4. Same as step 4.

STRAWBERRY-RHUBARB COMPOTE

⅔ **cup sugar**
1 **cup water**
2 **cups fresh strawberries, washed,**
   hulled, and halved
1 **pound rhubarb, cut into 1-inch**
   pieces
   Fresh mint sprigs

1. Combine sugar and water in a medium saucepan, stirring until well blended. Add strawberries, rhubarb, and 1 sprig mint, stirring well. Bring to a boil.

2. Cover and reduce heat; cook over medium heat 15 minutes or until rhubarb is tender, stirring occasionally. Chill mixture thoroughly.

3. Spoon mixture into individual serving dishes; garnish each serving with a mint sprig. Yield: 8 servings.

MicroMethod

1. Combine sugar and water in a 2-quart baking dish, stirring until well blended. Add strawberries, rhubarb, and 1 sprig mint, stirring well.

2. Cover with heavy-duty plastic wrap, and vent to allow steam to escape. Microwave at HIGH for 8 minutes or until rhubarb is tender, stirring after 4 minutes. Let stand 2 minutes. Chill thoroughly.

3. Same as step 3.

FRUIT WITH PEANUT YOGURT SAUCE

½ cup vanilla low-fat yogurt
1 tablespoon creamy peanut butter
1 (8¼-ounce) can pineapple chunks, drained
1 medium apple, cored and cut into cubes
1 banana, sliced
1 cup orange sections
1 cup fresh strawberry halves
2 tablespoons chopped peanuts

1. Combine yogurt and peanut butter in a small mixing bowl; stir well. Cover and refrigerate.
2. Combine pineapple, apple, banana, orange sections, and strawberries in a medium mixing bowl; toss gently.
3. Spoon fruit mixture into individual dessert dishes. Spoon 1 tablespoon plus 1½ teaspoons reserved yogurt mixture over each serving. Sprinkle evenly with chopped peanuts. Serve immediately. Yield: 6 servings.

Note: One cup fresh pineapple chunks may be used in place of canned pineapple chunks.

MIXED FRUIT DESSERT

1 (20-ounce) can pineapple chunks, undrained
1 (11-ounce) can mandarin oranges, undrained
2 cups strawberries, hulled and halved
1½ cups seedless grapes, halved
1 cup fresh blueberries
1 (3.5-ounce) package vanilla instant pudding mix
½ cup toasted pecan halves

1. Drain pineapple and oranges, reserving liquid.
2. Combine drained pineapple and oranges with remaining fruit in a large bowl.

3. Sprinkle pudding mix over reserved fruit liquids; beat with a wire whisk until smooth and thickened. Fold into fruit until all fruit is coated.
4. Spoon into individual serving dishes; garnish with pecans. Serve immediately or chill. Yield: 10 to 12 servings.

Note: Sliced bananas may be stirred into fruit mixture just before serving.

POTS DE CRÈME
(pictured on page 266)

1 cup half-and-half, scalded
1 (6-ounce) package semisweet chocolate morsels
2 egg yolks
3 tablespoons brandy
Whipped cream

1. Combine half-and-half, chocolate morsels, egg yolks, and brandy in the container of an electric blender; process until smooth.
2. Spoon mixture into 6 cordial glasses or demitasse cups. Cover each with plastic wrap, and chill overnight.
3. Garnish each serving with whipped cream. Yield: 6 servings.

EASY CHOCOLATE MOUSSE

1 (6-ounce) package semisweet chocolate morsels
1 teaspoon vanilla extract
Dash of salt
¾ cup whipping cream
3 eggs, separated
Whipped cream
Chocolate fans

1. Position knife blade in food processor bowl; add chocolate morsels, vanilla, and salt. Process 30 seconds.
2. In a small saucepan, heat ¾ cup whipping cream to just boiling. With processor running, add hot cream through

food chute; process 30 seconds or until chocolate completely melts. Add egg yolks; process 5 seconds or until smooth. Transfer mixture to a large mixing bowl; cool completely.

3. Beat egg whites (at room temperature) until stiff peaks form. Gently fold into chocolate mixture. Spoon into a 1-quart serving bowl or individual bowls. Cover and chill thoroughly.

4. To serve, garnish mousse with whipped cream and chocolate fans. Yield: 4 servings.

◆ CRÈME DE MENTHE CHOCOLATE PARFAITS

¼ cup butter or margarine, melted
1½ cups chocolate wafer crumbs (30 wafers)
 1 (10-ounce) package large marshmallows
¼ cup milk
¼ cup crème de menthe
 2 tablespoons white crème de cacao
 1 cup whipping cream, whipped
⅓ cup whipping cream
 2 tablespoons sifted powdered sugar
 Chocolate curls

1. Combine melted butter and chocolate wafer crumbs; mix well. Set aside.

2. Combine marshmallows and milk in a small Dutch oven; cook over low heat, stirring frequently, until marshmallows are melted. Remove from heat; place Dutch oven in a pan of ice water. Chill until thickened.

3. Combine crème de menthe and crème de cacao; stir into marshmallow mixture. Fold in 1 cup whipped cream.

4. Combine ⅓ cup whipping cream and powdered sugar in a small mixing bowl. Beat at high speed of an electric mixer until stiff peaks form; set aside.

5. Spoon alternate layers of chocolate crumb mixture and marshmallow mixture into chilled parfait glasses. Top with sweetened whipped cream, and garnish with chocolate curls. Chill. Yield: 4 servings.

COMING TO TERMS WITH CHOCOLATE...

For some people chocolate is one of several favorite flavors.....for others, it's a passion! Either way, these are the terms of cooking with chocolate know-how:

Unsweetened chocolate (also called baking, cooking, or bitter chocolate). This is pure chocolate, with no sugar added. It doesn't taste good to most people unless it's mixed with sugar.

Bittersweet chocolate. Baking chocolate with just enough sugar added to make it palatable, bittersweet chocolate has an intense flavor that true chocoholics love. It can be used interchangeably with semisweet chocolate.

Semisweet chocolate. Semisweet chocolate is composed of unsweetened chocolate with added cocoa butter and sugar. An all-purpose chocolate, semisweet can be eaten straight or used in cooking.

Milk chocolate. Milk or cream, and very often, vanilla are added to semisweet chocolate to make milk chocolate.

White chocolate. Not a true chocolate but used like chocolate in many kinds of recipes, white chocolate is a blend of cocoa butter, sugar, and whole milk. The cocoa butter is often removed and replaced by another vegetable fat. True chocolate, by legal definition, contains the pure form of chocolate called "chocolate liquor."

Chocolate morsels. These morsels, bits, or chips are semisweet in flavor, and they retain their shape when used in baking. Although they are a great convenience for cooks, there's no reason why you can't chop your favorite kind of chocolate bars in the food processor and use them instead.

CHEESECAKE SQUARES

1 (6-ounce) package butterscotch
    morsels
2 tablespoons butter or margarine
¾ cup graham cracker crumbs
1 (8-ounce) package cream cheese,
    softened
¼ cup sugar
3 eggs
1 teaspoon vanilla extract

1. Combine butterscotch morsels and butter in a medium saucepan. Cook over low heat until morsels melt. Stir in cracker crumbs. Remove and reserve ⅓ cup crumb mixture for topping.
2. Press remaining crumb mixture into bottom of an 8-inch square pan. Set aside.
3. Beat cream cheese, sugar, and eggs until smooth. Stir in vanilla. Pour into pan. Sprinkle with reserved crumb mixture. Bake at 325° for 25 minutes or until set.
4. Cool to room temperature; cut into squares. Yield: 3 dozen.

Note: Cheesecake Squares may also be refrigerated, and served chilled.

◆ CREAM CHEESE TARTS

2 (8-ounce) packages cream cheese
1 cup sugar
2 eggs
1 teaspoon vanilla extract
12 vanilla wafers
    Blueberry pie filling or whipped
    cream

1. Beat cream cheese in a medium mixing bowl until soft and creamy. Gradually add sugar, beating until light and fluffy. Add eggs, one at a time, beating well after each addition. Stir in vanilla.
2. Place vanilla wafers in paper-lined muffin cups. Spoon cream cheese mixture over wafers, filling cups full. Bake at 350° for 20 minutes. Leave Cream Cheese Tarts in muffin pans, and refrigerate overnight.
3. To serve, top with a small amount of blueberry pie filling or whipped cream. Remove paper liners, if desired. Yield: 1 dozen tarts.

Note: Other toppings, such as small dollops of melted raspberry jam, warm caramel sauce, or drained mandarin oranges, may be used with or without the whipped cream. Substitute gingersnaps or other plain cookies for vanilla wafers, if desired.

◆ BLUEBERRY CHEESECAKE

¼ cup plus 2 tablespoons butter
    or margarine, melted
1½ cups graham cracker
    crumbs
⅛ teaspoon ground
    nutmeg
2 (8-ounce) packages cream
    cheese, softened
1 cup sugar
4 eggs
1 teaspoon vanilla extract
1 teaspoon grated lemon rind
1 (21-ounce) can blueberry pie
    filling

1. Combine melted butter, graham cracker crumbs, and nutmeg in a 12- x 8- x 2-inch baking dish; stir well. Press mixture evenly into bottom of baking dish, and set aside.
2. Beat cream cheese with an electric mixer in a large mixing bowl until light and fluffy. Add sugar, eggs, vanilla, and lemon rind, mixing until smooth. Spread over crumb mixture. Bake at 375° for 25 minutes. Let baked mixture cool to room temperature on a wire rack. Spread blueberry pie filling over cheesecake; refrigerate overnight.
3. Cut Blueberry Cheesecake into 3- x 2½-inch bars to serve. Yield: about 1 dozen.

◆ CHOCOLATE CHEESECAKE
(pictured on page 266)

1 cup graham cracker crumbs
1¼ cups sugar, divided
¼ cup butter or margarine, melted
2 envelopes unflavored gelatin
½ cup water
4 (8-ounce) packages cream cheese,
    softened
    Dash of salt
1½ cups milk
8 (1-ounce) squares semisweet
    chocolate, melted and cooled
2 teaspoons vanilla extract
1 cup whipping cream, whipped
    Semisweet chocolate morsels
    Grated chocolate

1. Combine graham cracker crumbs, ¼ cup sugar, and butter in a small mixing bowl; stir well. Press mixture into bottom of a 9-inch springform pan. Set aside.

2. Soften gelatin in water in a small saucepan; cook over low heat, stirring constantly, until gelatin dissolves.

3. Beat cream cheese until light and fluffy; add gelatin mixture, remaining 1 cup sugar, salt, milk, melted chocolate, and vanilla, beating well. Refrigerate 10 minutes; fold in whipped cream. Spoon mixture into prepared pan. Cover and chill overnight.

4. Remove sides of pan; garnish cheesecake with chocolate morsels and grated chocolate. Yield: one 9-inch cheesecake.

◆ SAVANNAH TRIFLE

1½ quarts milk
1½ cups sugar
2 tablespoons cornstarch
6 eggs
½ cup cream sherry
1½ pounds sliced pound cake
2 cups whipping cream, whipped
    Maraschino cherries

1. Scald milk in top of a double boiler. Combine sugar and cornstarch, stirring

well. Add eggs to sugar mixture; beat with an electric mixer until well blended.

2. Stir one-fourth of hot milk into egg mixture; add to remaining hot milk in double boiler, stirring constantly. Cook, stirring constantly, until custard thickens and coats a metal spoon. Cool completely. Stir sherry into custard.

3. Arrange half of pound cake slices evenly in a 5-quart serving bowl. Pour half of custard over pound cake. Spread half of whipped cream over custard. Repeat layers.

4. Garnish top of trifle with cherries. Chill thoroughly before serving. Yield: 12 to 14 servings.

◆ RUM BERRY TRIFLE
(pictured on page i)

1 (3.5-ounce) package vanilla instant
    pudding mix
2 (6-ounce) packages commercial
    jellyrolls
¼ cup rum
¼ cup toasted slivered almonds
1 (10-ounce) package frozen
    raspberries, thawed and drained
1 cup whipping cream
1 tablespoon sugar
1 teaspoon vanilla extract
    Additional toasted slivered
    almonds

1. Prepare pudding according to package directions; chill.

2. Cut jellyrolls into ¾-inch-thick slices; brush slices with rum. Line a 2½ quart serving bowl with jellyroll slices. Spoon pudding over jellyroll slices; sprinkle evenly with ¼ cup slivered almonds. Spoon raspberries over almonds.

3. Beat whipping cream until foamy; add sugar and vanilla, beating until soft peaks form. Spoon whipped cream mixture over raspberries; garnish with additional toasted slivered almonds. Chill thoroughly.

4. Serve chilled. Yield: 8 servings.

QUICK ZUPPA INGLESE

1 (3.5-ounce) package vanilla instant pudding mix
½ (3-ounce) package ladyfingers
¼ cup Amaretto
2 tablespoons toasted slivered almonds, divided
  Frozen whipped topping, thawed

1. Prepare pudding according to package directions; set aside.
2. Line four individual dessert cups with ladyfingers; brush with Amaretto. Sprinkle half of almonds over ladyfingers, dividing evenly; spoon ½ cup reserved vanilla pudding over almonds in each cup. Chill thoroughly.
3. Garnish each serving with a dollop of whipped topping; sprinkle with remaining almonds, and serve immediately. Yield: 4 servings.

Note: Canned vanilla pudding may be substituted for vanilla instant pudding.

CREAMY RICE PUDDING

2 cups cooked rice
2 cups milk
¼ cup plus 1 tablespoon sugar
3 tablespoons butter or margarine
¼ teaspoon salt
½ teaspoon vanilla extract

1. Combine rice, milk, sugar, butter, and salt in a medium saucepan. Cook over medium heat, stirring frequently, 35 minutes or until thickened. Remove from heat; stir in vanilla.
2. Spoon into individual serving dishes. Serve hot or cold. Yield: about 3 cups.

Note: Creamy Rice Pudding may be topped with whipped cream, preserves, or dried fruit such as raisins or chopped apricots.

CHERRIES JUBILEE

1 (16½-ounce) can pitted dark sweet cherries, undrained
⅓ cup sugar
1 tablespoon plus 1 teaspoon cornstarch
½ teaspoon grated lemon rind
2 teaspoons lemon juice
¼ cup brandy
  Vanilla ice cream

1. Drain cherries, reserving liquid; set cherries aside. Combine sugar, cornstarch, and lemon rind in a medium saucepan, stirring until well blended. Add reserved cherry liquid and lemon juice; mix well. Cover and bring to a boil; reduce heat and cook, stirring constantly, until mixture thickens. Remove from heat; stir in reserved cherries, and keep warm.
2. Place brandy in a small long-handled pan; heat just until warm. Pour over cherry mixture, and ignite with a long match. Allow flames to die down.
3. Serve immediately over ice cream. Yield: 4 servings.

MicroMethod

1. Drain cherries, reserving liquid; set cherries aside. Combine sugar, cornstarch, and lemon rind in a 4-cup glass measure, stirring until well blended. Add reserved cherry liquid and lemon juice; mix well. Cover with waxed paper, and microwave at HIGH for 2 to 3 minutes or until mixture thickens, stirring after 1½ minutes. Stir in reserved cherries, and keep warm.
2. Place brandy in a 1-cup glass measure. Microwave at HIGH for 20 seconds or until warm. Pour over cherry mixture, and ignite with a long match. Allow flames to die down.
3. Same as step 3.

Note: This easy classic dessert is open to many flavor variations. You may substitute canned or frozen sliced peaches, canned plums, or blueberries for the cherries. You may use fruit packed in either juice or syrup.

PEACH MELBA

1 pint French vanilla ice cream
½ cup raspberry jam or preserves
1 tablespoon raspberry-flavored
    liqueur or cherry-flavored
    liqueur
6 sponge cake dessert shells
1 (16-ounce) can peach halves,
    drained
    Fresh mint leaves (optional)

1. Divide ice cream into 6 equal scoops; cover and freeze until ready to use.
2. Combine jam and liqueur in a small saucepan; heat slowly, stirring frequently.
3. Place sponge cake shells on individual dessert plates; place one peach half cut side up in each shell. Top each peach with a scoop of ice cream. Pour raspberry sauce over top of ice cream.
4. Garnish each serving with a mint leaf, if desired. Serve immediately. Yield: 6 servings.

Note: Six slices of angel food cake may be substituted for sponge cake dessert shells.

CREAMY PEACH SHERBET

1 cup plain low-fat yogurt
2 cups sliced fresh or frozen
    peaches
½ cup orange juice
2 tablespoons sugar

1. Combine yogurt, peaches, orange juice, and sugar in the container of an electric blender; process until smooth. Pour mixture into a 9-inch square baking pan; freeze until set around edges of pan.
2. Spoon mixture into a large mixing bowl; beat at high speed of an electric mixer until smooth and fluffy. Return mixture to baking pan. Freeze until set.
3. Remove from freezer, and let stand 10 minutes. Scoop into individual serving dishes. Yield: 6 servings.

BITTERSWEET SHERBET

½ cup sugar
¼ cup cocoa
3½ cups milk
1 teaspoon vanilla extract
½ teaspoon grated lime
    rind

1. Combine sugar and cocoa in a medium saucepan; stir well. Gradually add milk, stirring well. Cook over low heat, stirring frequently, until sugar melts; cook an additional 5 minutes. Remove from heat, and stir in vanilla and lime rind.
2. Pour mixture into a 9-inch square baking pan; freeze until partially set. Spoon mixture into a large mixing bowl; beat at high speed of an electric mixer until smooth. Return mixture to baking pan; freeze until set.
3. Scoop Bittersweet Sherbet into individual serving dishes. Serve immediately. Yield: 8 servings.

TASTY FRUIT POPS

⅔ cup sugar
1 envelope unflavored gelatin
2 cups canned pineapple juice
1 cup water
2 tablespoons lemon juice
3 cups fresh strawberries,
    pureed

1. Combine sugar and gelatin in a large mixing bowl, stirring well; set aside.
2. Combine pineapple juice, water, and lemon juice in a small saucepan; bring to a boil. Pour over sugar mixture, stirring until sugar dissolves. Stir in strawberries. Pour mixture into twelve (5-ounce) paper cups; freeze until partially set. Insert wooden ice cream sticks in center of each pop. Freeze until firm.
3. Remove from freezer; let stand 5 minutes. Peel off paper cups.
4. Serve Tasty Fruit Pops immediately. Yield: 12 servings.

◆ CHOCOLATE ICE CREAM CARAMEL CRUNCH

1 cup all-purpose flour
¼ cup quick-cooking oats, uncooked
¼ cup firmly packed brown sugar
½ cup butter or margarine, softened
½ cup chopped pecans
1 (12.25-ounce) jar caramel ice cream topping
1 quart chocolate ice cream, softened

1. Combine flour, oats, and sugar in a medium mixing bowl. Cut in butter with a pastry blender until mixture resembles coarse meal; stir in pecans. Crumble mixture into a 15- x 10- x 1-inch jellyroll pan; bake at 400° for 10 minutes. Remove from oven; stir mixture while still warm. Let mixture cool.
2. Spread half of crumb mixture into a 9-inch square pan. Spoon ½ jar caramel topping over crumb mixture. Spread ice cream evenly over mixture; top with remaining caramel topping and crumb mixture. Cover and freeze until firm.
3. Let stand at room temperature 5 minutes before slicing into 3-inch squares. Yield: 9 servings.

◆▢ BRANDY CREAM PIE

4 egg yolks
¼ cup brandy
1 cup whipping cream
½ cup sifted powdered sugar
   Microwaved Graham Cracker Crust
2 tablespoons graham cracker crumbs

1. Beat egg yolks until thick and lemon-colored; add brandy, and beat well. Set aside.
2. Beat whipping cream until foamy; gradually add powdered sugar, beating until stiff peaks form. Fold yolk mixture into whipping cream, and pour over Microwaved Graham Cracker Crust; freeze until firm.
3. Remove from freezer; sprinkle crumbs over top. Let stand 10 minutes before serving. Yield: one 9-inch pie.

Microwaved Graham Cracker Crust:

1½ cups graham cracker crumbs
¼ cup firmly packed brown sugar
¼ cup butter or margarine, melted

1. Combine all ingredients; mix well, and press into a buttered 9-inch pieplate.
2. Microwave at HIGH for 2½ minutes or until firm, rotating dish after 1 minute. Let cool. Yield: one 9-inch pie crust.

◆ PUMPKIN CREAM PIE

1 pint vanilla ice cream, softened
1 baked (10-inch) pastry shell
1 (16-ounce) can pumpkin
1½ cups sugar
1 teaspoon ground cinnamon
½ teaspoon ground ginger
¼ teaspoon ground cloves
¼ teaspoon salt
1 teaspoon vanilla extract
½ cup whipping cream, whipped
½ cup slivered almonds (optional)
2 tablespoons sugar (optional)

1. Spread ice cream evenly in pastry shell; place in freezer.
2. Combine pumpkin, 1½ cups sugar, cinnamon, ginger, cloves, salt, and vanilla in a large mixing bowl; fold in whipped cream. Pour filling over ice cream; cover and freeze overnight.
3. Combine almonds and 2 tablespoons sugar in a small skillet; cook over medium heat, stirring constantly, 8 minutes or until sugar caramelizes. Spread on a greased cookie sheet; break apart when cooled.
4. Remove pie from freezer; garnish with caramelized almonds, if desired. Let stand 10 minutes before serving. Yield: one 10-inch pie.

NO-BAKE
PEANUT BUTTER PIE

1 quart vanilla ice cream, softened
1 cup frozen whipped topping,
   thawed
⅔ cup crunchy peanut butter
1 (6-ounce) prepared graham
   cracker crust
   Additional whipped topping
   (optional)

1. Combine ice cream, 1 cup whipped topping, and peanut butter in a large mixing bowl; stir until well blended. Spoon mixture into graham cracker crust; cover and freeze 3 hours or until set.

2. Remove from freezer 10 minutes before serving. Garnish with additional whipped topping, if desired. Yield: one 9-inch pie.

Note: Serve with commercial chocolate sauce for an extra-special treat.

BANANA-GINGER
CREAM PIE

   Vegetable cooking spray
15 gingersnaps
½ cup sugar
3 tablespoons cornstarch
¼ teaspoon salt
2 cups skim milk
3 egg yolks, beaten
1 teaspoon vanilla extract
2 medium bananas

1. Lightly coat a 9-inch pieplate with vegetable cooking spray. Cut 6 gingersnaps in half. Crush remaining 9 gingersnaps, and press into bottom of pieplate. Arrange cookie halves around rim of pieplate; set aside.

2. Combine sugar, cornstarch, and salt in a medium saucepan; gradually stir in milk. Cook mixture over medium heat 5 minutes, stirring constantly, or just until thickened.

3. Stir one-fourth of hot mixture into yolks; add to remaining hot mixture, stirring constantly. Cook an additional 2 minutes or until thickened and bubbly. Remove from heat; stir in vanilla.

4. Slice 1 banana; arrange slices evenly in pie shell. Pour filling over top of slices, and chill several hours or overnight.

5. Just before serving, slice remaining banana. Arrange slices on top. Yield: one 9-inch pie.

CHOCOLATE-COFFEE PIE
(pictured on page 266)

1 (4-ounce) package chocolate
   instant pudding mix
¼ cup milk
¼ cup strong coffee
1 pint coffee ice cream, softened
1 (9-inch) Chocolate Crumb Crust
¾ cup toasted pecans

1. Combine pudding mix, milk, coffee, and ice cream in a large mixing bowl. Beat at medium speed of an electric mixer until smooth and thickened.

2. Pour mixture into crust. Sprinkle with pecans. Refrigerate 3 hours or overnight. Cut into wedges to serve. Yield: 1 9-inch pie.

Chocolate Crumb Crust:

19 chocolate cookie wafers (about 6
   ounces)
¼ cup plus 2 tablespoons butter or
   margarine, melted

1. Break chocolate cookie wafers into pieces; place in processor bowl. Pulse 3 to 4 times until wafers are fine crumbs.

2. Pour melted butter through food chute with processor running. Process 5 seconds or just until blended.

3. Press mixture firmly and evenly into a 9-inch pieplate. Bake at 350° for 10 minutes. Cool before filling. Yield: one 9-inch pie shell.

◆ FRESH STRAWBERRY PIE

1 cup sugar
2 tablespoons cornstarch
1 cup water
¼ cup strawberry-flavored gelatin
2 cups fresh strawberries, halved
1 baked (9-inch) pastry shell
Whipped cream

1. Combine sugar and cornstarch in a saucepan; stir in water. Cook over medium heat, stirring constantly, until thickened and clear. Remove from heat; stir in gelatin. Cool.

2. Place strawberries in pastry shell. Pour glaze over berries. Chill thoroughly.

3. Top with whipped cream. Yield: one 9-inch pie.

ORANGE MERINGUE PIE

¼ cup plus 2 tablespoons cornstarch
1¼ cups sugar, divided
1½ cups water
3 eggs, separated
2 tablespoons butter or margarine
1 (6-ounce) can frozen orange juice
    concentrate, thawed and
    undiluted
1 baked (9-inch) pastry shell

1. Combine cornstarch and ¾ cup sugar in a medium saucepan. Gradually add water; stir until smooth. Cook over medium heat, stirring constantly, until thickened and smooth.

2. Beat egg yolks until thick and lemon colored. Gradually stir one-fourth of hot mixture into yolks; add to remaining hot mixture, stirring constantly. Cook over medium heat 2 minutes or until mixture thickens. Remove from heat; add butter and orange juice concentrate, stirring until butter melts. Pour filling into pastry shell.

3. Beat egg whites (at room temperature) until foamy. Gradually add remaining ½ cup sugar, 1 tablespoon at a time.

Beat until stiff peaks form and sugar dissolves. Spread meringue over hot filling, sealing to edge of pastry. Bake at 400° for 5 minutes or until meringue is golden brown.

4. Cool to room temperature. Yield: one 9-inch pie.

LEMON PUDDING CAKE

1 (18.25-ounce) package yellow cake
    mix without pudding
1 (3.5-ounce) package lemon instant
    pudding mix
¾ cup water
½ cup vegetable oil
4 eggs
1 cup sifted powdered sugar
½ cup lemon juice
1 tablespoon plus 1½ teaspoons
    butter or margarine

1. Combine cake mix, pudding mix, water, oil, and eggs in a large mixing bowl. Beat at medium speed of an electric mixer for 4 minutes. Pour batter into a greased and floured 13- x 9- x 2-inch baking pan. Bake at 350° for 40 minutes or until a wooden pick inserted in center comes out clean.

2. Combine sugar, lemon juice, and butter in a small saucepan. Place over medium heat until thoroughly heated.

3. Pierce hot cake several times with a long fork. Slowly pour glaze over cake; cool completely before serving. Yield: one 13- x 9- x 2-inch cake.

Note: Lemon Pudding Cake may be easily varied with these substitutions:

For a chocolate version, use devil's food cake mix and chocolate pudding; substitute strong brewed coffee for the lemon juice in the glaze.

For a banana spice cake, use banana cake mix and banana pudding, and add ½ teaspoon cinnamon and ¼ teaspoon nutmeg to the batter; substitute orange juice for lemon juice in the glaze.

▢ ROCKY ROAD CAKE

1 (18.5-ounce) package devil's food
   cake mix with pudding
1 cup water
⅓ cup vegetable oil
3 eggs
1 (6-ounce) package semisweet
   chocolate morsels
1 cup miniature marshmallows
½ cup chopped pecans
   Chocolate Glaze

1. Combine first 4 ingredients in a large
mixing bowl; beat at high speed of an
electric mixer 2 minutes. Fold in chocolate
morsels, marshmallows, and pecans.

2. Pour batter into a well-greased 10-
inch bundt pan. Bake at 350° for 55 minutes or until a wooden pick inserted near
center comes out clean. Cool in pan 10
minutes; remove from pan, and cool completely on a wire rack.

3. Drizzle Chocolate Glaze over cooled
cake. Yield: one 10-inch cake

Chocolate Glaze:

1 cup sifted powdered sugar
2 tablespoons cocoa
2 tablespoons butter or margarine,
   softened
2 to 3 tablespoons water
2 teaspoons vanilla extract

1. Combine powdered sugar, cocoa,
butter, water, and vanilla in a small mixing
bowl; mix until well blended.

2. Drizzle glaze over cooled cake. Yield:
glaze for one 10-inch cake.

MicroMethod

1. Grease a 10-inch bundt pan. Sprinkle
with sugar; set aside. Combine first 4 ingredients in a large mixing bowl. Beat at
high speed of an electric mixer 2 minutes.
Fold in chocolate morsels, marshmallows,
and pecans.

2. Pour batter into prepared pan. Microwave at MEDIUM (50% power) for 14
to 15 minutes, rotating a quarter-turn

every 3 minutes. Microwave at HIGH for 2
to 3 minutes or until cake starts to pull
away from sides of pan. Remove from
oven, and let stand 10 minutes. Cool completely on a wire rack.

3. Same as step 3.

ANGEL FOOD CAKE WITH SOUR CREAM

1 (10¾-ounce) loaf angel food cake
1 (16-ounce) carton commercial sour
   cream
1 pint fresh strawberries, hulled
   and sliced
2 tablespoons firmly packed brown
   sugar

1. Cut cake into 3 even horizontal slices.
Place bottom layer on serving dish; frost
with sour cream. Place a layer of strawberries over sour cream. Repeat layers. Frost
entire cake with sour cream. Garnish with
strawberries, and chill.

2. Immediately before serving, sprinkle
with brown sugar. Yield: 10 to 12 servings.

BLACK FOREST DUMP CAKE

1 (8-ounce) can crushed pineapple,
   undrained
1 (21-ounce) can cherry pie filling
1 (18.5-ounce) package devil's food
   cake mix without pudding
1 cup chopped pecans
½ cup butter or margarine, melted
   Whipped topping

1. Drain pineapple, reserving liquid.

2. Spread pineapple in a lightly greased
13- x 9- x 2-inch pan; add pie filling,
spreading gently. Sprinkle dry cake mix
over pie filling; top with pecans.

3. Combine butter and reserved pineapple liquid; drizzle on mixture in pan. Bake
at 350° for 35 to 40 minutes.

4. Cut into squares; top with whipped
topping. Yield: one 13- x 9- x 2-inch cake.

MANDARIN ORANGE CAKE

(pictured at right)

1 (18.25-ounce) box yellow butter
    cake mix without pudding
4 eggs
½ cup vegetable oil
1 (11-ounce) can mandarin oranges,
    undrained
    Pineapple Frosting

1. Combine cake mix, eggs, and oil in a large mixing bowl; beat at medium speed of an electric mixer until well blended. Add mandarin oranges, beating just until combined.
2. Pour batter evenly into 3 greased and floured 8-inch round cakepans; bake at 350° for 20 to 25 minutes or until a wooden pick inserted in center comes out clean. Cool layers in pans, 10 minutes; remove from pans and cool completely.
3. Spread frosting between layers and on top and sides of cooled cake. Refrigerate overnight. Yield: one 3-layer cake.

Pineapple Frosting:

1 (3.5-ounce) box vanilla instant
    pudding mix
1 (20-ounce) can crushed pineapple,
    undrained
1 (8-ounce) carton frozen whipped
    topping, thawed

1. Combine pudding mix and pineapple in a medium mixing bowl; beat at medium speed of an electric mixer until well blended.
2. Add whipped topping, mixing well. Yield: frosting for one 3-layer cake.

Note: To make a rectangular cake, spoon batter into a greased and floured 15- x 10- x 1-inch jellyroll pan. Bake at 350° for 20 to 25 minutes. Cool in pan 10 minutes; remove from pan, and cool completely. Slice crosswise into 3 equal portions. Spread frosting between layers and on top and sides of cooled cake. Refrigerate overnight.

CHOCOLATE-APPLESAUCE CAKE

1 (18.25-ounce) package devil's food
    cake mix without pudding
2 cups applesauce
4 eggs
    Chocolate Frosting

1. Combine cake mix, applesauce, and eggs in a large mixing bowl; beat at medium speed of an electric mixer until well blended.
2. Pour batter into 3 greased and floured 8-inch round cakepans. Bake at 350° for 25 to 30 minutes or until a wooden pick inserted in center comes out clean. Cool in pans 10 minutes; remove layers from pans, and cool completely.
3. Spread Chocolate Frosting between layers and on top and sides of cake. Yield: one 3-layer cake.

Chocolate Frosting:

¼ cup butter or margarine, softened
1 (16-ounce) package powdered
    sugar, sifted
3 tablespoons milk
2 (1-ounce) squares unsweetened
    chocolate, melted

1. Cream butter in a large mixing bowl; gradually add sugar alternately with milk, beating mixture well.
2. Add melted chocolate, and beat until frosting is well blended. Yield: frosting for one 3-layer cake.

Note: Dust pans for chocolate cakes with cocoa instead of flour to keep the outside of the cakes from being white when they are removed from the pans.

The bright and snappy flavor of this Mandarin Orange Cake (above) iced with a pineapple frosting is sure to add pizzazz to any menu.

CHOCOLATE CAKE

2 cups all-purpose flour
2 cups sugar
1 cup water
½ cup butter or margarine
½ cup shortening
¼ cup cocoa
½ cup buttermilk
2 eggs
1 teaspoon baking soda
1 teaspoon vanilla extract
Chocolate-Pecan Frosting

1. Combine flour and sugar in a large mixing bowl; set aside.
2. Combine water, butter, shortening, and cocoa in a heavy saucepan; bring to a boil. Pour chocolate mixture over flour mixture; blend well. Add buttermilk, eggs, soda, and vanilla; mix well.
3. Pour batter into a lightly greased 13- x 9- x 2-inch baking pan. Bake at 350° for 35 minutes or until a wooden pick inserted in center comes out clean. Cool. Frost with Chocolate-Pecan Frosting. Yield: one 13- x 9- x 2-inch cake.

Chocolate-Pecan Frosting:

¼ cup cocoa
½ cup butter or margarine
¼ cup plus 2 tablespoons buttermilk
3½ cups sifted powdered sugar
1 cup chopped pecans
1 teaspoon vanilla extract

1. Combine cocoa, butter, and buttermilk in a heavy saucepan; bring to a boil, stirring constantly.
2. Remove from heat; stir in powdered sugar, pecans, and vanilla. Mix well. Yield: frosting for one 13- x 9- x 2-inch cake.

Chocolate lovers, take your pick (clockwise from top): Chocolate Macaroons (page 270), Chocolate Cheesecake (page 257), Chocolate Coffee Pie (page 261), Pots de Crème (page 254), Chocolate Cupcakes (page 267).

MicroNote: To microwave step 1, place butter in a mixing bowl; microwave at HIGH for 1 minute or until melted. Whisk in cocoa and buttermilk until smooth. Microwave at HIGH for 1 minute; whisk until smooth.

CHOCOLATE CUPCAKES
(pictured at left)

1 teaspoon baking soda
½ cup hot water
1½ cups all-purpose flour
1 cup sugar
½ cup cocoa
½ cup butter or margarine, softened
½ cup buttermilk
1 teaspoon vanilla extract
1 egg
Sifted powdered sugar

1. Dissolve soda in hot water.
2. Combine all ingredients except powdered sugar in a large mixing bowl. Beat at medium speed of an electric mixer 4 minutes or until mixture becomes light in color.
3. Spoon batter into greased or paper-lined muffin pans, filling three-fourths full. Bake at 350° for 18 minutes or until cupcakes test done. Remove to wire racks to cool completely.
4. Sprinkle cupcakes with powdered sugar. Yield: 1½ dozen.

SPICY APPLE BARS

1¾ cups sifted cake flour
½ teaspoon baking soda
½ teaspoon salt
1 teaspoon ground cinnamon
½ teaspoon ground allspice
⅛ teaspoon ground cloves
¼ cup butter or margarine,
     softened
¾ cup sugar
1 egg
¾ cup unsweetened applesauce
½ cup raisins

1. Sift together flour, soda, salt, cinnamon, allspice, and cloves; set aside.
2. Cream butter; gradually add sugar, beating well. Add egg, mixing well. Add reserved flour mixture to creamed mixture alternately with applesauce, beginning and ending with flour mixture; mix just until blended. Stir in raisins.
3. Spoon batter into a greased and floured 10- x 6- x 2-inch baking dish. Bake at 375° for 25 minutes or until a wooden pick inserted in center comes out clean. Let cool in baking dish 10 minutes. Cut into 2½- x 1-inch bars.
4. Serve warm or cool. Store in an airtight container. Yield: 2 dozen.

RAISIN-NUT SPICE BARS

2 cups all-purpose flour
⅓ cup firmly packed brown
     sugar
1 teaspoon baking powder
½ teaspoon salt
1 teaspoon ground cinnamon
½ teaspoon ground nutmeg
⅛ teaspoon ground cloves
1 cup milk
⅓ cup vegetable oil
⅓ cup molasses
1 cup raisins
½ cup chopped pecans
     Old Fashion Spice Sauce

1. Combine first 7 ingredients in a large mixing bowl. Add milk, oil, and molasses; stir. Stir in raisins and pecans.
2. Pour into a greased 12- x 8- x 2-inch baking dish. Bake at 350° for 40 minutes or until a wooden pick inserted in center comes out clean. Cool; cut into 2-inch squares.
3. Serve with Old Fashion Spice Sauce. Yield: 2 dozen.

Old Fashion Spice Sauce:

½ cup sugar
1 tablespoon cornstarch
½ teaspoon ground nutmeg
2 tablespoons water
¼ cup butter or margarine
2 tablespoons brandy

1. Combine first 3 ingredients in a small saucepan, stirring well. Add water and butter; cook, stirring constantly, until mixture boils and thickens. Stir in brandy.
2. Serve warm. Yield: ⅔ cup.

DATE-NUT BARS

1 (8-ounce) package chopped
     dates
1 cup chopped pecans
1 cup water
⅓ cup butter or margarine
1 (18.5-ounce) package white cake
     mix with pudding
1 egg

1. Combine dates, pecans, and water in a medium saucepan. Bring to a boil. Reduce heat, and simmer until mixture thickens, stirring constantly. Set aside.
2. Cut butter into cake mix with a pastry blender until mixture resembles coarse meal. Reserve ½ cup cake mix mixture. Add egg to remaining mixture; stir well.
3. Pat mixture into bottom of a greased 13- x 9- x 2-inch baking pan. Spread date mixture evenly over cake mix mixture.

Sprinkle with reserved cake mixture. Bake at 350° for 35 minutes or until browned.

4. Cool completely and cut into 1½- x 1-inch bars. Yield: 6½ dozen.

PEANUT BARS

¼ cup butter or margarine
¼ cup creamy peanut butter
1⅓ cups all-purpose flour, divided
1¼ cups firmly packed brown sugar, divided
⅛ teaspoon salt
2 eggs
½ teaspoon baking powder
½ teaspoon vanilla extract
1 cup flaked coconut
1 cup chopped dry-roasted peanuts

1. Combine butter and peanut butter in a medium saucepan. Cook over low heat stirring constantly, until melted. Add 1 cup flour, ¼ cup brown sugar, and salt, stirring well to combine.

2. Press mixture evenly into bottom of a greased 12- x 8- x 2-inch baking dish. Bake at 325° for 15 minutes. Remove from oven.

3. Beat eggs (at room temperature) in a medium mixing bowl until foamy; gradually add remaining 1 cup sugar, beating until fluffy. Stir in remaining ⅓ cup flour, baking powder, vanilla, coconut, and peanuts; pour over crust. Bake at 350° for 30 minutes or until browned.

4. Cool completely, and cut into 2- x 1-inch bars. Yield: 4 dozen.

CARAMEL CRISP

24 graham cracker squares
2 cups miniature marshmallows
½ cup plus 2 tablespoons butter or margarine
¾ cup firmly packed brown sugar
1 teaspoon ground cinnamon
1 teaspoon vanilla extract
1 cup sliced almonds
1 cup flaked coconut

1. Place graham crackers in rows on an ungreased 15- x 10- x 1-inch jellyroll pan; sprinkle marshmallows evenly over top.

2. Combine butter, sugar, cinnamon, and vanilla in a heavy medium saucepan. Cook over medium heat, stirring constantly, 5 minutes or until sugar dissolves and butter melts.

3. Pour sugar mixture evenly over crackers and marshmallows. Sprinkle almonds and coconut over top. Bake at 350° for 8 to 10 minutes. Cool completely before cutting.

4. Cut into 2- x 1-inch bars. Yield: about 6 dozen.

DOUBLE FUDGE BROWNIES

⅔ cup butter or margarine, melted
1½ cups sugar
¼ cup water
1 (12-ounce) package semisweet chocolate morsels
2 teaspoons vanilla extract
4 eggs
1½ cups all-purpose flour
½ teaspoon baking soda
½ teaspoon salt
1 cup chopped pecans
1 (6-ounce) package semisweet chocolate morsels

1. Combine butter, sugar, and water in a large saucepan; bring to a boil. Remove from heat; add 12-ounce package of chocolate morsels and vanilla, stirring until chocolate melts. Add eggs, one at a time, beating well after each addition.

2. Combine flour, soda, and salt in a small mixing bowl; gradually stir into chocolate mixture. Stir in pecans and remaining chocolate morsels. Spread batter into a greased 13- x 9- x 2-inch baking pan. Bake at 350° for 50 minutes. Cool brownies completely before cutting.

3. Cut into 2-inch squares to serve. Yield: about 2 dozen.

EASY SURPRISE BROWNIES

1 (21.5-ounce) package family-size
    fudge brownie mix
2 cups miniature marshmallows
½ cup butter or margarine
¼ cup plus 2 tablespoons milk
¼ cup cocoa
1 (16-ounce) package powdered
    sugar, sifted
1 teaspoon vanilla extract
1 cup chopped pecans

1. Prepare fudge brownie mix according to package directions using a 12- x 8- x 2-inch baking dish. Remove brownies from oven; sprinkle marshmallows over top, and return to oven just until marshmallows are softened. Remove brownies from oven. Set aside.

2. Combine butter, milk, and cocoa in a medium saucepan. Bring mixture to a boil, and remove from heat. Add sugar, stirring until well blended. Stir in vanilla extract and pecans. Quickly spread warm icing on top of warm brownies. Cool completely.

3. Cut brownies into squares when icing has set and brownies have cooled. Yield: 2 dozen.

BUTTERSCOTCH CHOCOLATE BARS

⅓ cup butter or margarine, softened
⅓ cup shortening
⅓ cup sugar
⅓ cup firmly packed brown sugar
1 egg
1 teaspoon vanilla extract
1½ cups all-purpose flour
1 (6-ounce) package butterscotch
    morsels
1 (6-ounce) package semisweet
    chocolate morsels
½ cup chopped pecans

1. Cream butter and shortening; gradually add sugar, beating until light and fluffy. Add egg; beat well. Stir in vanilla. Stir in remaining ingredients.

2. Press dough into a 13- x 9- x 2-inch baking pan. Bake at 375° for 20 minutes.

3. Cool completely and cut into 1½-inch squares. Yield: about 4 dozen.

CHOCOLATE CHIP COOKIES

1 (14-ounce) can sweetened
    condensed milk
1 (6-ounce) package semisweet
    chocolate morsels
2½ cups graham cracker crumbs
1 cup chopped pecans

1. Combine all ingredients in a large mixing bowl.

2. Drop by teaspoonfuls onto greased cookie sheets. Bake at 325° for 10 minutes. Cool slightly on cookie sheets.

3. Cool completely on wire racks. Yield: about 4 dozen.

CHOCOLATE MACAROONS
(pictured on page 266)

1 (18.25-ounce) package devil's food
    cake mix without pudding
1½ cups regular oats, uncooked
1 cup flaked coconut, toasted and
    divided
¾ cup butter or margarine, melted
2 eggs, beaten
2 teaspoons vanilla extract
5 (1.45-ounce) milk chocolate bars,
    broken into rectangles

1. Combine cake mix, oats, ½ cup coconut, butter, eggs, and vanilla, stirring until well blended. Cover and chill 15 minutes.

2. Shape dough into 1-inch balls; place balls 2 inches apart on ungreased cookie sheets. Bake at 350° for 12 minutes or until tops are slightly cracked.

3. Remove from oven and immediately press one rectangle of milk chocolate into center of each cookie. Sprinkle with remaining coconut. Remove from cookie sheets, and cool. Yield: about 4½ dozen.

DEVIL'S FOOD COOKIES

1 (18.5-ounce) package devil's food
    cake mix without pudding
½ cup vegetable oil
2 eggs, beaten
½ cup chopped pecans
6 (1.45-ounce) milk chocolate bars,
    broken into squares
½ cup flaked coconut

1. Combine cake mix, oil, and eggs in a large mixing bowl; mix well. Stir in pecans.
2. Drop batter by teaspoonfuls 2 inches apart onto ungreased cookie sheets. Bake at 350° for 10 minutes. Place one square of milk chocolate on each cookie while still warm; spread gently to frost. Sprinkle with coconut.
3. Remove from cookie sheets, and cool completely on wire racks. Yield: about 5 dozen.

SLICE AND BAKE OATMEAL CRISPIES

¾ cup all-purpose flour
½ teaspoon baking soda
½ teaspoon salt
½ cup shortening
½ cup sugar
½ cup firmly packed brown sugar
1 egg
½ teaspoon vanilla extract
1½ cups regular or quick-cooking
    oats, uncooked
½ cup chopped dates
½ cup chopped raisins
¼ cup chopped pecans

1. Combine flour, soda, and salt in a large mixing bowl; stir well. Add shortening, sugar, egg, and vanilla; beat well. Stir in remaining ingredients.
2. Divide dough in half; shape each half into a roll, 1½ inches in diameter. Wrap in plastic wrap or waxed paper, and chill 3 hours or until firm.

3. Cut into ¼-inch slices; place slices 2 inches apart on ungreased cookie sheets. Bake at 350° for 10 minutes or until lightly browned.
4. Remove from cookie sheets, and cool on wire racks. Yield: about 4 dozen.

☺ PEANUT BUTTER CUP BITES

1 (20-ounce) package refrigerated
    ready-to-slice peanut butter
    cookie dough roll
60 miniature peanut butter cup
    candies

1. Cut dough into 10 equal portions; divide each portion into 6 equal pieces. Place dough into paper-lined 1¾-inch muffin pans.
2. Bake at 350° for 10 minutes or until lightly browned. Remove from oven, and immediately press a miniature peanut butter cup into each hot cookie. Cool before removing from pan.
3. Serve immediately or store in an airtight container in refrigerator. Yield: 6 dozen.

☺ CARAMEL SAUCE

¾ cup butter or margarine
1½ cups firmly packed brown sugar
1 cup whipping cream

1. Combine butter and sugar in a medium-size heavy saucepan; cook over low heat, stirring constantly, until blended.
2. Gradually add cream; cook, stirring constantly, over medium heat until mixture comes to a boil. Remove from heat, and stir well.
3. Serve Caramel Sauce warm over vanilla ice cream or pound cake. Yield: about 2½ cups.

Index